First World War
and Army of Occupation
War Diary
France, Belgium and Germany

19 DIVISION
58 Infantry Brigade
Headquarters
1 January 1918 - 31 December 1919

WO95/2089

The Naval & Military Press Ltd
www.nmarchive.com
Published in association with The National Archives

Published by

The Naval & Military Press Ltd

Unit 10 Ridgewood Industrial Park,

Uckfield, East Sussex,

TN22 5QE England

Tel: +44 (0) 1825 749494

www.naval-military-press.com

www.nmarchive.com

This diary has been reprinted in facsimile from the original. Any imperfections are inevitably reproduced and the quality may fall short of modern type and cartographic standards.

© Crown Copyright
Images reproduced by permission of The National Archives, London, England, 2015.

Contents

Document type	Place/Title	Date From	Date To
Heading	19th Division 58th Infy Bde Bde Headquarters Jan 1918-Mar 1919		
Heading	HQ 58 Infy Bde (19th Div) Vol 31 January 1918		
War Diary	Ribecourt (Nine Wood Marcoing 1/10,000)	01/01/1918	05/01/1918
War Diary	Ruyaulcourt	06/01/1918	18/01/1918
War Diary	Reserve Area	19/01/1918	23/01/1918
War Diary	Couillet Wood Sector Right (Nine Wood Sheet).	24/01/1918	31/01/1918
Miscellaneous	Amendments To Left Brigade Defence Scheme, 19th Division, Issued Under B.M.1147 Dated 2/1/18.	02/01/1918	02/01/1918
Miscellaneous	Left Brigade Sector, 19th Division. Defence Scheme. App A	02/01/1917	02/01/1917
Miscellaneous	Appendix "A" Orders For Counter-Attacking Battalion, Left Sector 19th Division.		
Miscellaneous	Appendix B. "Evict Scheme."		
Miscellaneous	Appendix B.		
Operation(al) Order(s)	58th Infantry Brigade Order No.211.	01/01/1917	01/01/1917
Operation(al) Order(s)	58th Infantry Brigade Order No.212.	02/01/1918	02/01/1918
Miscellaneous	Copy No.		
Operation(al) Order(s)	58th Infantry Brigade Order No.213	03/01/1918	03/01/1918
Miscellaneous			
Miscellaneous	58th Infantry Brigade Order No.214	03/01/1918	03/01/1918
Miscellaneous	Relief Table Issued With 58th Infantry Brigade Order No.214		
Miscellaneous	Copy No.		
Miscellaneous	58th Infantry Brigade Order No.215.	04/01/1918	04/01/1918
Miscellaneous			
Operation(al) Order(s)	58th Infantry Brigade Order No.216	04/01/1918	04/01/1918
Miscellaneous	58th Infantry Brigade Order No.217	06/01/1918	06/01/1918
Miscellaneous	58th Infantry Brigade Order No.218	08/01/1918	08/01/1918
Miscellaneous	58th Infantry Brigade Order No.219	10/01/1918	10/01/1918
Miscellaneous	58th Infantry Brigade Order No.220.	12/01/1918	12/01/1918
Miscellaneous	58th Infantry Brigade Order No.221.	13/01/1918	13/01/1918
Miscellaneous	58th Infantry Brigade Order No.222.	15/01/1918	15/01/1918
Miscellaneous	58th Infantry Brigade Order No.223.	15/01/1918	15/01/1918
Miscellaneous	58th Infantry Brigade Order No.224.	15/01/1918	15/01/1918
Miscellaneous	Amendment No.1 To 58th Infantry Brigade Order No.224.	17/01/1918	17/01/1918
Miscellaneous	58th Infantry Brigade Order No.225.	19/01/1918	19/01/1918
Miscellaneous	To Accompany 58th Inf. Bde. Order No.225.		
Miscellaneous	58th Infantry Brigade Operation Order No.226.	20/01/1918	20/01/1918
Miscellaneous	Amendment No.1 To 58th Infantry Brigade Operation Order No.226	20/01/1918	20/01/1918
Miscellaneous	58th Infantry Brigade Order No.227.	22/01/1918	22/01/1918
Heading	HQ 58 Infy Bde (19th Div) Vol 32 February 1918.		
Heading	19 Division		
War Diary	Couillet Wood. Right Sector.	01/02/1918	15/02/1918
War Diary	Rocquigny.	16/02/1918	22/02/1918
War Diary	Haplincourt	23/02/1918	28/02/1918
Miscellaneous	58th Infantry Brigade Order No.228.	31/01/1918	31/01/1918
Miscellaneous	Relief Table.		

Miscellaneous	Locations Of Units On Completion Of Moves Taking Place On Dates Shown In Left Column.		
Miscellaneous	58th Brigade No. B.M.1603.	01/02/1918	01/02/1918
Miscellaneous	Index To Couillet Sector, Right Sub-Sector Defence Scheme.		
Miscellaneous	Defence Scheme. (Couillet Sector-Right Sub-Sector).		
Miscellaneous			
Miscellaneous	Garrison Of Highland Ridge System.	01/02/1918	01/02/1918
Miscellaneous	Part Of Nine Wood Map Appendix.I.		
Map	Map 'B' Appendix II		
Miscellaneous	Appendix III Locations.		
Miscellaneous	Appendix IV. Instructions For The Counter-Attack Battalion Couillet Right Sector.		
Miscellaneous	Appendix V. Signal Communications.		
Miscellaneous	Appendix. VI. Administrative Arrangements.		
Miscellaneous	Amendment To 58th Infy. Bde. Defence Scheme. Couillet Right Sub-Sector.	04/02/1918	04/02/1918
Miscellaneous	Amendment No.2 To 58th Infy. Bde. Defence Scheme. Couillet Right Sector.	05/02/1918	05/02/1918
Miscellaneous	58th Infantry Brigade Order No.229.	03/02/1916	03/02/1916
Miscellaneous	Relief Table "A" Attached To 58th Inf. Bde. Order No. 229 Showing Locations Of Dates Shown In Column 1.		
Miscellaneous	Addendum No.1 To 58th Infantry Brigade Order No.229.	04/02/1918	04/02/1918
Miscellaneous	Amendment To Second Page Of Relief Table Attached To 58th Infantry Brigade Order No.230.	11/02/1918	11/02/1918
Miscellaneous	58th Infantry Brigade Order No.230.	11/02/1918	11/02/1918
Miscellaneous	Relief Table Attached To 58th Infantry Brigade Order No.230.		
Miscellaneous	Amendment To Table Attached To 58th Inf. Brigade Order No.230.	12/02/1918	12/02/1918
Miscellaneous	58th Infantry Brigade Order No.231.	22/02/1918	22/02/1918
Miscellaneous	March Table Issued With 58th Infantry Brigade Order No.231.		
Heading	19th Division War Diary A Wad Of Maps Will Be Found Under Separate Cover B.H.Q. 58th Infantry Brigade March 1918 Report On Operations Attached.		
War Diary	Haplincourt	01/03/1918	27/03/1918
Miscellaneous	Bayencourt	28/03/1918	28/03/1918
War Diary	Famechon Locre.	29/03/1918	31/03/1918
War Diary		06/04/1918	06/04/1918
Miscellaneous	Headquarters 19th Division.	05/04/1918	05/04/1918
Miscellaneous	58th Infantry Brigade. Narrative Of Events From March 21st To 28th 1918.	21/03/1918	21/03/1918
Miscellaneous	Headquarters 19th Division.	07/04/1918	07/04/1918
Miscellaneous	58th Infantry Brigade Administrative Instructions Issued In Connection With B.M.97. Action Of 58th Brigade In The Event Of An Enemy Attack.	09/03/1918	09/03/1918
Miscellaneous	Amendment No.1 To B.M.97.	09/03/1918	09/03/1918
Miscellaneous	Amendment No.2 To B.M.97 Dated 8/3/18.	08/03/1918	08/03/1918
Miscellaneous	58th Brigade No. B.M.97.	08/03/1918	08/03/1918
Miscellaneous	Action Of The 58th Infantry Brigade In The Event Of An Attack.	08/03/1918	08/03/1918
Miscellaneous	Appendix I Counter-attack against Doignies (Resuming That To Hold The Third System).		

Type	Description	Date From	Date To
Miscellaneous	Appendix II. Counter-Attack On Hermies. Assuming That We Hold The 3rd System.		
Miscellaneous	Reference 58th Inf. Brigade No. B.M.97 Dated 5.3.18. Communications.	08/03/1918	08/03/1918
Miscellaneous	58th Brigade No. B.M.97/4.	11/03/1918	11/03/1918
Miscellaneous	Appendix III. Counter-Attack On Havrincourt.		
Miscellaneous	58th Brigade No. B.M.97/5.	12/03/1918	12/03/1918
Miscellaneous	Appendix IV. Counter Attack On Louverval (By Day).		
Map	1st Objective Inf. A.D.V.O. 70		
Miscellaneous	Communications. Havrincourt Attack.		
Miscellaneous	Communications. Louverval Attack.		
Miscellaneous	Warning Order.	19/03/1918	19/03/1918
Miscellaneous	58th Infantry Brigade Order No.232. App E	20/03/1918	20/03/1918
Miscellaneous	Relief Table To Accompany 58th Infantry Brigade Order No.232		
Miscellaneous	58th Inf. Bde. Order No.233.	28/03/1918	28/03/1918
Miscellaneous	March Table Issued With 58th Inf. Bde. Order No.233.		
Miscellaneous	19th Division "G".	13/03/1918	13/03/1918
Map	Defence Map.		
Miscellaneous	Brigade Sectors C.O Map 2A.		
Miscellaneous	19th Division "G".	13/03/1918	13/03/1918
Miscellaneous	Location Of Headquarters.		
Heading	19th Division Maps To Accompany War Diary Of 58th Infantry Brigade March 1918		
Map	Special Sheet		
Map			
Map	19th Division 46 1091/44	19/03/1918	19/03/1918
Map	IG.17. (Amendment To Map IG13) A & B Sectors. 19.3.18		
Map	Map IG.18. (amendment To Map IG.13). F & G Sectors.		
Map	Ganisation.		
Map	Sheet 57c. N.W.		
Map	Defence Map.		
Map	1st Objective Inf. Adv. O+70		
Miscellaneous	19th Division G1091/43	18/03/1918	18/03/1918
Heading	19th Division. B.H.Q. 58th Infantry Brigade. April 1918. Operation Orders & Narrative Attached		
War Diary	Locre.	01/04/1918	07/04/1918
War Diary	Line	08/04/1918	08/04/1918
War Diary	N.29.c.4.5.	09/04/1918	19/04/1918
War Diary	L.35.d.	19/04/1918	21/04/1918
War Diary	Proven.	22/04/1918	25/04/1918
War Diary	G.10.c.3.3.	26/04/1918	26/04/1918
War Diary	G.10.c.3.5	26/04/1918	26/04/1918
War Diary	G.10.d.5.1.	27/04/1918	27/04/1918
War Diary	G.22.a.3.8.	27/04/1918	30/04/1918
Operation(al) Order(s)	58th Infantry Brigade Order No.235.	31/03/1918	31/03/1918
Operation(al) Order(s)	58th Infantry Brigade Order No.236.	02/04/1918	02/04/1918
Miscellaneous	March Table Issued With 58th Infantry Brigade Order No.236.		
Operation(al) Order(s)	58th Infantry Brigade Order No.237	04/04/1918	04/04/1918
Operation(al) Order(s)	58th Infantry Brigade Order No.238.	06/04/1918	06/04/1918
Miscellaneous	58th Infantry Brigade Order No.239.	08/04/1918	08/04/1918
Miscellaneous	58th Infantry Brigade Order No.240.	10/04/1918	10/04/1918

Miscellaneous	Narrative Of Action Of 58th Inf. Bde. From 10th To 20th April, 1918.	10/04/1918	10/04/1918
Miscellaneous			
Miscellaneous	58th Inf. Bde. No. B.M.145.	18/04/1918	18/04/1918
Miscellaneous	58th Inf. Brigade Order No.241.	20/04/1918	20/04/1918
Miscellaneous	March Table.		
Miscellaneous	B Form. Messages And Signals.		
Miscellaneous	A Form. Messages And Signals.		
Miscellaneous	C Form. Messages And Signals.		
Miscellaneous	A Form Messages And Signals.	12/04/1918	12/04/1918
Miscellaneous	To Recipients Of Operation Order No.811.		
Miscellaneous	C Form. Messages And Signals.		
Miscellaneous	1st South African Infantry Brigade Order No.183	13/04/1918	13/04/1918
Miscellaneous	B Form. Messages And Signals.		
Miscellaneous	C Form. Messages And Signals.		
Map	Belgium And Part Of France		
Miscellaneous	Belgium And Part Of France		
Heading	Headquarters, 58th Inf. Bde. (19th Div.) May 1918 Vol.3.		
Heading	On His Majesty's Service.		
War Diary	H.27.b.6.7.	01/05/1918	10/05/1918
War Diary	K.12.b.7.5.	11/05/1918	12/05/1918
War Diary	Herzeele	13/05/1918	19/05/1918
War Diary	Chepy.	28/05/1918	31/05/1918
Operation(al) Order(s)	58th Brigade Order No.243.	09/05/1918	09/05/1918
Miscellaneous	58th Brigade Order No.244.	10/05/1918	10/05/1918
Operation(al) Order(s)	58th Infantry Brigade Order No.245.	11/05/1918	11/05/1918
Miscellaneous	March Table Issued With 58th Infantry Brigade Order No.245.		
Miscellaneous	To All Recipients Of 58th Brigade Order No.246.	14/05/1918	14/05/1918
Miscellaneous	58th Brigade Order No.246.	14/05/1918	14/05/1918
Miscellaneous	19th Division No. A/466/C.	12/05/1918	12/05/1918
War Diary	19th Division No. A.466/C.	07/05/1918	07/05/1918
Miscellaneous	Second Army No. G.867.	03/05/1918	03/05/1918
Miscellaneous	58th Brigade No. B.M.558.	15/05/1918	15/05/1918
Operation(al) Order(s)	To All Recipients Of 58th Brigade Order No.246.	15/05/1918	15/05/1918
Miscellaneous	To All Recipients Of 58th Brigade Order No.246.	15/05/1918	15/05/1918
Miscellaneous	58th Infantry Brigade Order No.247.	28/05/1918	28/05/1918
Miscellaneous	March Table To Accompany 58th Infantry Brigade Order No.247.		
Miscellaneous	58th Infantry Brigade. Narrative Of Operations From May 28th To May 31st, 1918.	28/05/1918	28/05/1918
Heading	Headquarters, 58th Inf. Bde. (19th Div.) June 1918 Vol. 36.		
Heading	On His Majesty's Service.		
War Diary	Line Nr Chambrecy	01/06/1918	06/06/1918
War Diary	Bois De Courton	07/06/1918	11/06/1918
War Diary	Chamuzy	12/06/1918	19/06/1918
War Diary	Dizy-Magenta.	20/06/1918	20/06/1918
War Diary	Cramant.	21/06/1918	21/06/1918
War Diary	Broussy-Le Grand.	22/06/1918	30/06/1918
Operation(al) Order(s)	58th Infantry Brigade Order No.246.	09/06/1918	09/06/1918
Miscellaneous	Administrative Instructions Issued With Reference To 58th Brigade Order No.248 Of 9th June 1918.	09/06/1918	09/06/1918
Miscellaneous	58th Infantry Brigade Order No.249.	10/06/1918	10/06/1918
Miscellaneous	58th Brigade Order No.250.	18/06/1918	18/06/1918

Miscellaneous	March Table To Accompany Operation Order No.250.		
Operation(al) Order(s)	Addendum No.1 To 58th Infantry Brigade Order No.250.	20/06/1918	20/06/1918
Operation(al) Order(s)	58th Infantry Brigade Order No.251.	29/06/1918	29/06/1918
Miscellaneous	March Table To Accompany O.O. No.251.		
Miscellaneous	Amendment No.1 To March Table Accompanying O. O. 251.	29/06/1918	29/06/1918
Heading	HQ 58 Infy Bde (19th Div.) Vol 37 July 1918.		
Heading	D.A.G. G.H.Q. 3rd Echelon.		
Miscellaneous	Headquarters 19th Division.	02/08/1918	02/08/1918
War Diary	Vassimont.	01/07/1918	03/07/1918
War Diary	Coupelle Vieille.	04/07/1918	04/07/1918
War Diary	Campagne.	05/07/1918	11/07/1918
War Diary	Ligny Les Aire	11/07/1918	31/07/1918
Operation(al) Order(s)	58th Infantry Brigade Order No.252.	03/07/1918	03/07/1918
Miscellaneous	March Table To Accompany O.O. No.252.		
Operation(al) Order(s)	Addendum No.1 To 58th Inf. Brigade Order No.253.	10/07/1918	10/07/1918
Miscellaneous	58th Infantry Brigade Order No.253.	14/07/1918	14/07/1918
Miscellaneous	March Table To Accompany 58th Brigade O.O. No.253		
Miscellaneous	58th Brigade No, S.C. 8954	10/07/1918	10/07/1918
Miscellaneous	All Units. 19th Div G.	20/07/1918	20/07/1918
Miscellaneous	Scheme For The Assembly Of "C" Brigade For Counter-Attack On Mt. Bernenchon-Hinges Ridge (To Be Known As Scheme "A".	15/07/1918	15/07/1918
Miscellaneous	Table A (1)		
Miscellaneous	Addendum To B.M.986 Dated 20th July To Be Attached Thereto.	20/07/1918	20/07/1918
Miscellaneous	Scheme For The Assembly Of "C" Brigade For Counter-Attack On Beuvry-Bethune Ridge To Be Known As Scheme "B".	20/07/1918	20/07/1918
Miscellaneous	Table "B"		
Miscellaneous	58th Brigade No. B.M.971.	21/07/1918	21/07/1918
Miscellaneous	Scheme For The Move Of The 58th Brigade To The Second Army By March Route, To Be Known As Scheme "H".	21/07/1918	21/07/1918
Miscellaneous	Table "A"		
Miscellaneous	Scheme For The Embussing Of The 58th Inf. Bde. Group To Be Known As Scheme "J".	21/07/1918	21/07/1918
Miscellaneous	58th Brigade No. B.M.971.	21/07/1918	21/07/1918
Miscellaneous	Scheme For The Move Of The 58th Brigade To The Second Army By March Route, To Be Known As Scheme "H".	21/07/1918	21/07/1918
Miscellaneous	Table "A"		
Miscellaneous	Scheme For The Embussing Of The 58th Inf. Bde. Group To Be Known As Scheme "J".	21/07/1918	21/07/1918
Miscellaneous	All Battalions.	22/07/1918	22/07/1918
Map	Sheet 44B. N.E. 1.20,000		
Miscellaneous	Appendix I.		
Miscellaneous	Scheme "B" (Right (A) Brigade). Counter-Attack On Bethune-Beuvry Ridge.		
Miscellaneous	Scheme B (left (B) Brigade). Counter-Attack On Beuvry-Bethune Ridge.	21/07/1918	21/07/1918
Miscellaneous		22/07/1918	22/07/1918
Miscellaneous	Scheme "B". (A Bde.). Appendix I.		

Miscellaneous	Scheme "A" (Right (A) Brigade). Counter-Attack On Ht. Bernenchon-Hinges Ridge.	14/07/1918	14/07/1918
Miscellaneous	Appendix I.		
Heading	Headquarters, 58th Inf. Bde. (19th Div.) August 1918 Vol. 38.		
Heading	On His Majesty's Service.		
Miscellaneous	Headquarters 19th Division.	11/09/1918	11/09/1918
War Diary	Lighy Les Aire.	01/08/1918	06/08/1918
War Diary	Line Hinges Sector	07/08/1918	11/08/1918
War Diary	Line.	12/08/1918	20/08/1918
War Diary	Reserve Abbaye	21/08/1918	22/08/1918
War Diary	Noisy Nook. V.12.b.2.6. Sht. 36A. S.E.	23/08/1918	31/08/1918
Operation(al) Order(s)	58th Infantry Brigade Order No.254.	04/08/1918	04/08/1918
Operation(al) Order(s)	Addendum No.1 To 58th Bde. Order No.254.	05/08/1918	05/08/1918
Operation(al) Order(s)	58th Brigade Order No.255.	09/08/1918	09/08/1918
Operation(al) Order(s)	58th Infantry Brigade Order No.256.	13/08/1918	13/08/1918
Operation(al) Order(s)	58th Infantry Brigade Order No.257.	17/08/1918	17/08/1918
Miscellaneous	Addendum No.1 To 58th Infantry Brigade Order No.258.	20/08/1918	20/08/1918
Miscellaneous	58th Brigade Order No.258.	20/08/1918	20/08/1918
Miscellaneous	58th Infantry Brigade. Provisional Defence Orders For New Sector.	21/08/1918	21/08/1918
Miscellaneous	58th Brigade No. B.M.1420/1.	24/08/1918	24/08/1918
Miscellaneous	58th Infantry Brigade Order No.259.	21/08/1918	21/08/1918
Miscellaneous	Relief Table To Accompany 58th Brigade Order No.259.		
Miscellaneous	Addendum No.1 To 58th Infantry Brigade Order No.259.	22/08/1918	22/08/1918
Miscellaneous	58th Infantry Brigade Order No.260.	25/08/1918	25/08/1918
Miscellaneous	58th Infantry Brigade Order No.261.	28/08/1918	28/08/1918
Miscellaneous	58th Inf. Brigade Order No.262.	29/08/1918	29/08/1918
Heading	HQ 58 Infy Bde (19th Div.) Vol 39 September 1918		
Miscellaneous	D.A.G. G.H.Q. 3rd Echelon.		
War Diary		01/09/1918	01/09/1918
War Diary	X.2.a.5.8.	02/09/1918	04/09/1918
War Diary	R.29.b.2.1.	05/09/1918	05/09/1918
War Diary	Stink Inn.	06/09/1918	11/09/1918
War Diary	R.34.b.9.7.	12/09/1918	22/09/1918
War Diary	W.23.b.75.15.	23/09/1918	27/09/1918
War Diary	X.28.a.30.60.	28/09/1918	30/09/1918
Operation(al) Order(s)	58th Infantry Brigade Order No.264.	02/09/1918	02/09/1918
Miscellaneous	B Reports Etc.		
Miscellaneous	C.	04/09/1918	04/09/1918
Miscellaneous	58th Infantry Brigade. Provisional Defence Orders For Right Sub-Sector Of Divisional Front.	21/09/1918	21/09/1918
Miscellaneous	58th Infantry Brigade. Provisional Defence Orders For Left Subsector Of Divl. Front.	09/09/1918	09/09/1918
Operation(al) Order(s)	58th Infantry Brigade Order No.266.	09/09/1918	09/09/1918
Operation(al) Order(s)	58th Infantry Brigade Order No.267.	13/09/1918	13/09/1918
Operation(al) Order(s)	58th Infantry Brigade Order No.268.	17/09/1918	17/09/1918
Operation(al) Order(s)	58th Infantry Brigade Order No.269.	21/09/1918	21/09/1918
Operation(al) Order(s)	58th Infantry Brigade Order No.271.	27/09/1918	27/09/1918
Operation(al) Order(s)	58th Infantry Brigade Order No.270.	26/09/1918	26/09/1918
Miscellaneous	Relief Table To Accompany 58th Inf. Brigade Order No.270.		
Operation(al) Order(s)	58th Infantry Brigade Order No.272.	29/09/1918	29/09/1918

Type	Description	Start	End
Miscellaneous	Stokes Mortar Co-Operation Reference Para. 4 Of O.O. 272.	29/09/1918	29/09/1918
Operation(al) Order(s)	58th Infantry Brigade Order No.273.	30/09/1918	30/09/1918
Miscellaneous	March Table For Move Of 1st Line Transport, On 1st October.	01/10/1918	01/10/1918
Miscellaneous	Relief Table To Accompany O.O. 273.		
Miscellaneous	March Table To Accompany O.O. 273.		
Map	Locon Map B		
Map	Richebourg Map B		
Miscellaneous	Glossary.		
Miscellaneous	Trench Map Richebourg. 36 S.W. 3. Edition 11.A		
Heading	58th Inf Bde (19th Div) October 1918 Vol 40		
Heading	D.A.G. G.H.Q 3rd Echelon		
War Diary	X.28.a.30.60.	01/10/1918	01/10/1918
War Diary	Pernes.	02/10/1918	04/10/1918
War Diary	Barly.	04/10/1918	07/10/1918
War Diary	K.4.d.50.45.	07/10/1918	11/10/1918
War Diary	Cagnoncles T.28.d.45.25.	12/10/1918	16/10/1918
War Diary	Rieux	17/10/1918	18/10/1918
War Diary	St. Aubert.	19/10/1918	20/10/1918
War Diary	V.9.a.8.8. Haussy	20/10/1918	22/10/1918
War Diary	Sandpits V.5.a.4.3.	22/10/1918	24/10/1918
War Diary	Rieux.	24/10/1918	30/10/1918
Map	Map "A"		
Map	57th Bde XXII Corps.		
Operation(al) Order(s)	58th Infantry Brigade Order No.274.	03/10/1918	03/10/1918
Miscellaneous			
Miscellaneous	March Table To Accompany 58th Inf. Brigade Order No.274.		
Miscellaneous	Entraining Table "A"		
Operation(al) Order(s)	58th Inf. Brigade Order No.275.	05/10/1918	05/10/1918
Operation(al) Order(s)	March Orders No.3.	05/10/1918	05/10/1918
Miscellaneous	March Table In Conjunction With March Order No.3.		
Operation(al) Order(s)	58th Infantry Brigade Order No.276.		
Miscellaneous	Amendment No.1 To 58th Inf. Brigade Order No.277.	12/10/1918	12/10/1918
Operation(al) Order(s)	Addendum No.1 To 58th Inf. Brigade Order No.277.	10/10/1918	10/10/1918
Operation(al) Order(s)	58th Infantry Brigade Order No.277.	10/10/1918	10/10/1918
Operation(al) Order(s)	58th Infantry Brigade Order No.278.		
Operation(al) Order(s)	58th Inf. Brigade Order No.279.	12/10/1918	12/10/1918
Operation(al) Order(s)	58th Infantry Brigade Order No.280.	15/10/1918	15/10/1918
Operation(al) Order(s)	58th Brigade O.O. 281.	18/10/1918	18/10/1918
Operation(al) Order(s)	58th Bde. Order No.282.	18/10/1918	18/10/1918
Operation(al) Order(s)	58th Infantry Brigade Order No.283.	22/10/1918	22/10/1918
Heading	HQ 58 Inf Bde (19th Div.) Nov 1918. Vol.41		
Heading	D.A.G. G.H.Q. 3rd Echelon.		
War Diary	Rieux	01/11/1918	01/11/1918
War Diary	Sommaing	02/11/1918	08/11/1918
War Diary	Houdain	09/11/1918	10/11/1918
War Diary	Eth	11/11/1918	15/11/1918
War Diary	Avesnes	16/11/1918	25/11/1918
War Diary	Cambrai	26/11/1918	29/11/1918
War Diary	Halloy Les Pernois.	30/11/1918	30/11/1918
Miscellaneous	Reference 19th Div. No. 1,000 58th Bde. No.1001.	31/10/1918	31/10/1918
Operation(al) Order(s)	58th Brigade Order No.284.	01/11/1918	01/11/1918
Miscellaneous	March Table To Accompany 58th Brigade Order No.284.		

Type	Description	Start	End
Operation(al) Order(s)	58th Infy. Bde. Order No.285.	02/11/1918	02/11/1918
Operation(al) Order(s)	Addendum No.1 To 58th Bde. Order No.285.	03/11/1918	03/11/1918
Operation(al) Order(s)	Addendum No.2 To 58th Bde. Order No.285.	03/11/1918	03/11/1918
Operation(al) Order(s)	Addendum No.3 To 58th Brigade Order No.285.	03/11/1918	03/11/1918
Miscellaneous	Narrative Of Operations From November 3rd To 9th 1918.	03/11/1918	03/11/1918
Map	Edition 3. Sheet 51 A N.E. 1/20.000		
Map	Belgium And Part Of France		
Miscellaneous	B.M. Objective Map.		
Operation(al) Order(s)	58th Brigade Order No.286.	09/11/1918	09/11/1918
Miscellaneous	March Table To Accompany 58th Brigade Order No.286.		
Miscellaneous	To 58th Inf. Brigade.	11/11/1918	11/11/1918
Operation(al) Order(s)	58th Brigade Order No.287.	13/11/1918	13/11/1918
Miscellaneous	March Table To Accompany O.O. No.287.		
Operation(al) Order(s)	58th Brigade Order No.288.	14/11/1918	14/11/1918
Miscellaneous	March Table To Accompany O.O. No.288.		
Operation(al) Order(s)	58th Brigade Order No.289.	23/11/1918	23/11/1918
Operation(al) Order(s)	Addendum No.1 To 58th Bde. Order No.289.		
Miscellaneous	March Table To Accompany Addendum No.1 To 58th Brigade Order No.289.		
Miscellaneous	Amendment No.1 To 58th Bde. Order No.289.	24/11/1918	24/11/1918
Operation(al) Order(s)	58th Brigade Order No.290.	24/11/1918	24/11/1918
Miscellaneous	March Table To Accompany 58th Brigade Order No.290.		
Operation(al) Order(s)	58th Brigade Order No.291.	26/11/1918	26/11/1918
Operation(al) Order(s)	58th Brigade Order No.292.	27/11/1918	27/11/1918
Heading	Headquarters, 58th Inf. Bde (19th Div.) December 1918 Vol. 42.		
Heading	On His Majesty's Service.		
War Diary	Halloy-Les-Pernois.	01/01/1919	31/01/1919
Heading	Headquarters. 58th Infantry Brigade February 1919 Vol 44		
War Diary	Halloy-Les-Pernois.	01/02/1919	24/02/1919
War Diary	Villers-l'Hopital.	25/02/1919	19/03/1919
War Diary	Frohen-Le-Grand.	30/03/1919	07/06/1919
War Diary	Candas	16/06/1919	16/06/1919
War Diary	Mondicourt.	17/06/1919	17/06/1919
War Diary	Le-Havre	18/06/1919	20/06/1919
War Diary	Halloy les Pernois.	01/12/1919	31/12/1919

19TH DIVISION
58TH INFY BDE

BDE HEADQUARTERS
JAN 1918-MAR 1919

HQ 5 8 Infy Bde
(1st line)
Vol 31
January 1918

Jan '18
Mar '19

Army Form C. 2118.

WAR DIARY
INTELLIGENCE SUMMARY
(Erase heading not required.)

Instructions regarding War Diaries and Intelligence Summaries are contained in F.S. Regs., Part II. and the Staff Manual respectively. Title Pages will be prepared in manuscript.

Place	Date Jany.	Hour	Summary of Events and Information	Remarks and references to Appendices
RIBECOURT (NINE WOOD) MARCOING 1/10,000)	1.		A quiet day. Visibility poor.	App A
	2.		Left Brigade Sector Defence Scheme issued. The right sub-sector was extended to the right taking over from 57th Bde. as far as the Railway (exclusive).	App B
	3.		Greater enemy artillery activity over a wide area, especially in L.25., L.31., and L.32. A British aeroplane (one of a flight of four) was brought down over MARCOING at 8.30.a.m. by hostile M.Gun fire. Much hostile aerial activity. The Brigade extended its left taking over the front of 50th Inf. Bde. (17th Divn) as far as BEETROOT FACTORY - RAVINE AVENUE (exclusive) The 9th Welch Regt. relieved the 6th Wilts Regt. in the Right Sub-sector.	App C do.
	4th		142nd Bde. relieved 9th Welch Regt. and 9th R.W.Fusiliers with 20th and 21st London Regt. respectively 9th Welch R and 9th R.W.Fus. moved back on relief to Intermediate Line, 58th T.M.B. was relieved by 142nd T.M.Battery.	App D and E
	5th		142nd Bde. relieved 9th Cheshire R. and 6th Wilts Regt. with 23rd and 22nd Bns. London Regt. respectively. 9th Cheshire R. and 6th Wilts R. on relief moved back to Intermediate Line vacated by 9th R.W.Fus. and 9th Welch R. who had relieved 10th Worc. R. and 8th Glouc. (57th Brigade) in new Left Bde. sector. 58th Bde. H.Q. moved to RUYAULCOURT on command passing to G.O.C. 142nd Inf. Bde. Capt.CARPENTER, (Bde Major) returned from leave.	App F
RUYAULCOURT	6th		9th Cheshire Regt. relieved 8th N.Staffs R. in centre sub-sector, 6th Wilts R. relieved 10th Warwicks R. in Support. Bde.H.Q. moved from RUYAULCOURT to L.31.a.1.2. and on the above relief being complete the command of Left Bde Sector passed from G.O.C. 57th to G.O.C. 58th Bde.	App G.
	7th		G.O.C. 58th Bde. goes on leave and command of Bde. passes to Lt-Col. R.M.HEATH, 10/R.Warwick R. Re-adjustment of boundaries between Right and Centre Battalion takes place.	App H
	8th		A quiet day. Visibility poor, freezing and snowing again, trenches in a bad condition. Weather cleared up in the afternoon and visibility was better.	

Army Form C. 2118.

WAR DIARY
or
INTELLIGENCE SUMMARY

(Erase heading not required.)

Instructions regarding War Diaries and Intelligence Summaries are contained in F.S. Regs, Part II. and the Staff Manual respectively. Title Pages will be prepared in manuscript.

Place	Date	Hour	Summary of Events and Information	Remarks and references to Appendices
	Jany 9th		Blizzard from S.W. blowing all day, thaw set in during the night making the trenches in a very bad state. In the evening the 6th Wilts R. relieved the 9th Cheshire Regt. in the Centre Sub-sector of front line. Work carried on as usual widening and deepening trenches. Abnormal movement noticed on the CAMBRAI - NOYELLES Rd. both transport and infantry going towards NOYELLES mostly.	App J.
	10th		Had a telephone message from Divn. to say the Corps reported having seen the Germans massing in R.29.d. and R.28.a. b and c. Numbers calculated to be about 3000. Abnormal movement still going on behind the enemy's lines in the same area as yesterday. Our guns more active than usual also our aircraft. Enemy artillery active on back areas L.25. and L.31. receiving special attention. Visibility very good all day. The Coy. of 9th Cheshire Regt. accommodated in FORK AVENUE move back to trench running from L.32.c.12.86. to L.31.b.85.00. with Coy.H.Q. at L.32.a.23.00. and 9th Welch Regt. took over the accommodation vacated by 9th Cheshire Regt. and will establish their Bn.H.Q. there.	App K.
	11th		Corps artillery carried out a systematic bombardment of the enemy's trenches and all known assembly areas from 6.17.a.m. - 6.32.a.m. Otherwise a quiet day. Visibility good.	
	12th		The 9th Cheshire R. relieved the 9th R.W.Fusrs. in the right sub-sector with the exception of the right support company of the 9th R.W.Fusrs. which was relieved by the 8th N.Staffs Regt. Enemy artillery active on battery areas.	App L
	13th		Re-adjustment of Bde on a two Battn. front, to affect this (see App M). Visibility good.	App M.
	14th		Visibility poor owing to snow. Little artillery activity.	
	15th		9th R.W.Fusrs. from support relieved 9th Cheshire R. in Right sub-sector. On relief 9th Cheshire move to support.	App N.
	16th		9th Welsh R. from Reserve relieved 6th Wilts Regt. in Left sub-sector On relief 6th Wilts R (less one company) moved to Reserve area.	App O.

Army Form C. 2118.

MAP SHEET 57c
1/40000

WAR DIARY
or
INTELLIGENCE SUMMARY

(Erase heading not required.)

Instructions regarding War Diaries and Intelligence Summaries are contained in F.S. Regs., Part II. and the Staff Manual respectively. Title Pages will be prepared in manuscript.

Place	Date	Hour	Summary of Events and Information	Remarks and references to Appendices
	17th		2 battalions 56th Bde. from reserve relieve 2 battalions 58th Bde. in the line on night 17/18 6th Wilts R (less 1 Coy) relieved in the Intermediate line by 7th S.Lancs.R. (less 2 Coys) 9th Cheshire R. (Support Battn) relieved by 7th K.O.R.Lanc.R. (less 1 Coy) Weather misty and rainy.	App F.
	18th		Remaining 2 Battns 56th Bde. and Bde H.Q. took over from remaining 2 Battns. and Bde.H.Q. of 58th Bde.	" "
RESERVE AREA	19th		Units resting. Training on 100ˣ range at F.15.a.4.4. Warning order for first Group relief issued to units concerned. O.O.225 issued on system of Group reliefs.	
	20th		B.M. visited B.M. 57th Bde. to arrange details of first Group relief. O.O.226 issued. Reconnoitring parties 9th Cheshire R. and 6th Wilts R. visited Rt. sector. Amendment No. 1 to O.O.226 issued.	
	21/22		9th Cheshire R. relieved 8th Glouc. R. in Left sub-sector, and 6th Wilts R. relieved 10th Worc. R. in Right sub-sector both of right sector. 9th Cheshire R. and 6th Wilts R. passed under command of G.O.C. A Group.	
	22nd		58th Bde. School established and assembled at P.25.a.2.3. Courses for Platoon Commdrs, Sergts. and a L.Gun and F.T. & B.F. Course. Working parties. Range allotted to 9th R.W.Fusrs. and relief of A.A.Guns over Corps dumps in YPRES Area. O.O.227 issued.	
	23rd		Units training. Working parties.	
COUILLET WOOD Sector Right (NINE WOOD Sheet).	24th		G.O.C. 58th Inf. Bde. and B.M. went and reconnoitred Intermediate Line of Right Group. H.Q. relieved H.Q. 57th Bde. in Q.12.a.9.6. (Sht. 57 C. S.E.) G.O.C. assumed command of "A" Group (Right) at 2.O.p.m. 9th R.W.Fusrs. relieved 7th S.Lanc. R. in the right sub-sector, and 9th Welch R. relieve 7th R.Lanc.R. in the Left sub-sector (Left or "B" Group), and pass under command of G.O.C. "B" or Left Group. "A" Group consists of 9th Cheshire R., 6th Wilts R., 10th R.War. R. in the front line, 8th Glouc. R. in support, 10th Worc. R and 8th N.Staffs R. in Reserve Area.	

Army Form C. 2118.

WAR DIARY
or
INTELLIGENCE SUMMARY

(Erase heading not required.)

Instructions regarding War Diaries and Intelligence Summaries are contained in F.S. Regs., Part II. and the Staff Manual respectively. Title Pages will be prepared in manuscript.

Place	Date	Hour	Summary of Events and Information	Remarks and references to Appendices
	25th		Visited Support, Centre and Right Battns. in the line. Going in C.T's very bad.	
	25/26th		8th Glouc. R. relieved 9th Cheshire R. in Right Left sub-sector and 10th Worc. relieved 6th Wilts in Right sub-sector.	
	26th		G.O.C. visited all battalions in morning. and B.M. visited front line and posts of Right and Centre battalions at night and all Bn. H.Q. Necessary suggestions written to battalions concerned on return.	
	27th		G.O.C. visited Bns. and Posts and front line in detail of Left Bn. Between 11.p.m. and 1.a.m. on night of 27/28th enemy heavily gas shelled COUILLET WOOD and HIGHLAND RIDGE line	
	28th		New B.M. arrived. Captain L.J.A.WILL, M.C. Worc. Regt., Acting B.M. visited/with him. C.T's and Centre and Right Bns visited.	
	28/29		G.O.C. visited Post line of right battalion. Necessary work noticed as needed, ordered to be undertaken.	
	29th		G.O.C. and new B.M. visited line. Right and Centre Bns.	
	29/30		Enemy heavily gas shelled BOAR COPSE Valley and vicinity of Bde. H.Q. Bombardment from 5.15.a.m. to 6.15.a.m.	
	30th		Defence scheme drafted. G.O.C. visited battns. New B.M. assumed duties.	
	31st		G.O.C. visited Bns. in the line. Heavy mist. Little artillery activity.	

W.H. Hill Col.
Brigadier/Major for Brigadier General
Commanding 58th Infantry Brigade.

SECRET.

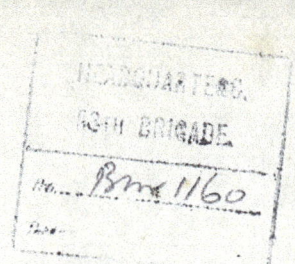

Amendments to LEFT BRIGADE DEFENCE SCHEME,
19th DIVISION,
issued under B.M.1147 dated 2/1/18.
----

1. Para. 2 (b) "BRIGADE FRONT". Insert full stop after "Reserve"; delete full stop after "hand".

2. Para. 3, line 9. "BOUNDARIES OF LEFT SECTOR". For L.20.d.0.8. read L.20.d.00.95.

3. Para. 4 (b), "MAIN LINE OF RESISTANCE": For th "The Salient L.21.c.45.90. - L.20.b.70.75." substitute "The Salient L.21.c.45.90. - L.21.b.02.61 - L.14.d.65 45. - L.20.b.70.75."

4. Para. 5, B, (c), (ii). For "STAT.AV." read "STATION AVENUE".

58th Brigade No. B.M.1147.

SECRET.   Copy No......

LEFT BRIGADE SECTOR, 19th DIVISION.
DEFENCE SCHEME.

Ref: Map: NINE WOOD, 1/10,000.
          MARCOING, 1/10,000.

DIVISIONAL FRONT. 1. (a). The 19th Divisional front extends from the Road (inclusive) L.34.a.5.0. to BEETROOT FACTORY (exclusive) L.13.c.75.85. a distance of 5,700 yards measured along front line.

(b). This front is held by 2 Brigades with one Brigade in Divisional Reserve.

BRIGADE FRONT. 2. (a). The Left Brigade sector 19th Divisional Front extends from the Railway inclusive at L.21.c.8.3. to BEETROOT FACTORY (exclusive) L.13.c.75.85.

(b). The sector is held by 3 Battalions in the Line, 1 Battalion being in Brigade Reserve in order to keep the command of the Salient in one hand. The Right Battalion in the Line is reinforced by 1 Company of Centre Battalion so that the Right Battalion consists of 5 Companies and Centre Battalion of 3 Companies.

(c). The Battalion in Brigade Reserve will be the counter-attacking Battalion. (See Appendix A.)
Two companies of this Battalion will be in a constant state of readiness. The remainder may take off boots and equipment but must have them ready to be immediately put on in case of alarm. Not more than two Companies will be taken at a time for work.

BOUNDARIES OF LEFT SECTOR. 3. Right Boundary L.21.c.8.3. (railway inclusive) - RAVINE (exclusive) at L.27.a.0.9. - along NORTH side of RAVINE (exclusive) to L.25.b.8.0. - L.25.d.3.0. - L.31.b.35.55.

Left Boundary BEETROOT FACTORY (exclusive) L.13.c.75.85. - L.19.a.0.1. - K.29.b.55.00. - K.29.c.7.6.

Rear Boundary L.31.b.35.55. - K.30.c.0.4. - K.29.d.5.3. - K.29.c.7.6.

Boundary between Right and Centre Battalions, L.20.b.4.8. - L.20.b.3.3. - L.20.d.0.8. - FREMY AVENUE (inclusive to RIGHT BATTALION) L.20.c.60.65.

Boundary between Left and Centre Battalions - L.20.a.1.7. - L.19.b.60.45. - L.19.b.60.00.

MAIN LINE OF RESISTANCE. 4. (a). The Main Line of Resistance will be the Front Line running from the railway (inclusive) at L.21.c.8.3. - L.21.c.45.90. - L.20.b.90.75. - L.20.b.75.55. - L.20.b.65.75. - L.13.c.70.85.

(b). The Salient L.21.c.45.90. - L.20.b.70.75. (known as DAGO and FREMY TRENCH) will be held as an Outpost Line by Posts only.

GENERAL PRINCIPLES OF DEFENCE. 5. IN THE EVENT OF ATTACK.

A. <u>Battalions in the Line.</u>

(1) The Outpost Line in the Salient will hold on and endeavour to prevent the enemy occupying any portion of their Line. In case of attack on a large scale, these posts will not be reinforced.

(ii) The Main Line of Resistance will be held at all costs. Battalion and Company Commanders on the spot will organise

                                                                 immediate.

immediate counter-attacks to regain any portion of it into which the enemy may have penetrated. For this purpose, every Commander, down to Platoon Commanders, must have a reserve definitely told off for counter-attack. In addition the Right Battalion will be prepared to carry out a deliberate counter-attack to recover the apex of the salient in the event of the enemy limiting his operations to the capture of this trench.

Each Battalion in the Line will have one Company definitely told off as the Counter-attacking Company, whose duty will be to support and, if necessary, retake any points of tactical importance. This counter-attacking Company will have written orders as to its action in the most probable contingencies. These orders will include the position of the counter-attacking Company, place and method of forming up and lines of advance. The orders should have an explanatory sketch attached.

B. BATTALION IN BRIGADE RESERVE.

(a). The Battalion in Brigade Reserve will be prepared to counter-attack on any portion of the Brigade front, or to form a defensive flank in the event of the enemy breaking through the front of the Brigade on either flank.

(b). For counter-attack the most probable lines are:-

(i). The PREMY CHAPEL Spur running in a North-easterly direction on the Southern side of the Valley in L.19.b. and L.14.c.

(ii). The Spur running in a North-Eastern direction on the Northern side of the Valley in L.19.b. and L.14.c.

If these two spurs are secured any enemy who may have penetrated up the valley between them, or up the main MARCOING - RIBECOURT Valley should be easily dealt with.

(c). For the purposes of forming defensive flanks.

(i) The line of PREMY AVENUE would form a convenient defensive flank which could be occupied in the event of the enemy breaking through the Brigade on our ~~left~~ RIGHT.

(ii) STAT. AV. would form defensive flank if enemy broke through Bde on left

(d). The O.C., Battalion in Brigade Reserve must be prepared to act at once without waiting for orders from Brigade H.Q. if the situation demands immediate action. He will at once report action taken. In the case of Alarm, the S.O.S. going up or heavy bombardment the Battalion in Brigade Reserve will "Stand to" in billets and the O.C. Battalion will send an Officer to Brigade H.Q. and an Officer (or selected N.C.O.) to the H.Q. of each Battalion in the Line to get in touch with and report on the situation. It must however be clearly understood that the O.C. Reserve Battalion is to act at once if he considers the situation demands it though no information may have been received from Brigade H.Q. or from their Liaison Officers or N.C.O's.

C. WORKING PARTIES.

Working parties will at once take up a suitable Defensive Position the Officer in command reporting in person to nearest Battalion H.Q.

ARTILLERY ARRANGEMENTS.
6. The Left sector is covered by the Left Group 19th Div.R.A. which at present consists of five 18 pdr. batteries, and one 4.5 Howitzer battery. The Left Group has a Junior Liaison Officer with each of the Battalions in the Line, and also a Senior Liaison Officer at Brigade H.Q. who is responsible for co-ordinating the work of the two Junior Liaison Officers. (See also App.B.).

MACHINE GUN ARRANGEMENTS.
7. The Left Sector is covered by the Left Group 19th Divl. M.Gs. composed of 56th and 57th M.G.Companies, each Company having 12 guns in the line.

This.

- 3 -

This Group is tactically under the orders of the D.W.G.O. but for all matters of trench discipline under the command of the Battalion Commander on the spot.

ARRANGEMENTS FOR DEALING WITH LOW FLYING E.A.
8. (a). <u>Lewis Guns.</u> In order to deal with low flying hostile aeroplanes each Battalion in the Line will have two Lewis Guns on anti-aircraft mountings detailed for this duty. These A.A. Lewis Guns will be sited in or near KAISER SUPPORT Trench.
Similarly the Battalion in Reserve will have four Lewis Guns detailed for A.A. work, these guns will be sited in positions in or near the village.

(b). <u>Vickers Guns.</u> Four of the M.Gs. in the Left Sector are detailed by O.C. Left Group M.Gs. for A.A. work by day.

S.O.S. ORDERS.
9. (a). All Officers, N.C.O's, Sentries and Machine Gunners will be made acquainted with the S.O.S. Orders.

(b). The S.O.S. signal will only be used when the enemy are actually seen to be forming up or advancing to attack.

(c). All available means of communication will be employed in sending the S.O.S. message.

(d). It should be impressed on all Officers that the <u>artillery must be informed immediately its fire is no longer required.</u>

TRENCH MORTARS.
10. The Trench Mortar Battery has four Mortars in the Line sited in defensive emplacements, one pair in FREMY SUPPORT about L.21.a.15.45. and one pair in FREMY SWITCH about L.20.b.45.45.
O.C. Trench Mortar Battery will prepare a number of alternative emplacements in other parts of the line, including the apex of the salient, so that he may be able to move his mortars quickly to any point where they may be required to assist in raids or counter the enemy's T.M. activity.

HEADQUARTERS.
11. Headquarters of Units are as under:-

Brigade H.Q.......... L.25.a.0.2.
Right Battalion...... L.20.d.05.80.
Centre Battalion..... L.19.c.50.00.
Left Battalion....... L.19.c.75.45.
Reserve Battalion.... L.25.a.85.65.
T.M.Battery.......... L.25.d.15.80.
Left Group R.A....... K.36.a.6.0.
Left Group M.G....... K.36.b.15.30.

TRENCH ORDERS.
12. Special attention is directed to 19th Division Standing Orders for the trenches, and the special instructions contained in 19th Division G.576, 611, and 613.

Acknowledge.

G.W. Dymond 2nd Lieutenant

A/Brigade Major 58th Infantry Brigade.

Brigade H.Qrs.
2nd January, 1917.

Copy No. 1 File.
2) War Diary.
3)
4 G.O.C.
5 19th Div. G.
6 56th Inf. Bde.
7 57th Inf Bde.
8 9.Cheshire R.
9 9.R.W.Fusrs.
10 9.Welch R.

11 6.Wiltshire R.
12 58.M.Gun Coy.
13 58.T.M.Batty.
14 Bde. Transport Offr.
15 81st Fld. Co.R.E.
16 50th Inf. Bde.
17 Staff Capt.
18 C.R.A. 19th Div.
19 C.R.E. 19th Div.
20 D.M.G.O.

(Issued to All Units & 19th Div.G. only).

APPENDIX "A"

Orders for Counter-attacking Battalion, Left Sector
19th Division.
------

1. The Battalion in Brigade Reserve is the Counter-attacking Battalion of the Brigade.

2. The Battalion is accommodated as under:-

    Hd.Qrs. at L.25.a.85.65.
    Companies billeted in cellars on both sides of road L.25.a.4.2. - L.25.b.4.5.

3. Two Companies will always be in a constant state of readiness. The remainder may take off boots and equipment but must have them ready to be put on immediately in case of alarm. Not more than 2 Companies of the Battalion will ever be taken for work at one time.

4. The Battalion will be prepared to counter-attack with the whole Battalion (or as much of it as is available should portions of it be away on work) on any portion of the Brigade Front, or to form a defensive flank in the event of the enemy breaking through the front of the Brigade on either flank.

5. The O.C. Battalion must be prepared to act at once without waiting for orders from Brigade H.Q. if the situation demands immediate action. He will at once report action taken. In the case of Alarm, of the S.O.S. going up, or of heavy bombardment, the battalion will "stand to" in its billets and O.C. will send an Officer to Brigade H.Q. and an Officer (or selected N.C.O.) to the H.Q. of each Battalion in the Line to get in touch and report on the situation. It must however be clearly understood that the O.C. Battalion is to act at once if he considers the situation demands it though no information may have been received from Brigade H.Q. or their Liaison Officers or N.C.O's.

6. The following are the general lines of action in the most probable contingencies that may arise (see attached Plan).

    A. In event of enemy breaking into FREMY SALIENT and occupying the CHORD (FREMY SUPPORT) only.

    Proceed by platoons up FREMY AVENUE to KAISER TRENCH and KAISER SUPPORT and form up one Company on each side of FREMY AVENUE in each Trench. Counter-attack with two leading Coys. each on a platoon front one Company on each side of FREMY AVENUE, one Company in Support, one Company in Reserve to remain in KAISER TRENCH in first instance.
    If only two Companies available launch attack on Northern side of FREMY AVENUE only with one Company, second Company in Support.

    B. In event of enemy breaking through Right or Centre Sub-sector and taking KAISER TRENCH or KAISER SUPPORT.

    Proceed by platoons and assemble in position about L.25.b.55.80. and form up for attack under cover of copse at that point. Counter-attack with two Companies side by side each Company on a one platoon front, 2 Companies in Support, taking FREMY AVENUE as a guiding line on the Right.
    If only 2 Companies available launch attack with one Company and one Company in Support.

    C. In event of enemy breaking through Left Sub-sector.

    Proceed by platoons and assemble in position in Sunken Road in L.19.c. and form up for attack under cover of the bank.

Counter.

Counter-attack with two Companies side by side each Company on a one platoon front, 2 Companies in Support. Counter-attack to be delivered in a North-easterly direction so as to get possession of the high ground on N. side of valley in L.19.b. and 14.c. If only two Companies available attack with one Company on a platoon front, one Company in Support.

D. In event of the enemy attacking on the whole Brigade front the O.C. Reserve Battalion will if necessary use his discretion as to where to launch his counter-attack without waiting for orders from the Brigade. Probably the most effective line of action would be a strong counter-attack along Northern side of PREMY AVENUE to recover possession of the PREMY CHAPEL Ridge which is the dominating position on the Brigade Front.

E. In event of enemy breaking through the Front of the Brigade on our Right.

Occupy PREMY AVENUE as a defensive flank.

F. In event of enemy breaking through the front of the Brigade on our Left.

Occupy STATION AVENUE as a protective flank pushing forward one platoon per Company to suitable position in RAVINE AVENUE.

Issued to all recipients of Left Sector
Defence Scheme.

APPENDIX B.

"EVICT SCHEME."

1. In the event of the enemy succeeding by a local attack, the most forward portion of the trenches in the Left Sector, the Left Artillery Group will assist the Infantry in the counter-attack by a short concentrated bombardment on the portion of our trenches seized.

2. This scheme will be known as "EVICT RIGHT" or "EVICT LEFT" and will be as follows:-

   EVICT RIGHT.   Barrage on DAGO Trench, FREMY TRENCH and NIGGER TRENCH from L.21. a 6.5   to L.20.b, 65.75   for 10 minutes at rapid rate.

   EVICT LEFT.   Barrage on NIGGER TRENCH and BEET TRENCH from L.20.b. 65.75 - L.13. d 5.1   for 10 minutes at rapid rate.

3. The order for putting the above into force will be sent in the following way:-   "EVICT RIGHT at (..........time...)
   At the time given batteries open fire on lines given in para. 2 for 10 minutes at a rapid rate of fire.

   After 10 minutes batteries continue on their present S.O.S. lines at alternate rates of normal and rapid fire until ordered to stop.

APPENDIX B.

1. In the event of the enemy succeeding in occupying by a local attack, the most forward portion of the trenches in the Left sector, the Left Artillery Group will assist the Infantry in the counter-attack by a short concentrated bombardment on the portion of our trenches seized.

2. In order to be able to put on this short concentrated bombardment rapidly, the following scheme has been worked out:-

3. The scheme will be known as "EVICT RIGHT" or "EVICT LEFT" and will be as follows:-

EVICT RIGHT. Barrage on DAGO TRENCH, FREMY TRENCH and NIGGER TRENCH from L.21.a.6.5. to L.20.b.65.75. for 10 minutes at rapid rate.

EVICT LEFT. Barrage on NIGGER TRENCH and BELT TRENCH from L.20.b.65.75. - L.13.d.5.1. for 10 minutes at rapid rate.

The order for putting the above into force will be sent in the following way :- "EVICT RIGHT at (....... time...)."
At the time given batteries open fire on lines given above for 10 minutes at a rapid rate of fire.

4. After 10 minutes batteries continue on their present S.O.S. lines at alternate rates of normal and rapid fire until ordered to stop.

4. The order for the time at which this bombardment is to begin ("EVICT RIGHT" or "EVICT LEFT" at...... "A.M." or "P.M.") would be 10 minutes before the time at which it is calculated the Counter-attack Battalion will be ready to assault.

SECRET. Copy No. 2. B.

58th Infantry Brigade Order No. 211.

1st January, 1917.

1. On night 2nd/3rd January 58th Infantry Brigade will extend its right and take over the front of the 57th Inf. Brigade as far as the Railway (inclusive) L.21.c.8.3.
   The Right Battalion Boundary will then run L.21.c.8.3. - RAVINE (exclusive) at L.27.a.0.9. - L.26.a.80.25.

2. On night 2nd/3rd January 1 Company 9th Bn Welch Regiment will take over from 57th Infantry Brigade (8th Bn Gloucester Regt.) the above new front, and will come under the orders of the O.C., Right Battalion (6th Bn Wiltshire Regiment) for tactical purposes.
   All details will be arranged direct between O's.C. concerned.

3. All trench stores will be handed over on relief.

4. Completion of relief will be wired to Brigade H.Q. in code.   Code word : NOT TO-NIGHT.

5. Acknowledge.

G. W. Dymond 2nd Lieutenant

A/Brigade Major 58th Infantry Brigade.

Issued at 8.0.p.m.

Copy No. 1 File.
2) War Diary.
3)
4 G.O.C.
5 19th Divn. "G"
6 19th Divn. "Q"
7 56th Inf. Bde.
8 57th Inf. Bde.
9 9.Cheshire Regt.
10 9.R.W.Fusrs.
11 9.Welch Regt.
12 6.Wiltshire Regt.
13 58.M.G.Coy.
14 58.T.M.Battery.
15 Staff Capt.
16 Bde. Transport Offr.
17 O.C. Signals.
18 Bde Int. Offr.
19 S.O. 58th Bde.
20 A.F.M. 19th Div.
21 19th Div. Train.
22 A.D.M.S., 19th Div.
23 C.R.E., 19th Div.
24 50th Inf. Bde.
25 81st Field Co.R.E.

SECRET.   Copy No. 2...

58th Infantry Brigade Order No. 212.

2nd January, 1918.

The following adjustment of the 19th Divisional front and inter-battalion reliefs will take place on the night 3rd/4th January.

A.

1. (a). The 58th Infantry Brigade (less M.G.C.) will extend its left and take over the front of the 50th Infantry Brigade as far as the BEETROOT FACTORY and RAVINE AVENUE (both exclusive).

   (b). 9th Bn Cheshire Regiment will take over:-

   (i). This new front from 50th Inf. Brigade (7/E.Yorks. R).
   (ii). The left Coy. front of 9th Bn R.W.Fusiliers.

2. The Company of the 9th Bn R.W.Fusiliers thus relieved will move back to RIBECOURT and there come under the orders of O.C. 6th Bn Wiltshire Regt. as part of the counter-attacking Battalion.

3. Completion of relief will be wired to 50th and 58th Brigade Hd.Qrs. in code. Code word:- CAN'T COME.

B.

1. The 3 Companies of 9th Bn Welch Regt. in RIBECOURT will relieve the 6th Bn Wiltshire Regt. (less counter-attacking Company) in Right Sub-sector.

2. On completion of relief 6th Bn Wiltshire Regt. (less counter-attacking Company) will move back to RIBECOURT and there become Counter-attacking Battalion.

3. The Counter-attacking Company of 6th Bn Wiltshire Regt. will remain in position and come under the orders of O.C., 9th Bn Welch Regt. for tactical purposes.

4. Completion of relief will be wired to Brigade H.Q. in code. Code word:- NOT THERE.

C.

On night 4th/5th January the following reliefs will take place.

1. The Company of 9th Bn R.W.Fusiliers in RIBECOURT will relieve the Company of 6th Bn Wiltshire Regt. attached to Right Battalion (9th Bn Welch Regt.) and will be under the orders of O.C. Right Battalion for tactical purposes.

2. The Company of 6th Bn Wiltshire Regt. thus relieved will rejoin its battalion in RIBECOURT.

3. Completion of relief will be wired to Brigade H.Q. in code. Code word:- THANK YOU.

D.

1. In A, B, and C above all details will be arranged between O's.C. concerned.

2. All trench stores, patrol suits, defences maps, will be handed over on relief and receipts forwarded to 58th Brigade H.Q.

3. Acknowledge.

G. W. Dymond.
2nd Lieutenant
A/Brigade Major 58th Infantry Brigade.

Issued at 12 noon.

Copy No. 1 File.
2) War Diary.
3)
4 G.O.C.
5 19th Divn. "G"
6 19th Divn. "Q"
7 56th Inf. Bde.
8 57th Inf. Bde.
9 9.Cheshire Regt.
10 9.R.W.Fusrs.
11 9.Welch Regt.
12 6.Wiltshire Regt.
13 58.M.Gun Coy.
14 58.T.M.Battery.
15 Staff Capt.
16 Bde. Transport Offr.
17 O.C. Signals.
18 Bde Int. Offr.
19 S.O. 58th Bde.
20 A.F.M. 19th Div.
21 19th Div. Train.
22 A.D.M.S. 19th Div.
23 C.R.E. 19th Div.
24 50th Inf. Bde.
25 81st Fld. Coy. R.E.

SECRET   Copy No..2....

58th Infantry Brigade Order No. 213.

3rd January, 1918.

1. The Brigade will be relieved on the night 4th/5th and 5th/6th January by 142nd Infantry Brigade.

2. On the night 4th/5th January the Right Battalion (9th Bn Welch Regiment plus 1 Company 6th Bn Wiltshire Regt. attached) will be relieved by 24th Bn London Regiment.
   The Centre Battalion (9th Bn R.W.Fusiliers less 1 Company) will be relieved by 21st Bn London Regiment.
   On relief 9th Bn Welch Regiment will move back to Left Sub-sector Intermediate Line, (Reserve Brigade Area).
   The attached Company of the 6th Bn Wiltshire Regiment will move back to RIBECOURT and rejoin its own battalion there.
   On relief 9th Bn R.W.Fusiliers including the Company at RIBECOURT will move back to the Right Sub-sector of the Intermediate Line (Reserve Brigade Area).

3. On the night 5th/6th 9th Bn R.W.Fusiliers will take over the Right Sub-sector of present 57th Inf. Brigade Sector.
   The 9th Bn Welch Regiment will take over the Left Sub-sector of present 57th Inf. Brigade Sector.
   The Left Battalion (9th Bn Cheshire Regiment) will be relieved by the 23rd Bn London Regiment.
   The Battalion in Brigade Reserve (6th Bn Wiltshire Regt.) will be relieved by 22nd Bn London Regiment.
   On relief the 9th Bn Cheshire Regiment will move back to Right Sub-sector of Intermediate Line (Reserve Brigade Area)
   On relief 6th Bn Wiltshire Regiment will move back to Left Sub-sector of Intermediate Line (Reserve Brigade Area).

4. On 6th January and night 6th/7th January the 9th Bn Cheshire Regiment and 6th Bn Wiltshire Regiment will relieve the two remaining battalions of 57th Inf. Brigade.

5. The relief of 58th Trench Mortar Battery by 142nd Trench Mortar Battery will take place either on 4th or 5th January.

6. The relief of ~~58th M.Gun Company~~ Machine Gun in present ~~Right~~ Brigade Sector will be arranged by D.M.G.O. - probably 12 guns being relieved on night 4th/5th January and the remainder the following night.

7. 58th Brigade H.Q. will move to RUYAULCOURT on night 5th/6th and will relieve 57th Brigade H.Q. on 6th January.

8. One officer and two guides per battalion will report to 58th Brigade H.Q. (L.25.a.O.2.) to-morrow 4th inst. (to show advanced parties of relieving units round the line and billets), as under:-

   Guides from 9th Bn R.W.Fusiliers, 9th Bn Welch Regiment, 6th Bn Wiltshire Regiment and 58th T.M.Battery - 9.45.a.m.

   Guides from 9th Bn Cheshire Regiment - 2.15.p.m.

10. ACKNOWLEDGE.

G. W. Dymond. 2nd Lieutenant

A/Brigade Major 58th Infantry Brigade.

Issued at 7pm

Copy No. 1 File.
2) War Diary.
3)
4 G.O.C.
5 19th Div. G.
6 19th Div. Q.
7 56th Inf Bde.
8 57th Inf Bde.
9 9.Cheshire Regt.
10 9.R.W.Fusrs.
11 9.Welch R.
12 6.Wilts Regt.
13 58.M.G.Coy.
14 58.T.M.Battery.
15 Staff. Capt.
16 Bde Transport Offr.
17 O.C. Signals.
18 Bde. Int. Offr.
19 S.O. 58th Bde.
20 A.P.M. 19th Div.
21 19th Div. Train.
22 A.D.M.S. 19th Div.
23 C.R.E., 19th Div.
24 81st Field Co. R.E.
25 50th Inf. Bde.
26 142nd Inf Bde.
27. CRA 19th Div.

SECRET.   Copy No....3.......

58th Infantry Brigade Order No. 214.

3rd January, 1918.

The following moves will take place on the night 4th/5th January in accordance with attached table.

1. (a). 9th Bn Welch Regiment plus 1 Company 6th Bn Wiltshire Regiment will be relieved by 24th Bn London Regiment.

   (b). On relief 9th Bn Welch Regiment will move into Left Sub-sector Intermediate Line.
   The attached Company 6th Bn Wiltshire Regiment will rejoin its Battalion in RIBECOURT.

2. (a). 9th Bn R.W.Fusiliers (less 1 Company attached to 6th Bn Wiltshire Regiment) will be relieved by 21st Bn London Regiment.

   (b). On relief 9th Bn R.W.Fusiliers including the Company in RIBECOURT will move to Right Sub-sector Intermediate Line.

3. 58th T.M.Battery will be relieved by 142nd T.M.Battery and will move to Left Sub-sector Intermediate Line where it will be attached to 9th Bn Welch Regiment for purposes of accommodation.

4. In 1, 2, and 3, above:-

   (a). All details not herein laid down will be arranged by O's.C. with the representatives of the units coming up on 4th inst.

   (b). Advanced billeting parties will be sent:

   (i). By 9th Bn Welch Regiment and 58th T.M.Battery to take over accommodation in Left Sub-sector Intermediate Line from 24th Bn London Regiment.

   (ii). By 9th Bn R.W.Fusiliers to take over accommodation in Right Sub-sector Intermediate Line from 7th Bn East Lancs. Regiment.

   (c). All trench stores, defences maps, aeroplane photographs will be handed over on relief.
   Patrol suits will NOT be handed over but will be kept by Battalions.

   (d). Completion of relief will be wired to 58th Bde.H.Q. in code.   Code word:- HAVE NONE.

   (e). Units will report arrival in Intermediate Line to 58th Brigade H.Q.

   (f). O.C., 58th T.M.Battery will report the location of his Hd.Qrs. in Intermediate Line to 58th Bde.H.Q. as soon as possible.

   (g). 21st and 24th Bns. London Regiment will report dispositions in Right and Centre Sub-sectors respectively to 58th Bde. H.Q. by NOON 5th inst.

5.   ACKNOWLEDGE.

                                        G. W. Dymond.   2nd Lieutenant

                                        A/Brigade Major 58th Infantry Brigade.

Issued at 7 a.m 4-1-18

Relief table issued with 58th Infantry Brigade Order No.214.

Unit.	From.	To.	Taking over from.
9th Bn Welch Regt.	Right Sub-sector.	Left Sub-sector, Intermediate Line, H.Q. K.36.d.7.9.	24th Bn London Regiment.
9th Bn R.W.Fusiliers (less 1 Company).	Centre Sub-sector.	Right Sub-sector. Intermediate line. H.Q. L.31.d.55.05.	7th Bn East Lancs. Regiment.
1 Coy. 9th Bn R.W.Fus. (attached 6/Wilts Regt).	RIBECOURT.		To be accommodated by arrangement with 9th Bn Welch Regiment.
58th T.M.Battery.	Line.	Left Sub-sector, Intermediate Line.	
1 Coy. 6/Wilts. Regt. (attached 9/Welch R.)	Right Sub-sector.	Rejoins its Battn. in RIBECOURT.	

```
Copy No.  1 File.
          2) War Diary.
          3)
          4 G.O.C.
          5 19th Divn. G.
          6 19th Divn. Q.
          7 56th Inf Bde.
          8 57th Inf Bde.
          9 9.Cheshire R.
         10 9.R.W.Fus.
         11 9.Welch Regt.
         12 6.Wilts Regt.
         13 58.M.G.Ccy.
         14 58.T.M.Battery.
         15 Staff Capt.
         16 Bde. Transport.
         17 O.C. Signals.
         18 Bde. Int. Offr.
         19 S.O. 58th Bde.
         20 A.P.M. 19th Div.
         21 19th Div Train.
         22 A.D.M.S. 19th Div.
         23 C.R.E. 19th Div.
         24 81st Fld. Co. R.E.
         25 50th Inf. Bde.
         26 142nd Inf Bde.
         27 C.R.A, 19th Div.
         28 21st Bn London Regt.
         29 24th Bn London Regt.
```

SECRET.   Copy No. 2.

58th Infantry Brigade Order No. 215.

4th January, 1918.

The following moves will take place on night 5th/6th January:-

1. 9th Bn Cheshire Regiment will be relieved in Left Sub-sector by 23rd Bn London Regt. (142nd Inf. Bde.) and on relief will move to Right Sub-sector Intermediate Line, vacated by 9th Bn R.W.Fusiliers.   H.Q:- L.31.d.55.05.

2. 6th Bn Wiltshire Regt. will be relieved in Brigade Reserve by 22nd Bn London Regt. (142nd Inf. Bde) and on relief will move to Left Sub-sector, Intermediate Line vacated by 9th Bn Welch Regt.   H.Q:- K.36.d.7.9.

3. 9th Bn R.W.Fusiliers will relieve 10th Bn Worcester Regt. in Right Sub-sector of present 57th Inf. Brigade Sector with 3 Companies in front and support lines from Railway (exclusive) at L.27.d.60.40. to present 57th Brigade Right boundary, (Road inclusive at L.34.a.55.85.).
   1 Company 9th Bn R.W.Fusiliers will be in close support in the new trench running from L.34.a.2.4. to L.34.c.1.7. (taking over from 1 Company 10th Bn Worcester Regt. or 8th Bn North Staffs Regt.).
   1 Company of a Battalion of 57th Inf. Brigade will be in reserve trench running from L.33.b.5.4. to L.33.d.80.85. and will be under the orders of O.C., 9th Bn R.W.Fusiliers for tactical purposes.
   Battalion Hd.Qrs:- L.33.b.3.7.

4. 9th Bn Welch Regt. will relieve the 8th Bn Gloucester Regt. in Left Sub-sector of present 57th Inf. Brigade Sector, from Railway (exclusive) at L.21.c.8.3. to L.27.b.20.25.
   Hd.Qrs:- L.20.d.25.05.

5. 58th T.M.Battery will relieve 57th T.M.Battery in present 57th Inf. Brigade Sector.   Hd.Qrs:- L.32.a.10.15.

6. In 1, 2, 3, 4, and 5 above:-

   (a). All details not herein laid down will be arranged between O's.C. concerned.

   (b). Trench stores, aeroplane photographs, defences maps, patrol suits will be handed over on relief, receipts obtained and forwarded to 58th Brigade H.Q.

   (c). Dispositions of 9th Bn R.W.Fusiliers, 9th Bn Welch Regt. and 58th T.M.Battery will be forwarded to 58th Brigade H.Q. by 6.p.m. 6th inst.

   (d). Completion of relief will be wired to 58th Brigade H.Q. in B.A.B. Code.

7. The command of present 58th Brigade sector will pass on 5th inst to G.O.C. 142nd Inf. Brigade at 4.p.m. at which hour 58th Brigade H.Q. will close at L.25.a.0.2. and re-open at RUYAULCOURT.

8. ACKNOWLEDGE.

G.W. Dymond, 2nd Lieutenant
A/Brigade Major 58th Infantry Brigade.

Issued at 8.0.p.m.

Copy No. 1 File
        2) War Diary.
        3)
        4 G.O.C.
        5 19th Div. G.
        6 19th Div Q.
        7 56th Inf. Bde.
        8 57th Inf. Bde.
        9 9.Cheshire R.
       10 9.R.W.Fusrs.
       11 9.Welch R.
       12 6.Wilts R.
       13 58.M.Gun Coy.
       14 58.T.M.Batty.
       15 Staff Capt.
       16 Bde. Transport Offr.
       17 O.C. Bde. Signals.
       18 Bde. Int. Offr.
       19 S.O. 58th Bde.
       20 A.P.M., 19th Div.
       21 19th Div Train.
       22 A.D.M.S., 19th Div.
       23 C.R.E., 19th Div.
       24 81st Fld. Co.R.E.
       25 50th Inf. Bde.
       26 142nd Inf. Bde.
       27 D.M.G.O.

SECRET   Copy No. 3

58th Infantry Brigade Order No. 216.

4th January, 1918.

On night 6th/7th January the following reliefs will take place:-

1. 9th Bn Cheshire Regt. will relieve 8th Bn N?Staffs. Regt. in centre sub-sector of present 57th Brigade sector, with 3 Companies in front and support lines.
    Battalion H.Q:- L.27.c.60.75.
    1 Company will relieve a company of a battalion of 57th Inf. Brigade in the reserve trench running from L.33.b.5.4. to L.33.d.80.85. and will come under the orders of O.C., 9th Bn R.W.Fusiliers for tactical purposes.

2. 6th Bn Wiltshire Regt. will relieve 10th Bn R.Warwick. Regt. in support in present 57th Brigade sector with 2 Companies in KABUL AVENUE and COUILLET AVENUE, 1 Company in FORK AVENUE 1 Company in trench running from L.26.d.45.95. to L.26.d.75.70.
    Battalion Hd.Qrs:- L.26.d.8.2.

3. In 1, and 2 above:-

    (a). All details not herein laid down will be arranged between O's.C. concerned.

    (b). Trench stores, aeroplane photographs, defences maps, patrols suits will be handed over on relief, receipts obtained and forwarded to 58th Brigade H.Q.

    (c). Dispositions will be forwarded to 58th Brigade H.Q. by NOON 7th inst.

    (d). Completion of reliefs will be wired to 58th Brigade H.Q. in code.   Code word:- UNDERSTOOD.

4. Command of present 57th Brigade sector will pass to G.O.C., 58th Inf. Brigade at 4.p.m. 6th inst. at which hour 58th Brigade H.Q. will close at RUYAULCOURT and open at L.32.a.15.15.

5. Acknowledge.

G.W. Dymond. 2nd Lieutenant
A/Brigade Major 58th Infantry Brigade.

Issued at 8.0.p.m.

Copy No. 1 File.
      2) War Diary.
      3)
      4 G.O.C.
      5 19th Divn. G.
      6 19th Divn. Q.
      7 56th Inf Bde.
      8 57th Inf Bde.
      9 9.Cheshire R.
      10 9.R.W.Fusrs.
      11 9.Welch R.
      12 6.Wilts R.
      13 58.M.Gun Coy.
      14 58.T.M.Batty.
      15 Staff Capt.
      16 Bde. Transport Offr.
      17 O.C. Bde. Signals.
      18 Bde. Int Offr.
      19 S.O. 58th Bde.
      20 A.P.M, 19th Div.
      21 A.D.M.S, 19th Div.
      22 19th Div. Train.
      23 C.R.E, 19th Div.
      24 81st Fld Co.R.E.
      25 50th Inf Bde.
      26 142nd Inf Bde.
      27 D.M.G.O.

Relief.   Copy No. 3.

56th Infantry Brigade Order No. 217.

6th January, 1918.

1. On night 7th/8th January the boundary between Right and Centre Battalions will be adjusted so as to run from L.29.c.0.2. to L.33.b.90.95. to L.33.b.45.5[?].

2. To effect this re-adjustment the Company of Centre Battn. (8th Bn Cheshire Regt) occupying the reserve trench running from L.33.b.60.65. to L.33.d.90.95. will take over left Company front of the Right Battalion (9th Bn R.S.Fusiliers), the Company of 9th Bn R.S.Fusiliers so relieved moving into the reserve trench L.33.b.60.65. to L.33.d.90.95. and becoming the counter-attack company of the Right Battalion.

3. This relief will be carried out platoon by platoon so that there will never be less than two platoons in the reserve trench L.33.b.60.65. to L.33.d.90.95.
   All other details of relief will be arranged between O's.C. Right and Centre Battns.

4. On completion of re-adjustment, Battalion boundaries will be as shown on attached map. (To Bns. concerned only.)
   Battalions will hold their lines as under:-

   Right Battalion:- 2 Companies in front and support lines.
                      1 Company in support of right flank in trench L.34.c.20.55. to L.34.c.1.7.
                      1 Counter-attacking Company in reserve trench L.33.b.60.65. to L.33.d.90.95. vacated by 8th Bn Cheshire Regt.

   Centre Battalion:- 3 Companies holding front and support trench, 1 counter-attacking company in reserve trench from approximately L.27.c.7.5. to L.27.d.0.1.

   Left Battalion:-   2 Companies in front and support lines.
                      1 Coy. in support and reserve lines on left.
                      1 Counter-attacking company in reserve line from YORK AVENUE to Right Boundary.

5. All trench stores will be handed over on relief.

6. Dispositions will be forwarded to 56th Brigade H.Q. by noon 8th inst.

7. Completion of relief will be reported to 56th Bde.H.Q. in B.A.B. code.

8. Acknowledge.

                                        G.W.Dymond
                                        Captain,
                                        Brigade Major 56th Infantry Brigade.

Issued at

   Copy No. 1 File.   6 8.Cheshire R.
           2 War Diary.   7 9.R.S.Fusiliers.
           3)   8 8.Welch R.
           4 T.O.C.   9 6.Wilts Regt.
           5 19th Division G.   10 Bn. M.Gun Co.
                                      11 83.T.M.Battery.

SECRET. Copy No. 3

58th Infantry Brigade Order No. 218.

8th January, 1918.

Ref: Secret Trench Map.

1. The 6th Bn Wiltshire Regiment will relieve the 9th Bn Cheshire Regiment in the Centre Sub-sector to-night January 9th/10th.
   All details will be arranged direct between O's.C. Battalions.

2. The 9th Bn Cheshire Regiment will detail two working parties
   (a). 2 Officers and 40 men.
   (b). 1 Officer and 20 men.
   to remain behind and continue the work which 6th Bn Wiltshire Regiment have been doing for 9th Bn Cheshire Regiment the last two nights.

3. All defence schemes, maps and photographs will be handed over and receipts forwarded to this office.

4. A list of trench stores taken and handed over will be forwarded to the Staff Captain by 12 noon 10th inst.

5. Dispositions will be forwarded to Brigade H.Q. by 12 noon 12th inst.

6. Completion of relief will be forwarded to Brigade H.Q. in B.A.B. Code.

7. Acknowledge.

S. Carpenter
Captain

Brigade Major 58th Infantry Brigade.

Issued at 12 noon.

```
Copy No. 1 File.
        2) War Diary.
        3)
        4  G.O.C.
        5  19th Div. G.
        6  19th Div. Q.
        7  56th Inf. Bde.
        8  57th Inf Bde.
        9  9.Cheshire Regt.
       10  9.R.W.Fusrs.
       11  9.Welch R.
       12  6.Wilts R.
       13  58.M.G.Coy.
       14  58.T.M.Batty.
       15  Staff Capt.
       16  Bde. Transport Offr.
       17  O.C. Bde. Signals.
       18  Bde. Int. Offr.
       19  S.O., 58th Bde.
       20  19th Div. Train.
       21  A.P.M., 19th Div.
       22  A.D.M.S., 19th Div.
       23  142nd Inf. Bde.
```

SECRET.   Copy No. 1

K

58th Infantry Brigade Order No. 219.

10th January, 1918.

Ref: Secret Trench Map.

1. The Company of 9th Bn Cheshire Regiment now accommodated in FORK AVENUE will move to-night to the trench running from L.32.c.12.86. to L.31.b.85.00. Company H.Q. will be at L.32.a.23.00. The Senior Liaison Officer will vacate this H.Q. at once, and will arrange billets for his Signallers with the Staff Captain.

2. 9th Bn Welch Regiment will take over the accommodation vacated by this Company of 9th Bn Cheshire Regiment and will establish their Battalion H.Q. there at about 8.30.a.m. to-morrow morning if the situation is quiet.

3. Completion of moves will be reported to Brigade H.Q.

4. 9th Bn Cheshire Regiment and 9th Bn Welch Regiment acknowledge.

S. Carpenter.
Captain

Brigade Major 58th Infantry Brigade.

Issued at 8.0.p.m.

Copy No. 1 File.
     2) War Diary.
     3)
     4 G.O.C.
     5 9.Cheshire R.
     6 9.R.W.Fusrs.
     7 9.Welch R.
     8 6.Wilts R.
     9 58.M.G.Coy.
    10 58.T.M.Battery.
    11 56th Inf. Bde.
    12 57th Inf Bde.
    13 142nd Inf Bde.
    14 19th Divn. G.
    15 Bde. Transport Offr.
    16 Bde. Int. Offr.
    17 Staff Capt.
    18 Senior Liaison Offr.

SECRET.   Copy No. 3.

58th Infantry Brigade Order No. 220.

12th January, 1918.

Ref: Secret Trench Map.

1. (a). The 9th Bn Cheshire Regiment will relieve the 9th Bn R.W.Fusrs. (less the Right Support Coy.) in the right sub-sector to-night 12th/13th inst.

   (b). A Company of 8th Bn N. Staffs. Regt. will relieve the Right Support Company of 9th Bn R.W.Fusiliers. All details will be arranged direct between O's.C. Battalions concerned.

   On relief 9th Bn R.W.Fusiliers will move into support in the area now occupied by 9th Bn Cheshire Regiment.

2. The 9th Bn R.W.Fusiliers will detail one company for work under 82nd Field Coy. R.E. on CABUL TRENCH after relief.

3. All maps, schemes, aeroplane photos, and trench stores will be handed over and receipts forwarded to Brigade H.Q. by 12 noon 13th inst.

4. Dispositions will be forwarded to Brigade H.Q. by 12 noon 13th inst.

5. Acknowledge.

                                                    [signature]
                                                    Captain

                                       Brigade Major 58th Infantry Brigade.

Issued at 3.p.m..

            Copy No. 1 File.
                    2) War Diary.
                    3)
                    4 G.O.C.
                    5 9.Cheshire R.
                    6 9.R.W.Fusrs.
                    7 9.Welch R.
                    8 6.Wilts R.
                    9 58.M.Gun Coy.
                   10 58.T.M.Battery.
                   11 56th Inf. Bde.
                   12 57th Inf. Bde.
                   13 140th Inf. Bde.
                   14 19th Divn. G.
                   15 Bde. Transport Offr.
                   16 Bde. Int. Offr.
                   17 Staff Capt.
                   18 Senior Liaison Offr.
                   19 O.C. Bde. Signals.

SECRET   M   Copy No. 3

58th Infantry Brigade Order No. 221.

13th January, 1918.

1. The 58th Infantry Brigade will re-organise on a two Battalion front to-night 13th inst.

2. To affect this the following changes will take place:-

   (a). The Right Battalion (9th Bn Cheshire Regiment) will extend its left to L.27.d.58.53. with three companies in front line and one Counter-attacking company in support. (A, B, C, D, as shown in attached sketch).

   (b). The Centre Battalion (6th Bn Wiltshire Regiment) will extend its left to L.21.c.84.30. taking over from 9th Bn Welch Regiment (less J. Coy.) see attached sketch.
      The 6th Bn Wiltshire Regiment will then consist of 5 companies, three, E, F, G, in the front line, H being counter-attacking company and J attached from 9th Bn Welch Regiment.

   (c). The 9th Bn Welch Regiment (less J. Coy.) on relief will move to the Intermediate Line taking over from 7/R.Lancs. Regt. with Headquarters at L.31.d.55.05.

3. All details will be arranged between O's.C. concerned.

4. All trench stores will be handed over on relief.

5. Dispositions will be sent to Brigade H.Q. not later than 24 hours after relief.

6. Relief complete will be wired to Brigade H.Q. by the code word DOCUMENTARY.

7. Acknowledge.

                                A. Bnett-Dampier Captain
                             Brigade Major 58th Infantry Brigade.

Issued at 12 noon.

   Copy No. 1 File.
          2) War Diary.
          3)
          4 G.O.C.
          5 9.Cheshire R.
          6 9.R.W.Fusrs.
          7 9.Welch R.
          8 6.Wilts R.   15 19th Div. G.
          9 58.M.Gun Coy.   16 Bde. Transport Offr.
         10 58.T.M.Battery.   17 Bde. Int. Offr.
         11 ~~58th Inf. Bde.~~   18 Staff Capt.
         12 140th Inf. Bde.   19 Senior Liaison Offr.
         13 56th Inf. Bde.   20 O.C. Bde. Signals.
         14 57th Inf. Bde.

SECRET.   Copy No. 3.

58th Infantry Brigade Order No.222.

15th January, 1918.

1. The 9th Bn R.W.Fusiliers will relieve the 9th Bn Cheshire Regiment in the Right Sub-sector on the 15th inst. and night 15th/16th inst. *On relief 9th Cheshire will move into present 9th RWF area, as Support Battalion.*

2. (a). The Support Company 9th Bn Cheshire Regiment at present in the trench from L.33.b.5.4. to L.33.d.80.85. will be relieved during daylight by a company of 9th Bn R.W.Fusiliers in KABUL AVENUE, and on relief will move to the accommodation in KABUL AVENUE thus vacated.

   (b). The relief of this company which will be complete by 5.p.m. will be wired in code to Brigade H.Q. Code word COMPLIED WITH.

3. All details not herein mentioned will be arranged direct between O's.C. concerned.

4. All trench stores and defences maps will be handed over on relief. Receipts will be forwarded to Brigade H.Q.

5. Dispositions will be reported within 24 hours of relief to Brigade H.Q.

6. Completion of relief will be wired to Brigade H.Q. in code. Code word: MARCOING.

7. Acknowledge.

G. W. Dymond 2nd Lieutenant

A/Brigade Major 58th Infantry Brigade.

Issued at 12 noon.

Copy No. 1 File.
2) War Diary.
3)
4 G.O.C.
5 9.Cheshire R.
6 9 R.W.Fusrs.
7 9.Welch R.
8 6.Wilts R.
9 58.M.Gun Coy.
10 58.T.M.Battery.
11 140th Inf. Bde.
12 56th Inf Bde.
13 57th Inf Bde.
14 19th Divn. G.
15 Bde Transport Offr.
16 Bde. Int Offr.
17 Staff Capt.
18 Senior Liaison Offr.
19 O.C. Bde Signals.
20 82nd Fld. Co. R.E.

SECRET.   Copy No. 3

58th Infantry Brigade Order No.223.

15th January, 1918.

1. 9th Bn Welch Regiment will relieve the 6th Bn Wiltshire Regiment (less 1 company) in left sub-sector on night 16th/17th January.
   On relief 6th Bn Wiltshire Regiment (less 1 company) will move back to the portion of Intermediate Line vacated by 9th Bn Welch Regiment. and become the Reserve Battalion.

2. One Company 6th Bn Wiltshire Regiment will remain in the Left Sub-sector and be under the orders of O.C. 9th Bn Welch Regiment for tactical purposes. This company will move into the area at present occupied by the company of 9th Bn Welch Regiment attached 6th Bn Wiltshire Regiment. The company of 9th Bn Welch Regiment so displaced will remain in the Left Sub-sector.

3. All details will be arranged between O's.C. concerned.

4. All trench stores, defences maps and schemes will be handed over on relief and receipts forwarded to Brigade H.Q. by NOON 17th inst.

5. Dispositions will be forwarded to Brigade H.Q. by NOON 17th inst.

6. Completion of relief will be wired to Brigade H.Q. in code. Code word: HYSTERICAL.

7. ACKNOWLEDGE.

G. W. Dymond. 2nd Lieutenant

A/Brigade Major 58th Infantry Brigade.

Issued at 8.0.p.m.

Copy No. 1 File.
2) War Diary.
3)
4 G.O.C.
5 9.Cheshire R.
6 9.R.W.Fusrs.
7 9.Welch R.
8 6.Wilts R.
9 58.M.G.Coy.
10 140th Inf Bde.
11 56th Inf Bde.
12 57th Inf Bde.
13 19th Divn. G.
14 58.T.M.Battery.
15 Bde. Transport Offr.
16 Bde. Int. Offr.
17 Staff Capt.
18 Senior Liaison Offr.
19 O.C. Bde Signals.
20 82nd Fld. Coy.R.E.

SECRET.   Copy No. 2.

58th Infantry Brigade Order No. 224.

15th January, 1918.

The 58th Infantry Brigade (less M.Gun Coy.) will be relieved on the nights 17th/18th and 18th/19th January by the 56th Inf. Brigade.

On relief 58th Infantry Brigade will become the Brigade in Divisional Reserve.

A. On night 17th/18th the following reliefs will take place:-

1. 6th Bn Wiltshire Regiment less one company (Battalion in Intermediate Line) will be relieved by 7th Bn South Lancs. Regt. (less 2 companies). On relief 6th Bn Wiltshire Regiment will move to F.18.d. HAWES CAMP (EAST), taking over from 7th Bn South Lancs Regt. *See A3 below.*

2. 9th Bn Cheshire Regiment (Support Battalion) will be relieved by 7th Bn K.O.R.Lanc. Regt. (less 1 company). 7th Bn K.O.R.Lanc. Regt. will garrison KABUL AVENUE with one instead of 2 companies as at present. On relief H.Q. and 2 companies 9th Bn Cheshire Regiment will move to LECHELLE by train from TRESCAULT and will occupy accommodation vacated by 7th Bn K.O.R.Lanc. Regt. Further instructions will be issued later by Staff Captain. The remaining two companies will move by march route to HAWES CAMP (EAST).

3. The company of 6th Bn Wiltshire Regiment attached 9th Bn Welch Regt. will be relieved by 1 company of 7th Bn K.O.R.Lanc. Regt. which will then come under the orders of O.C. 9th Bn Welch Regt. for tactical purposes. This company of 6th Bn Wiltshire Regt. on relief will move back to HAWES CAMP (EAST), rejoining its battalion there.

4. 58th Trench Mortar Battery will be relieved by 56th Trench Mortar Battery and on relief will move back to accommodation occupied by 56th Trench Mortar Battery in HAWES CAMP.

5. Guides for 7th Bn South Lancs. Regt. and 58th T.M.Battery will be arranged between O's.C. concerned.

Guides in charge of an officer for 7th Bn K.O.R.Lanc. Regt. will be sent by 9th Bn Cheshire Regiment to L.32.a.2.0. (FORK AVENUE near 58th Brigade H.Q) at 3.0.p.m. on the 17th inst. at the scale of 1 per platoon, 1 per Coy. H.Q., 1 per Battn. H.Q. Total 21.

B. On the night 18th/19th January the following reliefs will take place:-

(Right Sub-sector)
1. 9th Bn R.W.Fusiliers will be relieved by 7th Bn East Lancs Regt. On relief 9th Bn R.W.Fusiliers will proceed by Light Railway from TRESCAULT to LECHELLE and will occupy the accommodation vacated by 7th Bn East Lancs. Regt. Further instructions will be issued for this move by the Staff Captain.

(Left Sub-sector)
2. 9th Bn Welch Regt. will be relieved by 7th Bn L.N.Lancs Regt. On relief 9th Bn Welch Regt. will move by march route to HAWES CAMP (WEST) vacated by 7th Bn L.N. Lancs. Regt.

3. Guides in charge of an officer for 7th Bn East Lancs. Regt. and 7th Bn L.N.Lancs. Regt. will be sent by 9th Bn R.W.Fusiliers and 9th Bn Welch Regt, at 3.30.p.m. and 4.45.p.m. 18th inst. respectively to L.32.a.2.0. (FORK AVENUE near 58th Brigade H.Q.) at the scale of 1 per platoon, 1 per Coy. H.Q., 1 per Battn. H.Q. Total 21.

C. 1.   In A 1,2,3 and B 1, 2 all details not herein laid down will be arranged direct between C's.C. concerned.

2.   Each Battalion will send a billeting party in advance to its new quarters early on the day of relief.

3.   All trench stores including bass brooms, patrol suits, mud scoops, Food containers (11 per battalion), defences maps and schemes, will be handed over and receipts forwarded within 24 hours of relief to 58th Brigade H.Q.

4.   Completion of reliefs will be wired to 58th Brigade H.Q. in code.   Code word: HAVE HAD ENOUGH.

5.   58th Brigade H.Q. will close at L.32.a.15.15. at 4.0.p.m. 18th inst. re-opening at RUYAULCOURT at same hour; command of the LEFT SECTOR will pass from O.C. 58th Infantry Brigade to G.O.C. 56th Infantry Brigade on completion of relief.

6.   Units will ensure that the Anti-aircraft Lewis Gun positions in the camps in the back area are handed over to them by the relieving units.   At least 1 Lewis Gun is to be mounted for the protection of each camp.

7.   ACKNOWLEDGE.

G. W. Dymond. 2nd Lieutenant
Brigade Major 58th Infantry Brigade.

Issued at 12 mn.

Copy No. 1 File.
          2) War Diary.
          3)
          4 G.O.C.
          5 19th Div G.
          6 19th Div Q.
          7 56th Inf Bde.
          8 57th Inf Bde.
          9 9.Cheshire R.
         10 9.R.W.Fusrs.
         11 9.Welch R.
         12 6.Wilts R.
         13 58.M.Gun Coy.
         14 58.T.M.Battery.
         15 Staff Capt.
         16 Bde. Transport Offr.
         17 Bde. Int. Offr.
         18 O.C. Bde Signals.
         19 S.O. 58th Bde.
         20 19th Div Train.
         21 A.P.M. 19th Div.
         22 A.D.M.S., 19th Div.
         23 C.R.E. 19th Div.
         24 C.R.A 19th Div.
         25 82nd Field Co.R.E.
         26 94th Fld. Coy. R.E.
         27 140th Inf. Bde.
         28 D.M.G.O.

SECRET.

Amendment No. 1 to 58th Infantry
Brigade Order No.224.

17th January, 1918.

1. On 18th/19th January the following moves will take place:-

9th Bn R.W.Fusiliers will move by Light Railway from TRESCAULT to LECHELLE and will occupy accommodation in GRAZING CAMP P.25.b.; not as previously stated.

2. The 2 companies of 9th Bn Cheshire Regiment in HAWES CAMP (EAST) will join their Battalion at VALLULART CAMP in P.26.d.8.5.

The 2 companies of 9/Cheshire Regt. will not move till after dinner.

A. Bennett-Dampier, Captain for
Brigade Major, 58th Infantry Brigade.

Issued to all recipients of 58th Infantry Brigade Order No. 224.

SECRET　　　　　　　　　　　　　　　　　　　　　　　　Copy No. 2

58th Infantry Brigade Order No. 225.

19th January, 1918.

Reference to Sheet
57 (c) 1/40,000.

1. In order to admit of each front line battalion being relieved every 4 days the Battalions of the Division will be divided into two groups as under.

   A. Group.   4 Battns. 57th Inf. Bde.
               9th Ches. R.
               6th Wilts R.

   B Group.   4 Battns. 56th Inf. Bde.
               9th R.W.Fus.
               9th Welch R.

2. A. Group will be in the Right Sector of the Divisional front and will find the three front line battns., also one Battn. in Intermediate Line, one Battn. in HAWES CAMP and one Battn. in VALLULART WOOD. Front line battalions will be relieved every 4 days.

   B. Group will be in Left Sector of the Divisional front and will find the two front line Battns, Counter-attack Battn, also one Battn. in Intermediate Line, one Battn. in HAWES CAMP, and one Battn. in GRAZING CAMP. Front line battalions and Counter-attack battalion will be relieved every 4 days.

3. The first Group relief in the Right Sector will take place on night 21st/22nd Jan.

   The first Group relief of Left Sector will take place on night 24th/25th Jan.

   On completion of relief -

   G.O.C. 57th Inf. Bde. will command Right Group.
   G.O.C. 56th Inf. Bde. will command Left Group.
   G.O.C. and Hd.qrs 58th Inf. Bde. will be in rest at RUYAULCOURT.

4. On the nights 1/2nd and 2/3rd Feb. -

   A. Group will be transferred to Left Sector.
   B. Group will be transferred to Right Sector.

5. A programme of reliefs is attached which includes dates on which Group H.Q. relieve,

6. The Brigadier and Brigade Staff at rest will in case of tactical emergency assume command of the 4 battalions in Reserve and will be prepared to act with them as laid down for Reserve Bde. in 19th Div. Defence Scheme.

7. The battalion of Left Group in Intermediate Line and HIGHLAND TRENCH will be responsible for the defence of these lines as laid down in 19th Div. Defence Scheme.

8. Q. will arrange that if possible each relief is conveyed to and from the trenches by train.

9. Q. will issue necessary Administrative Instructions in connection with the Grouping system.

10. ACKNOWLEDGE.

A. Bennett-Dampier, Captain
A/Brigade Major 58th Infantry Brigade.

Issued at 12 noon.

To accompany 58th Inf. Bde. Order No. 225.

PROGRAMME OF RELIEFS.

Jany. 21/22nd.	Right) 6/Wilts R. (HAWES CAMP). (A)) 9/Ches. R. (VALLULART CAMP). Group)Bn of 57th Inf. Bde. in Intermediate Line.
	Relieve 3 Front Battns. of 57th Inf. Bde.
Jany. 24th.	G.O.C. 58th Inf. Bde. relieves G.O.C. 57th Inf. Bde. in command of Right (A) Group. G.O.C. 57th Inf. Bde. to reserve.
Jany 24/25th.	Left) 9/R.W.Fus. (GRILLING CAMP). (B)) 9/Welch R. (HAWES CAMP). Group)Bn of 56th Inf Bde. in Intermediate Line.
	Relieve Front and counter-attack battalions of 56th Inf. Bde.
Jany. 25/26th.	Right (A) Group relieves.
Jany. 28/29th.	Left (B) Group relieves.
Jany. 29/30th.	Right (A) Group relieves.
Feb. 1/2nd.	The 3 battalions of Left (B) Group who come out of the line on night 28/29th Jan. relieve the 3 Front line Battns. of Right (A) Group.
Feb. 2nd.	G.O.C. 57th Inf. Bde. relieves G.O.C. 56th Inf. Bde. in command of Left (B) Group. G.O.C. 56th Inf. Bde. to Reserve.
Feb. 2/3rd.	The 3 Battns of Right (A) Group in Reserve relieve the Battns. of Left (B) Group in Front Line and Intermediate positions.

	On completion of this relief the Right (B) Group will consist of:-
	      4 Bns. 56th Inf. Bde.
	      9th R.W.Fus.
	      9th Welch R.

	The Left (A) Group will consist of :-
	      4 Bns. 57th Inf. Bde.
	      9th Ches. R.
	      6th Wilts R.

Feb. 5/6th.	Right (B) Group relieves.
Feb. 6/7th.	Left (A) Group relieves.
Feb. 8th.	G.O.C. 56th Inf. Bde. relieves G.O.C. 58th Inf. Bde. in command of Right (B) Group. G.O.C. 58th Inf. Bde. to reserve.
Feb. 9/10th.	Right (B) Group relieves.
Feb. 10/11th.	Left (A) Group relieves.
Feb. 13/14th.	Right (B) Group relieves.

SECRET.
                                              Copy No. 5

           58th Infantry Brigade Operation Order No.226.

Ref: Maps Sheets :
     57 C. Ed.2. 1/40.000.   20th Jan. 1918.
     NINE WOOD

1.   In accordance with the Programme of Reliefs issued under
19th Division Order No. 202 of 18.1.18 and re-issued to units of
this Brigade under Order 225 of 19.1.18, the following reliefs
will take place on the night of the 21/22nd.
  (a). 9th Cheshire Regt. from VALLULART WOOD will relieve the
8th Gloucester Regt. in the left Battalion front of the
Right (57th Brigade) Sector, H.Qrs. at L.34.c.6.4.
Dispositions - Three Companies in the Front Line, one Company
in Support. 9th Cheshire Regt. will hand over VALLULART WOOD
Camp to the 10th Worcestershire Regt.

  (b) 6th Wiltshire Regt from EASTWOOD CAMP will relieve the 10th
Worcestershire Regt in the Right Battalion front of the Right
(57th Brigade) Sector, H.Qrs. at R.3.b.8.2. Dispositions -
Two Companies in the front line, one Company in Support, one
in Reserve. 6th Wiltshire Regt will hand over EASTWOOD CAMP
to the 8th N. Stafford Regt.

2.   Details of relief are as follows :-
  (a) Guides will be supplied by the 8th Gloucester Regt and 10th
Worcester Regt. for the 9th Cheshire Regt and 6th Wiltshire
Regt. respectively at the rate of :-
             1 per Platoon
             1 per Company H.Q.
             1 per Battalion H.Q.
Total per Battalion 21 Guides.
      These guides will be at the BENCHMARK, 82.7 at K.36.c.1.1.
at the following times :-
             8th Gloucester Regt at 4.45 p.m.
             10th Worcester Regt. at 5.30 p.m.
  (b) Route.
      The 9th Cheshire Regt will proceed from VALLULART CAMP
by Light Railway Train to TRESCAULT. Thence by march route
by Sections at distance of 100 yards between Sections.
Foremost Section will not pass East of TRESCAULT before 4.40 p.m.
      Details of above train will be notified by the Staff
Captain.
      The 6th Wiltshire Regt will proceed from EASTWOOD CAMP by
march route via METZ - TRESCAULT. Movement West of TRESCAULT
will be by platoons at 200 yards distance between Platoons,
and East of TRESCAULT by Sections at 100 yards distance
between Sections. Foremost Section will not enter TRESCAULT
before 5.15 p.m.

  (c) Flanks.
      On the night 21/22nd the flanking Battalions will be as
follows :-
           Left flank - 7th E. Lancs. Regt.
           Right flank - NELSON Battalion.

  (d) Trench Stores, Aeroplane photographs, Defence maps, schemes
of work will be taken over on relief.

  (e) Dispositions will be forwarded to 57th Brigade H.Q by
noon 23rd instant.

  (f) All details of relief not laid down in these orders will be
arranged by C.Os. concerned.

3. On completion of relief the 9th Cheshire Regt. and 6th Wiltshire Regt. will come under the Command of the G.O.C. 57th Brigade. Completion of relief will accordingly be wired in B.A.B. Code to 57th Brigade H.Q. Location Q.12.a.9.5.

The 10th Worcester Regt. and 8th N. Staffs. Regt. will report their arrival in Camp to 58th Brigade H.Q. Location RUYAULCOURT. In case of tactical emergency these two Battalions will immediately come under the Command of the G.O.C. 58th Brigade.

4. The 58th Brigade Signal Officer will be responsible for maintenance of communication to 10th Worcester Regt. and 8th N. Staffs. Regt.

5. Administrative Instructions have today been issued by the Staff Captain.

ACKNOWLEDGE.

Captain,
A/Brigade Major 58th Infantry Brigade.

Issued at 4.30 p.m.

Copy No. 1 File	14 58 T.M.Batty.
2) War Diary	15 Staff Captain.
3)	16 Bde Transport Off.
4 G.O.C.	17 O.C. Bde Signals.
5 19th Divn. G.	18 Bde. Int. Offr.
6 19th Divn. Q.	19 S.O. 58th Bde.
7 56th Inf. Bde.	20 A.F.M. 19th Divn.
8 57th Inf. Bde.	21 A.D.M.S. 19th Div.
9 9 Cheshire R.	22 19th Div. Train.
10 9 R.W.Fusrs.	23 C.R.E. 19th Div.
11 9/Welch R.	24 81st Field Coy, R.E.
12 6 Wilts R.	25 189th Inf. Bde.
13 58 M.G.Coy.	26 D.M.G.O.

SECRET.

AMENDMENT No. 1 to
58th Infantry Brigade Operation Order No.226 dated 20.1.18.

Reference para. 2 (b) Route.

The 6th Wiltshire Regt. will proceed from EASTWOOD CAMP by Train and **not** by march route as directed in above order. Details of entrainment have today been notified by the Staff Captain. 6/Wiltshire Regt. will detrain at TRESCAULT and will then proceed in accordance with above order.

W.F. Scammell
Captain,
A/Brigade Major 58th Infantry Brigade.

Brigade H.Q.
21.1.18.

Issued to all recipients of 58th Infantry Brigade Operation Order No. 226 dated 20.1.18.

SECRET   Copy No. 3

58th Infantry Brigade Order No.227.

22nd January, 1918.

Ref: Map Sheet 57.C. 1/40,000.
                                    No. 105
Reference 56th Inf. Brigade Order issued direct to 9th Bn R.W.Fusiliers and 9th Bn Welch Regiment, the following moves will take place on the 24th inst. and night of 24/25th.

A. In the LEFT Sector. (56th Brigade Group).

(a). 9th Bn R.W.Fusiliers will relieve 7th Bn S. Lancs. Regt. in the Right Sub-sector and will hand over GRAZING CAMP to 7/S. Lanc. Regt.

(b). 9th Bn Welch Regt. will relieve 7th Bn R.Lanc. Regt. in the Left Sub-sector and will hand over WESTWOOD CAMP to 7th Bn R.Lanc. Regt.

1. All details of relief including the provision of guides will be arranged direct between C.O's. concerned, except in so far as laid down in this order.

2. 9th Bn R.W.Fusiliers and 9th Bn Welch Regt. will send such reconnoitring parties as the C.O's think desirable, to report to 56th Inf. Bde. H.Q. at L.32.a.15.15. at or about 11.a.m. 23rd inst; accommodation in a Light Railway train going linewards will be arranged by the Staff Captain if possible, and details notified to units concerned.

3. It is also hoped that trains will be provided on the afternoon of the 24th as follows :-

    For 9th Bn R.W.Fusiliers departing YTRES at 3.15.p.m.
                           arriving TRESCAULT about 4.15.p.m.

    For 9th Bn Welch Regt.   departing HAVRINCOURT WOOD at 4.15.p.m.
                           arriving TRESCAULT about 4.45.p.m.

4. No movement is permitted E of TRESCAULT before 4.30.p.m. and will then be by platoons at 100 yards distance.

5. Trench stores, aeroplane photographs, defences maps and schemes of work will be taken over on relief.

6. Dispositions will be forwarded to 56th Inf Brigade Hd.Qrs. by noon 26th inst.

7. On completion of relief the 9th Bn R.W.Fusiliers and 9th Bn Welch Regt. will come under the command of the G.O.C. 56th Inf. Brigade. Completion of relief will accordingly be wired in B.A.B. Code to 56th Inf. Bde. H.Q.
The 7th Bn R. Lanc. Regt. and 7th Bn S. Lanc. Regt. will report their arrival in camp to the Resting Brigade H.Q. RUYAULCOURT. In case of tactical emergency these two battalions will immediately come under the command of the G.O.C. Resting Brigade.

8. Administrative Instructions concerning the above moves have been issued by the Staff Captain.

B. In the RIGHT Sector.

The following moves will take place on the 24th inst:-

1. The 58th T.M.Battery will relieve the 57th T.M.Battery in the Right Sector in accordance with 19th Div. G.703 already issued to O.C. 58th T.M.Battery. Details of relief will be

arranged between O's.C.T.M.B. and relief reported
to Group Headquarters at Q.12.a.9.5.

2.   Brigade Hd.Qrs. 58th Brigade will relieve the 57th
Brigade H.Q. in the Right Group. 58th Brigade Hd.Qrs.
will close at RUYAULCOURT at 2.0.p.m. 24th inst. and
open at Q.12.a.9.5. at 3.p.m. at which hour G.O.C.
58th Brigade will assume command of the Right Group.

   ACKNOWLEDGE.

                                     W.S.Scammell
                                       Captain
                         A/Brigade Major 58th Infantry Brigade.
Issued at 12 noon.

        Copy No. 1 File.
                2)War Diary.
                3)
                4 G.O.C.
                5 19th Divn. G.
                6 19th Divn. Q.
                7 56th Inf. Bde.
                8 57th Inf. Bde.
                9 9.Cheshire R.
               10 9.R.W.Fusrs.
               11 9.Welch R.
               12 6.Wilts R.
               13 58.M.G.Coy.
               14 58.T.M.Battery.
               15 Staff Capt.
               16 Bde. Transport Offr.
               17 O.C. Bde. Signals.
               18 Bde. Int. Offr.
               19 S.O. 58th Bde.
               20 A.P.M. 19th Divn.
               21 A.D.M.S. 19th Divn.
               22 19th Div. Train.
               23 C.R.E. 19th Divn.
               24 81st Fld. Coy.R.E.
               25 189th Inf Bde.
               26 D.M.G.O.

AO 53 Interstate
(19th Siècle)
Vol 32
February 1818.

On His Majesty's Service.

Army Form C. 2118.

WAR DIARY
or
INTELLIGENCE SUMMARY.

(Erase heading not required.)

Instructions regarding War Diaries and Intelligence Summaries are contained in F.S. Regs., Part II. and the Staff Manual respectively. Title pages will be prepared in manuscript.

Place	Date	Hour	Summary of Events and Information	Remarks and references to Appendices
COUILLET WOOD. RIGHT SECTOR.	Feb. 1st		Following reliefs were complete by 9.30.p.m. under O.O. 228 attached:- 9th R.W.Fusiliers relieved 6th Bn Wiltshire Regt. in the Right front sub-section. 9th Bn Welch Regt. relieved 8th Bn N.Staffs. Regt. in the Centre front sub-section. 7th E.Lancs. Regt. relieved 9th Bn Cheshire Regt. in the Left front sub-section. Poor visibility. G.O.C. visited front line battalions before relief.	1.
	2nd		Poor visibility. G.O.C. visited front line battalions before relief. Army and Divisional Commanders visited Brigade Headquarters during the afternoon. COUILLET WOOD (RIGHT SECTOR) DEFENCE SCHEME issued. Following reliefs in accordance with O.O.223 attached were complete by 10.15.p.m. 7th Bn L.N.Lancs. Regt. relieved by 8th Glouc. Regt. proceeded to GRAZING CAMP. 7th Bn E.Lancs. Regt. relieved by 10th Bn Worcestershire Regt. proceeded to HAWES W. Camp. 7th Bn R.Lancs. Regt. relieved by 8th Bn N.Staffs. Regt. proceeded to Support Area. Brigade Major visited Right Front battalion (9th R.W.F.) and examined posts and saps. Platoon Posts were sited in NEW NELSON SUPPORT by the Brigade Major and 2nd in command of 9th R.W.F. An unusually quiet night.	2. 1.
	3rd		G.O.C. visited the front line battalions. The Major-General visited Brigade Hd.Qrs. during the morning. The Right Group now disposed as follows:- Right Front line – 9th Bn R.W.Fusiliers. Centre Front line – 9th Bn Welch regiment. Left Front Line – 7th Bn E. Lancs. Regiment. Support line Bn. – 7th Bn R. Lancs. Regiment. HAWES Camp west. – 7th Bn S.Lancs. Regiment. GRAZING Camp. – 7th Bn L.N.Lancs. Regiment. Operation Order No. 229 detailing the reorganisation of the Division on a 3 Battalion Brigade basis and detailing future reliefs issued.	3.
	4th		G.O.C spent the day in the line. The Major-General visited Brigade H.Q. at 8.45.a.m. 7th Bn S.Lancs. Regt. relieved 7th E.Lancs. Regt. in Left sub-section. 7th L.N.Lancs. Regt relieved 7th Bn R.Lancs. Regt. in Support Area.	3.

Army Form C. 2118.

WAR DIARY
or
INTELLIGENCE SUMMARY.

(Erase heading not required.)

Instructions regarding War Diaries and Intelligence Summaries are contained in F. S. Regs., Part II. and the Staff Manual respectively. Title pages will be prepared in manuscript.

Place	Date	Hour	Summary of Events and Information	Remarks and references to Appendices
	5th		G.O.C. visited front line battalions. Brigade Major visited the Stokes Mortars and Machine Gun Company. G.S.O.I visited Brigade H.Q. Visibility good. 1/4th K.S.L.I. relieved 9th Bn Welch Regt. in Centre Sub-section. 9th Bn Cheshire Regiment relieved 9th Bn R.W.Fusiliers in Right Sub-section. Relief complete 10.30.p.m.	3.
	6th		G.O.C. visited front line battalions. Divisional Commander visited Brigade Hd.Qrs. 7th Bn L.N.Lancs. Regt. relieved 7th Bn S.Lancs.Regt. in Left Sub-section. 7th Bn S.Lancs. Regt. proceeded to Support Line.	3.
	7th		G.O.C. visited front line battalions. Poor visibility.	
	8th		G.O.C. visited front line battalions. Weather rainy. Brigade Hd.Qrs. relieved by 56th Infy. Bde.H.Q., proceeded to YTRES.	
	9th		Brigade Headquarters in rest at LITTLEWOOD CAMP, YTRES.	
	10th		G.O.C. reconnoitred	
	11th		G.O.C. inspected transport. Brigade Major attended demonstration of co-operation between Tanks and Infantry.	
	12th		In rest at LITTLEWOOD CAMP, YTRES.	
	13th		58th Machine Gun Company moved from line to BEAULENCOURT in accordance with 0.0.230 attached.	4.
	14th		6th Bn Wiltshire regiment moved from line to VALLULART CAMP. Following moves in accordance with 0.0.230 took place:- 6th Bn Wiltshire Regt from VALLULART Camp to ROCQUIGNY. 9th Bn Welch Regt from line to ROCQUIGNY. 58th T.M.Battery from line to ROCQUIGNY. 9th Bn R.W.Fusiliers from HAWES Camp W. to VALLULART Camp.	4.
	15th		9th Bn R.W.Fusiliers moved from VALLULART Camp to ROCQUIGNY and Brigade H.Q. moved from LITTLEWOOD Camp, YTRES to ROCQUIGNY.	4.
ROCQUIGNY.	16th		Brigade cleaning up.	
	17th		Brigade Major and 5 officers from each battalion reconnoitred the Corps Battle Zone Defences.	
	18th		G.O.C. visited the Corps Counter-Battery Officer.	
	19th		Brigade in Training at ROCQUIGNY.	

Army Form C. 2118.

WAR DIARY
or
INTELLIGENCE SUMMARY.
(Erase heading not required.)

Instructions regarding War Diaries and Intelligence Summaries are contained in F. S. Regs., Part II. and the Staff Manual respectively. Title pages will be prepared in manuscript.

Place	Date	Hour	Summary of Events and Information	Remarks and references to Appendices
ROCQUIGNY	20th		Brigade in Training at ROCQUIGNY.	
	21st		Brigade in Training at ROCQUIGNY.	
	22nd		Brigade in Training at ROCQUIGNY.	
HAPLINCOURT	23rd		Brigade Group moved to huts on HAPLINCOURT - BERTINCOURT Road in accordance with O.O.231 attached. New locations:-	5.
			Brigade Hd.Qrs. - HAPLINCOURT (O.5.c.8.8.)	
			9th Bn R.W.Fusiliers. - HERRICK CAMP.	
			9th Bn Welch Regiment - PHIPPS CAMP.	
			6th Bn Wilts Regiment - SANDERS CAMP.	
			59th T.M.Battery. - PHIPPS CAMP.	
	24th		Brigade in Training.	
	25th		Brigade in Training.	
	26th		Brigade in Training.	
	27th		Brigade in Training.	
	28th		Brigade in Training.	
	1.3.18.			

Brigadier General

Commanding 5th Infantry Brigade.

SECRET.   Copy No. 25

58th Infantry Brigade Order No.228.

31st January, 1918.

Ref: Map Sheet 57.C. 1/40,000.

1. The Battalions of "A" Group and "B" Group will be transferred to the Left and Right Sectors respectively of the Divisional front on the nights 1/2nd and 2/3rd February 1918.

2. On the night 1/2nd Feby. the following reliefs will take place in accordance with Table A attached.

    9th Bn Royal Welch Fusiliers will relieve the 6th Bn Wiltshire Regt. who proceed to GRAZING CAMP.
    9th Bn Welch Regt. will relieve the 8th Bn N. Staffs. Regt. who proceed to the Intermediate Support Left Sector.
    7th Bn E. Lancs. Regt. will relieve the 9th Bn Cheshire Regt. who proceed to HAWES CAMP WEST.

3. On the night 2/3rd Feby. the following moves will take place:-

    The 7th Bn R.Lanc. Regt. will take over the accommodation in the INTERMEDIATE SUPPORT to the Right Sector vacated by the 8th Bn Glouc. Regt.
    The 7th Bn S.Lancs. Regt. will take over the accommodation in HAWES CAMP WEST vacated by the 9th Bn Cheshire Regt, who move to HAWES CAMP EAST.
    The 7th Bn L.N.Lancs. Regt. will take over the accommodation in GRAZING CAMP vacated by the 6th Bn Wiltshire Regt, who move to VALLULART CAMP.
    After the departure of the 6th Bn Wiltshire Regt. and 9th Bn Cheshire Regt. from GRAZING CAMP and HAWES CAMP WEST on 2.2.18 these camps will be used by battalions of the "A" Group. Right

4. A Table of future reliefs is attached marked B.
    All details not laid down herein will be arranged between C.O's concerned.

5. All maps, defence schemes, aeroplane photographs, plans, orders, trench stores, documents referring to the sector, and L.G. Drums stored at Battn.H.Q. will be handed over on relief.

6. Completion of all reliefs will be wired in B.A.B.Code to "A" Group H.Q. and repeated to Brigade H.Q.

7. No movement by formed bodies of troops EAST of TRESCAULT will take place before 4.40.p.m.

8. Acknowledge.

                                        Captain
                        Brigade Major 58th Infantry Brigade.

Issued at 8.0.p.m.

    Copy No. 1 19th Div. G.
            2 19th Div. Q.   15 58.M.Gun Coy.
            3 56th Inf. Bde.   16 58.T.M.Battery.
            4 57th Inf. Bde.   17 C.R.A.
            5   6th Inf Bde.   18 C.R.E.
            6 9.R.W.Fusrs.   19 O.C.19th Div.Train.
            7 9.Welch R.   20 A.D.M.S.
            8 7.E.Lanc.R.   21 Staff Capt.
            9 7.S.Lanc.R.   22 Bde Signal Offr.
           10 7.R.Lanc.R.   23 Bde Int. Offr.
           11 7.L.N.Lancs.R.   24 Liaison Offr.
           12 9.Cheshire R.   25) War Diary.
           13 6.Wilts Regt.   26)
           14 8.N.Staffs. Regt.   27 File.

A

RELIEF TABLE.

Unit.	From.	To.	Relieving.	Rendezvous for Guides.♣	Remarks.
9/Welch Regt.	Intermediate Support. Left Sector.	Centre Front Right Sector.	8th Bn. Staffs. Regt.	Bn.H.Q. L.31.d.5.5. at 2.0.p.m.	8th N. Staffs. Regt. proceed to Intermediate Support Left Sector.
9/R.W.Fusrs.	GRAZING CAMP.	Right Front. Right Sector.	6th Bn Wilts Regt.	Junction of HIGHLAND Rd. and RIDGE TRENCH (R.2.b.0.5.) at 6.0.p.m.	6th Wilts Regt. proceed to GRAZING CAMP.
7/S.Lancs. Regt.	HAWS. W.	Left Front Right Sector.	9th Bn Cheshire Regt.	Junction of HIGHLAND Rd. and RIDGE TRENCH (at R.2.b.0.5.) at 6.45.p.m.	9th Cheshire Regt. proceed {signature}

♣ 1 Officer and 17 Men (1 for each platoon and Bn. H.Q.)

Locations of Units on completion of moves taking place on dates shown
in Left Column.

Dates.	Right.	Centre.	Left.	Intermediate.	HAWES W.	GRAZING.
Feb. 1st.	9/R.W.Fus.	9/Welch Regt.	7/L.Lancs.R.	2/Glouc. Regt.	9/Cheshire R.	6/Wiltshire R.
" 2nd.	"	"	"	7/R.Lan. Regt.	7/S. Lancs. R.	7/L.N.Lancs. R.
" 3rd.	"	"	"	"	"	"
" 4th.	"	"	"	"	"	"
" 5th.	7/L.N.Lancs.	7/R.Lan. R.	7/S.Lancs. R.	9/R.W.Fusrs.	9/Welch Regt.	7/E. Lancs. R.
" 6th.	"	"	"	"	"	"
" 7th.	"	"	"	"	"	"
" 8th.	"	"	"	"	"	"
" 9th.	9/R.W.Fusrs.	9/Welch Regt.	7/E.Lancs. R.	7/S. Lancs. Regt.	7/R.Lan. Regt.	7/L.N.Lancs. R.
" 10th.	"	"	"	"	"	"
" 11th.	"	"	"	"	"	"
" 12th.	"	"	"	"	"	"

SECRET   Copy No. 24

                    58th Brigade No. B.M.1603.

          Herewith Copy No. 24 Defence Scheme COUILLET
Right Sub-sector.

          This defence scheme cancels all previous defence
schemes issued with reference to this sector, which should now be
destroyed.

          Please acknowledge receipt.

                                        [signature]
                                                    Captain

                              Brigade Major 58th Infantry Brigade.

Brigade H.Q.
     1st February, 1918.

Copies to: 1 19th Div. G.
           2 19th Div. Q.
           3 56th Inf. Bde.
           4 57th Inf. Bde.
           5 6th Inf. Bde.
           6 9.R.W.Fusrs.
           7 9.Welch R.
           8 7.R.Lan. R.
           9 7.E.Lancs.R.
          10 7.S.Lancs. R.   18 94th Fld. Co. R.E.
          11 7.L.N.Lancs.R.   19 58th Bde. Sig. Offr.
          12 58.T.M.B.   20 G.O.C.
          13 Rt.Group R.F.A.   21 Staff Capt.
          14   "   " M.G.   22 R.F.A. Liaison Offr.
          15 C.R.A., 19th Div.   23) War Diary.
          16 C.R.E.   "   24)
          17 A.D.M.S. "   25 File.
                                     26 Bn in Reserve in Left
                                         Group Intermed. Line.

INDEX TO COUILLET SECTOR, RIGHT SUB-SECTOR DEFENCE SCHEME.

1. Front and Boundaries.
2. The general principles of defence.
3. Organisation of the defence.
4. Method of holding the line.
5. Action in case of attack and orders for counter-attack.
6. Artillery Arrangements.
7. S.O.S. Orders.
8. Organisation of Machine Guns.
9. Organisation of Trench Mortars.
10. Action against E.A.
11. Precautions against Gas.
12. Responsibilities for work.
13. Signal Communications.

APPENDICES.

I. Map A.
II. Map B.
III. Locations.
IV. Orders for counter-attack of Support Battalion.
V. Signal Communications.
VI. Administrative Arrangements.

SECRET.   Copy No. 24

DEFENCE SCHEME.
(COUILLET SECTOR - RIGHT SUB-SECTOR).

1. **Front and Boundaries.**

    The Divisional Front extends from OSTRICH AVENUE (Inclusive) in R.10.a. to the Railway (exclusive) in L.21.d. It is divided into a Right and Left Sector.
    The Right Sector extends from OSTRICH AVENUE (inclusive) in R.10.a. to L.34.a.6.2. (road at that point being exclusive).
    The forward boundaries are shown on Map A App.I.

2. **General Principles of Defence.**

    The Front Line System is the main line of defence.
    (i). The garrison of every trench post and locality will offer the greatest resistance of which it is capable against hostile attack. The above applies equally to troops holding the outpost line.

    (ii). Troops will not fall back because their flanks are turned. The stubborn resistance of a post or a section of a trench even though temporarily isolated, is often the deciding factor in the success or failure of a counter-attack.

    (iii) Every Commander down to a Platoon Commander must have a definite reserve earmarked for counter-attack.
    The success or failure of the counter-attack will probably depend almost entirely on the rapidity with which it is launched. If the counter-attack be launched by however small a force whilst the enemy is still disorganised its chance of success is great.

    (iv). Units will be disposed on the principle of Defence in Depth.

3. **Organisation of the Defences.**

    (a). The front line system consists of a Front, Support and Reserve Line as shown on Map A. App. I. The Support and Reserve Lines are at present in a very incomplete state and can only be occupied in parts.

    (b). The Front Line System is held by three battalions in the line one battalion (The Counter-attack Battalion) being in close Support. Each battalion in the line will have one company definitely earmarked for counter-attack.

    (c). In addition two companies of the Reserve Battalion of the Left Group Sector which are accommodated in the HIGHLAND RIDGE Line about R.2.b. and c. (see Map. A. App.I) are under the orders of G.O.C. Right Group for tactical purposes.
    These companies form a tactical permanent garrison of the HIGHLAND RIDGE Defences and may not be moved forward for the purpose of counter-attack. Of these not more than one company is available for carrying and work in the Right Group Sub-sector.

4. **Method of holding the Line.**

    The Divisional front is divided into 2 sub-sectors, each held by one group of 6 battalions. THE RIGHT Group holds the Right Sub-sector and is disposed as follows:-

    Front Line. - Three battalions distributed in depth as far as possible. THE DIVIDING LINES BETWEEN THESE BATTALIONS ARE SHOWN ON MAP A. APPENDIX I.

    Support Battalion (Counter-attacking Battn).
    One battalion accommodated in the HINDENBURG Line in the vicinity of WOOD AVENUE. No more than two companies may be detailed at any one time for carrying etc out of the Support Battn. area, so that there will never be less than 2 companies immediately available.

(d). (i). It appears probable from a study of a recently captured German order that Minenwerfer will be used prior to an assault to a greater extent than in the past. It is quite possible that the bombardment of front line trenches will be left entirely to Minenwerfer, Guns and Howitzers being used only on battery areas and communications.

(ii). If this method of preparation is used a very short and violent Trench Mortar bombardment is indicated, and the assault may be expected at any time after the bombardment has been in progress for a few minutes.

(iii). A steady fire on the S.O.S. Lines will be opened by the Artillery immediately a <u>general</u> Trench Mortar bombardment is started on any sector of our front and all known T.M. Emplacements will at the same time be engaged. M.Guns will also open sharp bursts of fire on S.O.S. lines.

(iv). It is, therefore, of the greatest importance that any <u>General</u> Trench Mortar bombardment of any sector of the front should be reported <u>with the least possible delay</u>.

Garrison of HIGHLAND RIDGE SYSTEM.

Two companies of reserve battalion of Left or "B" Group accommodated in HIGHLAND RIDGE Defences. (See para. 3 (b).

The remaining two battalions of the Group are back in HAVRINCOURT WOOD and GRAZING or VALLULART CAMP. These Battalions are under the orders of G.O.C. Reserve Brigade for tactical purposes.

5. **Action in case of attack and orders for counter-attack.**

(a). **Front Line Battalions.**
Troops will "Stand to" in their normal positions and will act in accordance with the principles laid down in para. 2.
The Counter-attack Company of each Battalion will under the orders of its Battalion Commander be employed normally to restore the situation on the battalion front, if required. They should also be prepared to assist the battalions on their flanks should such assistance be required.
The Company Commanders of these Companies will be in possession of written orders as to their action in the most probable contingencies.

(b). **The Support or Counter-attack Battalion.**
The retention in our hands of the commanding Welsh Ridge is of extreme importance as, should it be lost, the whole FLESQUIERES Salient would be in danger. Should therefore the enemy penetrate any portion of the front, and the local counter-attack by the Counter-attacking Coys of Battalions fail to eject him, the Counter-attack Battn. will deliver a counter-attack to re-establish the line.
The line of action which will probably give the best prospect of success is to strike rapidly and in the greatest strength possible to regain a position on the top of this ridge thence working along it in a Northerly direction if necessary.
Instructions for the Counter-attack Battalion are contained in Appendix IV.

(c). All working and carrying parties in front of and including the Intermediate Line will report to the nearest Company Commander for orders, other working parties will immediately rejoin their units.

6. **Artillery Arrangements.**

(a). The Right Sector is covered by the Right Group R.F.A.
The number of batteries are liable to be varied from time to time. At present the Group consists of:-

  3 18 pdr. Batteries.
  2 4.5 How.

1 Anti-Tank Gun is available for defence of the sector and is at present located at R.1.c.9.1.
6" Newton Mortars are also being installed.

(b). **Liaison.**
There is a Senior Liaison Officer at Brigade H.Q. and 1 Junior Liaison Officer with each of the 3 front line battalions; also 1 with the Support Battalion.

(c). **S.O.S. Barrages.**
The S.O.S. Barrage put down by the Artillery is supplemented by a Machine Gun S.O.S. Barrage. Barrage lines and battery zones are liable to variation and will be communicated from time to time.

7.

7. S.O.S. Orders.

(a). The S.O.S. Location Call for Right Sub-sector is "S.O.S. COUILLET RIGHT".

(b). All Officers, N.C.O's and Machine Gunners will be made acquainted with the S.O.S. Orders.

(c). The S.O.S. Signal will only be used when the enemy are actually seen to be assembling or advancing to the attack.

(d). All available means of communication will be employed in sending the S.O.S. message viz: Telephone, Rocket, Buzzer, Wireless and Visual and Runner. The S.O.S. takes priority over all other messages.

(e). It should be impressed on all officers that the Artillery must be informed immediately its fire is no longer required.

8. Organisation of Machine Gun Defence.

The Right Sub-sector is covered by the Right Group 19th Divl. M.G. composed of 24 guns. These guns are divided into - Forward Guns (6), Main Line Guns (6), Reserve Line Guns (12). Present positions of M.G's are contained in Map B.

This Group is tactically under the orders of the D.M.G.O. but for all matters of trench discipline is under the orders of the Battalion Commander on the spot.

9. Organisation of Trench Mortars.

One L.T.M.Battery is allotted to the Sub-sector. The number of guns in the line varies. At present there are 5 T.Mortars in the line, their dispositions are shown on Map B. attached.

10. Action against E.A.

In order to deal with low flying hostile aeroplanes (flying at 3000 ft. and under) each of the 3 battalions in the will have at least one L.G. on an anti-aircraft mounting detailed for this duty. Similarly the battalion in support will have at least 2 L.G's detailed for A.A. work.

Special precautions will be taken to deal with low flying aeroplanes attempting to fly up the MARCOING - COUILLET WOOD Valley.

The number and positions of Vickers guns detailed for A.A. work is laid down by D.M.G.O. from time to time.

11. Precautions against Gas.

(a). The box respirator will always be worn in the alert position.

(b). The entrances to all deep dug-outs and concrete shelters will be provided with double blanket protection.

Every dug-out should be equipped with AYRTON Fans which should be handed over on relief as Trench Stores.

(c). A sentry will be posted near the entrance to each deep dug-out or concrete emplacement, or group of dug-outs, and must know that in addition to his duties he is also responsible for giving warning in case of gas, and he should be instructed as to his action

      a. In case of Gas Shelling.
      b. In case of Gas Cloud.

(d). Every sentry will have a Gas alarm of some sort within reach of his post.

12. Responsibility for work.

The Front Line Battalions, will be entirely responsible for the upkeep of all trenches, posts, wire, etc., within their areas as well as the construction of any new defences that may be necessary unless R.E. or Pioneers are specially allotted for the work.

The Support Battalion will be responsible for the upkeep of defences within its area and will also be called upon for working parties in the forward area.

13. Signal Communications.

See Appendix V.

[signature] Captain

Brigade Major 58th Infantry Brigade.

Brigade H.Qrs.

1st February, 1918.

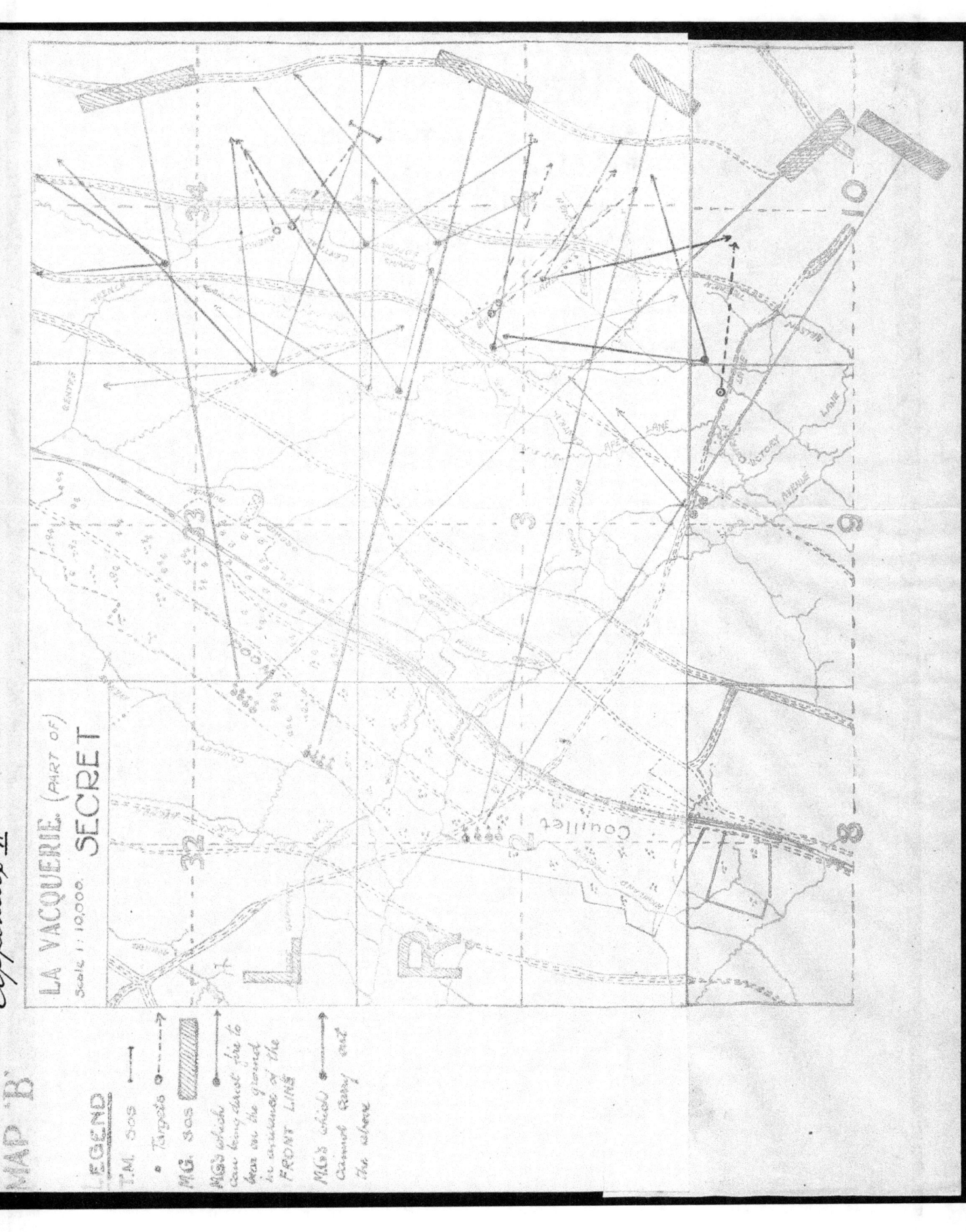

APPENDIX III
LOCATIONS.

Divl. Headquarters......... NEUVILLE BOURJONVAL.

Hd.Qrs. "A" Group......... Q.12.a.9.5.

"   "B" Group.......... L.32.a.15.15.

"   Rt. Group R.F.A.... Q.12.a.2.6.

"   "   "   M.G...... R.3.a.2.9.

"   T.M.Battery......... R.2.b.2.8.

Right Battalion............ R.3.b.70.05.

Centre Battalion........... R.4.a.25.35.

Left Battalion............. L.34.c.55.45.

Support Battalion.......... R.3.c.02.88.

Battalion of "B" Group in) L.31.d.55.05.
    Intermediate Line.)

Field Coy. R.E. affiliated) L.31.c.4.4.
    to "A" Group.   )

Pioneer Battalion (5/S.W.B) Q.10.b.2.3.

Signals Adv. Bde. Report... R.3.a.3.6.
    Centre.

APPENDIX IV.

Instructions for the Counter-attack Battalion
COUILLET RIGHT SECTOR.

1. The Counter-attack battalion of the Right Sector is located as under:-

   H.Qrs.... R.3.c.02.88.

   Companies. R.2.b.12.42.
   R.2.b.87.70.
   R.3.a.20.60.
   R.3.c.38.52.

2. The battalion will stand to in the trenches in which it lives which will be its normal defensive position. It will however be prepared to form up for attack in an Easterly direction in ORCHID AVENUE and the road running through R.3.c. and a.

   The battalion will be prepared to counter-attack to re-capture any part of the Brigade front in which the enemy may have gained a footing and will have plans for counter-attack on the Right, Centre or Left Sub-sectors of the Brigade front.

3. With this object in view forward routes will be carefully reconnoitred both by day and night and any necessary gaps cut in the wire.

   At least one overland route will be prepared and marked to each of the Right, Centre and Left Sub-sectors of the Brigade front. Although routes to all three Battalion sub-sectors will be marked out it will probably be best in most cases to strike at once for the top of the ridge and then if necessary work along it in a Northerly direction.

4. In case of alarm, S.O.S. being sent up, or a heavy bombardment, the Battalion will "Stand to" and man its defensive positions. It will then be ready to hold its ground and break up an attack in force, or to launch a counter-attack as ordered.

   The O.C. Battalion will send one officer or N.C.O. to the H.Q. of each of the front line battalions to get in touch with the situation and report.

5. Normally, provided the telephone lines are holding, the counter-attack battalion will not leave its defensive position to counter-attack without orders from the Brigadier. Where, however, telephone communication is interrupted or the O.C. considers that immediate action is necessary, he will act at once on the lines indicated above without waiting for orders, reporting his action immediately to Brigade H.Q.

   Under no circumstances will the battalion leave its defensive position, except for counter-attack as explained above, without orders from Brigade H.Q.

6. Ammunition, etc. will be maintained on the same scale as for a battalion holding the front line, and will be distributed throughout the area to be defended, and always ready for use.

7. During a preliminary bombardment of our defensive area, the troops of this battalion will, as far as possible, be kept under shell proof cover, double sentries only being kept above ground. Men sheltering in dug-outs in this case will be fully equipped and ready to get out the moment the bombardment lifts. With this object in view dug-out accommodation will be provided for as many men of the battalion as is possible.

8. All trenches will be kept in a state of repair and well wired.

9. Whenever any part of the battalion goes forward to work, definite orders in the event of attack will be given to all concerned.

10. Men will not be allowed to walk about on the top of the trenches indiscriminately by day.

NOTE I.

When a battalion becomes the Counter-attack Battalion, the O.C. will ascertain from O.C. Battalion he is relieving exactly what arrangements have been made with regard to para. 2 and 3 above and will report the following day to Brigade H.Q. whether he considers all arrangements satisfactory and, if not, what alterations he proposes.

NOTE II.

Suggested routes for counter-attack are as under:-

(a). In counter-attack on Right Sub-sector. Line of road running through R.3.c. and d. - R.9.b. - R.10.a.

(b). In counter-attack on Centre Sub-sector. Line of CENTRAL AVENUE

(c). For counter-attack on Left Sub-sector. Line of ORCHID AVENUE, SAILOR ALLEY, SUNKEN ALLEY, or CENTRAL AVENUE, to R.4.a. and thence Northward along the Spur.

APPENDIX V.
SIGNAL COMMUNICATIONS.

General

Conversation forward of Brigade is strictly forbidden unless of a very important nature.

Lines.

The lines in use in the Brigade sector are overland as shown on the straight line diagram at Brigade Signal Office, copies of which can be had on application.

To the forward battalions in the line, the line runs as follows:

From Brigade H.Q. re Advanced Brigade H.Q. at R.3.a.3.6. 3 pairs overland.

All Battalions are joined on to this exchange.

Right Battalion.	3 pairs. 2 direct and 1 via Centre Battn.
Left Battalion.	3 pairs. 2 direct and 1 via Centre Battn.
Centre Battalion.	4 pairs. 2 direct, 1 via Right Battn., and 1 via Left Battn.
Support Battalion.	2 pairs direct.
Bde. on Right.	1 pair.
Bde. on Left.	2 pairs, 1 via Adv. Div. Report Centre Q.5.a. 85.15, and 1 direct.
M.G. Hd.Qrs.	1 pair direct.
Divl. H.Q.	3 pairs overland. 1 direct and 2 via Adv. Div. Report Centre. The direct pair is superimposed for Sounder working.
Transport Lines.	The Transport Lines are in HAVRINCOURT WOOD. 1 pair via Divl. H.Q.

Runners.

The following runner service is in force:-

Brigade Headquarters...... 7 Orderlies.
Advanced Brigade......... 7 Orderlies.

All despatches are taken to R.C. and collected and delivered by Battalion runners to this place at times to be laid down by the Group Signal Officer.

Pigeons.

1 pair of pigeons is collected daily from Div. Adv. H.Q. and taken to the Left Battalion H.Q. These are collected and delivered every day. Pigeons may now be retained 48 hours in the line. On relief pigeons are sent from the Left Battalion to the Right, whence they are available to be released with a message, weather permitting. If they are not released they must be returned to H.Q. Right Group by the first runner of the second day after the day of arrival in the line.

Visual.

A visual station is established and working at R.8.b.1.1. direct to the Right and Centre battalions. The situation reports are sent daily at 4.0.a.m. and 4.0.p.m.

Another visual station works from Bde.H.Q. to Adv. Div. report Centre at the same times. Tests are carried out every 3 hours.

- 2 -

Fullerphones.
These are in use as shewn below:-

```
Brigade Headquarters...  2.
Right Battalion H.Q.....  1.
Left Battalion H.Q......  1.
Centre Battalion H.Q....  1.
Support Battalion H.Q...  1.
                         ----
                          65.
```

Wireless.
There is one wireless set in the Brigade sector at present at Brigade Headquarters.
This works back to Corps directing station at METZ, and YTRES, or if those stations are engaged to the ARMY DIRECTING STATION.

Power Buzzer.
There are 5 power buzzers and 2 amplifiers on the brigade front.
There is one power buzzer at each Battalion H.Q. in the line. These work to P.B. and A. at R.C. it is then transmitted back by P.B. and A. to Brigade H.Q.

APPENDIX. VI.

ADMINISTRATIVE ARRANGEMENTS.

1. **Rations.**

    Rations are taken up by limber via TRESCAULT and VILLERS PLOUICH (reaching TRESCAULT not earlier than 4.0.p.m.) to dumps as follows:-

    Right Battn....... R.3.c.1.8.
    Centre Battn...... R.3.b.2.9.
    Left Battn........ L.33.d.6.5.
    Support Battn..... R.3.c.1.8.

    Bde Transport Officer will arrange that Battns. are given a Time Table.

2. **Water.**

    There is a well at L.33.d.5.6. which supplies Left Battn. Water for remainder is taken up in petrol tins and water carts can be left as follows:-

    Right & Support... R.3.c.1.8.
    Centre............ R.3.b.2.9.

    Nearest water point - TRESCAULT.

3. **Cooking.**

    Solidified alcohol is used by 3 front line battalions.
    One soyer stove will be taken over on relief by each Battn. In addition cookhouses have been improvised and can be used by night. Hot food is also brought up, with rations in food containers.

4. **Medical.**

    Regimental Aid Posts are as follows:-

    Right Battalion..... R.3.d.4.5.
    Centre   "   ..... R.4.a.2.2.
    Left   "   ..... L.33.d.7.6.
    Support   "   ..... R.2.b.6.4.

    A.D.S. - Q.18.b.8.8. (2nd Divn).
    Cemetery at R.3.c.5.9.

5. **Bomb Stores.**

    Divisional - RIBECOURT, TRESCAULT.
    Brigade.   - R.3.c.1.8.
                 Adv. dump at R.3.c.3.3.

6. **Reserve Ration Dumps.**

    Dump "A" - R.3.c.1.8.

7. **R.E. Arrangements.**

    R.E. Dump - R.3.c.1.8. material may be drawn on application to R.E. N.C.O. i/c.

8. **Salvage.**

    Every possible effort will be made to salvage. Salvage will be collected at R.3.c.1.8. and brought back from there by ration limbers.

9. **Gum-boots and Socks.**

    A store of dry gumboots and socks is situated at R.3.c.1.8. Units can draw these in exchange for wet on application to Bomb Storeman.

S E C R E T.

Amendment to 58th Infy. Bde. Defence Scheme.
"COUILLET RIGHT SUB-SECTOR."

The following alterations in Map B, Appendix II of 58th
Infy. Bde. Defence Scheme "COUILLET RIGHT SUB-SECTOR are made:-

Machine guns at present shown at R.5.b.63.91. and
R.4.c.59.90. have been moved to R.3.a.15.03. and R.4.a.4.1.
respectively.

                                                           W.A.Bill. Captain

                          Brigade Major 58th Infantry Brigade.

4.2.18.

   Copies to 19th Div G.
          56th Inf. Bde.   58th T.M.B.
          57th Inf. Bde.   Rt.Group R.F.A.
          6th Inf. Bde.   M.Guns.
          9/R.W.F.   94th Field Co. R.E.
          9/Welch R.   H.Q.C.
          7/R.Lancs.R.   War Diary
          7/N.Lancs.R.
          7/S.Lancs   File.
          7/N.Lancs.R.   Bn in reserve in Left Group
                                                  Intermediate Line.

SECRET 58th Brigade No. B.M.1603/3.

Amendment No. 2 to 5th Infy. Bde.
Defence Scheme.

COUILLET RIGHT SECTOR.

5th February, 1918.

Para. 6 (a).

Instead of R.1.c.9.1. read R.2.c.55.00. for location of Anti-Tank Gun.

Para. 6 (b).

Delete "also 1 with the Support Battalion".

L.J.A.Bill. Captain

Brigade Major 58th Infantry Brigade.

Copy to all recipients of 58th Bde. Defence Scheme.
"COUILLET RIGHT SECTOR".

SECRET   Copy No......

58th Infantry Brigade Order No. 229.

3rd February, 1918.

Ref: Map Sheet 57.C. 1/40,000.

1. (a). The Infantry Brigades of the 19th Division are to be re-organised from 4 battalions to 3, the process commencing on 4/2/18.

   (b). The present battalions of the 56th Infantry Brigade are to be disbanded.
   On completion of the re-organisation, the order of battle of the Infantry of the Division will be as under:-

   ### 56th Infantry Brigade.

   9th Bn Cheshire Regiment.
   1/4th Shropshire Light Infantry.
   8th Bn North Staffordshire Regiment.

   ### 57th Infantry Brigade.

   10th Bn Royal Warwickshire Regiment.
   8th Bn Gloucestershire Regiment.
   10th Bn Worcestershire Regiment.

   ### 58th Infantry Brigade.

   9th Bn Royal Welch Fusiliers.
   9th Bn Welsh Regiment.
   6th Bn Wiltshire Regiment.

2. Detailed instructions for the transfer of the 9th Bn Cheshire Regiment to the 56th Infantry Brigade will be issued by the Staff Captain.

3. The Divisional front will continue to be held by two Groups.

4. (a). Relief Table "B" issued with O.O. No. 228 is hereby cancelled and Table "A" attached is substituted.

   (b). Reliefs will be carried out as therein laid down without further orders unless any alterations or modifications are found necessary.

   (c). Subject to the provisions laid down in the following sub-paragraphs, all details of relief (including time and meeting place of guides) will be arranged direct between Commanding Officers concerned:-

   (i). The Staff Captain of the Brigade concerned will arrange for trains or lorries for battalions moving up from and returning to the Reserve Brigade Area and will issue instructions to units concerned.

   (ii). The Battalion in Support moving up to relieve a front line battalion will arrange the time of leaving the Support area so as not to block battalions arriving from the Reserve Area.

   (iii). All maps, defence schemes, aeroplane photographs, plans, orders, trench stores, documents referring to the sector, and Lewis Gun drums stored at Battalion Headquarters will be handed over on relief.

   (iv). Lists of trench stores and ammunition taken over on relief will be forwarded in duplicate to Right Group H.Q. by 12 noon on the day after relief.

(v). Disposition reports will be forwarded to reach Right Group H.Q. by 2.0.p.m. on the day after relief.

(vi). Completion of all reliefs will be wired in B.A.B. code to Right Group H.Q.

5. Acknowledge.

[signed] Captain

Brigade Major 58th Infantry Brigade.

Issued at 11.0.a.m.

```
Copy No.  1 19th Divn G.           15 Right Group M.G.Co.
          2 19th Divn Q.           16 58.T.M.B.
          3 56th Inf. Bde.         17 Right Group R.A.
          4 57th Inf Bde.          18 C.R.E., 19th Div.
          5 6th Inf Bde.           19 O.C. Div. Train.
          6 9.Cheshire R.          20 A.D.M.S., 19th Div.
          7 9.R.W.Fusrs.           21 G.O.C.
          8 9.Welch R.             22 Staff Capt.
          9 K.S.L.I.               23 Bde. Signal Offr.
         10 7.R.Lanc. R.           24 Bde. Intelligence Offr.
         11 7.S.Lanc. R.           25 6.Wilts R.
         12 7.E.Lanc. R.           26) War Diary.
         13 7.N.Lanc. R.           27)
         14 8.N.Staffs. R.         28 File.
```

Relief Table "A" attached to 58th Inf. Bde. Order No. 229
Showing locations of dates shown in Column 1.

Date. Feb.	Right Sector. Right.	Centre.	Left.	Intermediate.	Reserve Area HAWES.W.	HAWES.E	GRAZING	PIONEER	Remarks.
3rd	9/R.W.F.	9/Welch.	7/E.Lan.	7/R.Lanc.R.			7/S.Lanc.	7/N.Lan.	
4th	"	"	"	"		"	"	"	K.S.L.I. transferred from 63rd Div.
5th	"	"	"	7/S.Lan.	7/N.Lanc.R.		7/E.Lan.	7/R.Lanc.	
6th	9/Ches.R. (from HAWES) EAST	K.S.L.I.	"	"	"	9/R.W.F.	"	9/Welch	E.Lanc.R. and R.Lanc.R. in process of disbandment.
7th	"	"	"	7/N.Lanc.	7/S.Lanc.R.		9/R.W.F.	9/Welch	
8th	"	"	"	"	"		"	"	
9th	"	"	"	9/R.W.F.	9/Welch R		7/N.Lan.R.	7/S.Lanc.R	Orders for disbandment of N.Lancs.R. & S.Lancs.R are being issued later.
10th	8/N.Staffs. (from VALIUL-LART).	9/Welch.	"	"	K.S.L.I.		9/Ches.R.		
11th	"	"	"	"	"		"		
12th	"	"	"	"	"		"		
13th	"	"	"	9/Ches.R	"		9/R.W.F.		

SECRET.

Addendum No. 1 to 56th Infantry Brigade
Order No. 229.

Para. 4 (c).

(vii). There will be no movement EAST of TRESCAULT before 4.45.p.m., except when visibility is so low as to render enemy observation impossible.

(viii). All movement will be by Platoons at 200 yards distance.

[signature]
Captain

Brigade Major 56th Infantry Brigade.

4.2.18.

Copy to all recipients of 56th Inf. Bde. Order No. 229.

SECRET.

Amendment to second page of Relief Table attached
to 58th Infantry Brigade Order No. 230.

The moves of the 9th Bn R.W.Fusrs. (less depot) from
WESTWOOD CAMP and of the 58th T.M.Battery (less depot) from the
Right Group front take place on 14th and night 14th/15th Feby.
respectively.

In the date column insert these dates opposite these moves.

signature, Captain

11.2.18.   Brigade Major 58th Infantry Brigade.

Issued to the following recipients of 58th Inf. Bde. Order
No. 230.

19th Div. G.	58.T.M.Battery.
19th Div. Q.	A.F.M., 19th Div.
9.R.W.Fusrs.	A.F.M. 47th Div.
9.Welch Regt.	O.C. 19th Div. Train.
6.Wilts Regt.	S.O. 58th Inf. Bde.
58.M.Gun Coy.	188th Inf. Bde.

SECRET.   Copy No. 23

                 58th Infantry Brigade Order No. 230.

                                                    11th February, 1918.

Reference
    Sheet 1/40,000. 57.C.

1.   The 19th Division will be relieved in the line by the
63rd Division on the nights 13th/14th and 14th/15th February
1918.
     On relief the 19th Division will be in Corps Reserve in
the BARASTRE Area with Divisional Headquarters at HAPLINCOURT.

2.   The 58th Infantry Brigade (less the 58th Machine Gun Coy)
will be located at ROCQUIGNY (O.33.b.central).
     The 58th Machine Gun Company will be located in BEAULENCOURT
for training under the D.M.G.O.

3.   Moves will be carried out in accordance with the attached
Table.

4.   Distances of 100 yards will be kept between Companies on the
march.

5.   The Staff Captain will issue Administrative Instructions
which will include:-

        (a). Train arrangements from the Line.
        (b). Lorry arrangements.
        (c). Billeting arrangements and Camps.

     Billeting parties from units in the line will be at the
depots the evening before the move of their units to the
ROCQUIGNY Area.

6.   Defence Schemes and Area Stores will be handed over to
relieving units and written receipts obtained. Units in
VALLULART CAMP and GRAZING CAMP will return the Reserve
Brigade Defence Schemes to Brigade Headquarters on vacating
these camps.

7.   Completion of moves will be notified to this office.

8.   Brigade Headquarters will close at LITTLEWOOD CAMP, YTRES
on 15.2.18 at 12 noon and will re-open at ROCQUIGNY at same
hour.

9.   ACKNOWLEDGE.

                                              J.A.Bill. Captain
                                      Brigade Major 58th Infantry Brigade.

Issued at 10.30.a.m.

        Copy No. 1 19th Divn. G.   14 A.P.M., 19th Div.
                 2 19th Divn. Q.   15 A.P.M. 47th Div.
                 3 9.R.W.Fusrs.   16 O.C. 19th Div. Train.
                 4 9.Welch Regt.   17 S.O. 58th Inf. Bde.
                 5 6.Wilts Regt.   18 188th Inf. Bde.
                 6 7.L.N.Lancs. Regt.   19 G.O.C.
                 7 58.M.Gun Coy.   20 Staff Capt.
                 8 58.T.M.Battery.   21 Bde. Sig. Offr.
                 9 56th Inf. Bde.   22 Bde. Int. Offr.
                10 57th Inf. Bde.   23) War Diary.
                11 A.D.M.S., 19th Div.   24)
                12 C.R.E.   25 File.
                13 D.M.G.O.   26 Bde. Transport Offr.

Relief Table attached to 58th Infantry Brigade Order No. 230.

Date.	Unit.	From.	To.	Route.	Starting Point.	Time.	Remarks.
13th Feb.	Depot, 58th M.Gun Coy.	HAVRINCOURT WOOD.	BEAULENCOURT.	NEUVILLE BOURJONVAL -YTRES - Road Junction F.19.b.8.8. - BUS - ROCQUIGNY.	Cross Roads F.17.d.central	2.p.m.	
13/14th Feby.	58th M.G.Coy. (less depot).	Right Group.	BEAULENCOURT.	Light Railway.	-	-	Under orders to be issued by D.A.M.G.O.
do.	6/Wilts Regt. (less Depot).	Left Group.	VALLULART CAMP.	March route.	-	-	Under orders to be issued by G.O.C. Left Group.
14th Feb.	Depot 6/Wilts Regt.	HAVRINCOURT WOOD.	ROCQUIGNY.	NEUVILLE BOURJONVAL -YTRES - Road Junction F.19.b.8.8. - BUS.	Cross roads F.17.a.central	2.15.p.m.	
	6/Wilts Regt. (less depot).	VALLULART CAMP.	ROCQUIGNY.	Road junction at F.32.d.2.4. - LECHELLE - BUS.	VALLULART CAMP.	2.30.p.m.	Transport required at VALLULART CAMP will move with Battalion.
	Depot 58/T.M.Battery.	HAVRINCOURT WOOD.	ROCQUIGNY.	-	-	-	By lorry
	Depot, 9/Welch Regt.	HAVRINCOURT WOOD.	ROCQUIGNY.	NEUVILLE BOURJONVAL -YTRES - Road junction F.19.b.8.8. - BUS.	Cross roads F.17.a. central.	2.25.pm.	

Date.	Unit.	From.	To.	Route.	Starting Point.	Time.	Remarks.
14/15th Feby.	9/Welch Regt. (less depot).	Right Group (Centre Sub-sector).	ROCQUIGNY.	Light railway.	-	-	Under orders to be issued by O.C. Right Group.
	9/R.W.Fusrs. (less depot).	WESTWOOD CAMP.	VALLULART CAMP.	NEUVILLE - BOURJONVAL.	-	On relief time of which will be notified later.	
	58/T.M.Battery (less depot).	Right Group Front.	ROCQUIGNY.	Light Railway.	-	-	Under orders to be issued by O.C Right Group.
15th Feb.	Brigade Hd.Qrs.	LITTLE WOOD CAMP, YTRES.	ROCQUIGNY.	Road junction F.19.b.8.8. - BUS.	LITTLE WOOD CAMP, YTRES.	On relief.	
	Depot, 9th R.W.Fusrs.	HAVRINCOURT WOOD.	ROCQUIGNY.	NEUVILLE BOURJONVAL - YTRES - Road junction F.19.b.8.8 - BUS.	Cross roads F.17.a. central.	2.15 pm.	
	9/R.W.Fusrs. (less depot).	VALLULART CAMP.	ROCQUIGNY.	Road junction F.32.d.2.4; - LECHELLE - BUS.	VALLULART CAMP.	2.30.pm.	Transport required at VALLULART CAMP will move with Battalion.

SECRET.

Amendment to Table attached to 58th Inf. Brigade Order No. 230.

The moves of the Depot of the 9th Bn R.W.Fusiliers as shown in the above Table are hereby cancelled and those shown below are substituted:-

Date.	Unit.	From.	To.	Route.	Starting Point.	Time.	Remarks.
14th Feb.	Depot, 9/R.W.Fus.	HAVRINCOURT WOOD.	LECHELLE (Lines occupied by transport of 1/4th K.S.L.I.)	NEUVILLE BOURJONVAL - YTRES - ROAD JUNCTION. P32.d.4.8.	Cross roads F.17.d. central.	1.45.p.m. 1.30 p.m	
15th Feb.	Depot, 9/R.W.Fus.	LECHELLE.	ROCQUIGNY.	via BUS.	LECHELLE Camp.	2.15.p.m.	

V.J.W.W. Captain

Brigade Major 58th Infantry Brigade.

12.2.18.

Issued to all recipients of 58th Infy.-Brigade Order No. 230. 9/R.W.Fusiliers and Brigade Transport Officer to ACKNOWLEDGE.

SECRET. Copy No. 24

58th Infantry Brigade Order No. 231.

22nd February, 1918.

Ref: Map Sheet 57.C. 1/40,000

1. The 58th Infy. Brigade Group (less 59th Field Ambulance) will move to the HAPLINCOURT BERTINCOURT Area on 23rd instant in accordance with the attached march table.

2. (a) First Line Transport and baggage wagons will accompany units. The whole of a unit's transport will march together 100 yards in rear of the troops.

   (b) Normal halts will be observed after passing Starting Point.

   (c) Dress - Marching Order.
   Steel helmets will be worn and packs carried.

   (d) Distances between Units.

   Between Companies...................... 100 yards.
   Between unit and its transport......... 100 yards.
   Between Battalions..................... 500 yards.

   Brigade Headquarters and T.M.Battery will be counted as a Company. T.M.Battery will join Brigade Hd.qrs. at the Starting Point.

3. Camps and transport lines will be taken over as already arranged by Staff Captain. Advance Parties will be sent to new camps before 12 noon 23rd instant. Orders with reference to lorries for blankets and extra kit will be issued later.

4. Area Stores, and Training equipment and material which belong to the ROCQUIGNY Area will be handed over to the Area Commandant.

5. Brigade Headquarters will close at ROCQUIGNY at 2.0.p.m. and will open at O.5.c.8.8. at the same hour.

6. Acknowledge.

[signature] Captain

Brigade Major 58th Infantry Brigade.

Issued at 12 noon

Copy No. 1 19th Div G.
        2 19th Div Q.
        3 9.R.W.Fus.
        4 9.Welch R.
        5 6.Wilts R.
        6 58.T.M.Battery.
        7 58.Fld. Amb.
        8 59.Fld. Amb.
        9 82.Fld. Co.R.E.
       10 52nd Inf. Bde.
       11 A.D.M.S., 19th Div.
       12 C.R.E., "
       13 A.P.M. "
       14 19th Div. Train.
       15 S.O. 58th Bde.
       16 G.O.C.
       17 Staff Capt.
       18 Bde. Sig. Offr.
       19 Bde. Int. Offr.
       20) war Diary.
       21)
       22 File
       23 Bde. Transport Offr.
       24

March Table issued with 58th Infantry Brigade Order No. 231.

Serial No.	Unit.	Starting Point.	Time.	Route.	Destination.	Remarks.
1.	58th Brigade Hdqrs.	Road Junction ROCQUIGNY (O.27.d.50.95.)	2.20.p.m.	via BARASTRE - HAPLINCOURT.	O.5.c.8.8.	
2.	58th T.M.Battery.	-do-	2.24.p.m.	-do-	PHIPPS CAMP (O.6.d.)	
3.	9/Welch Regt.	-do-	2.39.p.m.	-do-	PHIPPS CAMP (O.6.d.)	
4.	9/R.W.Fusiliers.	-do-	3. 4.p.m.	-do-	HERRICK CAMP (O.5.d.).	
5.	6/Wilts Regt.	-do-	3.19.p.m.	-do-	SANDERS CAMP (O.4.b.&.d.)	
6.	82/Field Coy.R.E.	-do-	3.25.p.m.	-do-	F.1.b.O.2.	
7.	58/Field Ambulance.	-do-		-do-	SANDERS CAMP (O.4.b.&.d.)	

19th Division

WAR DIARY

A WAD OF MAPS WILL BE FOUND UNDER SEPARATE COVER

B. H. Q.

58th INFANTRY BRIGADE

MARCH 1918

Report on Operations attached.

Army Form C. 2118.

WAR DIARY
or
INTELLIGENCE SUMMARY.
(Erase heading not required.)

HQ 58 Infy Bde

Vol 33

Instructions regarding War Diaries and Intelligence Summaries are contained in F.S. Regs., Part II. and the Staff Manual respectively. Title pages will be prepared in manuscript.

Place	Date	Hour	Summary of Events and Information	Remarks and references to Appendices
HAPLINCOURT	1.3.18. to 8.3.18.)		Brigade in Training. The 2nd and 3rd Systems in V Corps area and in Southern portion of IV Corps area were reconnoitred by all units in the Brigade with a view to occupying any portion of these systems in case of a hostile attack. Special counter-attack schemes (see Appendices A, B, C, D) were issued for counter-attacks against the following villages :- HERMIES, DOIGNIES, HAVRINCOURT, and LOUVERVAL. Throughout this period the weather with a very few exceptions was fine with slight frosts at nights.	A,B,C,D.
	9.3.18.		Brigade took part in a practice assembly and later moved to assembly positions for DOIGNIES counter-attack.	
	10.3.18) to 15.3.18.)		Brigade in Training. Reconnoitring as above continued.	
	16.3.18.		Brigade Tactical Exercise carried out with Contact Aeroplane. 9th Bn WELCH Regiment carried out the attack.	
	17.3.18.		Brigade in Training. Final of R.A. Competition held at ROCQUIGNY range. 6th Bn Wiltshire Regiment were 2nd in Division.	
	18.3.18.		Brigade Exercise carried out with Tanks. Attack behind Tanks practised. 9th Bn R.W.Fusiliers carried out exercise.	
	19.3.18.		Brigade in Training.	
	20.3.18.		Second Tactical Exercise with Tanks carried out by 6th Bn Wiltshire Regiment. Brigade Order No. 232 for relief of 50th Inf. Bde. by 58th Inf. Bde. issued.	E.

Army Form C. 2118.

WAR DIARY
or
INTELLIGENCE SUMMARY.
(Erase heading not required.)

Instructions regarding War Diaries and Intelligence Summaries are contained in F. S. Regs., Part II. and the Staff Manual respectively. Title pages will be prepared in manuscript.

Place	Date	Hour	Summary of Events and Information	Remarks and references to Appendices
	21.3.18. to 27.3.18.		Brigade engaged in contesting enemy offensive. (See detailed narrative attached).	F
BAYENCOURT	28.3.18.		Brigade left BAYENCOURT by march route for FAMECHON. Brigade Order No. 233 attached.	
FAMECHON	29.3.18 to 31.3.18.		Brigade left FAMECHON by march route for DOULLENS and CANDAS where it entrained for STRAZEELE and GAESTRE and from these places was conveyed by lorry to LOCRE.	G
LOCRE.			Brigade billeted in LOCRE. Battalions at WAKEFIELD HUTS, DONCASTER HUTS and BIRR BARRACKS. Brigade Order No. 234 attached. Battalions re-organising.	H
	6.4.18.		One composite company from 9th R.W.Fusiliers attached to 8th Gloucesters, 57th Inf. Bde. on relief of 5th Australian Bde. by 19th Divn.	

Brigadier General
Commanding 58th Infantry Brigade.

S E C R E T.

Headquarters

    19th Division.

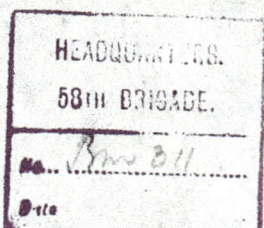

    Herewith narrative of battles of 58th Brigade during period 21st - 28th March, 1918.

                                                    Brigadier General

                                  Commanding 58th Infantry Brigade.

5.4.18.

SECRET

58th Infantry Brigade.

Narrative of events from March 21st to 28th 1918.

March 21st. On the morning of March 21st the 58th Bde. was situated in camps along the BERTINCOURT - HAPLINCOURT Road. Bde. H.Q. at O.5.c.8.8.

5.0.a.m. At about 5.a.m. the enemy opened a heavy barrage on our front line trenches.

5.12.a.m. At 5.12.a.m. orders received from Division to "Stand by".

11.30.a.m. At 11.30.a.m. information received from Division that enemy was reported to have reached 2nd system between LOUVERVAL and LAGNICOURT. One Coy. of the 6th Wilts Regt. was moved to the high ground between BEUGNY and LE BEUCQUIERE to form a line of posts and to keep the Bde. in touch with the situation on the front. This Coy. was relieved during the night by a Coy. from the 56th Bde.

11.44.a.m. At 11.44.a.m. orders from Division to move to "Assembly Positions" in GAIKA COPSE. At the same time the 9th Welch Regt was ordered to send a Coy. and establish strong posts along the HERMIES - BEAUMETZ Ridge from HERMIES to Cross roads in J.28.a. inclusive, one Coy. of 57th Bde. continuing the line to BEAUMETZ.

12.35.p.m. The Brigade was concentrated in GAIKA COPSE by 12.35.p.m. and remained there until about 4.45.p.m. The vicinity of GAIKA COPSE was shelled intermittently both during the morning and afternoon.

4.45.p.m. About 4.45.p.m. in accordance with verbal orders received from Div. (subsequently confirmed in writing) the Brigade was ordered to move to the Ridge West of HERMIES as far as J.27. central and entrench itself there. 57th Bde. was at the same time to form on left of 58th Bde. preparatory to attacking DOIGNIES. At this time information was that the enemy were in possession of both LOUVERVAL and DOIGNIES. Battalions arrived on the HERMIES Ridge about 6.45.p.m. and started entrenching as under:-

9th Welch Regt. on Right from HERMIES to J.28.a.9.2. (Junction of 3rd system and Railway Line), 9th R.W.Fusiliers from this point to J.27.central, 6th Wilts Regt. in Support. 82nd Field Coy. R.E. and 1 Coy. of Pioneers were detailed to assist in digging the line.
Observation Posts were pushed forward to occupy HERMIES SWITCH.

8.30.p.m. At 8.30.p.m. orders received from Division for the Bde. to occupy HERMIES SWITCH. Orders issued accordingly but before this movement was completed verbal orders received from Division that the Brigade would probably have to move en bloc to West of LEBUCQUIERE. Orders at once despatched for Battalions to concentrate behind HERMIES Ridge.

11.25.p.m. At 11.25.p.m. orders from Division to concentrate the Bde. in a position of readiness West of LEBUCQUIERE and to push out patrols to MORCHIES to keep in touch with the situation on the BEAUMETZ - MORCHIES Line.

March 22nd. This move was completed by 4.a.m. Battalions being then concentrated along the road running in I.29.a. and b.

1.26.a.m. At 1.26.a.m. orders were received from Division that the Bde. was to be prepared to counter-attack, assisted by Tanks, if the enemy broke through the BEAUMETZ - MORCHIES Line. No. 6 M.M.G.Battery were in position in I.23.a.

- 2 -

March 22nd.

10.a.m. At 10.a.m. orders from Division that situation N. and N.W. of MORCHIES was insecure and that the Bde. was to move forward at once and dig in on the spurs in I.10.a., I.11.a. and I.17.b. with one battalion allotted for the defence of BEUGNY. "C" Coy. 19th M.G. Battn. and No. 6 M.M.G. Battery placed under orders of Bde.

11.a.m. Brigade occupied this position as under:-

6th Wilts Regt. 3 Coys. in front "dug in" along a line of posts E. of Sunken Road MORCHIES - SUGARBEET Factory on BAPAUME - CAMBRAI Road left flank swung back to meet 9th R.W.Fus. about I.11.a.8.2. 1 Coy. in Support.

9th R.W.Fus. were on the left of the 6th Wilts R. and were dug in on a line covering the two ridges in I.10. and I.11. about 500 yards S.W. of MORCHIES Village the left being about I.10.a.1.5. 3 Coys. in line and 1 Coy. in Support. Battn.H.Q. of 9th R.W.F. and 6th Wilts R. in Sunken Road I.17.a.5.7. The 9th Welch R. were detailed to garrison and hold the village of BEUGNY. Three Coys. occupied a line extending from I.15.d. through I.16.a. and d as far as the main BAPAUME-CAMBRAI Road. The fourth Coy. was in the village in Reserve. The 56th Bde. were on the right S. of the BAPAUME - CAMBRAI Road. Bde. H.Q. moved from O.5.c.8.8. to old Div. H.Q. in I.34.a.

2.30.p.m. As 9th R.W.F. were unable to obtain any touch with troops on their left two companies of the 9th Welch R. and a section of M.G's were sent forward at 2.30.p.m. to endeavour to gain touch with troops on our left flank or failing that to form a defensive flank back to GREEN Line in I.14.b. At the same time the enemy could be seen massing in large numbers on the high ground between VAULX and MORCHIES. Repeated requests for Artillery fire met with no response. It appeared at this time that some of our troops were still in positions North and West of MORCHIES but they subsequently withdrew through our line leaving no troops in front of 9th R.W.F.

3.30.p.m. The enemy developed a heavy attack about 3.30.p.m. along the front held by the 9th R.W.F. although no attack developed on the front held by the 6th Wilts Regt. The attack was beaten off at all points with much loss to the enemy. Cavalry could be seen in readiness to support this attack on the high ground between VAULX and MORCHIES.

5.p.m. About 5.p.m. a counter-attack by Tanks was launched. This attack drove back the enemy to about the MORCHIES - VAULX Road and inflicted heavy casualties on him.

8.p.m. The enemy attempted to raid the post of the 6th Wilts R. nearest MORCHIES. The raid was repulsed leaving 1 killed.

Night 22/23rd. During the night 2 battalions of the 123rd Brigade came up and took over the line as far as the road in I.10.b. The two Coys. of 9th Welch Regt. on left flank of 9th R.W.F. then rejoined their Battalion in BEUGNY and one Coy. of the R.W.F. from the left relieved the left Coy. of the 6th Wilts Regt. the 6th Wilts Regt. then extending their right down to the BAPAUME - CAMBRAI Road. The R.W.F. line then ran approximately from I.10.central to I.11.b.6.3. Three Coys. in line and 1 Coy. in support.
The 6th Wilts line ran from I.11.b.6.3. to the Beetroot Factory in I.17.d. keeping East of the Sunken Road. Three Coys. in line and one in support.
The 9th Welch Regt. were in and around BEUGNY as before, but 1 Coy. had again to be sent out to form a defensive flank back from the 123rd Bde. left as they could get no touch with the troops who should have carried on the line to the left.
1 prisoner and 1 light Machine gun were captured by the 9th R.W.F. during the night.
Consolidation was continued during the night 22nd/23rd and the early morning of the 23rd

- 3 -

March 23rd.   Patrols sent out by 6th Wilts R. in the early morning reported that the enemy held MORCHIES - CRUCIFIX Line and that troops of 56th Bde. with whom the right of the battalion had been in touch had disappeared. To meet this situation two companies of a Cheshire Battn. of 25th Divn. (whose Battn. H.Q. was with R.W.F. and Wilts) were sent to form a line from Beetroot Factory in a S.W. direction.

7.a.m.   Between 7.a.m. and 8.a.m. the enemy opened a heavy bombardment on the 6th Wilts R. and small portions of the enemy could be seen moving across the front of the Wilts to the BAPAUME Road at a range of about 1200 yards. No frontal attack was attempted by the enemy at this time. The shelling in I.17.a. and particularly round Bn. H.Q. of the R.W.F. and Wilts became very heavy and machine gun fire swept all the slopes between BEUGNY and MORCHIES makkng movem-ent very difficult.

9.a.m.   At about 9.a.m. orders were received from the Division for a withdrawal to the GREEN or ARMY Line after dusk. The Bde. to hold the line from the BEUGNY - FREMICOURT Road (inclusive) to the Grid running E. and W. through I.14.central.
Orders were at once issued to Battalions to withdraw at 9.30.p.m. 9th Welch to withdraw to GREEN Line and hold it R.W.F. and Wilts to send parties to N. and E. of BEUGNY, remainder retiring through them.

11.a.m.   Bde. H.Q. moved to BANCOURT.

Later in the morning information was received through Div. that the K.O.S.L.I. on the right of 6th Wilts R. had retired on to GREEN Line thus leaving the right flank of 6th Wilts and 9th Welch completely in the air. Orders sent to Battalions giving this information and ordering 6th Wilts and 9th R.W.F. to withdraw to the outskirts of BEUGNY and complete movement to Green Line at dusk. This order reached the front line battalions about 2.30.p.m. by which time the whole line was very heavily engaged and a strong enemy attack had developed behind the 6th Wilts from between LE BUCQUIERE and BEUGNY. Orders were there-upon sent out to advanced Coys. to commence the withdrawal but owing to an intense barrage on Battn.H.Q. few runners succeeded in getting through. Personnel of Battalion H.Q. endeavoured to form a defensive flank to assist the withdrawal of the forward Coys. but most of the men were killed or wounded. By 5.p.m. however it was evident that Coys. were endeavouring to fight their way back and O.C. 6th Wilts and 9th R.W.F. with such of their H.Q. as were left withdrew. Before doing so all codes and maps etc. were burnt as escape seemed most improbable.
Meanwhile 9th Welch in BEUGNY had been compelled to bring nearly all their men on to the East and Southern edges of BEUGNY and were very heavily engaged. O.C. had sent up word to forward Battalions that enemy were attacking heavily from the South and that there appeared to be none of our troops in front South of the main road.

3.10.p.m.   A message was received from O.C. 9th Welch timed 3.10.p.m. stating that evacuation of forward line was proceeding and that he was holding enemy attack well. A later message stated that no considerable number of Wilts or R.W.F. had come through and he feared many must have been cut off.

5.20.p.m.   A further message timed 5.20.p.m. stated that he was very heavily engaged and that all other troops appeared to have retired to GREEN Line but that he would hang on till dusk to cover withdrawal of any more of Wilts or R.W.F. who might possibly get back. The 9th Welch held the village till dusk when they withdrew in good order to the Green Line. They had however suffered very heavy casualties. I am of opinion that had it not been for the fine defence of the village by 9th Welch none of the Wilts or R.W.F. would have got away at all.

- 4 -

Bde. H.Q. moved to between BANCOURT and BAPAUME.

1.p.m.   By 11.p.m. the remnants of the Bde. were re-organised in the GREEN Line Welch and Wilts holding the front line. R.W.F. and 1 Coy. S.W.B. in support. At this time the GREEN Line was full of troops of many different units. These subsequently side-stepped Northwards.
The remainder of the night was spend in consolidating and no further attack by the enemy was made.
During the evening all available men (about 120 in all) from depots were sent up and reinforced their Battalions.

March   About 8.a.m. on 24th the enemy attacked the 9th Cheshire and
8.a.m.   9th Welch holding the GREEN Line but was repulsed — about noon
1.30.p.m. these attacks were renewed and by 1.30.p.m. the troops on the
2.30.p.m. right began to retire. At about 2.30.p.m. it was decided to commence withdrawal to RED Line. Welch and Wilts accordingly withdrew covered by 9th R.W.F. and S.W.B. The retirement was continued to a position East of FREMICOURT where a further stand was made and several local counter-attacks delivered to relieve the pressure. The withdrawal was then continued to a line East of BAPAUME. Here the Brigade was re-organised and occupied a line from Brickyard in H.28.c. to BAPAUME - BEUGNATRE Road on the Left. The 9th Cheshire were on the right and later the 10th Worcesters extended on the left of 55th Bde.
Bde.H.Q. had meanwhile moved to GREVILLERS.

9.30.p.m.   At 9.30.p.m. orders were received from Division that the Division was to occupy the line LIGNY THILLOY to Railway at H.25.a.8.3. inclusive. The 58th Bde. to hold from ALBERT Road at N.1.a.5.8. exclusive to H.31.a.7.3. All available men that could be collect-ed from the transport and about Bde.H.Q. (including the guard on dumps of blankets in GREVILLERS) Bands, Cooks, etc were at once sent out to occupy the line pending the arrival of the remainder of the Brigade. These reinforcements amounted to some 50 to 60 men per battalion. The remainder of the Bde. withdrew unmolested from the Eastern side of BAPAUME and by midnight were re-organised on their new line. Including the reinforcements that had been sent in the whole Bde. at this time did not amount to more than about 270 rifles. Bde.H.Q. then moved to IRLES.
The night was spent consolidating and passed quietly.

March 25th.   By the morning of 25th telephonic communication had been established between Bde. H.Q. and Battn.H.Q. of 9th R.W.F. and 9th Welch.

5.30.a.m.   Patrols pushed forward into BAPAUME reported it unoccupied by enemy up to 5.30.a.m.

7.a.m.   About 7.a.m. an attack developed South of the BAPAUME - ALBERT Road and by 9.a.m. was general along the whole front but mainly South of the road. About this time the troops South of the road withdrew some 500 yards and the right of 9th Welch was thrown back to keep touch.

11.a.m.   About 11.a.m. as the right was still giving way a withdrawal was made to the high ground running from East of LOUPART Wood to West of GREVILLERS about G.29. This position was a good one and could have been held for many hours but for the fact that the enemy still continued to press forward South of LOUPART Wood beyond the flank of the Division.
The position was held till about 2.p.m. when a further retirement was made to a position West and N.W. of the Wood. Here a gallant stand by a portion of 10th R. Warwicks held up the
3.15.p.m.   enemy's outflanking movement for nearly an hour. At about 3.15.p the withdrawal was continued to a line in front of IRLES.
5.p.m.   At about 5.p.m. the remnants of the Bde. withdrew to PUISIEUX where they were re-organised on a line just East of the village

10.30.p.m.	At 10.30.p.m. the Bde. (with 56th and 57th Bdes.) withdrew to HEBUTERNE and occupied that village with outposts on the Eastern and Southern outskirts of the village. 58th Bde. being responsible for the portion from Road in K.16.b. (inclusive) to road running through K.16.a. - K.16.d.5.8. (exclusive). The Bde. was re-organised as a Battn. each Battn. forming one Coy. with from 1 to 3 platoons.
March 26th. 9.45.a.m.	At about 9.45.a.m. reports were received that the enemy were on the S.W. outskirts of the village. Patrols were at once pushed forward, the Bde. stood to arms, and took up a position in K.9.a., North of the village, the 57th Bde. taking up a position further back in the direction of the CHATEAU de la HAIE. Fighting patrols and mopping parties were then sent through the village to establish a line of posts on the far side. This was eventually done but desultory fighting went on throughout the day in the village, during which a few prisoners and 1 machine gun were captured.
10.30.p.m.	At about 10.30.p.m. a Bde. of the 4th Australian Division relieved the Bde. in front of HEBUTERNE and the Brigade withdrew to BAYENCOURT pushing out an outpost line West and South of the village.
March 27th.	On 27th the Bde. remained in BAYENCOURT and on 28th marched to FAMECHON.

The casualties incurred by the Brigade during these operations amounted to -

    52 Officers
   1362 Other Ranks.

CONFIDENTIAL.

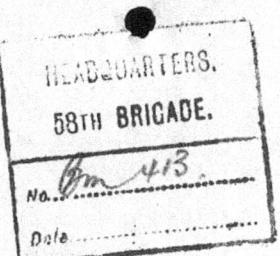

Headquarters

   19th Division.

Herewith War Diaries for March 1918 of the following Units

   58th Brigade H.Q.
   9th Bn R.W.Fusiliers.
   9th Bn Welch Regiment.
   6th Bn Wiltshire Regiment.
   58th Trench Mortar Battery.

                                        Brigadier General

                            Commanding 58th Infantry Brigade.

7.4.18.

SECRET.

58th INFANTRY BRIGADE ADMINISTRATIVE INSTRUCTIONS
issued in connection with B.M.97. Action of 58th
Brigade in the event of an enemy attack.

----------::::----------

1. **SUPPLIES.**
   The Normal system of loading at ROCQUIGNY Railhead in supply wagons will be continued.
   Brigades will keep Divisional H.Q. "Q" informed of all moves of units and first line Transport.
   The Train will select the necessary refilling Points inform "Q", who will inform Brigades.
   The latter are responsible for sending guides to the Refilling Points to conduct Supply Wagons to first line Transport Camps.
   It is of the utmost importance that these guides should arrive punctually.

2. **AMMUNITION.**
   It has been decided not to form a Divisional Dump at VELU WOOD.
   Requirements in S.A.A. and Fireworks may be drawn from the Dumps situated in the Areas of the Division in which the operations may be taking place.
   Situation and contents of dumps are shown on attached list (Sent to Battalions and T.M.Battery only).

3. **WATER POINTS.**
   Water points are situated as follows :-

   51st Division area.
FREMICOURT	I 20 c 3.8.
FREMICOURT VILLAGE	I 25 b.
HILL CROSS	I 27 c.
BANCOURT ROAD	H 34 c 3.7.

   17th Division area.
VELU.	J 31 a 5.8.
BERTINCOURT	F 7 c central.

   19th Division area.
HERMIES	J 30 d 1.2.

4. **TRAFFIC.**
   The A.P.M. will be responsible for controlling the traffic between BEAULENCOURT, HAPLINCOURT, BARASTRE and VELU.
   Units as under will hold the following personnel in readiness to report to the A.P.M. if required :-

	Officer.	N.C.O.	Men.
9th Bn Welch Regt.	1	-	3
9th Bn R.W.Fusiliers	-	1 Sgt.	3

5. Transport Officer, 7th Bn S. Lancs. Regt. will on receipt of orders "Stand to" send 2 limbers to report to 58th T.M.Battery at PHIPPS CAMP.
   O.C. 58th T.M.Battery will on no account wait for these should they not arrive in time. He should leave two men to load up any ammunition he has not been able to take and the limbers will then proceed to assembly position.

6. Baggage wagons will be despatched to units by O.C. No. 4 Company, Train, immediately "Stand to" has been ordered.

7. The personnel not moving with Battalions will be accommodated in their present camps.

8.   The present camps will be handed over to units of the 56th Brigade. Transport Lines will not be handed over.

9.   All blankets, Officers' kits, etc, will be stored in present Camps. On no account will more than 3 huts in each Camp be occupied by personnel or kits.

The move of Battalions will on no account be delayed through this, but arrangements must be made for the guards or other personnel left behind to get the stores, etc together.

A.L. May. Captain,
A/Staff Captain 58th Infantry Brigade.

Brigade H.Q.

9th March 1918.

Copies to :-

G.O.C.	T.O. 7/S.Lancs.R.
P.M.	Bde Transport Off.
9/R.W.Fus.	19th Division "Q".
9/Welch.	56th Inf. Brigade.
6/Wilts.	19th Div. Train.
58 T.M.Bty.	File.
No 4 Coy, Train.	

SECRET.

Amendment No 1 to B.M.97.

Para. 3 (b). Add at end of para.

    Lewis Gun limbers carrying the remainder of Lewis Gun drums not carried by the men and Maltese cart with medical equipment will proceed direct from Transport lines to the Assembly Area in GAIKA. COPSE.

    Cookers and water-carts will proceed at once to Transport lines and await further orders. Water carts will be refilled before returning to Transport lines.

                                              Captain

                              Brigade Major 58th Infantry Brigade.

Brigade H.Q.

    9th March, 1918.

        Issued to all recipients of B.M. 97. dated 8.3.18.

SECRET.

Amendment No. 2 to B.M.97 dated 8/3/18.

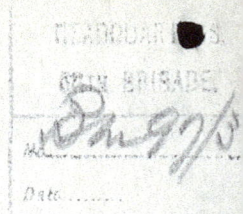

Add para. 4 (a).

On arrival in the Assembly Area the O.C. Reserve Battalion will despatch an Officer's patrol to the high ground W. of HERMIES to keep Brigade Hd.Qrs. informed as to the situation on that part of the 51st Division front.

Reference Appendix I para. 8.

Battalion Hd.Qrs. of Assaulting Battalions will be in Sunken Road at J.26.b.30.05.
Battalion Hd.Qrs. of the Reserve Battalion will be in the bank at J.26.d.5.2.

Reference Appendix II para. 3.

K.9.a. should read K.25.a.

Captain

Brigade Major 58th Infantry Brigade.

Brigade H.Q.

10/3/18.

Issued to all recipients of B.M.97 dated 8.3.18.

SECRET.

58th Brigade No. B.M. 97.

War Diary

Herewith "Action of the 58th Infantry Brigade in the event of an attack" and Appendix I.

Appendix II and Signal Instructions will be issued later

[signature]
Captain

8.3.18.

Brigade Major 58th Infantry Brigade.

SECRET   Copy No. 15

HEADQUARTERS
58TH BRIGADE.

Action of the 58th Infantry Brigade in the event of an attack.

1. B.M. 87 dated 7.3.18 is cancelled.

2. Probable operations for 58th Infantry Brigade are :-

    (a) To occupy any portion of the 2nd or 3rd Systems of the Battle Zone on the Northern portion of V Corps or Southern portion of IV Corps front.

    (b) To counter-attack and recapture HERMIES, DOIGNIES or HAVRINCOURT.

    (c) To move to any part of the 3rd Army front that may be ordered.

3. It will be necessary for the Brigade, whenever it is required to move, to act with rapidity.
    The following messages will be sent by priority wire, all previous instructions on this subject being cancelled:-

    (a) "Stand by" each unit (less transport) will prepare to move on 20 minutes notice in fighting order having previously issued tools, extra S.A.A. and grenades etc. from camp dumps.

    (b) "Move to Assembly position" each unit (less transport) will move to its allotted assembly area in GAIKA COPSE with the least possible delay reporting time of departure to Brigade H.Q.

    (c) "Prepare Rail - Road or Bus" each unit will prepare to move on shortest possible notice taking packs, transport being ready to move also. Units will report to Brigade H.Q. when ready to move.

4. On the order "Move to Assembly Positions" units will move from their present camps to their assembly positions in GAIKA COPSE I.36.d. with the least possible delay. The positions have been pointed out to Units and any further marking out required will be carried out at once.
    While in the Assembly area Brigade H.Q. will be at I.36.b.9.5.

5. While in the Assembly Area units will take special precautions against the possibility of attack by hostile low flying aeroplanes and at least 2 Lewis Guns per Battalion will be mounted immediately on arrival for A.A. protection. Sites to be selected and the necessary posts erected by units concerned at once and report made when they are up.

6. From the Assembly Area routes will be reconnoitred to the following "Positions of Deployment" :-

    (a) The portion of the Third System from the CANAL in J.34.c. to J.28.c.9.0. with a view to a counter-attack to recapture HERMIES and the occupation of the Second System N.E. of the village.

    (b) Behind the road about J.27.central to J.27.a.0.7. with a view to a counter-attack to recapture DOIGNIES and the Second System beyond the village.

    NOTE:- If the attack mentioned in sub-para. (b) takes place at dawn the "Position of Deployment" will be in front of the Third System. Routes forward as far as Third System must therefore be reconnoitred.

    (c) The occupation of the Second System between the TRESCAULT - FLESQUIERES Road and the Canal, with a view to a counter-attack to recapture HAVRINCOURT.

7. Routes to Positions of Deployment from Assembly Area are shown on attached map.

Routes A and D will be used by Right Battalion for moving to Position of Deployment mentioned in sub-para. 6 (b) above if HERMIES is in our hands.

Routes B & D will be used if HERMIES is held by the enemy.

Routes B & C will be used by Left and Reserve Battalions for moving to Position of Deployment mentioned in sub-para. 6 (b).

Routes A, B, D & E will be used by all three Battalions for moving to Position of Deployment mentioned in sub-para 6 (a). Right Battalion will move first.

8. ACKNOWLEDGE.

F. H. Fraser
Captain

Brigade Major 58th Infantry Brigade.

Brigade Hd. Qrs.

8th March, 1918.

Copy No. 1 19th Div. G.
2 19th Div. Q.
3 9.R.W.Fusrs.
4 9.Welch R.
5 6.Wilts R.
6 58.T.M.Battery.
7 56th Inf. Bde.
8 57th Inf. Bde.
9 C.R.A, 19th Div.
10 8th Bn Tanks.
11 D.M.G.C.
12 G.O.C.
13 Staff Capt.
14 Bde. Sig. Offr.
15 Bde. Int. Offr.
16) War Diary.
17)
18 File.
19 B. T. O.
20 T. O., S. Lancs. Regt.

APPENDIX I

Counter-attack against DOIGNIES
(Assuming that we hold the Third System).

1. Positions of deployment, boundaries, and objectives are shown on attached Map "A".
   The 58th Inf. Brigade will probably be the Right Brigade of the Attack.
   The attack would be carried out by 2 Battalions with 1 Battalion in Reserve.
   Probable distribution:-

   On the Right.   6th Bn Wiltshire Regiment.
   On the Left.   9th Bn R.W.Fus. with 1 Coy. of 9th Bn Welch Regiment attached.

   In Brigade Reserve.   9th Bn Welch Regiment (less 1 Coy).

   Dividing line between Battalions is shown on Map A.
   One Company of TANKS (probably "A" Coy. No. 8 Battalion) will co-operate in the attack, main body Tanks moving about 100 yards in advance of the leading wave. Should any or all of the Tanks break down Infantry are on no account to stop but will carry on without them.
   A portion of the Tanks will be detailed to move through DOIGNIES.

2. Two "Positions of Deployment" are shown. The rear one in J.27.a., b., and d, will be for a day-light assembly. Should however the assembly be carried out at night for a dawn attack "Position of Deployment" will be the forward one in J.21.b., J.22.a. This position is in front of the wire of the Third System.

3. The attack will be carried out as follows:-

   (a). Each Attacking Battalion will attack on a three company front. Right Battalion with 1 Company in Reserve. Left Battalion 1 Company specially detailed to clear the portion of the village allotted to the Battalion. One Company (attached from 9th Bn Welch Regt.) in Reserve

   (b). Assaulting Companies will be in Normal attack formation. Each Company in four waves of 1 platoon each. There will be no leap-frogging.

   (c). Assaulting Companies which have to pass through DOIGNIES will carry the attack right through the village and capture the final objective beyond. The Clearing Company will follow and complete the clearing of the village. Arrangements for clearing the village must be very carefully worked out, the village being divided in sectors for this purpose.

   (d). Assaulting Battalions having gained the final objective will reorganise and consolidate in depth.

   (e). Reserve Companies of Assaulting Battalions (unless required earlier by Battalion Commanders) will follow Assaulting Companies as far as the Third System. After capture of final objective they will move up and consolidate the BLUE Line shown on Map "A" within their respective Battalion Boundaries.
   The Reserve Company of Right Battalion will be prepared, if necessary, to form a defensive flank along the spur marked approximately by the line of the Right Boundary of the Right Battn.
   It is to be clearly understood that these instructions in no way prevent Battalion Commanders using their Reserve Companies as they think best should there be any check in the attack.

(f).

- 2 -

(f). Reserve Battalion will assemble in J.26 as shown on Map "A".
   The O.C. Battalion will move forward to a position in or near the 3rd system where he can watch the battle and be prepared to use his reserve to push home the attack. He will act if necessary without waiting for orders. Unless the Battalion has had to move earlier it will move from assembly position at Zero plus 45 minutes into the 3rd system and garrison it within the limits of the Brigade Area.

(g). The O.C. Right Battalion will take special precautions to guard his right flank during the advance. He will arrange to drop special parties (not less than half a platoon each) on the ridge making his right flank about Sunken Road at J.16.d.8.0. and at about J.17.a.4.0. (see also machine guns). Should the enemy be occupying the 2nd system beyond his Right Flank on the final objective he will have bombing parties told off to bomb them out.

4. Two sections of Machine Guns will be allotted to the Brigade. One section will follow the rear wave of the attack approximately along the dividing line between Battalions and will take up position on the spur about J.16.b. or 17.a. to cover consolidation.
   The remaining section will follow rear wave of Right Battalion on the Right Flank and occupy position to be selected by O.C. Section, on spur running through J.16.d. and 17.c. and a. to protect the Right Flank. (The Machine Gun Sections mentioned above will join the Battalions with whom they are going to operate in the Assembly Area).

5. One Mortar will be attached to each Assaulting Battalion. It will follow the attack and take up position to cover the final objective when captured.
   2 Mortars will be attached to Reserve Battalion.
   Mortars detailed to operate with Battalions will join their respective Battalions in the Assembly Area.

6. The rates of advance will be as follows:-

   From Position of Deployment to 3rd System 100^X in 3 mins.

   Pause of 3 mins. on clearing wire of 3rd system.

   From outside wire of 3rd system to S.W. outskirts of DOIGNIES 100^X in 3 mins. (Line shown on Map A RR).

   From S.W. outskirts of DOIGNIES (RR) to 2nd system 100^X in 5 mins.

7. At the moment when the infantry and tanks leave the Position of Deployment the Field Artillery will place a standing barrage on the S.W. edge of DOIGNIES and arrangements will be made to put smoke on DEMICOURT, DOIGNIES and LOUVERVAL. Machine Guns will also cover the advance with barrage fire.

8. On leaving Assembly Area

   Brigade Hd.Qrs. will be established at J.26.d.5.1.
   Battalion Hd.Qrs. will be in J.27.a. or c. exact location will be notified later.
   Battn. Forward command post will be established at J.16.c.5.1 for both Battns. Battn. HQ being established there when final objective is taken.

9. Signal Instructions are attached.

APPENDIX II.

Counter-attack on HERMIES.
Assuming that we hold the 3rd System.

1. The Position of Deployment, Boundaries and objectives of the attacking Battalions are shown on the attached Map "A".
    The Brigade will probably be the Right attacking Brigade of the Division.
    Probable distribution:-

    On the Right.   6th Bn.Wiltshire Regiment.
    On the Left.   9th Bn.R.W.Fusiliers plus 1 Company of the 9th Bn Welch Regt. attached.

    In Brigade Reserve.   9th Bn Welch Regiment (less 1 Coy).

    Dividing line between Battalions is shown on Map "A".

    One Company of Tanks will co-operate with the Brigade in the attack. Main body Tanks will advance about 100^x in advance of the leading wave. Should any or all of the Tanks breakdown infantry are on no account to stop but to carry on without them.

2. The attack will be carried out as follows:-

    (a). Each attacking Battalion will attack on a three Company front. Right Battalion with 1 Company in Reserve. Left Battalion 1 Company specially detailed to clear the portion of the village allotted to the Battalion. One Coy. (attached from 9th Bn Welch Regiment) in Reserve.

    (b). Assaulting companies will be in Normal Attack Formation. Each Company in four waves of 1 platoon each.

    (c). Assaulting Companies which have to pass through HERMIES will carry the attack right through the village and capture the final objective beyond. The Coy. of Left Battalion detailed to clear the village will follow the assault Companies and complete clearing the village. In order to facilitate this task the village will be divided in sectors.

    (d). Assaulting Battalions having gained the final objective will reorganise and consolidate in depth.

    (e). Reserve Companies of Assaulting Battalions will move forward in a series of bounds, to definite lines to be fixed by Battalion Commanders, so as to keep them well in hand, and sufficiently close up to be used quickly if necessary.

    (f). Reserve Battalion will assemble in 3rd System in J.34.a. at Zero.
    The O.C. Battalion will move forward at Zero plus 45 mins. to a position from which he can watch the progress of the battle and be prepared to use his reserve to push home the attack. He will act if necessary without waiting for further orders.
    As soon as the final objective has been captured, if the Battalion has not already moved, it will be ordered to consolidate on the approximate line of the road J.30.c.7.4. J.36.b.5.5.

3. Two sections of machine guns are allotted to the Brigade.
    These sections will move forward behind the attack in a series of bounds. Lines of advance and positions to be selected by O's.C. Sections concerned with a view to carrying out the following tasks:-

- 2 -

One Section - During the advance to assist the Left Battalion if necessary by bringing fire to bear along the Southern edge of the village should the enemy attempt to enfilade the advance from position.

After capture of final objective take up position in vicinity of spur in Northern portion of K.9.a. to cover consolidation.

One Section - During the advance to assist the Right Battalion if necessary by bringing oblique fire to bear across the front. This can best be done by selecting a line of advance as far North as possible without coming under direct fire from HERMIES till the village is captured. *Subsequently to cover consolidation*

Above sections will assemble immediately in rear *from a position approximately in K 26.a.* of Assaulting Companies of the two leading Battalions.

4. STOKES MORTARS One Mortar will be attached to each Assaulting Battalion. It will follow the attack and take up position to cover the final objective when captured.

2 Mortars will be attached to Reserve Battalion.

Mortars detailed to operate with Battalions will join their respective Battalions in the Assembly Area.

5. At Zero the Field Artillery will place a standing barrage on the line A - B, and arrangements will be made to smoke K.19. and K.20. central, the SUGAR FACTORY RIDGE and DOIGNIES, if latter is occupied by the enemy.

At O plus 40 the Field Artillery barrage will concentrate on the line X - Y and will form a thick creeping barrage moving up the shaded rectangle at the rate of 100 yards in 6 mins. The Infantry will follow as close as possible behind this barrage.

At O plus 118 the Field Artillery barrage will lift on to the final objective from the CANAL to SUNKEN ROAD in J.24.a. until just before the Infantry arrive there at O plus 157.

6. On approaching within 200 yards of the line A - B the Tanks will wheel outwards and keep outside the shaded rectangle, unless they see a portion of the Infantry are held up and are losing the barrage, in which case they will turn inwards and help the Infantry forward. No Tank will cross the final objective East of the Sunken road in J.24.a. before O plus 155

7. On leaving the Assembly Area Brigade Hd.Qrs. will be established at J.26.d.5.1.

Battalion Hd.Qrs.
At Position of Deployment.

Right Battalion. - J.34.b.25.20.
Left Battalion. - Sunken road at J.34.a.9.9.
Reserve Battn. - In or close to 3rd system.

Battalions will establish Forward Command Posts as under and will move their H.Q. to them when final objective is captured.

Right Battalion in vicinity of SQUARE COPSE K.25.d.
Left Battalion K.25.a.6.1.
Reserve Battalion - Quarry in J.36.a.1.9.

8. SIGNALLING ARRANGEMENTS. See Signalling Instructions attached.

Reference 58th Inf. Brigade No. B.M.97 dated 8.3.18.

COMMUNICATIONS.

A. **DOIGNIES ATTACK.**

1. Telegraph. A 4th Corps buried cable runs from BZ at J.20.c.8.3. (Hd.Qrs. of Centre Bde. 51st Divn) through J.21.central to near the 2nd system about J.17.a.central. This will be connected to Advanced Brigade Hd.qrs. and can be tapped at test boxes every ¼ mile along its length. Brigade Forward Station will be established at BO Dug-out on the cable at J.16.c.4.1.

2. A Brigade Visual Station will be at J.20.d.7.3. Call BZ. Visible from (a) Sunken road in J.16.c. and (b) 3rd system in J.21.b. and d.

3. Pigeons will be issued if available.

4. Wireless will not be employed elsewhere than from Brigade Forward Station to Advanced Bde.

5. Runners. On assembly of Brigade near VELU WOOD 5 runners will report to Brigade Signalling Officer from each Battalion.

B. **HERMIES ATTACK.**

1. Telegraph. A 5th Corps buried cable exists from LS Test point J.28.c.central to HS Test Point J.30.d.5.0.
 LS will be connected to Advanced Brigade H.Q. and the cable can be tapped at test points along its length. Brigade Forward Station will be established in or near HS Test Point J.30.d.5.0.

2. Visual. Brigade Station at J.32.a.5.9. will work direct to Battalions in Position of Deployment.
 At Zero a Brigade Station will be established on the slag heap in J.34.d.

3. Pigeons. Pigeons will be issued if available.

4. Wireless will not be employed elsewhere than from Bde. Forward Station to Advanced Bde.

5. Runners. On assembly of Brigade near VELU WOOD 5 runners will report to Brigade Signal Officer from each Battalion.

58th Brigade No. B.M.95/3.

SECRET.

W.D.

Herewith Appendix III to "Action of 58th Infantry Brigade in the event of an Attack".

Please acknowledge receipt.

F.W. Fraser, Captain

Brigade Major 58th Infantry Brigade,

Brigade H.Q.
11th March, 1918.

SECRET

APPENDIX III.

Counter-attack on HAVRINCOURT.

On the assumption that we hold the Second System S. of the village, or that HERMIES is being attacked simultaneously.

---

1. **Positions of Deployment, Boundaries, & Dispositions.**

    The Positions of Deployment, Boundaries and objectives of the attacking Battalions are shown on attached Map A.
    The Brigade will probably be the Right Attacking Brigade of the Division.
    Probable distribution:-

On the right.	9th Bn Welch Regiment.
In the centre.	6th Bn Wiltshire Regt.
On the Left.	9th Bn R.W.Fusiliers.
In Bde. Reserve.	9th Bn Cheshire Regt. (attached from 56th Inf. Brigade).

2. **Assembly.**

    (a). Assembly areas are shown on Map A.

    (b). Assaulting Battalions must be formed up in front of the moat running round the southern end of the Chateau grounds.

    (c). The Company of the 9th Bn Welch Regt. detailed to form a defensive flank will assemble immediately behind the 4th wave of the Right Company of the 6th Bn Wiltshire Regiment. (see para. 3 (b).

    (d). One Company of the 9th Bn Cheshire Regiment will assemble immediately behind the Reserve Coy. of the 6th Bn Wiltshire Regiment and one immediately behind the Reserve Coy. of the 9th Bn R.W.Fusiliers. These two Companies will be detailed to "Mop up" the Southern portion of the village. These two Companies may assemble in the moat provided they are in a place where they can readily get out of it.

    (e). Routes to be used to Assembly Area will be notified later.

3. **Method of Attack.**

    The attack will be carried out as follows:-

    (a). The main attack on the final objective marked C,D will be carried out by the
    6th Bn Wiltshire Regt. on the Right.
    9th Bn R.W.Fusiliers on the left.

    Each Battalion will attack on a three company front, each company being in four waves. One company will be in reserve.
    The two leading waves of assaulting companies will go straight through to the final objective, the 3rd and 4th waves being responsible for "Mopping up" the village forward of the line XY (Marked Infantry arrive plus 75). These two waves having completed "Mopping up" this portion of the village will consolidate a support line to the final objective on the northern outskirts of the village.
    The Reserve Companies of the Assaulting Battalions will follow closely behind the 4th wave to the line E F G H and thence forward to the line XY and will systematically clear the village. On completing this task they will re-organise and take up positions in CHEYNE and MILE ROW respectively in Reserve to their Battalions.

(b).

(b). The 9th Bn Welch Regiment will be responsible for the capture of the final objective from K to L and for forming a defensive flank from the right of the 6th Bn Wiltshire Regiment on final objective at D back to K.

Two companies will be employed to capture objective from K to L where they will consolidate in depth.

One Company will assemble immediately behind the right flank of 6th Bn Wiltshire Regiment and will follow the last wave of their assault establishing a series of platoon posts between K and D as a defensive flank.

The remaining Company will be in Battalion Reserve at disposal of C.O. for use as required to complete his tasks.

(c). The 9th Bn Cheshire Regiment will be responsible for the systematic clearing of the village up to the line E F G H, and also the portion North of this line should assaulting Battalions not have been able to complete their task.

One Company will follow close behind the reserve Companies of each of the 6th Bn Wiltshire Regt. and 9th Bn R.W.Fusiliers and will commence "mopping up" the village from the Southern edge immediately the Reserve Companies have gone into the village. On completing this task they will withdraw to the southern edge of village and consolidate a line there.

The two remaining companies will assemble in the Old Second System in K.33.d. At Zero two platoons of each Company will open a steady covering fire on to the Chateau Wood and Southern edges of HAVRINCOURT keeping well in advance of the infantry, whose position will be known by the position of the creeping barrage. Fire must be carefully controlled and discontinued as soon as there is any danger to our own troops, Fire will not be continued in any case after Zero plus 25. If necessary the two platoons detailed for this task will be pushed out in advance of the 2nd System to gain the required fire positions. These two Companies will not move without orders from Brigade H.Q.

4. Machine Guns.

Two sections Machine Guns are allotted to the Brigade.

One section will follow in rear of the 6th Bn Wiltshire Regiment and be disposed by the O.C. Section for the defence of the right flank from D to K.

These guns must follow the attack closely and get into action as soon as possible.

One section from position in K.33.d. or K.34.c. will open fire at Zero and cover the advance by direct fire on the slopes of the Chateau Wood and southern slopes of the village until the leading waves of the assaulting Companies are nearing the village.

As soon as the fire of these guns is masked, two guns will be pushed forward to position about the N.E. portion of Square K.28.a. to cover consolidation.

These guns should be sited with the special object of dealing with an enemy attack from the direction of FLESQUIERES

At Zero plus 75 min. the remaining two guns will move to positions in N.W. portion of Square K.28.a.

5. Stokes Mortars.

One gun will be attached to the 6th Bn Wiltshire Regt. and 9th R.W.Fusiliers respectively to follow the attack and assist to overcome local opposition during the advance.

After capture of final objective one mortar (No. 1) will get into position about K.28.a.7.9. to cover the corner of the Salient. One Gun (No. 2) will

/get

get into position about K.28.a.2.9. to deal with Sunken Road in K.22.c.

Two Mortars will move forward after capture of final objective, one to a position near (No.1) and the other to about K.27.b.6.8.

6. Rates of Advance.

Rates of advance will be as follows.

From Position of Deployment to the line A - B 100 yards in 5 minutes.

From line A - B to final objective 100 yards in 8 minutes.

7. Artillery & M.G. Barrage

At Zero Field Artillery will open a Creeping Barrage and arrangements will be made to smoke HAVRINCOURT Ridge, the valley and the high ground East and North of that village and FLESQUIERES.

The Assaulting Companies will follow as close as possible to the creeping barrage.

Machine Guns will be employed in covering the advance with barrage fire, and in protecting the right flank against counter-attacks coming from the direction of FLESQUIERES or up the valley leading westward from RIBECOURT.

8. Headquarters.

Advanced Brigade Hd.Qrs. will be at Q.7.d.8.8.

Battalion Hd.Qrs. while at Position of Deployment.

The three leading Battalion Hd.Qrs. will be in the "Moat".

Battalion Hd.Qrs. Reserve Battn. will be at MONS POST Q.3.b.65.80.

Brigade Report Centre - K.34.c.2.4.

The 9th Bn R.W.Fusiliers and 6th Bn Wiltshire Regt. will establish Forward Command Posts at the A.D.S. K.27.d.8.5. Both Battalions will move their Hd.Qrs. there as soon as the village is captured.

Battalion Hd.Qrs. of 9th Bn Welch Regt. and 9th Bn Cheshire Regt. will not move.

Brigade Forward Station A.D.S. at K.27.d.8.5.

9. Communications.

These will be issued separately.

SECRET.

58th Brigade No. B.M.97/5.

......W.D..........

    Herewith Appendix IV to "Action of 58th Inf.Brigade in the event of an attack".

    Please acknowledge receipt.

[signature]
Captain,

12.3.1918.   Brigade Major, 58th Infantry Brigade.

Issued to all recipients of B.M.97.

APPENDIX IV.

Counter attack on LOUVERVAL (By day)

(On the assumption we hold the Third System and DOIGNIES or that the latter is being attacked simultaneously.)

1. **Position of Deployment.**
   Boundaries & Objectives.

   (a) The Position of Deployment, Boundaries and Objectives of the attacking Battalions are shown on Map "A".
   The Brigade will probably be the Right Attacking Brigade of the Division.
   Probable distribution:-

   On the Right.   6th Bn. Wilts Regt.
   One the Left.   9th Bn. R.W.Fus.
   In Brigade Reserve. 9th Bn. Welch Regt.

   (b) **Forming up position.**
   The 58th Brigade and Tanks will form up in the low ground N.W. of BEAUMETZ as shown on Map "A".
   At ZERO - 55 the advance will commence in Artillery Formation till the wire of Third System is cleared, Battalions deploying East of the wire. Ten minutes will be allowed to clear the trench and wire of Third System. The Tanks will not halt, but will check their pace slightly until the Infantry regain the correct distance behind them.

2. **Method of Attack.**

   The attack will be carried out as follows:-

   (a) **Assaulting Battalions** will attack on a three Company Front with one Company in reserve.
   Reserve Companies will follow Battalions 300 yards behind 4th wave and consolidate the 1st Objective.

   (b) **Reserve Battalion.** One Company with two Machine Guns will follow the reserve Company of the Right Battalion, and as soon as the Final Objective has been captured will occupy the old mill buildings on the spur just West of BOURSIES. One section of Tanks will cooperate in this movement. Officer Commanding 9th Bn. Welch Regt will get into touch with Officer Commanding "A" Company, 9th Bn. Tanks and arrange details as regards this operation. The two Machine Guns will follow close behind the Infantry and occupy positions sited to cover the exits of BOURSIES (See para 3.M.G.)
   One Company will advance 300 yards behind the reserve Company, the 9th R.W.Fus., and will occupy the left portion of the 1st objective, reinforcing the reserve Company of the 9th Bn. R.W.Fus. if the Company has not had to be used to hold the final objective.
   The remainder of the Battalion will advance at ZERO to the Third System whence Officer Commanding Battalion will move to a position from which he can observe the battle. If necessary he will utilize his reserve without waiting for orders from Brigade Headquarters, but this should only be done if he considers immediate action necessary.

3. **Machine Guns.**

   Two sections of Machine Guns are allotted to the Brigade. One section will advance in rear of the Left Battalion along the spur in J.8.b. J.3.c & d. During the advance they will assist the advance of the Right Battalion by cross fire across the valley, if necessary. As soon as the final objective is captured two guns will take up position about J.3.b.1.2 in order to bring fire to bear in a north-easterly direction to cover the ground in J.3.b and D.27.d.

   Two guns will take up a position about J.4.a.6.7. to cover the valley leading from D.29.central.

   The two guns of the second section will move with the Company of the reserve Battalion detailed to occupy the Old Mill Buildings spur, just west of BOURSIES (see para 2 (b).). The remaining two guns will follow the advance of the Right Battalion, & eventually take up a position about J.4.c, to cover slopes leading from spur in J.10.b and J.5.c.

4. **Stokes' Mortars.**

   One Mortar will follow each of the 6th Bn. Wilts Regt. and 9th. Bn. R.W.Fus. to deal with local opposition during the advance. When final objective has been captured, one mortar will take up a position about J.4.a.6.1 to enfilade the BOURSIES Sunken Road. One mortar will take up a position about J.4.a.3.4. to fire down road in D.28.c.

   Two mortars will remain with reserve Battalion ready to move forward when ordered.

5. **Tanks.**

   One Company of Tanks will cooperate with the Brigade. They will advance about 200 yards in front of the Infantry, see para 1 (b)

6. **Rates of Advance.**

   From Forming up Position to Position of Deployment in Third System 100 yards in 3 minutes. Pause of 10 minutes at Position of Deployment to deploy on far side of wire.

   From Position of Deployment to 1st objective 100 yards in three minutes.

   From 1st objective to Final objective 100 yards in six minutes.

7. **Artillery & M.Gun Barrage.**

   At 0 minus 20 the Field Artillery will place a standing barrage on the 1st objective. The Factory in J.9.b. if occupied by the enemy will also be shelled until 0 plus 25. At 0 plus 70 the standing barrage on the 1st objective will lift and commence to creep forward at the rate of 100 yards in 6 minutes. over the shaded Area to the final objective, putting a protective barrage 350 yards outside the final objective.

   Arrangements will be made to smoke the high ground North of LOUVERVAL and the spur west of BOURSIES during the advance from the Forming up Position.

   A Machine Gun Barrage will also cover the advance.

8. Headquarters.

Brigade Headquarters on leaving the position of Assembly at GAIKA COPSE will be at I.17.b.central.

Brigade forward Station will be established at J.8.c.0.6. before operations if possible. This would move subsequently to J.3.c.8.8.

Battalion Headquarters will move forward with Battalions, as far as 3rd System, where temperary Headquarters will be established at J.8.c.0.6. Forwarded Command Posts to which Battalion Headquarters will move later.

      Right Battalion, near Beet Root Factory, in J.9.b.5.1.
      Left Battalion.   J.3.c.8.8

9. Signal Arrangements.

These will be issued separately.

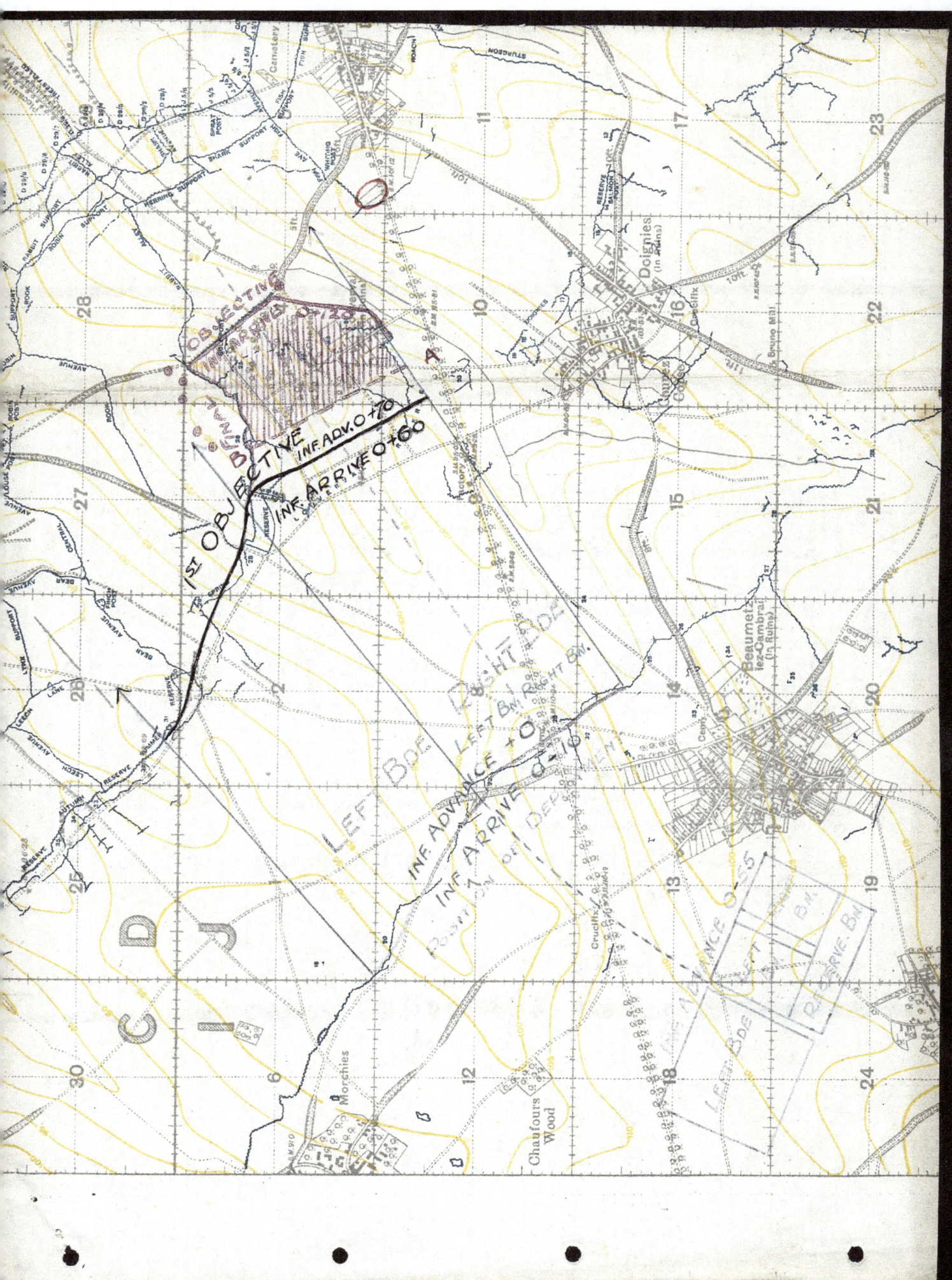

Communications.
HAVRINCOURT Attack.

1. **Telegraph.** Brigade Report Centre (Call A.C.) while attacking Battalions are at Position of Assembly will be at trench and road crossing K.34.c.8.4. Reserve Battalion will be connected thereto, as well as assaulting Battalions. Brigade Forward Party will be under Officer i/c Signals, Right Battalion and will move forward after Zero at his orders and establish Brigade Forward Station at A.D.S., K.28.c.05.00. Headquarters Right and Reserve Battalions will remain connected to Brigade Report Centre.

2. **Visual.** While Battalions are in Position of Deployment there will be no visual signalling to Brigade. At the time when barrage lifts off final objective a Brigade Visual Station will open at about Q.b.(Call S.H.)

3. **Pigeons.** Will be issued if available.

4. **Wireless.** Wireless will not be employed elsewhere than from Brigade Forward Station to Advanced Brigade.

5. **Runners.** The Brigade Report Centre will be the 1st Relay Post back from Brigade Forward Station.

Communications.
LOUVERVAL Attack.

1. **Telegraph.** While Battalions are in position of Deployment they will be connected direct to Brigade Headquarters in J.17.b. A Brigade Forward Station will meanwhile be established in Sunken Road at J.8.c.0.6. to which Battalion Headquarters will connect on their arrival there. Brigade Forward Party will move under Orders of Officer i/c Signals, Left Battalion to 2nd Position Brigade Forward Station at J.3.c.8.8. A buried cable runs from L.L.Test Point at J.4.a.4.9 via N.N.Test Point at J.7.b.9.1. to N.L.Test Point in J.17.b., which can be tapped every ¼ mile. Arrangements will be made to connect Officer Commanding, Reserve Battalion to this line.

2. **Visual.** A Visual Station, manned by Brigade personnel will open at Zero at Farm J.8.c.7.2. to receive messages back from Battalion Forward Parties, and, on establishment of Battalion Headquarters near LOUVERVAL will transmit messages from Brigade Forward Station back to Brigade.

3. **Pigeons.** Will be issued if available.

4. **Wireless.** Wireless will not be employed elsewhere than from Brigade Forward Station to Advanced Brigade.

5. **Runners.** The 1st Runner Relay Post back from Brigade Forward Station will be at J.7.b.9.1.

SECRET.

HEADQUARTERS Copy No. 13
58TH BRIGADE
No. BM272

WARNING ORDER.

1. The 19th Division will relieve the 17th Division in the Canal Sector on the nights 22nd/23rd and 23rd/24th March.

2. The 58th Inf. Bde. will relieve the 50th Inf. Bde. in the Left Sector on the night 22nd/23rd March.

3. If the sector is still being held in the same way as it was when previously reconnoitred the dispositions will be as follows:-

    6th Bn Wiltshire Regt. on the Right.
    9th Bn R.W.Fusiliers on the Left.
    9th Bn Welch Regiment in Reserve.

4. Lorries for reconnoitring parties etc. are being asked for as follows:-

    20th March. 1 lorry for reconnoitring parties.

    21st March 1 lorry for reconnoitring parties.
              1 lorry for advance parties who will remain in line till their units arrive.

    22nd March 2 lorries for advance parties, Signallers, Runners etc.

Seats in the above mentioned lorries will be as follows:-

    Battalions... 7 places.
    T.M.Battery.. 2 places.
    Bde. H.Q..... 2 places.

Lorries will start from Brigade H.Q. at times to be notified later.

5. Acknowledge.

F.H.Fraser
Captain
Brigade Major 58th Infantry Brigade

19th March 1918. Issued at 8.0.a.m.

Copy No. 1 9.R.W.Fusrs.
    2 9.Welch R.
    3 6.Wilts R.
    4 T.M.Battery.
    5 G.O.C.
    6 Staff Capt.

7 Bde. Sig. Offr.
8 Bde. Transport Offr.
9 19th Div. G.
10 S.O., 58th Bde.
11 O.C. No. 4 Coy. Train.
12 File.
13) War Diary.
14)

S.C.37.   Copy No. 18

58th Infantry Brigade Order No. 232.

App E

March 20th, 1918.

Ref. Map. FRANCE 57.C. 1/40,000.
and MOEUVRES Special Sht. 1/20,000.

1. The 58th Inf. Bde. will relieve the 50th Inf. Bde. in the Left Sub-sector of the GOUZ.L Sector on the night 22/23rd March in accordance with attached Relief Table.

2. All details not mentioned herein will be arranged direct between Commanding Officers concerned.

3. Battalions and T.M.Battery will detail advance parties to proceed to the line on the 21st inst. and remain in the line until their units arrive. A lorry will report at Brigade H.Q. at 1.0.p.m. to convey these parties. Seven places will be allotted to each Battalion and 4 to T.M.Battery in this lorry.
   Parties will be rationed up to the 23rd inclusive.
   On March 22nd 2 lorries will report at Brigade H.Q. at 10.0.a.m. to convey advance parties of signallers, runners, etc to the line. 14 places to each Battn., 4 to T.M.Battery, and 4 to Bde. H.Q. will be allotted in these lorries.

4. All maps, aeroplane photos, defence schemes, programmes of work and trench stores will be taken over and receipts forwarded to Brigade H.Q. by 10.a.m. March 24th.
   All Counter-attack schemes and orders, Training Facilities will be handed over to units taking over present camps.

5. Completion of relief will be wired to Brigade H.Q. using the code word "ONCE MORE".

6. Units will report their dispositions in detail to Brigade H.Q. by 12 noon March 23rd.

7. During daylight movements of troops East of BERTINCOURT will be by Coys. at 200 yards intervals and East of 3rd System by Platoons at 100 yards intervals.

8. Brigade H.Q. will close at O.5.c.8.8. at 9.0.p.m. 22nd March and will re-open at Canal Bank J.36.b.8.3. at the same hour.

9. Acknowledge.

                                                    F.W. Fraser,
                                                    ———————, Captain
                                          Brigade Major 58th Infantry Brigade.

Issued at 8.0.p.m.

    Copy No. 1 9.R.W.Fus.   10 G.O.C.
            2 9.Welch R.   11 Staff Capt.
            3 6.Wilts R.   12 Bde. Sig. Offr.
            4 58.T.M.Battery.   13 Bde. Transport Offr.
            5 56th Inf. Bde.   14 Bde Supply Offr.
            6 57th Inf. Bde.   15 O.C. No. 4 Coy. Train.
            7 50th Inf. Bde.   16 File.
            8 Right Bde. 51.Div.   17) War Diary.
            9 19th Division G.   18)

Relief Table to accompany 58th Infantry Brigade Order No.232

All Units will move by train.

Unit.	To.	Relieving.	Entraining. Point.	Time.	Detraining Pt. Meet platoon guides at.	Time.	Remarks.
6/Wilts Regt.	Line, Right Front.	10/W. Yorks.R.	PHIPPS CAMP.	To be notified later.	HERMIES YARD. J.29.d. near WINDY CORNER.	7.30.p.m.	2 guides will be supplied for Battn. H.Q. at detraining point.
9/R.W.Fusrs.	Line, Left Front.	6/Dorsets.R.	do.		do.	3.15.p.m.	do.
9/Welch Regt.	Support.	7/E. Yorks.R.	do.		do.	9.0.p.m.	do.
58/T.M.Batty.	Line.	50/T.M.Batty.	do.		do.	7.30.p.m.	Will travel by same train as 6/Wilts Regt.

SECRET. G. Copy No. 7

58th Inf. Bde. Order No. 233.

28.3.18.

Ref. map:- LENS 11 1/100,000.

1. The 19th Division is being withdrawn from the line. The 58th Bde. Group composed as under will move to THIEVRES and FAMECHON by march route to-day the 28th inst. in accordance with attached march table:-
    58th Brigade H.Q.
    9/R.W.Fusiliers.
    9/Welch Regt.
    6/Wilts Regt.
    58/T.M.Battery.
    94th Field Coy. R.E.

2. Orders as regards billeting parties have already been issued by the Staff Captain. Billeting representative of Brigade will meet the Brigade at the Eastern outskirts of THIEVRES and notify units exact location of billets.

3. 1st and 2nd line transport of battalions will move under orders of the Brigade Transport Officer.
   No. 4 Coy. of Train will not move.

4. 1 lorry will report at Brigade H.Q. at 12 noon to convey stragglers and men unable to march to new billets. Units will notify Brigade H.Q. as soon as possible the numbers they wish to send by this lorry.

5. Brigade H.Q. will close at BAVINCOURT at 11.30.a.m.

6. ACKNOWLEDGE.

Captain

Brigade Major 58th Infantry Brigade.

Issued at 4.30.a.m.

Copy No. 1 9/R.W.Fusrs.   5 94th Field Coy. R.E.
        2 9/Welch R   6) War Diary.
        3 6/Wilts Regt.   7)
        4 58/T.M.Battery.   8 File.

March Table issued with 59th Inf. Bde. Order No. 233.

Unit.	From.	To.	Starting Point.	Time of passing S. Point.	Route.	Remarks.
Bde. H.Q.	BAYENCOURT.	THIEVRES or FAMECHON.		11.37.am.	COIGNEUX-St.LEGER les AUTHIE- & AUTHIE.	
/R.W.Fus.	do.	do.		11.40.am.	do.	
/Welch R.	do.	do.		11.43.am.	do.	
/Wilts R.	do.	do.		11.46.am.	do.	
3/T.M.Bty.	do.	do.		11.49.am.	do.	
4/Fld.Co.RE.	SOUASTRE.	do.				Will march independently am under orders of O.C. Coy. so as to join column at COUIN.

A distance of 200 yards will be maintained between Battalions and similar units.

S E C R E T.

19th Division "G".
9th Bn. R.W.Fusiliers,   58th T.M.Battery.
9th Bn. Welch Regt.
6th Bn. Wiltshire Regt.
57th Inf.Brigade.

B.M.185.

---

1. Herewith Map showing Second and Third Systems divided into probable Brigade and Battalion Sectors for defensive purposes in the event of the Brigade being ordered to man any portion of these Systems.

2. The position of Brigade and Battalion Hd.qrs. will be notified as soon as possible. Should the Brigade be ordered up before these have been selected Battalion Commanders will select their own Hd.qrs. and report their position to Brigade H.Q. as soon as possible.

3. Positions would most probably be occupied as under:-

   Two Battalions in Front Line - Each Battalion with three Coys. in front line, and 1 Coy. in Battn. Reserve available for counter-attack or to hold reserve position. Each Coy. in front line should have at least 1 Platoon in support.

   One Battalion in reserve.

   2 Stokes Mortars with each Front Line Battalion sited for defence of Front Line.

   4 Stokes Mortars with Reserve Battalion.

4. Although Battalions will have to be prepared to occupy any of the sub-sectors in any of the above roles, in order to get plans for occupation settled as quickly as possible Battalions will first have reconnaissances made for their Units in following positions.

   6th Bn. Wiltshire Regt. as Right Front Battalion of each Sector.
   9th Bn. R.W.Fusiliers as Left Front Battalion of each Sector.
   9th Bn. Welch Regt. as Reserve Battalion.

5. The approaches to each Sector are to be reconnoitred and detailed plans made for method of holding it. Os.C. Battalions are to pass to each other their arrangements so that every Battalion will as quickly as possible have a scheme for holding any position in a Sector. They can modify these if necessary later after personal reconnaissance of sub-sectors other than those which they reconnoitre first (vide para 4.)

6. In order to get arrangements made quickly it will be necessary for Os.C. Battalions to depute as many Officers as they can rely on to arrange for the occupation of different sub-sectors. Thus they can get preliminary arrangements for many different sub-sectors made on the same day.

7. The following general principle for Reserve Coys. and Reserve Battalion should be adhered to as far as possible.

   (A) Reserve Coys. should be distributed by platoons sufficiently close together to be fairly handy should the Coy. be required to counter-attack, but so arranged so that they can mutually support each other if required to hold on. They then constitute 3 or 4 points of resistance (not necessarily in one line) and after occupation

- 2 -

these points of resistance should be strengthened as quickly as possible.

(b) Reserve Battalion should be distributed by Coys. on the same principle. If required for counter-attack they are then fairly handy, if required to hang on they form a series of points of resistance (not necessarily in one line).

8. The following notes are to help Os.C. Battalions by giving likely approximate positions for Reserve Coys. of Battalions and for Reserve Battalion. The line marking the 2nd and 3rd systems indicates the general line of the front trenches of these systems only and are not in all cases quite accurately marked. In some small places the trench is not dug but the wire always marks the line.

The principle of distribution in depth is to be adhered to as far as possible. In many cases it will be necessary for troups to dig themselves in where existing trenches are not available. In all cases front line Companies will occupy the fronts shown with at least one platoon in support.

(i). Sector A. Dividing line between Battalions Ravine about K.34.a.95.75. Ravine inclusive to Right Battn.

Right Sub-sector. Reserve Coy. in area about S.E. portion of K.33.d. Several old trenches exist about here.

Left Sub-sector. Reserve Coy. in area about Eastern portion K.33.b. and K.34.a.2.6. There is a trench in the Chateau Wood in this locality.

Reserve Battalion. In old second system about K.33.c. and d.

(ii). Sector B. Dividing Line between Battalions - The point where LONDON Trench cuts new second system about K.21.d.2.1. LONDON Trench inclusive to Right Battalion.

Right Sub-sector. Reserve Coy. in area K.27.b. MILE END ROW and LONDON Support in this area might be suitable.

Left Sub-sector. CITY Trench or Sunken Road in K.26.d and K.27.c.

Reserve Battalion. Yorkshire Spoil Heap and South City Support.

(iii). Sector C. Dividing Line between Battalions K.19.c.7.3. Railway inclusive to Right Battalion.

Right Sub-sector. Reserve Company SOUTH CITY Support in K.26.c DERRY SWITCH and MAXWELL AVENUE.

Left Sub-sector. Reserve Coy. Trenches on Northern Edge of HERMIES about J.30.b. and J.24.d.

Reserve Battalion. Maxwell Avenue South of HERMIES Sunken Rd. and Trenches near Cemetery in J.36.a.

(iv). Sector D. Dividing line between Battalions - J.17.central. The line of Bank inclusive to Right Battn.

Right Sub-sector. Reserve Coy. HERMIES SWITCH in J.23.a.

Left Sub-sector. Reserve Coy. Sunken Road in J.18.d.

Reserve Battalion. Sunken Road in J.22.a. HERMIES SWITCH J.22.c. and d. or DOIGNIES - HERMIES Road.

- 3 -

(v). Sector E. Dividing line between Battalions. Road along edge of wood at J.4.c.9.7. Road inclusive to Left Battn.

Right Sub-sector. Reserve Coy. Road in J.9.d.

Left Sub-sector. Reserve Coy. Existing bits of trench in J.3.d. running about 200x yds. of the wood or Sunken road running from J.3.d.0.5. to J.9.b.5.6.

Reserve Battalion. 3rd System in J.8.d. and J.14.a.

(vi). Sector F. Dividing line between Battalions. Road at K.34.c.3.5. Road inclusive to Left Battalion.

Right Sub-sector. Reserve Coy. in existing trenches in Q.4.a.

Left Sub-sector. Reserve Coy. in existing trenches in Q.3.b.

Reserve Battalion. Area about Q.3.c. and d.

(vii). Sector G. Dividing line between Battalions. Cross roads K.32.b.8.8. YORKSHIRE SPOIL HEAP inclusive to Right Battalion.

Right Sub-sector. Reserve Coy. in CHELTHAM SWITCH or existing SHROPSHIRE SPOIL HEAP Strong Point.

Left Sub-sector. Reserve Coy. about WEST TRENCH or CAGE TRENCH in K.26.a. or K.26.c. (West of Canal).

Reserve Battalion. Area West of SQUARE COPSE about K.25.c. & d.

(viii). Sector H. Dividing line between Battalions. Road at F.4.d.6.3. Road inclusive to Right Battalion.

Right Sub-sector. Reserve Coy. Trenches East edge of RUYAULCOURT.

Left Sub-sector. Trenches North edge of RUYAULCOURT or road in F.4.c.

Reserve Battalion. Area immediately West of RUYAULCOURT where various bits of trenches and wire already exist.

(ix). Sector I. Dividing line between Battalions. J.34.a.2.5. Point on 3rd system 100 yds. North of Railway Line.

Right Sub-sector. Reserve Coy. Area J.33.d. Would probably have to dig itself in.

Left Sub-sector. Reserve Coy. Area J.27.d. Would also probably have to dig itself in.

Reserve Battalion. About road in Valley in J.26.d. Would have to prepare positions on spur in between Squares J.26. & J.27.

(x). Sector J. Dividing line between Battalions. About J.21.d.8.9. Junction of HERMIES SWITCH with 3rd Line inclusive to Right Battalion.

Right Sub-sector. Reserve Coy. About road in J.21.d. This is a sunken road in places.

Left Sub-sector. Reserve Coy. Sunken road in J.20.b.

Reserve Battalion. Area J.20.c. and J.26.a. and b. The road running through these squares is sunken in many places.

- 4 -

(xi). <u>Sector K.</u>   Dividing line between Battalions. J.14.a.8.9.
Point on 3rd system 200 yards south of main BAPAUME - CAMBRAI Road.

Right Sub-sector. Reserve Coy. Sunken road J.14.a. or trenches in vicinity.

Left Sub-sector. Reserve Coy. Sunken road in J.8.c. until it could dig itself in further back.

Reserve Battalion. CRUCIFIX - MORCHIES Road in J.7.c. and J.13.a. and b. and BEETROOT FACTORY - MORCHIES Road in I.17.b.

9.   O's.C. Units will report their proposed distribution as soon as they have decided it for each Sub-sector.

10.   As frontages to be held by Battalions are large and as much depth as possible is wanted in the defence it is essential that if the Brigade is ordered to occupy a sector of the 2nd or 3rd system. Units should take every available man.

F.H. Fraser, Captain

Brigade Major 58th Infantry Brigade.

Brigade H.Q.
13th March, 1918.

BRIGADE SECTORS   C.O
C.O
M-m 2A?

S E C R E T.

19th Division "G".
9th Bn R.W.Fusiliers.
9th Bn Welch Regiment.
6th Bn Wiltshire Regiment.
57th Infantry Brigade.

1. Herewith map showing Second and Third Systems divided into probable Brigade and Battalion Sectors, in the event of the Brigade being ordered to man any portion of these systems.

2. The position of Brigade and Battalion Hd.Qrs. will be notified as soon as possible. Should the Brigade be ordered up before these have been selected Battalion Commanders will select their own Hd.Qrs. and report their position to Brigade H.Q. as soon as possible.

3. Positions would most probably be occupied as under:-

Two Battalions in front line - Each Battalion with three Coys. in front line, and 1 Coy. in Battn. Reserve available for counter-attack or to hold reserve position. Each Coy. in front line should have at least 1 platoon in support.

One Battalion in Reserve.

    2 Stokes Mortars with each front line battalion sited for defence of Front Line.

    4 Stokes Mortars with Reserve Battalion.

4. Although Battalions will have to be prepared to occupy any of the sub-sectors in any of the above roles, in order to get plans for occupation settled as quickly as possible Battalions will first have reconnaissances made for their units in following positions.

    6th Bn Wiltshire Regt. as Right Front Battn. of each Sector.
    9th Bn R.W.Fusiliers as Left Front Battn. of each Sector.
    9th Bn Welch Regiment as Reserve Battalion.

5. The approaches to each sector are to be reconnoitred and detailed plans made for method of holding it. O's.C. Battalions are to pass to each other their arrangements so that every Battalion will as quickly as possible have a scheme for holding any position in a sector. They can modify these if necessary later after personal reconnaissance of sub-sectors other than those which they reconnoitre first (vide para. 4).

6. In order to get arrangements made quickly it will be necessary for O's.C. Battalions to depute as many Officers as they can rely on to arrange for the occupation of different sub-sectors. Thus they can get preliminary arrangements for many different sub-sectors made on the same day.

7. The following general principle for Reserve Coys. and Reserve Battalion should be adhered to as far as possible.

(A). Reserve Coys. should be distributed by platoons sufficiently close together to be fairly handy should the Coy. be required to counter-attack, but so arranged so that they can mutually each other if required to hold on. They then constitute 3 or 4 points of resistance (not necessarily in one line) and after occupation

- 2 -

these points of resistance should be strengthened as quickly as possibl

(B). Reserve Battalion should be distributed by Coys. on the same principle. If required for counter-attack they are then fairly handy, if required to hang on they form a series of points of resistance (not necessarily in one line).

9. The following notes are to help O's.C. Battalions by giving likely approximate positions for Reserve Coys. of Battalions and for Reserve Battalion. The line marking the 2nd and 3rd systems indicates the general line of the front trenches of these systems only and are not in all cases quite accurately marked. In some small places the trench is not dug but the wire always marks the Line.

The principle of distribution in depth is to be adhered to as far as possible. In many cases it will be necessary for troops to dig themselves in where existing trenches are not available. In all cases front line Companies will occupy the fronts shown with at least one platoon in support.

(i). <u>Sector A.</u> Dividing line between Battalions Ravine about K.34.a.95.75. Ravine inclusive to Right Battn.

Right Sub-sector. Reserve Coy. in area about S.E. portion of K.33.d. Several old trenches exist about here.

Left Sub-sector. Reserve Coy. in area about Eastern portion K.33.b. and K.34.a.2.6. There is a trench in the Chateau Wood in this locality.

Reserve Battn. In old second system about K.33.c. and d.

(ii). <u>Sector B.</u> Dividing line between Battalions - The point where LONDON Trench cuts new second system about K.21.d.2.1. LONDON Trench inclusive to Right Battalion.

Right Sub-sector. Reserve Coy. in area K.27.b. MILE END ROW and LONDON Support in this area might be suitable.

Left Sub-sector. CITY TRENCH or SUNKEN Road in K.26.d. and K.27.c.

Reserve Battalion. Yorkshire Spoil Heap and South City Support.

(iii). <u>Sector C.</u> Dividing line between Battalions K.19.c.7.3. Railway inclusive to Right Battalion.

Right Sub-sector. Reserve Coy. SOUTH CITY Support in K.26.c. DERRY SWITCH and MAXWELL AVENUE.

Left Sub-sector. Reserve Coy. Trenches on Northern edge of HERMIES about J.30.b. and J.24.d.

Reserve Battalion. Maxwell Avenue South of HERMIES Sunken Rd. and trenches near cemetery in J.36.a.

(iv). <u>Sector D.</u> Dividing line between Battalions - J.17.central. The line of Bank inclusive to Right Battn.

Right Sub-sector. Reserve Coy. HERMIES SWITCH in J.23.c.

Left Sub-sector. Reserve Coy. Sunken Road in J.16.d.

Reserve Battalion. Sunken Road in J.22.a. HERMIES SWITCH J.22.c. and d. or DOIGNIES - HERMIES Road.

- 3 -

(v). <u>Sector E.</u> Dividing line between Battalions. Road along edge of wood at J.4.c.9.7. Road inclusive to Left Battn.

    Right Sub-sector. Reserve Coy. Road in J.9.d.

    Left Sub-sector. Reserve Coy. Existing bits of trench in J.3.d. running about 200x west of the wood or Sunken Road running from J.3.d.0.5. to J.9.b.5.6.

    Reserve Battalion. 3rd system in J.8.d. and J.14.a.

(vi). <u>Sector F.</u> Dividing line between Battalions. Road at K.34.c.3.5. Road inclusive to Left Battalion.

    Right Sub-sector. Reserve Coy. in existing trenches in Q.4.a.

    Left Sub-sector. Reserve Coy. in existing trenches in Q.3.b.

    Reserve Battalion. Area about Q.3.c. and d.

(vii). <u>Sector G.</u> Dividing line between Battalions. Cross roads K.32.b.8.8. YORKSHIRE SPOIL HEAP inclusive to Right Battalion.

    Right Sub-sector. Reserve Coy. in CHEATHAM SWITCH or existing SHROPSHIRE SPOIL HEAP Strong point.

    Left Sub-sector. Reserve Coy. about WEST TRENCH or CAGE TRENCH in K.26.a. or K.26.c. (West of Canal).

    Reserve Battalion. Area West of SQUARE COPSE about K.25.c. & d.

(viii). <u>Sector H.</u> Dividing line between Battalions. Road at P.4.d.6.3. Road inclusive to Right Battalion.

    Right Sub-sector. Reserve Coy. Trenches East edge of RUYAULCOURT.

    Left Sub-sector. Trenches North edge of RUYAULCOURT or road in P.4.c.

    Reserve Battalion. Area immediately West of RUYAULCOURT where various bits of trenches and wire already exist.

(ix). <u>Sector I.</u> Dividing line between Battalions. J.34.a.2.5. Point on 3rd system 100 yards North of Railway Line.

    Right Sub-sector. Reserve Coy. Area J.33.d. Would probably have to dig itself in.

    Left Sub-sector. Reserve Coy. Area J.27.d. Would also probably have to dig itself in.

    Reserve Battalion. About Road in Valley in J.26.d. Would have to prepare positions on spur in between Squares J.26. and J.27.

(x). <u>Sector J.</u> Dividing line between Battalions. About J.21.d.8.0 Junction of HERMIES SWITCH with 3rd Line inclusive to Right Battalion.

    Right Sub-sector. Reserve Coy. About road in J.21.d. This is a Sunken Road in places.

    Left Sub-sector. Reserve Coy. Sunken Road in J.20.b.

    Reserve Battalion. Area J.20.c. and J.26.a. and b. The road running through these Squares is sunken in many places.

(xi). **Sector K.** Dividing line between Battalions. J.14.a.8.9.
Point on 3rd System 200 yards South of main
BAPAUME - CAMBRAI Road.

Right Sub-sector. Reserve Coy. Sunken road J.14.a. or trenches in vicinity.

Left Sub-sector. Reserve Coy. Sunken road in J.8.c. Until it could dig itself in further back.

Reserve Battalion. CRUCIFIX - MORCHIES Road in J.7.c. and J.13.a. and b. and BEETROOT FACTORY ~~FACTORY~~ - MORCHIE Road in I.17.b.

9. O's.C. Units will report their proposed distribution as soon as they have decided it for each sub-sector.

10. As frontages to be held by Battalions are large and as much depth as possible is wanted in the defence it is essential that if the Brigade is ordered to occupy a sector of the 2nd or 3rd systems Units should take every available man.

Captain

Brigade Major 58th Infantry Brigade.

Brigade H.Q.

13th March, 1918.

LOCATION OF HEADQUARTERS.

Sector A.   Brigade Hd.Qrs.

                Battn.H.Q. Right.
                  "   " Left.
                  "   " Reserve.

Sector B.   Brigade H.Q.

                Battn.H.Q. Right.
                    "   " Left.
                  "   " Reserve.

Sector C.   Brigade H.Q.

                Battn.H.Q. Right.
                    "   " Left.
                  "   " Reserve.

Sector D.   Brigade H.Q.

                Battn. H.Q. Right.
                  "   " Left.
                  "   " Reserve.

Sector E.   Brigade H.Q.

                Battn.H.Q. Right.   BEETROOT FACTORY.
                  "   " Left.   J.3.c.9.7.
                  "   " Reserve. J.8.c.0.6.

Sector F.   Brigade H.Q.

                Battn.H.Q. Right.
                  "   " Left.
                  "   " Reserve.

Sector G.   Brigade H.Q.

                Battn.H.Q. Right.
                  "   " Left.
                  "   " Reserve.

Sector H.   Brigade H.Q.

                Battn.H.Q. Right.
                  "   " Left.
                  "   " Reserve.

Sector I.   Brigade H.Q.

                Battn.H.Q. Right.
                  "   " Left.
                  "   " Reserve.

Sector J.   Brigade H.Q.
                Battn.H.Q. Right.
                  "   " Left.
                  "   " Reserve.

Sector K.   Brigade H.Q.
                Battn.H.Q. Right.
                         Left.

19th Division

M.A.P.S

TO ACCOMPANY WAR DIARY OF 58th INFANTRY BRIGADE

MARCH 1918

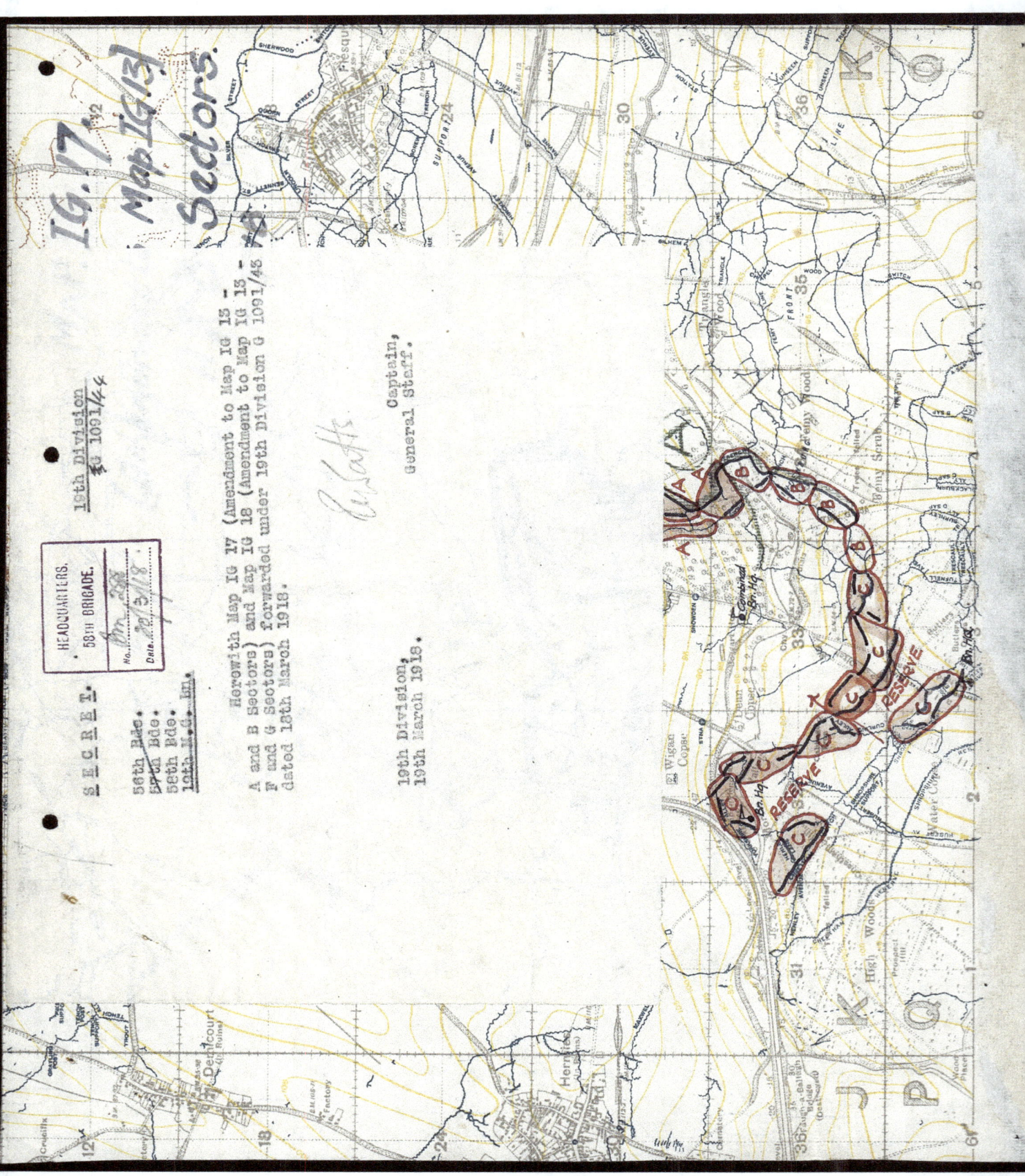

SECRET.

19th Division
G 1091/44

HEADQUARTERS,
58TH BRIGADE.
No. ....
Date. 20/3/18

56th Bde.
57th Bde.
58th Bde.
19th M.G. Bn.

Herewith Map IG 17 (Amendment to Map IG 15 - A and B Sectors) and Map IG 18 (Amendment to Map IG 15 - F and G Sectors) forwarded under 19th Division G 1091/43 dated 18th March 1918.

Captain,
General Staff.

19th Division,
19th March 1918.

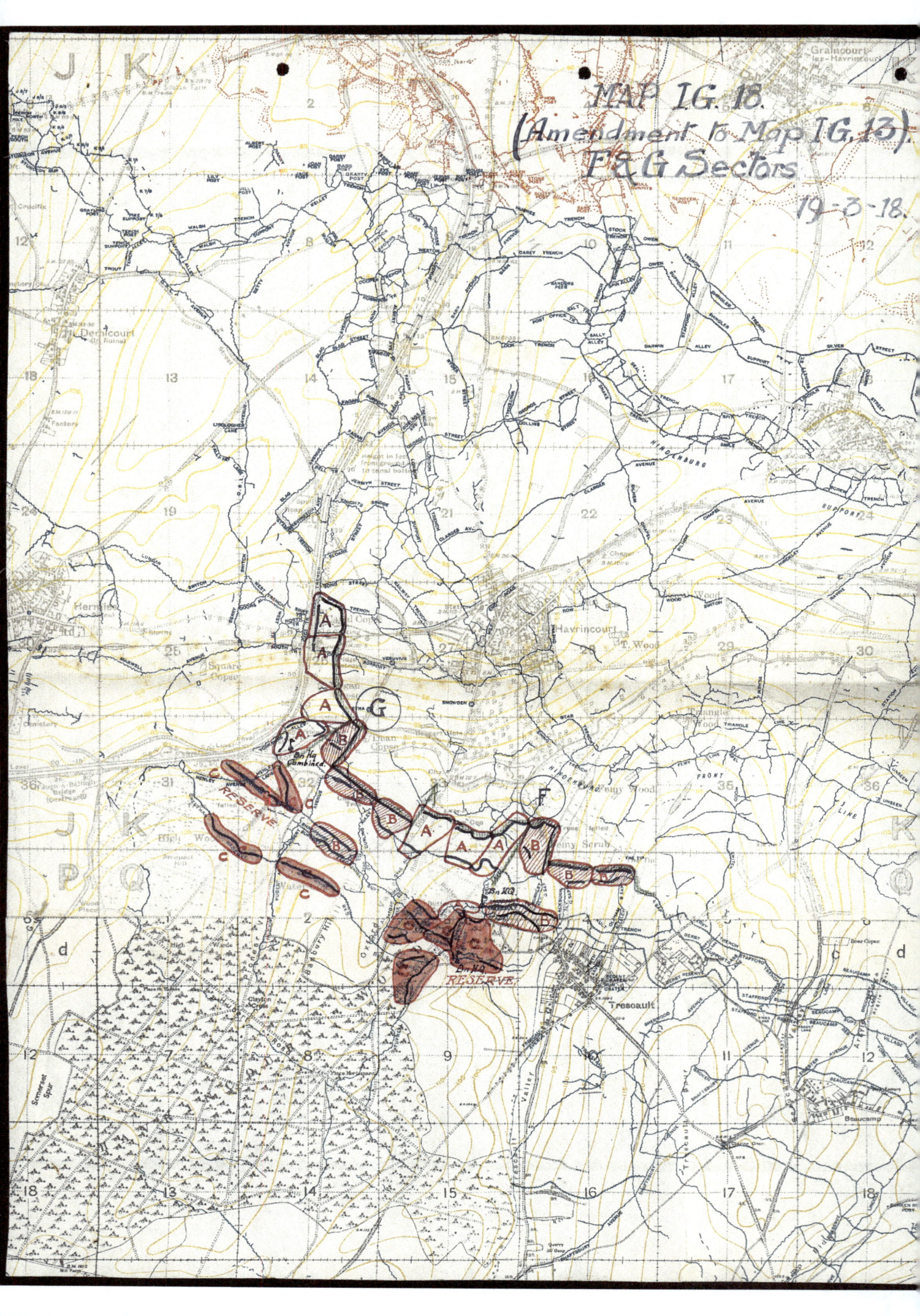

19th Division.

B. H. Q.

58th INFANTRY BRIGADE.

APRIL 1918.

OPERATION ORDERS & NARRATIVE ATTACHED

Army Form C. 2118.

WAR DIARY
or
INTELLIGENCE SUMMARY.
(Erase heading not required.)

Instructions regarding War Diaries and Intelligence Summaries are contained in F. S. Regs, Part II. and the Staff Manual respectively. Title pages will be prepared in manuscript.

Place	Date	Hour	Summary of Events and Information	Remarks and references to Appendices
LOCRE.	April 1st		Battalions re-organising and training. 1 Composite Coy. 9th Welch reported to 10 R.Warwicks and 1 Composite Coy. 6th Wilts reported to 10th Worcesters for tour of duty in line with 57th Bde. (58th Bde. Order No.235 attached). Inspection by Army Commander.	A
	2nd		Bde moved by march route to NEUVE EGLISE Area. Brigade H.Q. at SHANKHILL CAMP, FUSILIER CAMP and LINDENHOEK CAMP. (58th Bde. Order No. 236 attached).	B
	3rd		Battalions re-organising and training.	C
	4th		Battalions re-organising and training. Brigade H.Q. moved to APEX CAMP, N.33.a.3.5. (58th Bde Order No. 237 attached).	D
	5th) 6th)		Battalions re-organising and training.	
	7th		Bde. relieved 62nd and 64th Bdes. in line in WYTSCHAETE Sector on night 7th/8th. 3 Battalions in front line, Brigade H.Q. at REGENT'S Dug-outs, N.29.c.4.5. (58th Bde Order No. 238 attached).	D
LINE N.29.c.4.5.9th)	8th) 9th)		Situation normal. Night 9th/10th 26th (Highland) Bde took over portion of front as far South a-s 0.11.d.10.75. Remainder divided between 9th R.W.F. and 6th Wilts. 9th Welch moved into Bde. Reserve. (58th Bde Order No. 239 attached).	E
	10th		Orders received for relief by 26th Bde and Bde Order No. 240 (copies attached) issued. This relief was not carried out.	F
	10th to 18th)		Copy of Narrative of Action attached.	G
	18/19th		Bde relieved by 22nd French Regt and moved to canvas camps in L.35.d. (58th Bde B.M.145 attached)	H

Army Form C. 2118.

WAR DIARY
or
INTELLIGENCE SUMMARY.
(Erase heading not required.)

Instructions regarding War Diaries and Intelligence Summaries are contained in F.S. Regs., Part II. and the Staff Manual respectively. Title pages will be prepared in manuscript.

Place	Date	Hour	Summary of Events and Information	Remarks and references to Appendices
L.35.d.	19th) 20th)		Battalions re-organising.	
	21st		Bde. moved by march route to PROVEN. Battalions in FENTON, PADDINGTON and CENTRAL Camps. Bde. H.Q. at CENTRAL Camp. (58th Bde. Order 241 attached).	I
PROVEN.	22nd) 23rd)		Battalions re-organising and training.	
	24th		Battalions re-organising and training. Working party of 400 found by WILTS for digging new line E. of POPERINGHE.	
	25th		Same working party found by 9th WELCH. Remainder re-organising and training.	
		12.35.pm.	Units to be held in readiness to move at short notice.	
		8.7pm.	56th Bde. moved to RENINGHELST. Div. under orders of XXII Corps.	
G.10.c.3.3.	26th	1.10.am.	Verbal message from G.S.O.1 that Bde would move to Square G.15 at 5.am. Bde. to be in Divisional Reserve and be prepared to occupy position in LA CLYTTE - G.24.central, line. Line to be reconnoitred.	
		3.am	Wire from Division confirming G.S.O.1 message.	
		5.am	Bde on move to G.15 via PROVEN - POPERINGHE Road through POPERINGHE.	
		8.am	Head of Brigade at Cross roads G.15.b. Looking for accommodation.	
		8.25am	Battalions under cover. R.W.F. in PENGUIN Camp G.9.c.6.6. Welch beside the road G.15.c.5.9. Wilts in huts and standings G.15.a.9.5.	
		10.30am	Welch moving to a camp in G.22.a.	
		3.25.pm	Major-General visited Brigade H.Q. and warned us that if 56th Bde. was put at disposal of 49th Div. 58th Bde. would take place of 56th Bde. Warning (B.M.164) issued to units (copy attached).	
		6.45.pm	Orders that in case of emergency 56th Bde. would be at disposal of G.O.C. 49th Div. 57th Bde. to keep in touch with situation at Junction between British and French. 58th Bde. and 82nd and 94th Field Coys R.E. to reconnoitre defensive line from HALLEBAST to VLAMERTINGHE.	

Army Form C. 2118.

WAR DIARY
or
INTELLIGENCE SUMMARY.
(Erase heading not required.)

Instructions regarding War Diaries and Intelligence Summaries are contained in F. S. Regs., Part II. and the Staff Manual respectively. Title pages will be prepared in manuscript.

Place	Date	Hour	Summary of Events and Information	Remarks and references to Appendices
G.10.c.3.5	26/4	10.30pm.	Following situation report received. Main Line of Resistance is YPRES RAMPARTS, SHRAPNEL CORNER, CHATEAU SEGARD, EIZENWAAV, West End of ZILLEBEKE LAKE, LOCK 8, VOORMEZEELE. 56th Bde. will be prepared to assist 49th Div. if required. During the night the vicinity of Bde.H.Q. was shelled and it was decided to move H.Q.	
G.10.d.5.1.	27/4	8.am.	Bde.H.Q. established in cottage about G.10.d.5.1. Situation at 7.30.a.m. VOURMEZEELE definitely in our hands.	
		10.am.	Bde.H.Q. moved to G.22.a.3.8.	
G.22.a.3.8.		12.35pm	Orders to construct HALLEBAST - VLAMERTINGHE - YPRES Rd. Line as soon as possible and Bde. to be prepared to man same in case of emergency.	
		2.30pm.	Written orders as to construction of this line issued confirming verbal instructions given previously (B.M.130/A).	
		5.45pm.	Written orders received to occupy line. 58th Bde. in front 2nd N.Z. Entrenching Battalion in Reserve.	
		9.pm.	Written orders issued to units for occupying line. (B.M.132/A).	
		10.15pm	Verbal message from G.S.O. 1 giving boundary between 6th Div. and 58th Bde. on the Northern end of the HALLEBAST - VLAMERTINGHE Line.	
		11.5pm.		
	28th	2.am.	Above message confirmed by wire from Division.	
		3.15.a.m.	Some doubts as to the whereabouts of the 2nd N.Z. Entrenching Battalion.	
		9.a.m.	Orders issued to all units under orders of Bde. re re-adjustment of line (B.M.133/A).	
		12noon	Dispositions received from 9th R.W.F. and 9th Welch.	
		3.30pm.	Message from Div. (T.B.102) saying there were indications of an attack on YPRES from S.E. either during the afternoon or in the early morning.	
		3.45pm.	Increase of Artillery fire on both sides.	
		4.pm.	Telephone message from G.S.O. 1 saying that in case of serious attack Bde. would come under orders of 21st Division.	
		8.55pm.	Wire from 19th Div. that Bde. might be placed at disposal of 21st Div. in event of attack on YPRES. Bde. to be prepared to move at ½ hour's notice.	
		10.5pm.	19th Div. wire 56th and 58th Bdes. to be held in readiness to move at ½ hour's notice. 58th is at disposal of 21st Div.	
	29th	3.am.	Heavy barrage on front opened.	

Army Form C. 2118.

WAR DIARY
or
INTELLIGENCE SUMMARY.
(Erase heading not required.)

Instructions regarding War Diaries and Intelligence Summaries are contained in F.S. Regs., Part II and the Staff Manual respectively. Title pages will be prepared in manuscript.

Place	Date	Hour	Summary of Events and Information	Remarks and references to Appendices
G.22.a.3.8.	29th	6.45am.	Division report no infantry action up to 5.30.am.	
		7.am.	Reports received from N.Z. Battalion, R.W.F. and Welch state area being shelled with H.E. and Gas,	
		9.am.	Verbal message from 56th Bde. French attacked this morning by enemy but was driven off.	
		9.30am.	Wire from Div. 57th Bde. to move to G.14 and 15 at once and be prepared to take over portion of line held by 58th Bde.	
		10.40.am.	Div. report enemy on MONT ROUGE and MONT VIDAIGNE. 57th Bde. to move to Square. L.24. and ascertain position. 56th Bde. to ascertain situation Mt. ROUGE and SCHERPENBERG.	
	30th	12.30pm	Welch report G.H.Q. Line opposite their Battalion front held by a Battn. of LEICESTERS and Righting going on in SCOTTISH WOOD. Situation reported by Battalions to be quieter. Situation report from 21st Div. states Right and Centre Battalions of Right Bde. were attacked but enemy driven off.	
		12.50pm.	19th Div. report that lines held by 39th French Div. and 25th Div. are intact.	
		1.pm.	19th Div. report that lines held by 39th French Div. and 25th Div are intact and that French hold SCHERPENBERG, LOCRE, Mt ROUGE and Mt. VIDAIGNE.	
		2.35am.	Warning order from Div. that if situation permitted 19th Div. would relieve 21st Div. in line 58th Bde. to relieve 110th. Battalions warned.	
		9.15am	Div report from 22nd Corps that French counter-attacked took LOCRE HOSPICE and 45 prisoners.	
		12.30pm	3 Coys N.Z. organised under 1 Coy. to be placed under orders of 25th Div forthwith.	
	30th	4.pm.	Wire from Div. saying M.G. Coy. in the VLAMERTINGHE Line to remain in after Bde. moved forward for relief. The 3 remaining Coys of N.Z. Entrenching Battalion would take over line from Bde. putting their men in selected strong points etc.	
		4.4.pm.	Relief orders issued.(B.M.139/4. copy attached).	
		7.pm.	Bde. H.Q. closed at G.22.a.3.8.	
		8.30pm	Bde.H.Q. opened at H.27.b.6.7.	

15.5.18.

[signature]
for Brigadier General
Commanding 58th Infantry Brigade.

SECRET.   Copy No. 13

58th Infantry Brigade Order No. 235.

31-3-18.

Ref: Map. FRANCE Sht. 28.S.W. 1/20,000.

1. The 19th Division is taking over the MESSINES Sector from 5th Australian Inf. Bde. on the nights 31st March/1st April and 1st/2nd April.
    The Sector is 3,200 yds. in width and extends from the DOEUVRE to the WAMBEEK.

2. This sector is being taken over by a composite Brigade of 57th and 58th Inf. Brigades under the command of G.O.C., 57th Inf. Bde.
    The Battalions of the 58th Inf Brigade will send a Company to each of the Battalions of the 57th Inf. Bde. as follows:-

    1 Coy. 9th Welch R. to 10th R.War. Regt.
    1 Coy. 9th R.W.Fus. to 8th Gloucester Regt.
    1 Coy. 6th Wilts R. to 10th Worc. Regt.

    Each of these companies will include all the available rifles in the Battn., but this company need not be more than 200 strong, including sufficient Lewis Gunners to man 4 Lewis guns and 5 Signallers.
    Each of the Companies being attached must be organised into 4 platoons. It is hoped to take over L.G. Drums in the sector.

3. The 10th R. War. Regt. are relieving the 18th Battn. on night 1st/2nd April in Left Sub-sector.
    8th Glouc. Regt. are relieving the 17th Battn. on night 31st March/1st April in Right Sub-sector.
    10th Worc. Regt. are relieving 19th Battn. on night 1st/2nd April in Centre Sub-sector.

4. The Companies will report to the Battalions to whom they are being attached as follows:-

    The Coy. 9th R.W.F. to report to 8th Glouc. R. Hd.Qrs. at
    ROSSIGNOL CAMP N.21.b.8.0. at 2.0.p.m. March 31st.
    The Coy. 9th Welch R. to report to 10th R. War. R.   ) both on
    H.Q. at KEMMEL SHELTERS N.19.d.6.4.   ) morning of
    and the Coy. 6th Wilts. R. to report to 10th Worc. R.) 1st April.
    H.Q. at ROSSIGNOL CAMP N.21.b.8.0.   )

5. Advance parties from each Battn. consisting of

        The O.C. Composite Coy.
        One Platoon Officer.
        and 4 Platoon Sergeants

    will report as follows:-

    9th R.W.Fus. to H.Q. 8th Glouc. Regt. as soon as possible.
    9th Welch R. to H.Q. 10th R.War. Regt. at 2.0.p.m. March 31st.
    6th Wilts. R. to H.Q. 10th Worc. Regt. at 2.0.p.m. March 31st.

6. Coy. and Platoon H.Q. and as many Platoon Sergeants and Section Commanders as possible of remaining Coys. of Battalions will remain out of line and will be formed into complete Coys. as reinforcements arrive.

7. Brigade H.Q. will remain at LOCRE.

8. Acknowledge.

[signature] Captain

Brigade Major 58th Infantry Brigade.

Issued at 2.30.p.m.

Copy No.
1 G.O.C.
2 Staff Capt.
3 9.R.W.Fus.
4 9.Welch R.
5 6.Wilts. R.
6 58.T.M.Battery.
7 19th Div. "G"
8 56th Inf. Bde.
9 57th Inf. Bde.
10 Bde. Transport Offr.
11 Bde. Sig. Offr.
12 O.C. No. 4 Coy. Div. Train.
13) War Diary.
14)
15 File.

B

SECRET.   Copy No. 13

58th Infantry Brigade Order No. 236.

2nd April, 1918.

Ref. map: Sht. 28 S.W.
1/20,000.

1. The 58th Inf. Brigade (less 1 Coy. per Battn. in the line) will move by march route to NEUVE EGLISE Area to-day 2nd April in accordance with attached march table.

2. 1st Line Transport and Baggage wagons will accompany Units. After arrival in new camps such transport as is not required in camps will move to Brigade Transport Lines HILLSIDE NORTH CAMP T.14.c.

3. Intervals of 100 yards between Companies (or groups approximately equal in strength to a Coy.), and 100 yards between Unit and transport will be maintained during the march.

4. No lorries are available to assist in the move. Baggage wagons are reporting to units in the morning.

5. Brigade H.Q. will close at LOCRE at 10.15.a.m. and re-open at NEUVE EGLISE at the same hour.

6. Completion of moves to be reported to Brigade H.Q.

7. ACKNOWLEDGE.

F.W. Fraser.
Captain

Brigade Major 58th Infantry Brigade.
Issued at 1.30.a.m. 2.4.18.

Copy No. 1 G.O.C.
2 Staff Capt.
3 9.R.W.Fus.
4 9.Welch R.
5 6.Wilts R.
6 58.T.M.Bty.
7 19th Div. G.
8 56th Inf. Bde.
9 57th Inf. Bde.
10 Bde. Transport Offr.
11 Bde. Sig. Offr.
12 O.C. No. 4 Coy. Div. Train.
13) War Diary.
14)
15 File.

March Table issued with 58th Infantry Brigade Order No.236.

Unit.	From.	To.	Route.	Leave Present Camp.	Remarks.
Brigade H.Q.	LOCRE.	NEUVE EGLISE.	DRANOUTRE.	10.15.a.m.	
9/R.W.Fusrs.	WAKEFIELD HUTS.	SHANKHILL CAMP (T.15.b.4.4.)	DRANOUTRE NEUVE EGLISE.	10.40.a.m.	Halt for 5 minutes from 11.10. to 11.15.a.m. and subsequently usual halts from 10 minutes to clockhour to the clockhour.
58/T.M.Bty.	LOCREHOFF FM.			10.45.a.m.	
6/Wilts Regt.	BIRR BARRACKS.	LINDENHOEK N.27.c.9.2.	HOSPICE - N.19.c. S.O. KEMMEL.	10.45.a.m.	
9/Welch Regt.	DONCASTER HUTS.	FUSILIER CAMP. T.3.c.9.9.	DRANOUTRE - DONEGAL FM N.31.d. AIRCRAFT FM. N.32.b. N.33.c.	10.45.a.m.	

SECRET   Copy No 4

58th Infantry Brigade Order No. 237

Ref; Map Sheet 28 S.W.
1/20.000.

58th Brigade Headquarters will move from NEUVE EGLISE at 3 p.m. on April 4th and reopen at the same hour at APEX CAMP N.33.a.3.5.

Captain,
Brigade Major 58th Infantry Brigade.

Brigade H.Q.
    4th April 1918.

Issued at 9 a.m.

Copy No. 1	G.O.C.	10.	19th Division "G"
2	Staff Captain.	11.	19th Division "Q"
3)		12	56th Inf. Bde.
4)	File.	13	57th Inf. Bde.
5	War Diary.	14	Bde Transport Offr.
6	9/R.W.Fus.	15	Bde Signalling Offr.
7	9/Welch	16	No 4 Coy, Train.
8	6/Wilts.		
9	58/T.M.Battery.		

SECRET.   Copy No. 16

58th Infantry Brigade Order No. 238.

6th April, 1918.

Ref. map Sht. 28.S.W. 1/20,000
HOLLEBEKE Sht. 1/10,000.

1. The 58th Inf. Bde. will relieve the 62nd and 64th Inf. Bdes. in the WYTSCHAETE Sector on the night 7th/8th April as under :-

    6th Bn Wiltshire Regt. will relieve 1st Bn Lincolns, 62nd Bde. in Right Sub-sector. Battn. H.Q. TORREKEN FARM, O.20.d.1.2.

    9th Bn R.W.Fusiliers will relieve the 2nd Bn Lincolns, 62nd Bde. in Centre Sub-sector. Battn.H.Q., PRINCE RUPERT'S DUG-OUTS, O.20.b.2.1.

    9th Bn Welch Regt. will relieve the 9th K.O.Y.L.I., 64th Bde. in Left Sub-sector. Battn.H.Q. ONRAET FARM, O.14.a.2.1.

    58th T.M.Battery will relieve 62nd and 64th T.M.Batteries.

2. Boundaries between Battalions on front line will be as follows:-

    Right Battn. from the WAMBEEK, O.23.c.2.1., to WALL FARM, O.23.a.2.6. (inclusive).

    Centre Battn. from WALL FARM, O.23.a.2.6., (exclusive) to the ROOZEBEEK about O.11.c.8.0.

    Left Battn. from the ROOZEBEEK about O.11.c.8.0. to HOLLEBEKE about O.11.b.9.5.

3. Guides (numbers to be arranged by C.O's direct) will be at LAMP POST CORNER N.24.d.1.2. for the 9th Bn Welch Regt. at 6.45.p.m. for the 6th Bn Wiltshire Regt. at 7.0.p.m. C.O. 9th Bn R.W.Fusiliers will arrange direct with C.O. 2nd Lincolns a meeting place for guides but will not pass WYTSCHAETE till 6th Bn Wiltshire Regt. are clear.
    All further details of relief will be arranged direct between C.O's concerned.

4. No troops will move East of WYTSCHAETE until 8.0.p.m. unless the visibility is bad.
    West of WYTSCHAETE movement will be by Coys. at 200 yards intervals East of WYTSCHAETE by platoons at 200 yards intervals.

5. Brigade H.Q. will close at APEX CAMP at 6.0.p.m. on April 7th and re-open at the same hour at REGENT'S DUG-OUTS N.29.c.4.5.
    G.O.C. 58th Inf. Bde. will assume command of the sector on completion of relief.

6. Relief complete will be reported to Brigade H.Q. by the Code words "NO SUGGESTIONS TO MAKE".

7. All maps, plans of defences, defence schemes, aeroplane photos and programmes of work will be taken over and copies of receipts given forwarded to Brigade H.Q. by 6.0.p.m. on 8th inst.

8. Dispositions to be reported to Brigade H.Q. by 12 noon 8th April.

9. Administrative Instructions are being issued separately by the Staff Captain.

10. Acknowledge.

F. H. Fraser

Captain

Brigade Major 58th Infantry Brigade.

Issued at 8.0.p.m.

Copy No. 1 G.O.C.
2 Staff Captain.
3 9.R.W.Fusrs.
4 9.Welch R.
5 6.Wilts. R.
6 58.T.M.Battery.
7 19th Divn. "G"
8 19th Divn. "Q".
9 56th Inf. Bde.
10 57th Inf. Bde.
11 62nd Inf. Bde.
12 64th Inf. Bde.
13 Bde. Transport Offr.
14 Bde. Signalling Offr.
15 No. 4 Coy. Train.
16) War Diary.
17)
18 File.

SECRET.   Copy No. 14

58th Infantry Brigade Order No. 239.

8th April, 1918.

1. In continuation of Warning Order issued this evening the 26th Highland Brigade, 9th Division will take over the Northern portion of the Brigade Front as far S. as S.P.2.O.11. (O.11.d.10.75) inclusive on the night 9th/10th April.

2. On completion of relief the Northern boundary of the Brigade will run as follows:-

   S.P.2.O.11.(exclusive) - CHARITY FM. (exclusive) - OLIVE LANE (inclusive) - S. of ENGLEBRIEN FM. - S.P.2.O.9. (joint liaison Post) - thence along road to In den JAGER CART. - thence to the S. edge of OATEN WOOD and BOIS CONFLUENT where it joins the present boundary at O.1.c.5.0.

3. Joint Liaison Posts of 9th Bn R.W.Fusiliers and 26th (Highland) Brigade will be established as follows:-

   (a). In Support System. S.P.3.O.10.
   (b). In Reserve System. S.P.2.O.9.

   Not less than two sections will be allotted to each liaison post.

4. On the night 9th/10th April the remainder of the Brigade front will be organised on a two battalion front with one Battalion in Brigade Reserve.

   Dividing Line between Battalions will be -
   Junction Buildings (inclusive to Left Battn) - Ridge Fm. (inclusive to Left Battn) - thence to PIONEER LANE O.16.c.6.5. - thence along PIONEER LANE to S.P.2.O.15. (O.15.d.2.6.), S.P.2.O.15. inclusive to Right Battn. - thence to OOSTAVERNE-ST. ELOI Road at O.15.c.7.6.

   Battn.H.Q. Right Battn. PRINCE RUPERT'S DUG-OUTS, O.20.b.2.1.
   Battn.H.Q. Left Battn. ONRAET FM, O.14.a.2.1.

5. To effect this re-adjustment -

   (a). 6th Bn Wiltshire Regt. will extend its left so as to take over from 9th Bn R.W.Fusiliers on front, support, and reserve lines as far N. as the dividing line between Battalions laid down in para. 4.

   (b). 9th Bn R.W.Fusiliers will extend its left so as to take over from 9th Bn Welch Regiment on front, support, and reserve lines as far N. as the new Northern Bde. Boundary laid down in para.2.

   (c). On relief by 9th Division and 9th Bn R.W.Fusiliers the 9th Bn Welch Regt. will withdraw into Brigade Reserve. Locations to be notified later.

6. No post is to be withdrawn until definitely relieved.

7. 6th Bn Wiltshire Regt. and 9th Bn R.W.Fusiliers will each hold their sub-sectors as follows:-

   2 Coys. each organised in depth holding front and support lines.
   2 Coys. holding Reserve Line.

8. All other details of relief will be arranged direct between C.O's. concerned.
   Orders as to rendezvous for guides from 9th Bn Welch Regt. for 26th Highland Brigade will be issued.

9. Completion of relief of 9th Bn Welch Regiment will be wired by O.C. 9th Bn Welch Regiment to Brigade H.Q. by code words "PAPERS NOT YET RECEIVED" and arrival in Brigade Reserve Area by code words "PAPERS NOW RECEIVED"

Completion of adjustment of line by 6th Bn Wiltshire Regt. and 9th Bn R.W.Fusiliers will be wired to Brigade H.Q. by code words "CERTAINLY".

10. Detailed dispositions will be forwarded to Brigade H.Q. by 4.0.p.m. April 10th.

11. ACKNOWLEDGE.

                                                        Captain

                        Brigade Major 58th Infantry Brigade.

Issued at 12.20 a.m.

Copy No. 1 G.O.C.
         2 9.R.W.Fusrs.
         3 9.Welch R.
         4 6.Wilts R.
         5 58.T.M.Battery.
         6 19th Div. "G".
         7 56th Inf. Bde.
         8 57th Bde.
         9 26th Bde.
        10 Staff. Capt.
        11 Bde. Transport Offr.
        12 Bde. Int. Offr.
        13 Bde. Sig. Offr.
        14) War Diary.
        15)
        16 File.

SECRET   Copy No. 23

58th Infantry Brigade Order No. 240.

10th April, 1918.

Ref. map. Sheet 28.S.W. 1/20,000.
and WYTSCHAETE 1/10,000.

1. The 58th Brigade will be relieved in the WYTSCHAETE Sector by the 26th Brigade, 9th Division on the night 10th/11th April as under:-

   6th Bn Wiltshire Regt. will be relieved in the Right Sub-sector by the 8th Bn The Black Watch.
   9th Bn R.W.Fusiliers will be relieved in the Left Sub-sector by the 7th Bn Seaforth Highlanders.
   The 9th Bn Welch Regt. in Brigade Reserve will withdraw without being relieved. Withdrawal will commence at 8.30.p.m.
   58th T.M.Battery will be relieved by 26th T.M.Battery. Any mortars not being relieved will be withdrawn after dark.

2. On relief units of the 58th Brigade will proceed to the BEAVER Area. The Staff Captain will notify units the locations of camps later.
   On arrival in new area (BEAVER Area) the Brigade Group composed as under will be ready to move at an hour's notice.

58th Brigade H.Q.	
9/R.W.Fusrs.	59/Field Ambulance.
9/Welch Regt.	Divl H.Q. Units.
6/Wilts Regt.	No. 4 Coy. Train.
58/L.T.M.B.	No. 3 Sec. D.A.C.
82/Field Coy.R.E.	H.Q., "C" and "D" Coys. 19th M.G.Battn.

3. Each front line Battalion will supply 5 guides per Coy. and 2 per Battn.H.Q. to be at The Red Chateau, O.18.b.9.2., for the 8th Black Watch at 7.45.p.m. and for the 7th Seaforths at 8.15.p.m.
   If these arrangements do not suit, C.O's may make other arrangements provided that they ensure that incoming units do not clash.
   All further details will be arranged between C.O's concerned.

4. All documents, maps, defence schemes and air photos, relating to the sector will be handed over to incoming units.

5. The parties from each Battn. attached to the 82nd Field Coy. R.E. will remain with this unit.

6. Completion of relief will be wired to Brigade H.Q. by the code word "VICTOR".
   Arrival in camps in BEAVER Area will also be reported to Brigade H.Q. by all units in 58th Brigade Group.

7. Brigade H.Q. will close at REGENT'S DUG-OUTS on completion of relief and re-open on arrival in BEAVER Area. Location of Brigade H.Q. will be notified later to all concerned.

8. Acknowledge.

                                                  Fraser
                                                  Captain

Brigade Major 58th Infantry Brigade.

Issued at 8.0.a.m.

Copy No.			
1 G.O.C.	5. 58.L.T.M.B.	15 82nd Fld. Coy.R.E.	
2 9.R.W.Fusrs.	6. 19th Div. G.	16 59th Field Amb.	
3 9.Welch R.	7. 56th Inf. Bde.	17 No. 4 Coy. Train.	
4 6.Wilts R.	8. 57th Inf. Bde.	18 No. 3 Sec. D.A.C.	
	9. 26th Inf. Bde.	19 H.Q. 19th M.G.Bn.	
	10. 27th Inf. Bde.	20 C Co. do.	
	11. Staff Capt.	21 D Co. do.	
	12 Bde. Transport Offr.		
	13 Bde. Int. Offr.	22 File.	
	14 Bde. Sig. Offr.	23) War Diary.	
		24)	

NARRATIVE OF ACTION OF 58th INF. BDE. FROM 10th to 20th APRIL, 1918.

9.4.18. Brigade holding the line from WAMBEEK to CHARITY HO. 6th Bn Wiltshire Regt. on Right. 9th Bn R.W.Fusiliers on Left. 9th Bn Welch Regt. in Support.

10.4.18. At 5.30.a.m. enemy opened heavy barrage on front system mainly South of the WAMBEEK, and attacked South of that Stream. Information was received from 6th Bn Wiltshire Regt shortly afterwards that Warwicks on their Right had retired. At 7.0.a.m. 57th Brigade reported that enemy were believed to be in MESSINES.

By 9.a.m. it became apparent that the 57th Brigade had been driven back and the nearest troops of that Brigade that could be found were some WARWICKS at PICK HOUSE. 6th Bn Wiltshire Regt. were ordered to hold a flank along ridge North of WAMBEKE more or less along line of MANCHESTER STREET and thence via TORREKEN HO. to PICK HOUSE. O.C., 6th Bn Wiltshire Regt. was told to take the Coy of 9th Bn Welch Regt. in CATACOMBS to help form his flank towards TORREKEN HOUSE.

9.5.a.m. Wire received from Division stating that all details of 19th Division in NEUVE EGLISE under command of Lieut-Colonel SOLE were at once to man the high ground from MAEDELSTEDE FM. - SPANBROK-MOLEN - T.6.central - BRISTOL Castle. All available machine guns were also put in this line.

At 10.a.m. the situation on the MESSINES RIDGE being very obscure 9th Bn Welch Regt. were ordered to send 2 Coys. to occupy the Cutting South and East of WYTSCHAETE to protect WYTSCHAETE itself and to get in touch with WILTS defensive flank.

At 12 mid-day and again at 1.30.p.m. O.C. 6th Bn Wiltshire Regt reported his line intact, and defensive flank in position. Welch Coys in Cutting were now in touch, O.C. Welch had visited O.C. 6th Wilts and latter were in touch with WARWICKS at PICK HOUSE. The defensive flank was however very weak owing to its great extent, something like 2,000 yards.

Meanwhile information received from 57th Bde. that 2 Coys. N.Staffs had counter-attacked on MESSINES and got to Western edge of village and that S.A. Bde. would counter-attack during the afternoon.

At 2.p.m. R.W.F. reported attack on their front and that one post had been driven back. He also reported 9th Division troops at and North of CHARITY HOUSE were retiring. As this left both flanks of Bde. in the air WILTS and R.W.F. were ordered to withdraw to the Support Line.

At 3.30.p.m. WILTS were holding Support Line. R.W.F. had been very heavily shelled especially in the RAVINE where one Company had been nearly wiped out and troops were coming back on the Reserve Line. Orders were then issued to WILTS to conform to this movement if they found it necessary to leave the Support Line. The Coys of this Bn in the Support Line did not however retire until much later after the enemy had broken through behind them from the TORREKEN FARM direction.

Meanwhile the 82nd Field Coy.R.E. and "D" Coy. S.W.B. had been placed under the orders of the Bde. and were sent forward to ONRAET WOOD. These were eventually used to link up the MAEDELSTEDE FARM Line with 9th WELCH in cutting South of WYTSCHAETE.

At 4.p.m. the Bde came under the orders of G.O.C. 9th Division G.O.C. 9th Division reported Right of his Division about the WHITE CHATEAU Stables and not in touch with 58th Bde. R.W.F. reported their Left on Reserve Line in Northern portion of DENYS WOOD not in touch with 9th Division. The remaining Coy of 9th Welch in ONRAET Wood was therefore sent forward to try and fill this gap.

About 4.p.m. 2 Battalions of 9th Division were ordered to move up to make the position round WYTSCHAETE more secure and to connect up with 57th Bde. This order was however afterwards cancelled and the 2 Battalions were sent up to connect up from DENYS WOOD to WHITE CHATEAU Stables instead. This information did not reach this Brigade till 7.5.p.m.

About 7.30.p.m. the Signalling Sergeant of 6th Wilts reached Bde.HQ. and reported that the H.Q. of 6th Wilts had been driven out of their dug-out the enemy having approximately broken through from the

PICK HOUSE - TORREKEN FARM direction and being all round them. A portion of one Coy. of 9th Welch Regt. were in position between SONEN and SOMER FARMS to prevent enemy breaking through North of SONEN FARM.

The O.C. Battalion had therefore taken his Headquarters personnel to try and hold up enemy in direction of TORREKEN FARM (This information proved correct, and the C.O. was killed and the Adjutant wounded in endeavouring to stop the enemy coming through from the South.

About 7.30.p.m. O.C. R.W.F. reported that the enemy had got into OOSTAVERNE WOOD apparently behind the Reserve Line.

He was ordered to find out exact situation and then remove his H.Q. with that of 9th WELCH to PALMER Dump.

As a result of reconnaissance the situation by 10.30.p.m. was found to be as follows :-

The 9th WELCH were holding the Cutting South and East of WYTSCHAETE with 2 Coys and a portion of a third Coy. The remainder of the third Coy had been attached to WILTS holding defensive flank from about GUN FARM Westwards. No news could be got of them and they were evidently cut off by the enemy who had broken through further West. The fourth Coy which had been sent up to join up between DENYS WOOD and WHITE CHATEAU Stables was in position near PHEASANT WOOD.

the 9th R.W.F. had one Coy holding the Reserve Line in DENYS WOOD. One Coy was believed to be about GOUDEZENE FARM but no news could be got of it. (This Coy did actually hold its position till 3.a.m. on 11th when finding no other troops on either flank it withdrew to the GRAND BOIS). The original Front and Support Line Companies were known to have lost heavily during the withdrawal. Elements of them were with the DENYS WOOD Coy but no further information of them could be got and very few of them ever got back.

The 6th WILTS had been completely cut off by the enemy's break through from the TORREKEN FARM direction. One party of about 50 succeeded in withdrawing Northwards and joined the Coy of 9th WELCH near PHEASANT WOOD. Elements of the Battn. were believed to be about the STAENYZER CAB - ONRAET WOOD Line but no formed bodies could be found and only small isolated parties succeeded in getting back through the enemy after dark.

At 9.30.p.m. Bde.H.Q. moved back to FARRET CAMP there joining Bde.H.Q. of 26th and 62nd Bdes.

<u>11th April.</u> The enemy did not press his attack during the night. About 2.am. 2 Battalions of 62nd Bde. were ordered to occupy a line from Southern end of ONRAET WOOD along the ONRAET WOOD-MESSINES Road to PICK HO. before daylight and at 5.30.am. to occupy the Corps Line on that front. These Battalions succeeded on the Left in occupying the Corps Line. On the Right they remained holding the line of the road joining up with 9th Welch in the cutting.

The situation throughout the 11th remained much the same. On the left the BLACK WATCH and SEAFORTH HIGHLANDERS with one Coy. R.W.F. and one Coy 9th Welch formed a line from STABLES along DAMMESTRASSE to ZERO WOOD.

Reinforcements which had arrived for the Brigade were organised into a Battalion and held in readiness to man the VIERSTRAAT Line from LA POLKA to VIERSTRAAT if required.

<u>Night 11/12th.</u> In accordance with orders of G.O.C. 9th Division it was the intention to withdraw the Bde on this night into Reserve WEST of the VIERSTRAAT Ridge. The situation however was not sufficiently settled to admit of this and the Bde. (with the exception of the 50 men of 6th WILTS who were withdrawn) remained holding their positions.

<u>12th April.</u> The 12th passed comparatively quietly except for occasional heavy shelling. During the afternoon the Composite Bn of Drafts was broken up and drafts sent to their respective Bn.H.Q.

<u>Night 12/13th.</u> On the night 12/13th the Bde was withdrawn from the line and concentrated in the LA CLYTTE Area. Bde.H.Q. moved to BARBADOES CAMP, LA CLYTTE.

- 3 -

13th April. At 10.47.am. orders were received from 9th Division to occupy a position of assembly astride the road between LA CLYTTE and KEMMEL there to come again under the orders of 19th Division. Bde moved out at once and occupied position WELCH on Right of Road, WILTS on Left. 9th R.W.F., "D" Coy S.W.B., portions of "C" and "D" Coys 19th M.G.Bn, 58th T.M.B. were in support behind AU POMPIER ESTAMINET. 58th T.M.B. were later attached to WILTS as riflemen. G.S.O.2 19th Division brought orders there to occupy LINDENHOEK - SPANBROEKMOLEN Line from SPY FARM to SPANBROEKMOLEN at once and to be prepared to relieve S.A.Bde. in MAEDELSTEDE - SPANBROEKMOLEN Sector at night. 9th WELCH were ordered to occupy the SPY FARM Line, remaining two Battalions to stand by to take over S.A. Bde front. Bde.H.Q. moved to KEMMEL Dug-outs N.26.b.4.1. Commanding Officers of relieving Battalions going first to this place (H.Q. S.A. Bde) and then to see C.O's in the Line.

Night 13/14th. Brigade relieved S.A. Bde in MAEDELSTEDE - SPANBROEKMOLEN Line. WILTS on Right, R.W.F. on Left, WELCH in Support with 2 Coys in SPY FARM - SPANBROEKENMOLEN Line, one Coy about N.23.c. and one Coy N.29.a. Relief complete about 2.30.am.

14th April. A good deal of shelling, some of it very heavy, during the day and enemy attack in the NEUVE EGLISE Sector. No heavy Infantry attack developed on the Brigade front.

Night 14/15th April. Orders received from 19th Division for the line to be withdrawn commencing at 1.30.am. to line approximately T.2.b.8.0. - 3.b.0.4. - 5.a.5.3. - N.36.c.2.4. - DURHAM Road N.36.central and thence along former line. This withdrawal did not actually affect the Bde. whose front remained as before. Bde.H.Q. moved to dug-outs N.25.b.9.1.

15th April. 108th Bde on our right reported early that they were being attack and their left flank was being driven in. To meet this situation 1 Coy of 9th Welch was moved up in close support to 6th Wilts suffering severely from shell fire in doing so. In order to maintain touch with 108th Bde the 6th Wilts found it necessary to extend their right flank by about 400 yards. They succeeded in doing this effectually and remained in touch throughout the day.

10.35.a.m. Owing to the situation still being somewhat obscure the 10th Worcesters were moved up into support, two Coys about N.22.d. and 23.c. two Coys in N.29.a.

12.55.p.m. One Coy of the 10th R.War. Regt. was sent to assist the 6th Wilts and put under direct orders of the O.C. that Bn. This Coy was not employed.

There was heavy shelling at intervals throughout the day.

Night 15/16th April. During the evening orders were received that the 9th Division (62nd Bde) were to take over the line as far South as SPANBROEKENMOLEN inclusive and that the 19th Division line was to be withdrawn at 2.am. to the REGENT STREET Line (LINDENHOEK - SPANBROEKMOLEN). This involved 9th R.W.F. and portion of 6th Wilts being relieved by 62nd Bde. The portion of 6th Wilts South of SPANBROEKENMOLEN to withdraw at 2.am. leaving outposts in position till 2.45.am. 108th Bde and troops to the right of them to withdraw through the 9th WELCH Line which then became front line. 9th Welch to extend their left to make effective junction with 62nd Bde at Southern edge of SPANBROEKMOLEN where strong liaison post was ordered to be established. On relief 9th R.W.F. to withdraw into Left Support, 6th Wilts to Right Support, each Bn with one Coy pushed up in close support to Left and Right half of 9th Welch respectively. Above movements were successfully carried out and completed before daylight.

Bde.H.Q. moved to FAIRY HOUSE at 4.0.am.

16th April. In the morning about 6.am. enemy put down a very heavy barrage and attacked from WYTSCHAETE Southwards. He quickly drove 62nd Bde from the MAEDELSTEDE - SPANBROEKMOLEN Line and occupied the MOLEN. 9th WELCH were therefore compelled to withdraw their left flank and throw it back in a Northerly direction. The line then ran as before as far East as N.29.d.2.8. thence Northwards to

(4)

In the evening 2 Coys of the French Bn in this Sector, attacked SPANBROEKMOLEN but did not get further than 200yds & eventually withdrew back to our Line.

KEMMEL - WYTSCHAETE Road about N.29.b.1.6. As the left did not join on to any troops of 62nd Bde the 9th R.W.F. (Left Supporting Batt: moved up two Coys and continued the line to LAGACHE FARM where touch with troops of 9th Division was gained.

9.55.a.m. Orders received from Division that in the event of the 9th Division on our left, being driven back from WYTSCHAETE the Boundary between 19th and 9th Divisions on the VIERSTRAAT Line would run through LA POLKA in N.22.c.

3.p.m. Message received from Division that the 9th Division in co-operation with a French Division would be carrying out an operation on our left in the afternoon.

Later in the day information was received that WYTSCHAETE had fallen.

No further heavy infantry attack developed but the line was subjected at intervals to very heavy shelling.

Bde.H.Q. moved to Farmhouse near SCHERPENBERG, M.11.d.2.7.

Later information was received that the 28th French Division would attack the General line WULVERGHEM - WYTSCHAETE. 19th Division to co-operate. Attack was timed for 6.p.m.

A heavy barrage was put down at 6.p.m. and again at 7.p.m. Owing apparently to faulty liaison arrangements the barrage was put down behind our front line and we suffered many casualties from it. No attack by the French however materialized though a Battalion of French Infantry came into the line.

Night 16/17th. A fairly quiet quiet night.

17th April. Heavy shelling at intervals especially about 6.p.m. when a local infantry attack developed on the extreme right of the Bde and on left of 57th Bde on our right. This was easily dealt with.

In the evening 2 Coys of a French Battalion in the sector attacked SPANBROEKMOLEN but did not get further than 200 yards and eventually withdrew back to our line.

Night 17/18th. The 62nd Bde were ordered to take over the portion of line held within their boundary from LAGACHE FARM to STORR FM. This relief however did not materialize. The 6th Wilts relieved 3 Coys of 9th Welch in front line.

18th April. A comparatively quiet day except for bursts of heavy shelling on front and Reserve Line and Battalion H.Q. (PARRIN FM) area at 4.a.m., 5.a.m., 9.a.m., 10.a.m., 2.30.p.m. and 6.p.m. No infantry attack followed.

Night 18/19th. In the evening a Regt. of 28th French Division took over the line, Units on relief withdrawing first to positions near SCHERPENBERG 19th and after a meal on to positions in L.35.d. where they remained until morning of 21st when the Brigade marched to the PROVEN Area.

The casualties incurred by the Brigade during these operations amounted to :-

	Killed.	Wounded.	Missing.	Total.
Officers.	5	12	8	25
O.R's.	81	320	770	1171
Total.	86	332	778	1196

58th Inf. Bde. No. B.M.145.

9th R.W.F.	56th Inf. Bde.	Captain E.O. Lauderdale.
9th Welch.	57th " "	M. Schloss, Liaison Officer
6th Wilts.	62nd " "	with 22nd Inf. Regt.

1. The 58th Inf Bde. will be relieved in the line to-night, night 18th/19th inst by the 22nd French Inf. Regt. The French will only take over as far North as the KEMMEL - WYTSCHAETE Road at N.29.b.7.6. Troops holding the line from this point to LAGACHE FARM will be relieved by troops of the 19th Division and will not withdraw until relieved.

2. The French are coming in under their own arrangements.

3. The Headquarters of the 22nd French Regt. are at the BREWERY, BEAVER CORNER about N.15.c.2.3.

4. Captain E.O. Lauderdale will report forthwith to the Colonel Commanding the 22nd Inf. Regt. to take up duties of Liaison Officer.

5. Colonel L.F. SMEATHMAN will send two runners forthwith to report to Captain Lauderdale at N.15.c.2.3.

6. The Colonel Commanding the 22nd French Regt. will inform Captain Lauderdale when he is satisfied that his troops are in position and that he is prepared for the 58th Inf. Bde. (less the portion North of the KEMMEL - WYTSCHAETE Road) to withdraw.

7. Captain Lauderdale will thereupon send the code words "ALL CORRECT" to the three Battalion H.Q. at FARRIN Fm. N.28.b.7.9. by runner repeating it to Brigade H.Q.

8. Troops of 58th Bde. will not withdraw on arrival of relieving troops.

9. On receipt of code words "ALL CORRECT" from Captain Lauderdale and not until then will troops of the 58th Bde. withdraw.

10. The withdrawal will be carried out as ordered in B.M.143 dated "D" Coy of the 5th S.W.B. will withdraw direct to BABINGTON CAMP.

11. Captain Lauderdale will remain with the French Colonel at N.15.c.2.3. until 6.a.m. April 20th.

12. Bde.H.Q. will close at M.11.d.2.7. at a time to be notified later and re-open on arrival at or near L.35.d.1.9.

13. Units will report arrival in new area,

14. Acknowledge.

Captain

Brigade Major 58th Infantry Brigade.

Issued at 6.15.p.m.
18.4.18.

SECRET.   Copy No. 1.......

58th Inf. Brigade Order No. 241.

Ref. Map Belgium & France.
       Sheet 27. 1/40,000.
----

1. The 58th Brigade will march to the PROVEN Area tomorrow 21st instant in accordance with the attached March Table.

2. 1st Line Transport will march with Units.

3. Dress - Marching Order, Steel Helmets.

4. The following intervals will be maintained on the line of march:-

    100 yards between Companies.
    500   "   "   Battalions.
    100   "   "   last Company and Transport.
     25. "   "   every section of six vehicles.

5. Administrative Instructions will be issued separately by the Staff Captain.

6. Units will report their arrival in the new Camps.

7. Brigade Headquarters will close at L.29.d.9.2. at 7-30 a.m. and open on arrival at CENTRAL CAMPS, F.7.b.3.3.

8. Acknowledge.

                                                    Captain,

20.4.1918.   Brigade Major, 58th Infantry Brigade.

        Issued at 1 a.m

Copy No. 1. G.O.C.   9. A.D.M.S.
        2. 9th Bn. R.W.Fus.   10. Staff Captain,
        3. 9th Bn. Welch Regt.   11. Bde. Signal Officer.
        4. 6th Bn. Wilts Regt.   12. Bde. Transport Officer.
        5. 58th T.M. Battery.   13. Bde. Supply Officer.
        6. 56th Brigade.   14. War Diary.)
        7. 57th Brigade.   15. War Diary.)
        8. 19th Division.   16. File.

MARCH TABLE.

Unit.	To.	Starting Point.	Time of passing Starting Point.	Route.	Remarks.
Brigade Hd.Qrs.	CENTRAL CAMPS, F.7.b.3.3.	Bend in Road. L.29.a.8.4.	7-40 a.m.	Road Junction L.23.c.0.2 - L.17.b.20.05 - Switchroad - Poperinghe - Proven Road - to Proven.	
6th Bn.Wilts Regt.	- do -	- do -	7-43 a.m.	- do -	
9th Bn.Welch Regt.	PADDINGTON CAMP, F.3.a.6.3.	- do -	8-8 a.m.	- do -	
9th Bn.R.W.Fus.	FENTON CAMP F.8.a.4.9.	- do -	8-23 a.m.	- do -	
58th T.M.Bty.	- do -	- do -	8-33 a.m.	- do -	

(1086) Wt.W16552/M1615 250,000 Pads. 21/3/17. J.R.& C. E 685 Forms/C2122/6.

"B" Form.
MESSAGES AND SIGNALS.

Army Form C2122 (In pads of 150)
No. of Message........

Prefix AM Code LXm.	Received At 12·12 a.m.	Sent At .... m.	Office Stamp
Office of Origin and Service Instructions: U7H 2 adds	Words 181 T	From CU7H By willis	To .... By ....

TO 58 Bde (1)

| Sender's Number. BM1022 | Day of Month. 10th | In reply to Number. | AAA |

Situation aaa OAK I support intact and SPO and OPAL support in front of WHITECHATEAU held in strength by BENCH aaa BENCH have made a line from STABLES to about O.H.C 2·5 with posts in front of DAMM STRASSE aaa 3 Coys of 7th Seaforths are in line about 40 yds in front of DAMM STRASSE and are feeling forward aaa a Coy of 7th Seaforths is sideslipping to get touch with STABLES and B Coy of 9th Welsh Regt are

From
Place
Time

* This line should be erased if not required.

(1086) Wt.W16552/M1615 250,000 Pads. 21/3/17. J.R.&C. E 685 Forms/C2122/6.

Army Form C2122
(In pads of 150)

"B" Form.

MESSAGES AND SIGNALS. No. of Message........

Prefix........Code...........m.		Received	Sent	Office Stamp
Office of Origin and Service Instructions.	Words	At 12/120 m.	At............m.	
		From Eu.ge	To................	
		By Wells	By................	

TO 58 Bde (2)

Sender's Number.	Day of Month.	In reply to Number.	AAA
VBM 1077			

in line on right of 7th Seaforths and report that RWF are holding posts in DENYS WOOD aaa other small elements of 19th Division carry line forward to O15B2.8 aaa Two Coys 8th Black Watch have been seen at this point one appears to be in support trench behind the welsh Regt aaa C Coy 8th Black Watch carry on to the right but it's position here is still obscure aaa 7th Seaforth Bn HQ are at EITHOE FM

From		
Place		
Time		

* This line should be erased if not required.

(1086) Wt.W16552/M1615 250,000 Pads. 21/3/17. J.R.&C. E 685 Forms/C2122/6.

Army Form C2122
(In pads of 150)

"B" Form.
MESSAGES AND SIGNALS. No. of Message........

Prefix......Code......m.	Received	Sent	Office Stamp
Office of Origin and Service Instructions. Words	At 12.17a m. From...... By......	At...... m. To...... By......	

TO 58 Bde (3)

Sender's Number.	Day of Month.	In reply to Number.	AAA
*19 M022			

O3D aaa 9th Seaforth Bn
HQ are at SHELLEY FARM
O2B and RAP at THE
MOUND O2D

From **Beak**
Place
Time

* This line should be erased if not required.

"A" Form.
MESSAGES AND SIGNALS.

Army Form C.2121 (in pads of 100).

Prefix	Code	m.	Words	Charge	This message is on a/o of:	Recd. at	m.
Office of Origin and Service Instructions.			Sent			Date	
			At	m.	Service.	From	
			To				
			By		(Signature of "Franking Officer.")	By	

TO — 8th Blackwatch
 — 58th Bde

Sender's Number.	Day of Month.	In reply to Number.	
20/21	10		AAA

Ref to 28 I nov
/already disposed hold a
Company in reserve behind GRAND
BOIS aaa There should elements
of 1½ battns 58th Bde
holding a line in front
of you aaa Battn HQ in
PARAET FARM (014c 6.7) aaa
of 58th Bde are holding
a satisfactory line dispose
yourself in reserve in depth
behind them aaa Addsed
8th BW repld 58th Bde aaa

From: 4th R Bde
Place:
Time: 4.38 pm

The above may be forwarded as now corrected. (Z)

Censor. Signature of Addressor or person authorised to telegraph in his name.

"A" Form.
MESSAGES AND SIGNALS.

Army Form C.2121 (in pads of 100).

Prefix...........Code...........m.	Words	Charge	This message is on a/c of:	Recd. at...............m.
Office of Origin and Service Instructions.				Date.................
	Sent		.......................Service.	From.................
	At........m.			
	To.................			By.................
	By.................	(Signature of "Franking Officer.")		

TO { 8th Black Watch
     58th Bde

Sender's Number.	Day of Month.	In reply to Number.	
To 21	10		A A A

Detail one company to proceed via WYSCHAETE to cutting S of WYTSCHAETE pt (O.19.d) to support troops of 58th Bde defending WYTSCHAETE aaa Acknowledge and say if this is posible aaa addsed 8th Black Watch reptd 58th Bde aaa

From 58th Bde
Place
Time

The above may be forwarded as now corrected. (Z)   C...... Capt for Bde

Censor.   Signature of Addressor or person authorised to telegraph in his name.

750,000. W 2186—M509. H. W. & V., Ld. 6/16.

"A" Form
MESSAGES AND SIGNALS.

Army Form C. 2121
(in pads of 100).

TO	OC 58th Bde

Sender's Number.	Day of Month.	In reply to Number.	
BM 42	10		AAA

26th Bde is sending 2 Batts
to 27th Bde by order of
G.O.C. 9th Div as the situation
on your front is considered
satisfactory & that of the
WHITE CHATEAU is not.

The two Batts ordered to make
good at WYCHAET have been
cancelled.

G.O.C. has 2 Batts in hand at
Parret Camp.

From 26 Bde

"C" Form.
MESSAGES AND SIGNALS.

Army Form C. 2123.
(In books of 100).

No. of Message..........

Prefix.... Code.... Words....	Received.	Sent, or sent out.	Office Stamp.
£ s. d.	From..........	At.......... m.	
Charges to collect	By..........	To..........	
Service Instructions.		By..........	

Handed in at **7762** Office **5.20** m. Received **7.5** m.

TO **7N28**

*Sender's Number	Day of Month	In reply to Number	A A A
5409	10		

1 Messines and Wytschaete are now reported to be in our hands large numbers of the enemy have been seen approaching Messines from the E. 2 the 25 Bde under orders from 19 Divn is being directed to establish the General line Messines Pick House (O 26 A) to which 19 Divn are sending one Coy from Wytschaete 3 26 Bde less 1 Battn are not now required to occupy the line L'ENFER O 25 D TORREKEN CORNER O 20 D they will establish a line between the

FROM
PLACE & TIME

"C" Form.
MESSAGES AND SIGNALS.

Army Form C. 2123.
(In books of 100).

Received 7.5 pm

TO Fh 28

left	of	the	58	Bde
and	the	right	of	the
27	Bde	if	the	situation
permits	OOSTAVERNE		should	be
included	in	this	line	26
Bde	will	report	the	actual
line	taken	up	by	his
Bde	+	58	Bde	19
Divn	has	been	placed	under
orders	of	GOC	9	Divn

FROM 9 Divn

PLACE & TIME 3·45 PM

"C" Form.
MESSAGES AND SIGNALS.

Army Form C. 2125.
(In books of 100.)

No. of Message _____

| Prefix ___ Code ___ Words ___ | Received. From _Hill_ By _Pads_ | Sent, or sent out. At ___ m. To ___ By ___ | Office Stamp. |

Charges to Collect ___
Service Instructions ___

Handed in at ___ 11/9 ___ Office 10.50 m. Received 11.15 m.

TO ___ 58 Bde. ___

Sender's Number.	Day of Month.	In reply to Number.	AAA
G 420	11		

Situation report   am   62
Bde   in   touch   with
19th   R   at   PETITS
PUITS 026A   and   62
Bde   R.C.R.   strong   point
at   O.19 D 8 6   and   STAENYZER
CABT   and   3   coys
are   on   the   line
approx STAENYZER CABT — SOMER
FARM   are   strong   patrols
have   been   sent   towards
WICK   HOUSE   and   a
coy   is   working   forward
towards TURKEN CORNER and   7 B
Bde   reports   at   7.10

FROM	
TIME & PLACE	

*This line should be erased if not required.
100,000.—John Rissan, Ltd.—3/17.—8141. Forms C2125.

"C" Form.
MESSAGES AND SIGNALS.

Army Form C. 2123.
(In books of 100.)

No. of Message _____

Prefix ___ Code ___ Words ___	Received.	Sent, or sent out.	Office Stamp.
£ s. d.	From _____	At _____ m.	
Charges to Collect	By _____	To _____	
Service Instructions.		By	

Handed in at _____ Office _____ m. Received _____ m.

TO (2/0) 58 Bde.

Sender's Number.	Day of Month.	In reply to Number.	AAA
am	aaa	In	touch
with	62nd	Bde	about
O14.D02.	Their	line	runs
O14.A4.0	to	O8.C9.0	to
Dome	House	along	DAMM
STRASSE	probably	with	posts
in	front	aaa	line
thence	runs	south	by
to	STRASSE	along	road
to	HOLLEBEKE	nth	nth
of	HOLLEBEKE	are	held
Lifft	line	by forward posts
R.F.	been	withdrawn aaa
19th	Divn	reports	our
line	runs	just	west
of	MESSINES	to	MINE
FARM	thence	northwards	on

FROM

TIME & PLACE

*This line should be erased if not required.

"C" Form.
MESSAGES AND SIGNALS.

Army Form C. 2123.
(In books of 100.)

No. of Message _____

Prefix	Code	Words	Received.	Sent, or sent out.	Office Stamp
		£ s. d.	From	At ___ m.	
Charges to Collect			By	To	
Service Instructions.				By	

Handed in at _____ Office _____ m. Received _____

TO (3rd) 50 Bde

*Sender's Number.	Day of Month.	In reply to Number.	AAA
General	Line	of	Main
Road	aaa	added	26
2)	38	62	64
Bdes	plans	Divising CM	
CRES	Q	for	Cofm

FROM
TIME & PLACE   9th Div   10 am

*This line should be erased if not required.

"C" Form.
MESSAGES AND SIGNALS.

Army Form C. 2123
(In books of 100.)

Prefix.	Code	Words	Received.	Sent, or sent out.	Office Stamp
		£ s. d.	From	At .... m.	
Charges to Collect			By	To	
Service Instructions.			Baddy	By	

Handed in at .... Office .... m. Received ....

TO

*Sender's Number.	Day of Month.	In reply to Number.	AAA
G422	11		

Following from 27 Bde reserve at 10 am aaa 6 am Germans attacked line at OAK SUPPORT trying to get on north aaa attack repulsed with heavy loss aaa Machine Guns got on to them aaa Germans very disorganised now attacked again at S of OAK SUPPORT aaa of 50 men got close to our machine guns aaa m/g got a target of about 1000 men at

FROM

TIME & PLACE

*This line should be erased if not required.

100,000.—John Rissen, Ltd.—8/17.—P141. Forms C2123.

"C" Form.
MESSAGES AND SIGNALS.

Army Form C. 2123.
(In books of 100.)
No. of Message

Prefix....... Code....... Words.......	Received.	Sent, or sent out.	Office Stamp.
£ s. d.	From.......	At....... m.	
Charges to Collect	By.......	To.......	
Service Instructions.		By.......	

Handed in at....... Office....... m. Received....... m.

TO 2nd 58 Bde

*Sender's Number.	Day of Month.	In reply to Number.	AAA

effective range and dropped a lot of their own. They went back in a SE direction SW of HOLLEBEKE aaa artillery also got on to them aaa at 9 am they also attacked the Stables from the S aaa the heavy was repulsed with at 9 am he also attacked the Stables Seaforth from the to zero House aaa attack to held and has been driven back

FROM
TIME & PLACE

*This line should be erased if not required.

"C" Form.
MESSAGES AND SIGNALS.

Army Form C. 2123.
(In books of 100.)

No. of Message ....

Prefix	Code	Words	Received.	Sent, or sent out.	Office Stamp.
		£ s. d.	From	At .... m.	
Charges to Collect			By	To	
Service Instructions.				By	

Handed in at .... Office .... m. Received .... m.

TO .... 52 Div

Sender's Number.	Day of Month.	In reply to Number.	AAA
on	right	an	advd
9th	Corps	flank	Divns
26th	58th	62nd	& 64th
Bdes	CRA		

FROM .... 9 Divison Hqrs
TIME & PLACE

*This line should be erased if not required.

"C" Form.
MESSAGES AND SIGNALS.

Army Form C. 2123.
(In books of 100.)

No. of Message ....

Prefix.......Code......Words........	Received.	Sent, or sent out.	Office Stamp.
£ s. d.	From	At ....m.	
Charges to Collect	By	To	
Service Instructions.	Badds	By	

Handed in at .... Office 12:15 m. Received 33 m.

TO ....

*Sender's Number.	Day of Month.	In reply to Number.	AAA
G425	11		

Right Divisional Boundary as follows aaa PIPK HOUSE (to 9th Divn) — N30A57 — along road to KEMMEL (Road to 19th Divn) along road to N19C500 (Road to 19th Divn) left Divisional Boundary unchanged aaa added 36th 58th 62nd fifty Bdes Q CRA CRE ADMS 9th

FROM
TIME & PLACE 9th Divn. 12.20pm

*This line should be erased if not required.

"G" Form.
MESSAGES AND SIGNALS.

Army Form C. 2123.
(In books of 100.)

No. of Message _____

Prefix ___ Code ___ Words ___	Received.	Sent, or sent out.	Office Stamp
£ s. d.	From _____	At _____ m.	
Charges to Collect	By _____	To _____	
Service Instructions. X62		By _____	

Handed in at _____ Office 1.37 m. Received 1.47 m.

TO 58 Div

*Sender's Number.	Day of Month.	In reply to Number.	AAA
437	11		

Following wire received from General PLUMER AAA Begins AAA Please convey my congratulations to 9th Divn on repulsing enemy attacks successfully this morning AAA their determined resistance is a great help AAA also AAA the Corps and Divnl Commanders wish to add their congratulations AAA

FROM Barnes
TIME & PLACE

"C" Form.
MESSAGES AND SIGNALS.

Army Form C. 2123.
(In books of 100.)

No. of Message

Prefix .... Code .... Words 56
Charges to Collect
Service Instructions. 3addio Urgent operation Priority

Received. From 48
By OShirley

Sent, or sent out.
At .... m.
To ....
By ....

Office Stamp.

Handed in at .... Office .... m. Received 1.16 p.m.

TO 26 Inf/Bde. 58 Inf/Bde. 62 Inf/Bde.
G Adm

*Sender's Number.	Day of Month.	In reply to Number.	AAA
G 428	11		
GOC	will	meet	Bde
Commanders 26	27	58	
62	64	Bdes	at
26	Bde	HQ	PARRITT
CAMP	N17A0.8	at	2
pm	today	aaa	Car
will	be	at	SPOIL
BANK	at	1.30	pm
to	fetch	Bde	Commanders
27	and	64	Bdes.
aaa	acknowledge	addso 26	
27	58	62	64
Inf	Bdes		

FROM 9th Div
TIME & PLACE 1pm

*This line should be erased if not required.

"A" Form
MESSAGES AND SIGNALS.

Army Form C. 2121
(In pads of 100)

Prefix	Code	m.	Words.	Charge.		No. of Message
Office of Origin and Service Instructions				This message is on a/c of:		Recd. at ... m.
Urgent			Sent			Date. 12.IV.18
Priority			At ...... m.	Service.		From
			To			
			By	(Signature of "Franking Officer.")		By

TO: 31 Inf Bde   62nd Inf Bde
    32 Inf Bde   64th " "
    58 " "   CRA   Q

Sender's Number	Day of Month	In reply to Number.	AAA
* G 452	12		

Our artillery is carrying out counter preparation this evening as follows AAA Field arty zero hour 7·30 pm for fifteen minutes on probable assembly area as AAA Heavy arty zero hour 7 pm for twenty four minutes added all Inf Bdes. and Q CRE

From: 9th Div
Place:
Time: 5·30 pm

The above may be forwarded as now corrected. (Z)

Censor.   Signature of Addressor or person authorised to telegraph in his name.

* This line should be erased if not required.

(7981) Wt. W. 90/M1647 130,000 Pads 5/17 D. D. & L. E1187

LW
88 Bde

To recipients of Operation Order No. 211.

G455   18.   AAA

Ref. 9th Div. Order No. 211 of to-days date
para 9 AAA Composite Bde. 29th Divn. is not under
orders of G.O.C. 9th Divn. But G.O.C. 9th Divn. can
call upon it in case of need AAA Location of Bde.
is as follows AAA Bde. H.Q., DUMFORD HOUSE and Bns.
are in close vicinity AAA Addvs. Recipients of
Order No. 211.

9th Division.

10.45 P.M.   [signature]

Lt.Col.
G.S.

"C" Form.
MESSAGES AND SIGNALS.
Army Form C 2123.
(In books of 100).
No. of Message.........

Prefix......Code......Words......	Received	Sent, or sent out.	Office Stamp.
£ s. d.	From...............	At ....m	
Charges to Collect	By..................	To	
Service Instructions		By	

Urgent Priority

Handed in at............... Office 1.59ᵃ m. Received 2.7ᵃ m.

TO: 58th Inf Bde

Sender's Number	Day of Month	In reply to Number	AAA
G 460	13		
Our	Artillery	will	carry
out	Counter	preparation	today
as	follows	aaa	Field
Arty	Zero	Hour	5.30
am	for	10	minutes
aaa	Heavy	Arty	Zero
Hour	5.30	am	for
30 minutes aaa	added	all	
2 f	Bdes		

FROM PLACE & TIME: 9th Div 1.40 am

"C" Form.   Army Form C 2123.
(In books of 100).
MESSAGES AND SIGNALS. No. of Message........

Prefix....Code....Words....	Received	Sent, or sent out.	Office Stamp.
£ s. d.	From................	At................m	
Charges to Collect	By................	To................	
Service Instructions MOST Urgent operations		By................	

Handed in at Urgent Office 9.40 m Received 10.46 m

TO 58 Bde

* Sender's Number	Day of Month	In reply to Number	AAA
G.14/4	1st		
58	Bde	will	move
at	once	by	the
ω̄	CLYTE + KINMEL	Road to	
a	position	of	assembly
astride	that	road inc	
NIM6	and	D	AM
58	Bde	will send	
an	officer	at	once
to	HQ 57	Bde	
at	N26.B9.1	Orders	
for	58	Bde	will
be	sent	to	HQ
57	Bde	by	9th
Divn			
	rec	10.47 am	

FROM PLACE & TIME	9th Divn 10.30 AM

* This line should be erased if not required
(5554). Wt.14832/M1523. 2/17. 400m Books, N.P.Co. (E930). A.F. C2123.

SECRET

1st SOUTH AFRICAN INFANTRY BRIGADE ORDER No 183

REF SHEET 28 SW   13.4.1918

1. The 1st SOUTH AFRICAN Bde and details of the 10th ROYAL WARWICKS and 6th S.W.B. will be relieved on the night of the 13th/14th April by the 58th Infantry Brigade.

2. The portion of the line held by the S.A. Brigade and details of the 57th Bde (from N.36.a.73 to MAGDELSTEDE Fm) will be taken over by the 6th WILTSHIRE Regt on the Right and the 9th ROYAL WELSH FUSILIERS on the left. The Boundary between the two battalions being approximately from Road junction at N.30.d.6.3 on Outpost Line to N.30.a.5.1.

3. All details of relief will be arranged by the Bn. Units concerned.

4. S.O.S. Rt Grenades and Reserve S.A.A. will be handed over to incoming Units on Relief.

5. On relief the SA Bde will march via KEMMEL to LA CLYTTE and will be billeted in camp to be arranged by Staff Captain who will meet units on arrival.

6. Rations will be dumped at and a hot meal prepared at for Units on arrival

7. 1st line Transport will not move for the present.

8. Completion of relief will be notified to Bde HQ by the question "WHEN ARE RATIONS COMING UP".

9. Bde HQ will close on completion of relief at N26 b.q.1 and open at LA CLYTTE on arrival

10 Acknowledge

Issued at 8.30 pm
1 – 4th Regts
9th Divn
19th "
57th Bde
58th "

[signature] Capt
Bde Major
1st SA Infy Bde

(S.O. 1074). Wt. W 4819/M920 11/16. 50,000 Pads. McC. & Co., Ltd.

"B" Form.
MESSAGES AND SIGNALS.

Army Form C. 2122.

688 703

No. of Message............

Prefix	Code	m.	Received	Sent	Office Stamp
Office of Origin and Service Instructions.	Words.	At _____ m	At _____ m	
	13	From	To 119	
		By	By	

TO: 58 Bde

Sender's Number.	Day of Month.	In reply to Number.	A A A

From: 4 Div
Place:
Time:

* This line should be erased if not required.

"C" Form.
MESSAGES AND SIGNALS.

Army Form C. 2123.
(In books of 100.)

No. of Message _____

Prefix	Code	Words	Received.	Sent, or sent out.	Office Stamp.
	£ s. d.		From	At m.	
Charges to Collect			By	To	
Service Instructions				By	

Handed in at _____ Office ____ m. Received 11.17 m.

TO .....58 Bde.....

* Sender's Number	Day of Month.	In reply to Number	A A A
508	15	—	
Ref	our	order	No
212	at 15th Inst	lines	
two	and three	of	
have	two	aaa	for
"which will be			at
SP	236 (2362)	read	
"which will be			at
SP	2230 (3022)	add	
aaa	recipients	20	No
212	2am	20th	Inf
Bde	to	acknowledge	

FROM
PLACE & TIME ....
8/30 pm

This line should be erased if not required

BELGIUM AND PART OF FRANCE

1:40,000

BELGIUM AND PART OF FRANCE   EDITION 3.   SHEET 28.

Vol. 3

Headquarters
58th Inf. Bde.
(19th Div.)
May 1916

On His Majesty's Service.

Army Form C. 2118.

WAR DIARY
or
INTELLIGENCE SUMMARY.
(Erase heading not required.)

Instructions regarding War Diaries and Intelligence Summaries are contained in F. S. Regs., Part II. and the Staff Manual respectively. Title pages will be prepared in manuscript.

Place	Date	Hour	Summary of Events and Information	Remarks and references to Appendices
H.27.b.6.7.	MAY 1st		Quiet day and night.	
	2nd	10.30.am.	Visit by Divisional Commander. A quiet day and night.	
	3rd	2.40pm.	Wire from Division giving warning of possible attack next morning. A moderately quiet day. Hostile barrage S of Bde. sector put down about 8.p.m.	
	4th		Night of 3/4th quiet. Counter-preparation shoot by Artillery in early hours. Four prisoners captured near BURLINGFORD FARM 2 by 9th R.W.F., 2 by 9th Welch Regt. Quiet day.	
	5th	12.30am.	Night of 4/5th quiet. Counter-preparation by artillery until 4.30.a.m. 1 prisoner captured by 9th Welch Regt. Quiet day and night.	
	6th		Quiet day and night.	
	7th		Situation normal. Usual shelling forward area and some of back area.	
	8th	3.am.	Night of 7/8th quiet until 3.a.m. Enemy barrage on our Right - also shelling of back areas - some gas.	
		5.45am.	2 prisoners captured by 98th Bde. state enemy proposed to attack at 7.30.a.m. English time from KEMMEL HILL N. on front of 3 kilos.	
		8.am.	Fire slightly decreased.	
		9.45am.	98th Bde report enemy broken through 30th Composite Bde. and advancing Westward from N.4.d. and N.5.c. 98th Bde hold defensive flank from RIDGE WOOD to DICKEBUSCH LAKE.	
		12.30.pm.	Order from Div. that 57th Bde. were to be prepared to assist 33rd Div. Verbal reports that 19th Bde. were coming up to restore situation	
		1.30.pm.	98th Bde. definitely not in RIDGE WOOD. line of 30th Composite Bde. given as KLEINE VIERSTRAAT CABT. N.4.d.5.9. 19th Bde. in conjunction with 32nd French Div. to counter-attack at 7.p.m.	
		7.p.m.	Counter-attack believed to have been successful and original line restored. Remainder of the night quiet.	
	9th	4.p.m.	A fairly quiet day, the usual shelling of our line and battery areas. Reserve Coy. 6th Wilts to relieve 1 Coy. of 9th R.W.F. (Copy Bde. Order No.243 attached and marked "A").	

WAR DIARY
or
INTELLIGENCE SUMMARY.
(Erase heading not required.)

Army Form C. 2118.

Place	Date	Hour	Summary of Events and Information	Remarks and references to Appendices
H.27.b.6.7.	9th		Wire received from Division in evening stating 56th Bde. would relieve us on night 10th/11th. A quiet night.	
	10th.		A quiet day. Preparation for relief. 56th Bde brought up by light railway to PIONEER JUNCTION H.16.c.6.0. 58th Bde taken back by train to L.17.d. and marched to Camps in Squares K & L. Bde.H.Q. K.12.b.7.5. Relief complete 5.30.a.m. (Copy Bde. Order No. 244 attd. and marked "B")	B.
K.13.b.7.5.	11th.		Battalions reorganising.	
	12th		Brigade moved by march route to HERZEELE Area (Copy Bde. Order No. 245 attd. and marked "C")	C.
HERZEELE	13th		Absorption of 6th Wilts by 2nd Wilts (Copies of instructions relating thereto attd. and marked S.G.	S.G.
	15th.			
to	15th.		Battalions reorganising and training.	
	16th.			
	17th.		Bde. moved by rail to CHALONS area Copy Bde order No. 246 and copies B.M.552 and S.C.8385 and S.C.8386 attd. and marked D.E.F. and G respectively).	D, E, F and G.
	19th.			
	28th.		Battalions Training.	
CHEPY.	28th.		Transport and mounted personnel and horses moved by road to area JUVIGNY - TOURS - BISSEUL. Copy Bde. Order No. 247nattached and marked"H").	H.
	28th.			
	31st.		See copy of narrative of Operations attached and marked "J".	J.
22.6.18.				

[signature]
for Lieutenant Colonel
Commanding 58th Infantry Brigade.

SECRET "A" Copy No. 6

58th Brigade Order No. 243.

1. 6th Bn WILTS Regt. will place his reserve Company at the disposal of O.C. 9/R.W.F. from to-night till further orders to relieve one Company of 9/R.W.F. in the Line.

2. The Coy. 9/R.W.F. so relieved will move into reserve to 6/WILTS and will then come under orders of O.C. 6/WILTS.

3. O.C. 9/R.W.F. will then command for tactical purposes 3 Coys of his own Battalion and 1 Coy. 6th WILTS. O.C. 6th WILTS will for tactical purposes command 3 Coys of his own Battalion and 1 Coy. 9/R.W.F.

4. For administrative purposes Coys. will remain under their own Battalions.

5. O.C. 9/R.W.F. will report completion of relief and O.C. 6/WILTS arrival of 1 Coy. R.W.F. in reserve position to G.H.Q.2 Line by wiring code "YES PLEASE".

6. 9/R.W.F. and 6/WILTS acknowledge.

Captain
Brigade Major 58th Infantry Brigade.

Issued at 4.p.m. 9-5-18.

Copy No. 1 9/R.W.F.
2 9/Welch.
3 6/Wilts.
4 10/Worc. R.
5 58/T.M.B.
6) War Diary.
7)
8 File.

SECRET.   Copy No.......

58th Brigade Order No. 244.

Ref. map YPRES. Sht. 1/40,000.
        28 N.W. 1/20,000
        Sheet 27, 1/40,000.

1. The 58th Inf. Bde. will be relieved by the 56th Inf. Bde. in the 19th Div. Sector on night 10/11th May as follows :-

   a. 9th Welch R. in the left sub-sector will be relieved by the 8/N.Staffs. Regt.

   b. 9th R.W.F. and troops under tactical command of O.C. 9th R.W.F. in the right sub-sector will be relieved by 1/4th K.S.L.I.

   c. 6th Wilts R. and troops under tactical command of O.C. 6th Wilts in support will be relieved by 9th Cheshire Regt.

   d. 58th T.M.Battery will be relieved by 56th T M.Battery.

   The 10th Worc. R. will remain in their present position and come under orders of G.O.C, 56th Bde. on completion of relief.

2. Advance parties from each unit of 56th Bde. will report at the Bn.H.Q. of the Bn. they will relieve at to-night at about mid-day.

3. Guides at the rate of 1 per Coy. and Bn H.Q. will be on the VLAMERTINGHE - KRUISSTRAAT Road at H.23.a.1.2. at 9.p.m. to guide their respective parties to Bn H.Q. Platoon guides will meet incoming Coys. at Bn H.Q.

4. On relief units of the 58th Bde. will proceed to PIONEER Junction H.16.c.6.0. and entrain as they arrive. Entraining arrangements will be supervised by the Staff Captain. The detraining point will be at FOUL WIND L.17.d.
   Guides from all units will meet each train at detraining point and guide their respective parties to their camps. These guides will be found from Depot personnel. Train journey takes approximately 1 hr. and 20 mins.
   The Coy. of the 6th Wilts Regt. at present in the line with 9th R.W.F. will rejoin its Bn in camp; similarly Coy. of 9th R.W.F. with 6th Wilts.   Units will report their arrival in camp to Bde. H.Q.

5. All orders and instructions as regards defence of the line, maps and aeroplane photos will be handed over to incoming units.

6. Administrative Instructions are being issued separately by Staff Captain.

7. Completion of relief will be wired to Bde.H.Q. using the name of the commanding officer as the code word.

8. Command of the sector will pass to G.O.C. 56th Bde. on relief at which hour Bde.H.Q. will close at WALKER CAMP H.27.b.5.7. and re-open on arrival at K.12.b.

9. Acknowledge.

                                                              Captain
                                         Brigade Major 58th Infantry Brigade.

Issued at 12 noon 10/5/18.

Copy No. 1 9.R.W.F.   5 Staff Capt   10. 18 Bde   15. War Diary
         2 9/Welch   6 Capt A.L. Wayne   11. 98 Bde   16.
         3 6/Wilts   7 19 Div   12. 245 Bde R.F.A   17. File
         4 58/T.m.B   8 56 Bde   13. 246 Bde R.F.A   18. 575 W.B
                          9 57 Bde   14. Signals   19. 82/Fd.Coy R.E
                                                                    20. 94/Fd.Coy R.E

SECRET.   Copy No. 19

58th Infantry Brigade Order No. 245.

11th May, 1918.

Map ref/ Sheet 19) 1/40,000.
         Sheet 27)

1. The 58th Infantry Brigade and No. 4 Coy. 19th Divl. Train will march to the HERZEELE Area to-morrow the 12th inst. in accordance with the attached March Table.
   Dress: Fighting Order.

2. The following intervals will be maintained during the march:-

   Between Battalions 500 yards.
   Between Companies. 150 yards.
   Between Rear Coy. and Transport 100 yards.
   Between every six vehicles 25 yards.

3. Lewis Gun Limbers, Cookers, Water-carts, *Maltese Carts* and Mess Carts will march with Battalions. The remainder of the transport will march brigaded under the orders of B.T.O.

4. Captain A.L.MAY, M.C. will arrange for guides to meet units and the transport en route.

5. Three lorries are allotted to the Brigade for surplus kit. Distribution of these will be arranged by the Staff Captain.

6. When reporting arrival in billets Battalions will give exact location of Battalion H.Qrs.

7. Brigade H.Q. will close at K.12.b.7.7. at 8.45.a.m.

8. The 94th Field Coy. will march independently from their transport lines to HERZEELE Area on 13th inst. O.C., 94th Field Coy. R.E. will report time of marching as early as possible, to Brigade H.Q. when arrangements will be made for guides to meet the Coy. on the HOUTKERQUE - HERZEELE Road.

9. 19th M.G.Battn. and 59th Field Ambulance are marching to HERZEELE Area under orders of 19th Div. They will report to Brigade H.Q. as early as possible date, time and place they wish guides to meet them to show them their billets.

10. Acknowledge.

                                                                    (signed)
                                                                    Captain
                                                 Brigade Major 58th Infantry Brigade.

Issued through Signals at *10.30 p.m.*

Copy No. 1 9.R.W.Fusrs.   11 56th Inf. Bde.
         2 9.Welch R.   12 57th Inf. Bde.
         3 6.Wilts. R.   13 No. 4 Coy. 19th Div. Train.
         4 58th T.M.B.   14 59th Fld. Amb.
         5 G.O.C.   15 19th M.G.Battn.
         6 Staff Capt.   16 94th Fld Coy. R.E.
         7 B.T.O.   17 A.P.M., 19th Div.
         8 Bde. Sig. Offr.   18 File.
         9 Bde. Int. Offr.   19) War Diary.
        10 19th Div. G.   20)
                                   21 *Capt. A.L.May. M.C.*

March Table issued with 58th Infantry Brigade Order No. 245.

Unit.	Starting Point.	Time of passing Starting Point.	Route.	Remarks.
58th Brigade H.Q.) 58th T.M.Battery.)	Cross Roads K.12.c.6.4.	9.0.a.m.	Starting Point to Cross Roads K.17.b. 55.90. - WATOU - HOUTKERQUE - HERZEELE.	
9th Bn R.W.Fusiliers.	-do-	9.4.a.m.	-do-	
6th Bn Wiltshire Regt.	-do-	9.19.a.m.	-do-	
9th Bn Welch Regiment.	-do-	9.34.a.m.	-do-	
Brigade Transport.			St. JAN-ter-BIEZEN - AU TROIS ROIS - HOUTKERQUE - HERZEELE	Will march under orders of B.T.O. not to pass Road Junction E.21.b.central before 11.a.m.
No.4 Coy. 19th Div. Train.				To march independently so as not to interfere with above moves.

To all recipients of 58th Brigade Order No.246.

  Reference para. 1 of above order for "15th instant" read "16th instant".

                Captain,
      for Brigade Major 58th Infantry Brigade.

14.5.18.

HEADQUARTERS,
58th BRIGADE.
No. B.16 547
Date.

SECRET   Copy No.....

58th Brigade Order No. 246.

Ref map Sheet 19, 1/40,000.
      Sheet 27, 1/40,000.   14th May, 1918.

1. The 58th Infantry Brigade Group consisting of the undermentioned units will entrain at REXPOEDE Station (V.3.d. Sheet 19) on the 15th instant. Times of entrainment will be notified later :-

    58th Brigade H.Q.   58th T.M.Battery.
    Bde. Signal Section.   19th M.G.Battalion.
    9th Bn R.W.Fusrs.   94th Field Coy. R.E.
    9th Bn Welch Regt.   59th Field Ambulance.
    2nd Bn Wiltshire Regt.   No. 4 Coy. 19th Divl. Train.
                                       No. 320 Employment Coy.

2. The senior Officer travelling on each train will be O.C. Train and will be responsible for the discipline of the troops travelling on his train.
    Attention is drawn to para. 15 of 19th Div. Q/474/C.
    O.C. Train will be responsible that these picquets are detailed.

3. Entraining and Detraining Officers will be detailed as follows :-

    Entraining Officers.
    9th Bn Welch Regt. will detail two Officers (one to be a Major or Captain) to report to R.T.O., REXPOEDE as laid down in para. 4 Q/474/C.

    Detraining Officers.
    9th Bn R.W.Fusrs. will detail two Officers (one to be a Major or Captain) to travel by No. 1 Train and report to R.T.O. detraining station vide para. 5 Q/474/C.

4. Advance parties.
    The following advanced parties will proceed by No. 1 Train vide para 23 Q/474/C.
              Brigade H.Q..... 2 O.R.
              T.M.Battery.... 1 Officer 1 O.R.
              Battalions..... 1 Officer 5 O.R. each.
              94th Field Co.. 1 Officer 2 O.R.
              59th Field Amb. 1 Officer 2 O.R.
              No. 4 Coy Train 1 Officer 1 O.R.

    Above party will report to Captain E.B.SAUNDERS, M.C., 9th Bn Welch Regt. at entraining station 2 hours before time of departure of No. 1 Train.
    Captain E.B. Saunders, M.C. will detail the senior officer of this party to take charge of the whole party who will report to the Staff Captain at the detraining station for further instructions.
    Two complete days' rations to be carried.

5. Loading and Unloading parties will be detailed as under :-

    Loading Party vide para. 6 Q/474/C.
    This party will be detailed from "C" and "D" Companies 19th M.G.Battalion.
    The Officer in charge of this party will thoroughly reconnoitre the entraining station forthwith.
    A billet for this party in the immediate vicinity of the station will be found by the Staff Captain.

- 2 -

Unloading Party vide para 7 Q/474/C. will be found by 9th Bn Welch Regt. This party accompanied by 1 Cooker will travel by No. 1 Train.

6. **Lorries for Surplus kit.**
Three lorries for the Brigade, divided as under, will report to Brigade H.Q. on the 15th inst. Battalions (not M.G. Battalion) and T.M.Battery will each detail a guide at a time to be notified later to report to Brigade H.Q. to guide lorries to Q.M. Stores.

Brigade H.Q. and 2nd Wilts Regt......... 1 lorry.
9th Bn R.W.Fusiliers and T.M.Battery.... 1 lorry.
9th Bn Welch Regt and Bde Canteen....... 1 lorry.

Instructions will be issued later with reference to the packs of the 2nd Wilts Regt.

7. Reference para 16 of 19th Div. Q/474/C for 9th Bn Welch Regt. complete read 9th Bn Welch Regt. less 1 Coy. and Cooker. This Coy. and Cooker will proceed by No. 1 Train vide para. 5 of this order.

8. Acknowledge.

F.H.Fraser
Captain

Brigade Major 58th Infantry Brigade.

Issued through Signals at 1.p.m. 14.5.18.

```
Copy No. 1 9.R.W.Fusrs.
       2 9 Welch R.
       3 2.Wilts R.
       4 58.T.M.B.
       5 G.O.C.
       6 Staff Capt.
       7 Bde. Sig. Offr.
       8 B.T.O.
       9 Bde. Int. Offr.
      10 19th Div. G.
      11 19th Div. Q.
      12 56th Inf Bde.
      13 57th Inf. Bde.
      14 A.P.M., 19th Div.
      15 19th M.G.Battn.
      16 94th Fld. Coy. R.E.
      17 59th Fld. Amb.
      18 No 4 Coy. 19th Div. Train.
      19 O.C. 220 Employment Coy
      20 Major E.L.MILLS, M.C., 9.R.W.F.
      21 Captain E.B.SAUNDERS, M.C., 9th Welch Regt.
      22 R.T.O.,RUXFOEDE.
```

19th Div. No. Q/474/C issued to units of 58th Bde. Major E.L.Mills and Captain E.B.Saunders only.

19th Division No. A/466/C.
58th Brigade No. ~~XXXX~~ S.C.8346.

58th Inf. Bde.

30th Div "Q" (for inf).

1. In continuation of this office No. A/466/C, dated 7.5.18.
The 2nd Bn Wilts Regt. complete with 1st Line Transport, less baggage and supply wagons, and consisting of about 250 All Ranks will arrive in your area to-morrow, the 13th instant, the personnel by bus and the transport by road.

2. On arrival of personnel please despatch the Battalion Training Staff of the 6th Wilts, accompanied by nominal roll, in the same busses to report to Rear H.Q. 21st Bde. at BUYSCHEERE where they will receive further instructions.

3. At the same time despatch to same destination from the 1st line transport of the 6th Wilts, the vehicles etc. as laid down in the Battn. Training Staff Schedule.

4. Further orders will be issued re the disposal of the balance of the 1st line transport of the 6th Wilts Regt.

5. The new 2nd Wilts (late 6th Wilts) will be made up to 40 Officers and 900 Other Ranks and will be known as the 2nd Bn Wiltshire Regiment from the 13th instant.

6. The surplus personnel left over after amalgamation will be despatched to CALAIS in accordance with Second Army letter No. A.1496 dated 4th May, 1918, on receipt of further orders from this office when train arrangements will be notified you.
Nominal rolls of Officers and Other Ranks will accompany each party to the Base.
Nominal rolls of Officers and Other Ranks despatched to the Base will be forwarded by the Battalion concerned direct to D.A.G., 3rd Echelon, and in the case of Officers 3 copies will be sent to this office.

7. Nominal rolls of Officers and Other Ranks transferred from the 6th Wilts to 2nd Wilts will be forwarded by the 6th Wilts direct to D.A.G. 3rd Echelon and in the case of Officers 3 copies will be forwarded to this office.

8. On completion of amalgamation a nominal roll of Officers forming the Battalion Training Staff will be forwarded to this office in triplicate and one copy direct by you to D.A.G. 3rd Echelon.

9. The Battalion Training Staff of 6th Wilts will take rations for consumption on 14th instant.

10. Baggage and supply wagons of 6th Wilts will remain with 2nd Wilts wil after amalgamation.

D.H.Q.
12.5.18.

(sd) GEORGE HAWES? Lieut-Colonel
A.A.&.Q.M.G., 19th Division.

6th Bn Wiltshire Regiment.

For information and necessary action.
Please note:-
1. The total numbers sent away will be as laid down in S.C.111 less the following
 (a). Qr.Mr. and Hon. Capt. W.B. HARRIS who will join Training Staff as soon as fit.
 (b). 2nd Lieut. ROBINSON and his servant who will join Training Staff on completion of Course.

(c).
P.T.O.

Second Army. XXII Corps   19th Division No. A.466/C.
A.1496,   A.4154/26.

XXII Corps.

1.   Reference to Second Army G.867 dated 3.5.1918 (O.B.2216 dated 2.5.1918) and Second Army G.863 dated 3.5.1918 (O.B.1851.A. dated 2.5.18)

     x   x   x   x   x   x

     x   x   x   x   x   x

5.   Personnel for withdrawal to the Base will be despatched by you to CALAIS by empty supply trains from Divisional Railheads under arrangements to be made by you with Traffic, ST.OMER.

6.   (a) Nominal roll of Officers and other ranks will accompany each party.

   (b) Nominal rolls of Officers and other ranks despatched to the Base will be forwarded by Units concerned direct to D.A.G., 3rd Echelon.

   (c) Nominal rolls of Officers despatched to the Base will be forwarded by the Units concerned direct to A.G., G.H.Q.

7.   Base Commandant, CALAIS should be informed by wire of the despatch of this personnel.

Headquarters,   (Sgd) J.C.CHAYTOR, Lieut-Colonel.
  Second Army.   A.A.G., Second Army.

2.

Headquarters,
  58th Inf.Brigade.

   For information and necessary action in due course.

   The personnel composing the Battalion Training Staff of the 6th Bn. Wiltshire Regt is to be detailed in readiness to be transferred to the 30th Division at short notice.

D.H.Q.   (Sgd) G. HAWES, Lieut-Colonel.
7.5.18.   A.A. & Q.M.G., 19th Division.

Second Army No. G.867.
3rd May, 1918.

XXII Corps.

In consequence of the shortage of Infantry reinforcements, the following transfers and amalgamations will take place forthwith. In each case the Battalion which is absorbed will form a Training Staff on the approved establishment and be transferred to a cadre Division, while personnel rendered surplus will be sent to the Base to be held as Reinforcements for Battalions of their own Regiment.

The following transfers and amalgamations to take place shortly; further orders to be issued.

(c). 2nd Wilts Regt. from 30th Division to 19th Division to absorb 6th Wilts Regt.

Battalion Training Staffs of 6th Yorks, 6th Wilts, and 7th Bedfords to be transferred to the 30th Division.

Instructions as to the disposal of personnel and as to the re-adjustment and disposal of transport will be issued by the D.A.&.Q.M.G.

(sd) L.H. MANTEN, Captain
for M.G., G.S.
Second Army.

SECRET.   58th Brigade No. C.R.558.

E.

Reference 58th Infantry Brigade C.O. 246 of the 11th inst.

1. The times of departure of trains are being notified by the Staff Captain.

2. The following are the routes to be used to reach the entraining station :-

(a). BAMBECQUE - V.22.c.4.9. - V.15.a.4.6. - V.9.d.6.6. - V.9.a.9.9. Station V.3.d.

(b). D.12.d.8.1. - V.19.c.5.1. - V.20.a.3.2. - V.20.a.2.6. - V.9.d.6.6. V.9.a.9.9. Station V.3.d.

3. Troops proceeding by trains No's 4 and 13 will march to the entraining station in accordance with the following table. All other troops will march independently using either of above routes suitable. Troops to arrive 1½ hours transport 3 hours before departure of train.

Unit.	From.	To.	Starting Point.	Time of passing S.P.	Route.
Train No. 4.					
58th Bde.H.Q. & Sig. Sec.	HERZEELE.	Station V.3.d.	Road junc. D.10.c.35.80.	4.20.p.m. 16th inst	Route (a) as laid down in para. 2 above.
58th T.M.B.	"	"	"	4.23.p.m. 16th inst	"
59.Fld. Amb.	"	"	"	4.25.p.m. 16th inst	"
1 Coy. 2nd Bn Wiltshire Regt	"	"	"	4.30.p.m. 16th inst	"

Transport of the above units will march under the orders of the B.T.O. and will use route (a) so as to arrive at station by 4.32.p.m. 16th inst.

Train No. 13.					
94th Fld.Co. R.E.	Billets.	Station V.3.d.	Cross roads V.25.a.5.5.	3.25.a.m. 17th inst	Route (b) as laid down in para 2 above.
No.4 Co.Train.	Billets.	"	"	3.35.a.m. 17th inst	Route (b) from V.19.c.5.1.
220.Employment Coy.	March to entraining station independently and report to O.C., 94th Field Coy. R.E. 1½ hours before departure of the Train.				

4. The usual distances between Companies and between vehicles will be maintained during march to entraining station and march from detraining station.

5. Dress "Fighting Order". Unit Commanders will ensure that their men commence the journey with full waterbottles.

6. A representative of Brigade H.Q., Captain E.O. LAUDERDALE, will remain behind until the Brigade Group has entrained. He will establish his H.Qrs. at the R.T.O's. Office REXPOEDE.

7. Acknowledge.

[signature]
Captain

Brigade Major 59th Infantry Brigade.

Brigade H.Q.

15th May, 1918.

Issued to all recipients of 58th Inf. Bde. O.O. No. 246.

To all recipients of 58th Brigade Order No. 246.

[Stamp: HEADQUARTERS, 58TH INFANTRY BRIGADE. No. SG 8385 Date.......]

Reference 58th Brigade Order No. 246 :-

1. Herewith Appendix "A" giving Supply Arrangements. Units should arrange to have Camp kettles loaded on the train where there can be easily got at for use at halts.

2. There are three halts, viz at :- NOYELLES, PONTOISE and CHATEAU THIERY. Duration of halts are not known but will probably be between 2 - 4 hours.

3. Train journey is believed to be about 36 hours. Troops will detrain at one of the following Stations :- VITRY-LA-VILLE - CHALONS COOLUS or CHALONS LANGRIERE.

4. Trains are timed to leave as under :-

    Train No. 1   15.32   on   16th.
           4   19.32   "   "
           7   23.32   "   "
          10   3.32   "   17th.
          13   7.32   "   "
          16   11.32   "   "
          19   15.32   "   "
          22   19.32   "   "

5. Breast ropes will be issued to units at the Station by a representative of D.A.D.O.S.

6. Lorries will report at HERZEELE CHURCH as follows :-

    1 lorry for Bde H.Q. and 2/Wilts - 10 a.m. 16th inst.
    1   "   " 9/R.W.F. and 58/T.M.B - 12 noon "   "
    1   "   " 9/Welch. and Bde Canteen 12 m/n 16/17th inst.

Units will arrange to have all Quartermaster's Stores, surplus kits and any mens packs at present with units carried to the Station on these lorries where they will be loaded on to the train by which units are travelling.

Units will send guides to meet lorries at place and time stated. In the case of the first two lorries Brigade H.Q. and T.M.Battery will load first and Battalions afterwards. If absolutely necessary lorries may do two journeys but this must be avoided if possible.

                                           Captain,
                          for Staff Captain 58th Infantry Brigade.

Brigade H.Q.

    15th May 1918.

G

58th Brigade No S.C.3385.

To all recipients of 58th Brigade Order No. 246.

Reference S.C.8385 dated 15.5.18 :-

WATERING HORSES.

Transport Officers must make the necessary arrangements to ensure that all animals get at least one gallon of water every four hours during the journey. It is suggested that the Petrol tins at present on charge of Quartermasters be filled before entraining and distributed along that part of the train in which the animals are.

All Water Carts should be entrained full and two should be placed on the train at a convenient spot near the animals.

A.L.May Captain.
for Staff Captain 58th Infantry Brigade.

Brigade H.Q.
15th May 1918.

SECRET.

Copy No. 12

58th Infantry Brigade Order No. 247.

26th May, 1918.

Refce maps:-
   CHALONS SHEET No. 17 1/20,000
   Chalons Sheet) 1/80,000
   REIMS   ")

1. The Divisional Artillery and all Transport, Mounted Personnel and Horses will move to-day under command of Brig-General W.P. Monkhouse, C.M.G., M.V.O. by road to the area JUVIGNY - TOURS - BISSEUL.
   The March will be continued on the 29th inst.
   The Brigade Transport plus 31st M.V. Section will move under command of the B.T.O. in accordance with attached march table.

2. Dismounted personnel including M.G.Battalion with machine guns and a proportion of ammunition will be moved by motor bus at a date to be notified later.

3. Arrangements in regard to cooking, Lewis Guns and signalling Equipment will be as stated in S.C.112/1 issued on the 27th inst.

4. Acknowledge.

E. Lauderdale
Captain
for Brigade Major 58th Infantry Brigade.

Issued at 7am.

   Copy No. 1. C.O.C.
        2. 9/...F.
        3. 9/ elch R.
        4. 2/Wilts R.
        5. 58.M.G.B.
        6. 31. M.V.S.
        7. Staff Capt.
        8. B.T.O.
        9. S.T.O.
        10. 19th Div. G.
        11. O.C. Signals.
        12) War Diary.
        13)
        14 File.

March Table to accompany 58th Infantry Brigade Order No. 247.

Unit.	Starting Point.	Hour of passing Starting Point.	Route.
H.Q. 58th Brigade.	Cross roads in CAMPY Village on the ST. GERMAIN - CAMPY - MINGEM Road.	11.15.a.m.	MEMPY - CAMPY - CHALONS thence by road north of MARNE.
9th Bn N.F.Fus.	- do -	11.17.a.m.	- do -
9th Bn Essex Regt.	- do -	11.19.a.m.	- do -
2nd Bn Wilts Regt.	- do -	11.21.a.m.	- do -
21st Mob. Vet. Sectn.	- do -	11.23.a.m.	- do -

58th INFANTRY BRIGADE.

NARRATIVE OF OPERATIONS
From May 28th to May 31st, 1918.

May 28th. 4.0.p.m.	At about 4.p.m. a message was received from Division intimating that the Division would probably embus that evening, in any case units were to be prepared to embus at short notice.
7.0.p.m.	Message received that fighting portion of Brigade would embus as soon as busses arrived. Surplus personnel and T.M.B. to be prepared to embus at 9.30.p.m.
10.30.p.m.	Busses commenced to arrive and troops commenced to embus, each Battalion embussing from its billets. Destination was not known but was to be communicated to the Officer Commanding each column en route.
May 29th. 5.0.a.m.	After driving all night the Brigade debussed at the cross roads at the Y in CHAMBRECY, (SOISSONS Sheet 1/100,000). From the crossroads Battalions marched to BLIGNY arriving about
6.30.a.m.	6.30.a.m. The 2nd Bn Wiltshire Regiment were ordered to take up an Outpost position on the high ground N and N.W. of the village.
7.30.a.m.	Warning received from Division that the Brigade was to be ready to move at a moment's notice. Units were warned accordingly. It appears a gap existed in our line between SERZY and PRIN, the 19th Division would probably be ordered to fill the gap.
8.20.a.m.	Orders received that the 19th Division would take up the line FAVEROLLES - COEMY - LHERY. The 58th Brigade were ordered to hold the line from FAVEROLLES to COEMY, the 57th Brigade continuing the line on the left. Brigade ordered to gain touch with the 154th French Division on the right. The IX Corps Cyclists were holding an Outpost Line in front of the above mentioned line. One Company of the Divisional Machine Gun Battalion was placed at the disposal of the G.O.C. 58th Brigade for the defence of the line. Dispositions of the 58th Brigade were as follows :- 9th Bn R.W.Fusiliers holding the front from FAVEROLLES to COEMY. 9th Bn Welch Regt. in support about TRAMERY. 2nd Bn Wiltshire Regt. in reserve on the eastern outskirts of SARCY. Brigade H.Q. was established at SARCY. Battalions were in position soon after mid-day.
12.15.p.m.	Divisional Order received stating that once the FAVEROLLES - LHERY Line had been established every endeavour was to be made to push on to the SAVIGNY - PRIN Line. The 9th Bn R.W.Fusiliers sent forward Officers' patrols with the object of discovering if this was possible but both places were found to be strongly held by the enemy.
1.10.p.m.	In accordance with orders received from the Division Battalions were warned that the 74th Brigade were withdrawing from positions in front of FAVEROLLES to the FAVEROLLES - COEMY Road and were there to reform behind the 19th Division.
2.0.p.m.	Owing to the situation being somewhat obscure on the right flank the 2nd Bn Wiltshire Regt. were ordered to move via SARCY and POILLY and take up a position on a wide front on the high ground N. of BOULEUSE. This Battalion dug in on a front of 1500 yards and at the time heavy fighting was in progress on the ridge immediately North of the BOULEUSE Spur in the neighbourhood of TRESLON and GERMIGNY. Later elements of the 8th and 25th Divisions commenced to withdraw to the position taken up by the 2nd Bn Wiltshire Regt., these elements were reformed and helped to strengthen the line. By nightfall the line held by the 2nd Bn Wiltshire Regt. was the front line.
6.35.p.m.	2nd Bn Wiltshire Regt. was placed under orders of G.O.C. 8th Division.
6.50.p.m.	A platoon of Corps Cyclists was placed at the disposal of the Brigade for reconnaissance work.

- 2 -

May 29th. 7.40.p.m.	Information received from Division that two Battalions of the 56th Brigade were to counter-attack to restore the high ground N. of MERY PREMECY. The counter-attack never materialised as the high ground was still in our possession.
7.54.p.m.	The 56th Brigade less 1 Battalion (9th Bn Cheshire Regt) were placed under orders of G.O.C. 8th Division. At the same time the 2nd Bn Wiltshire Regiment came under orders of the G.O.C. 56th Brigade. The 9th Bn Cheshire Regt. were placed at the disposal of G.O.C. 58th Brigade but were not to be used without reference to Divisional Hd.Qrs. The night of May 29th/30th passed quietly.
May 30th. 3.0.a.m.	The enemy were endeavouring to push forward by means of patrols on the front held by the 9th Bn R.W.Fusiliers and some prisoners were taken.
3.30.a.m.	The troops on the immediate right of the 9th Bn R.W.Fusiliers had been compelled to withdraw, and it was found that about a platoon of the 9th Bn R.W.Fusiliers on the N.E. outskirts of FAVEROLLES had been cut off. Orders were issued for the 9th Bn R.W.Fusiliers to withdraw to the line held by the 9th Bn Welch Regt., i.e., the COEMY - TRAMERY line, but the 9th Bn R.W.Fusiliers did not withdraw from the FAVEROLLES - COEMY Line until about 9.0.a.m.
8.15.a.m.	The 2nd Bn Wiltshire Regt., who were still under the orders of the G.O.C., 56th Brigade, reported that the enemy were attacking and had heavily engaged their flanks who had been forced to give ground. The 57th Brigade also reported that the enemy was advancing towards ROMIGNY.
11.0.a.m.	About this time an order was received from the Division stating that if the G.O.C., 57th Bde. considered that it was absolutely necessary for the Division to withdraw then the following line should be taken up - from the road junction due South of the Y in TRAMERY - in a S.W. direction along road to the farm at the junction of the track 2 Kms. N. of the BOIS D'AULNAY thence to HILL 225 S.E. of LHERY to the right flank of the 74th Brigade. Great care was to be taken to ensure that touch was maintained between units. By this time the 9th Bn R.W.Fusiliers and 9th Bn Welch Regt. were endeavouring to take up a line a position on the POILLY - BOIS D'AULNAY Line owing to the troops on their left having been forced back.
11.30.a.m.	The 9th Bn Cheshire Regt. were ordered to be prepared to occupy the high ground N.W. of SARCY at a moment's notice. The 9th Bn Cheshire Regt. reported that our troops could be seen retiring from the BOIS D'AULNAY.
12.25.p.m.	After consulting the G.O.C. 57th Brigade the G.O.C., 58th Bde. ordered the 9th Bn Cheshire Regt to take up a position on the high ground about the word SARCY getting touch with the 56th Brigade on the SARCY - BOULOUSE Road and with the 57th Brigade about the SARCY - ROMIGNY Road. The 9th Bn R.W.Fusiliers and 9th Bn Welch Regt. were to withdraw behind this line and re-organise subsequently taking up positions on the high ground ½ mile N. of CHAMBRECY.
1 p.m.	The O.C. 9th Bn R.W.Fusiliers reported that practically the whole of his Battalion had been cut off and had either been killed or captured only 50 O.R. being left. Later information was received that 3 Companies of the 9th Bn Welch Regt had shared the same fate. The remainder of these two battalions and the 58th T.M.B. were placed at the disposal of O.C., 9th Bn Cheshire Regt. and were sent to fill up a gap which existed between the right of the 9th Bn Cheshire Regt and the 2nd Bn Wiltshire Regiment.
3.0.p.m.	The G.O.C. 58th Brigade having been wounded the G.O.C. 56th Bde took command of the 58th Bde. and established his Hd. Qrs. at the cross roads at the Y in CHAMBRECY, the combined Hd.Qrs. subsequently moved to CHAUMUZY. The 2nd Bn Wiltshire Regiment had maintained their position till about 2.0.p.m. when they were forced to withdraw to the high ground E. of SARCY and subsequently owing to their right flank

	having been turned they were ordered to withdraw to a position S.W. of BLIGNY with their left flank on the River ARDRE. At 9.30.p.m. the Battalion advanced and re-occupied its old position E. of SARCY but by this time French troops had already occupied the position and the Battalion retired to its position S.W. of BLIGNY.
8.30.p.m.	The line held by the 58th Brigade was re-organised and consolidated. The 9th Bn Cheshire Regt. were on the left and in touch with the 8th Bn Gloucester Regt. of the 57th Brigade, the R.W.F. and Welch were on the right and were in touch with the French. The 58th T.M.B. with remnants of the 8th and 25th Divisions were in reserve about the kink in the CHAMBRECY - BLIGNY Road. The night of May 30th/31st passed without incident.
May 31st.	On the morning of the 31st the enemy having shelled our troops out of the posts dug by them on the previous night a further small withdrawal became necessary. This line was finally made in front of the knoll on the MONTAGNE de BLIGNY. The rmenants of the 9th Bn R.W.Fusiliers and 9th Bn Welch Regt. were organised into one Company and placed under the orders of the O.C., 9th Bn Cheshire Regiment. The 2nd Bn Wiltshire Regt. had become reserve Battalion of the 56th Brigade and available for counter-attack on either the 56th or 58th Brigade fronts.
5.0.p.m.	O.C., 2nd Bn Wiltshire Regt. received orders to counter-attack the farm on the river due N. of CHAMBRECY village. The position having been reconnoitred and the Battalion assembled, the attack
7.20.p.m.	commenced at 7.20.p.m. The attack met with very heavy machine gun fire from the flanks and considerable heavy artillery fire, but the Battalion pressed on and finally reached its objective and in due course joined up with the French on the left, later after the position had been consolidated touch was maintained with the R.W.F. on the right. The casualties sustained during the attack had been fairly heavy and some French troops were sent up in support. The night of May 31st June 1st passed quietly.

Vol. 36.

Headquarters,
58th Inf. Bde.
(19th Div.)
June 1918

On His Majesty's Service.

Army Form C. 2118.

WAR DIARY
or
INTELLIGENCE SUMMARY.

(Erase heading not required.)

Instructions regarding War Diaries and Intelligence Summaries are contained in F. S. Regs., Part II. and the Staff Manual respectively. Title pages will be prepared in manuscript.

HQ 58th Infy Bde
WO 36

Place	Date	Hour	Summary of Events and Information	Remarks and references to Appendices
LINE nr CHAMBRECY	June 1st – 6th		See Narrative of Operations (copy attached and marked A).	A.
BOIS DE COURTON	7th – 11th		58th Composite Battn. in Divisional Reserve (Copy Bde. Order 248 attached and marked B).	B.
CHAMUZY	12th		58th Composite Bn relieved 151st Comp. Bn (50th Div) in Bde Reserve in front of CHAMUZY.	
	13th – 17th		58th Composite Bn remained in Bde. Reserve. Situation normal.	
	18/19th.		58th Comp. Bn relieved by 1/51st Bn ITALIAN Regt of 8th ITALIAN Div. and marched to HAUTVILLERS where remnants of Bns were taken over by respective Headquarters (Copy Bde. Order No. 249 attached and marked C.).	C. D
DIZY - MAGENTA.	20th		Brigade moved by march route to billets at CRAMANT (Copy Bde.Order No.250 attached and marked D)	
CRAMANT.	21st		Brigade moved by lorries to billets at BROUSSY-le-GRAND Area. Transport moved by road. (Copy Addendum No. 1 to Brigade Order No. 250 attached and marked E).	E.
BROUSSY-le-GRAND.	22nd to 29th		Brigade reorganizing and training.	
do.	30th		Brigade marched to billets at HAUSSIMONT & VASSIMONT preparatory to entraining for BRITISH ZONE (Copy Bde. Order No. 251 attached and marked F).	F.

Brigadier General
Commanding 58th Infantry Brigade.

SECRET.   Copy No... 15

B

58th Infantry Brigade Order No. ~~258~~ 248.

9th June, 1918.

1. The Infantry now serving in the 19th Division will be grouped into three Infantry Brigades as follows :-

   (a). <u>19th Division Composite Brigade</u> (consisting of 3 Battns.).

   56th Comp. Bn. (formed from 56th Bde.).
   57th Comp. Bn. (formed from 57th Bde.).
   58th Comp. Bn. (formed from 58th Bde.) plus 1/6.Cheshire R.)

   Total Strength approximately 2,000 rifles.

   (b). <u>50th Division Composite Brigade</u> (consisting of 3 Battns).

   149th Comp. Bn.
   150th Comp. Bn.
   151st Comp. Bn.

   Troops of 50th Div. Comp. Bde. to be distributed amongst the above.
   Total Strength approximately 1,700 rifles.

   (c). <u>7th Composite Brigade</u> (consisting of 5 Battalions).

   1/8th and 2/8th Comp. Bns.
   1/25th, 2/25th and 3/25th Comp. Bns.

   Total strength approximately 2,800 rifles.   TOTAL 6,500.

2. In addition there will be the following M.G.Coys.

   3 M.G.Coys. of 19th Div. 12 guns each = 36
   1 M.G.Coy. of 8th Div. 16 guns.
   1 M.G.Coy. of 25th Div. 10 guns.
   1 M.G.Coy. of 50th Div. 16 guns.
              Total 78 guns.

   %6 guns to be added.

3. The Divisional Front will be held with 2 Brigades with one Brigade and 5th S.W.B. in Divisional Reserve.
   The 7th Comp. Bde. will hold the line on a 3 Battalion front. from present Left Div. Boundary to a point about 2162.2718 (point where track from CHAMBRECY cuts the front line on 1/20,000 sheet).
   The 19th and 50th Div. Comp. Bdes. will relieve one another and hold the remainder of the Divnl. front.

4. The 50th Div. Comp. Bde. is holding the Right Sector, the 7th Comp. Bde. will hold the Left Sector of the 19th Div. Front.
   The 19th Div. Comp. Bde. under command of Brig-General R.M.HEATH, D.S.O. will be in Divisional Reserve disposed as follows:
      57th Comp. Bn. in the vicinity of NAPPES.
      56th and 58th Comp. Bns. in the Eastern portion of the BOIS de COURTON.
      5th S.W.B. are to be accommodated near LES HAIES and will be in Divisional Reserve.

5. The 58th Infantry Brigade plus 1/6th Cheshire Regiment will be organised into a Composite Bn. as follows :-

   (a). The Battalion will consist of 4 Coys. each representing one Battalion Unit. Companies will be as strong as possible, only personnel of Battalion H.Q. being withdrawn.

(b).

- 2 -

  (b). The Battalion will be commanded by Major W.S.SHEPPARD, M.C. 2nd Bn Wiltshire Regiment.
    Battalion H.Q. Staff will be found from 2nd Bn Wiltshire Regiment.
    Company Signallers and Runners will be found from the respective Companies.

  (c). Personnel of Headquarters of the 9th Bn R.W.Fusiliers and 9th Bn Welch Regiment not required will be withdrawn to their transport lines forthwith.
    Personnel of Headquarters of 1/6th Bn Cheshire Regiment not required will be withdrawn to 7th Bde. Transport Lines S.E. of BOURSALT to-morrow 10th inst.

  (d). The personnel of 58th T.M.B. will remain affiliated with the 9th Welch Coy.

6. The Staff Captain will issue Administrative Instructions separately.

7. Acknowledge.

              F H Fraser
                 Captain

           Brigade Major 58th Infantry Brigade.

Issued at 7 p.m.

Copy No. 1 G.O.C.
   2 1/6th Ches.Regt.
   3 9.R.W.F.
   4 9.Welch R.
   5 2.Wilts R.
   6 58.T.M.B.
   7 Staff Capt.
   8 B.T.O.
   9 19th Div.
   10 19th Div. "G"
   11 56th Bde.
   12 57th Bde.
   13 7th Bde.
   14) War Diary.
   15)
   16 File.

SECRET.   56th Brigade No. S.G.8604.

ADMINISTRATIVE INSTRUCTIONS issued with reference to
58th Brigade Order No.248 of 9th June 1918.
--------- ::: ---------

RATIONS. The 2nd Bn Wiltshire Regt. will be entirely responsible for the rationing of the Composite Battalion. The 9th Bn. R.W.Fus, 9th Bn Welch Regt and the 1/6th Cheshire Regt. will detail at least one reliable C.Q.M.S. to live at the Quartermaster's Stores of the 2nd Bn. Wiltshire Regt and look after the interests of their respective Companies.

TRANSPORT. Transport for Rations, S.A.A, Lewis Guns, etc., will be found by the 2nd Bn Wiltshire Regt, but the Brigade Transport Officer will arrange for any transport required to draw Stores from D.A.D.O.S. Coal, etc, to be provided by the two other Battalions of the 58th Brigade.
While the Composite Battalion is in reserve each unit will detail 1 Cooker and Cooks for its Company; the 2nd Bn Wiltshire Regt will detail a Cooker and Cooks for the Company of the 1/6th Cheshire Regt. These Cookers will be withdrawn to the Transport Lines at HAUTVILLERS when the Composite Bn. goes into the line.

ORDERLY ROOM. Each Battalion will establish an Orderly Room, with an Adjutant or Assistant Adjutant, at the Transport Lines at HAUTVILLERS.
Careful touch must be maintained by these offices with the Companies of the Composite Bn. as well as with Brigade H.Q.

SUPPLIES. Units are responsible for ensuring that Mail and any extra supplies which the 2nd Bn Wiltshire Regt. cannot administer are sent up to their Companies.

CASUALTIES. O.Cs. Companies of the Composite Bn. will forward daily Casualty returns to Battalion H.Q. The O.C. Composite Bn. will forward Daily Casualty returns to Brigade H.Q. stating casualties by units. Brigade H.Q. will repeat these to the Battalion Orderly Rooms at HAUTVILLERS.

SUPPLY and TRANSPORT. The 9th Bn R.W.Fusiliers and 9th Bn Welch Regt. will in turn relieve the 2nd Bn. Wiltshire Regt. Transport and Depot personnel at dates to be notified later.

SURPLUS PERSONNEL. Details as to the disposal of that portion of the Surplus Personnel which joined the Brigade Transport Lines at HAUTVILLERS today, will be issued later.
For the present they will be rationed by the 2nd Bn. Wiltshire Regt.

LOCATION of TRANSPORT etc. The following will be the location of Transport, Orderly Rooms etc :-

At HAUTVILLERS, W. of the Main road, opposite the H. in HAUTVILLERS :-

Bde Transport Officer and Brigade H.Q. Transport.
Adjutant (or Assistant Adjutant) Orderly Room and 1 Limber from each Battalion.
Depot and Transport Lines, complete, of the 2nd Bn. Wiltshire Regt.

At least 1 C.Q.M.S. of the 9th R.W.Fusiliers, 9th Welch R. and 1/6th Cheshire Regt.

At <u>RIFLE RANGE, S.E. of EPERNAY</u>.

The remainder of Transport and Depot of the 9th R.W.Fus. and 9th Welch Regt.

At <u>7th Brigade Transport Lines, S.E. of BOURSAULT</u>.

The remainder of Transport and personnel of 1/6th Cheshire Regt. other than that detailed above, and the 1/6th Cheshire Coy of the 58th Composite Bn.

ACKNOWLEDGE.

H.W. House

Major,
Staff Captain 58th Infantry Brigade.

Brigade H.Q.
9th June 1918.

Copies to :-

G.O.C.	56th Bde.
1/6th Cheshire Regt.	57th Bde.
9th R.W.Fus.	7th Bde.
9th Welch.	19th Div. Train.
2nd Wilts.	Depot 9th R.W.F.
58th T.M.Bty.	Depot 9th Welch.
Bde Major.	No. 4 Coy, Train.
B.T.O.	War Diary.
19th Div "G"	File.
19th Div "Q"	

SECRET.

C

58th Infantry Brigade Order No.249.

16th June 1918.

1. The 19th Division will be relieved in the line by the 8th Italian Division. The Relief will be completed by 8-0 a.m. 19th June, at which hour command of the 19th Divisional Front will pass to G.O.C., 8th Italian Division.

2. On relief the Infantry of the Division will move to a back area either (a) by bus, or (b) by march route.
   In the event of (a) - The Transport of Brigade H.Q. 9th Bn. R.W.Fusiliers and 9th Bn. Welch Regiment will move off tomorrow, 17th instant under orders of the Brigade Transport Officer.
   In the event of (b) - Orders will be issued later.
   Orders for the move of the 2nd Bn. Wiltshire Regiment will be issued separately.

3. Orders for the relief and move of the 58th Composite Battalion will be issued by the 19th Div.Comp.Brigade.

4. Administrative Instructions are being issued separately by the Staff Captain.

5. All further details will be issued when known.

6. ACKNOWLEDGE.

Captain,

Brigade Major, 58th Infantry Brigade.

Issued at 7-45 p.m.

Copies to all concerned.

SECRET.   D   Copy No. 22

58th Brigade Order No. 250.

18th June, 1918.

Reference to
CHALONS Sheet 1/80,000.
SOISSONS Sheet 1/100,000.

1. The 58th Brigade Group composed as under will on relief proceed by march route to CRAMANT

   Brigade H.Q.   94th Fld Coy. R.E.
   9/R.W.Fusrs.   59th Fld Ambulance.
   9/Welch R.   No. 4 Coy. 19th Div. Train.
   2/Wilts R.   19th M.G.Battn.
   58/T.M.Bty.

2. On the night of the 18th/19th June after relief the 58th Composite Battalion will proceed to the clearing in the BOIS de COURTON near the Keeper's Lodge about 1 kilo. South of the N in BOIS de COURTON under orders of the 19th Div. Comp. Bde.

3. A hot meal will be served to the troops in the "clearing" after which the 58th Comp. Battalion will be broken up. A senior Officer from each unit, (preferably the Second-in-Command), will be sent to the "clearing" to take command of the troops of his Battalion.
   Command will pass from O.C., 58th Comp. Battalion to Senior Officer i/c Battalions at 5.0.a.m.
   At 5.30.a.m. on the 19th inst. Units will move off to bivouacs in the Wood W. of HAUTVILLERS (present Transport lines of 2nd Bn Wiltshire Regiment) in the following order at 200 yards intervals, 9th Bn R.W.Fusiliers, 9th Bn Welch Regt. and T.M.B. 2nd Bn Wiltshire Regt: Route NANTEUIL - HAUTVILLERS Road.
   Each unit will provide transport to bring back its Lewis Guns from the BOIS de COURTON. 2nd Bn Wiltshire Regt. will provide transport for the guns of the 1/6th Bn Cheshire Regt. as far as HAUTVILLERS.

4. (a). O.C., 94th Field Coy. R.E. will make his own arrangements for moving his Company to Transport Lines at HAUTVILLERS.

   (b). O.C., 59th Field Ambulance will make his own arrangements for moving his Ambulance to Transport Lines at PIERRY.

5. Special orders will be issued to 1/6th Bn Cheshire Regt. direct with regard to their move.
   For the whole of the forthcoming move the 58th T.M.Battery will be affiliated to the 9th Bn Welch Regiment.

6. On the 20th inst. the 58th Bde. Group, less personnel of the 19th Bn M.G.Corps, will march to CRAMANT in accordance with the attached march table. The personnel of the 19th Bn M.G.Corps is being conveyed from the forward area to CRAMANT on the 20th inst. by lorry.

7. During the march on the 20th inst. each Battalion Transport will be responsible for carrying the Lewis Guns and Officers' kits of its own Battalion. Lorries are being provided for surplus stores and the conveyance of men unable to march.

8. From CRAMANT to the MONDEMENT Area the personnel of the Brigade will move by bus, Transport moving by road. Further orders regarding this move will be issued later.

9. Brigade H.Q. will close at NANTEUIL at 10.a.m. on the 19th inst. and re-open in the Wood at HAUTVILLERS at the same hour.
   On the 20th inst. Brigade H.Q. will close at HAUTVILLERS at 7.a.m. and re-open at CRAMANT on arrival.

10. Acknowledge.

Issued at 12 noon.

F.W.Fraser.
Captain
Brigade Major 58th Infantry Brigade.

Ref. to CHALONS 1/80,000. March Table to accompany Operation Order No. 250.

Unit.	From.	To.	Route.	Starting Pt.	Hour head of column passes S.P.	Remarks.
Bde.H.Q.	HAUTVILLERS.	CRAMANT.	DIZY-MAGENTA - EPERNAY - Road on E.side of the Quartier de Cavalerie thence via track across Champ de manoeuvres past the S in Sarran Sal. to CRAMANT.	Road Junction ½ kilo. N. of DIZY-MAGENTA.	8.0.a.m.	
9/R.W.Fusrs. (less Transpt).	"	"	do.	do.	8.5.a.m.	
9/Welch R. & T.M.B. less Transport.	"	"	do.	do.	8.10.a.m.	
2/Wilts Regt.	"	"	do.	do.	8.20.a.m.	
94th Fld.Coy.R.E. dismounted portion.	"	"	do.	do.	8.33.a.m.	
Transport 19th Bn M.G.Corps.	"	"	do.	do.	8.38.a.m.	
59th Fld. Amb.	PIERRY.	"				} To march independ -ently but not to arrive in CRAMANT before 12 noon.
No. 4 Coy. 19th Divl. Train.	"	"				

P.T.O.

Unit.	From.	To.	Route.	Starting Point.	Hour head of Col. passes S.P.	Remarks.
Transport 9th R.W.Fusrs.	Rifle Range.	CRAMANT.				To join in behind their respective units as Column passes the Rifle Range.
Transport 9th Welch Regt.	"	"				
94th Fld Coy. R.E. transport.	"	"				

NOTE:

(1). Intervals of 200 yards will be maintained between Battalions, and between Units and their transport.

(2). Intervals of 50 yards will be maintained between each series of 10 vehicles.

(3). The strictest march discipline is to be maintained throughout by all units.

SECRET. Copy No. 22.

Addendum No. 1 to 58th Infantry Brigade Order No. 250.

20th June, 1918.

1. The 58th Brigade Group (less personnel of M.G.Battalion and Transport), will move by lorry route to the BROUSSY LE GRAND Area. Details as to the allotment and time of departure of lorries will be issued separately by the Staff Captain.

2. All transport and mounted personnel of the 58th Brigade Group will move by march route on the 21st inst. from CRAMANT to the BROUSSY LE GRAND Area under orders of the Brigade Transport Officer.

3. (a) ROUTE: AVIZE-OGER - VERTUS - BERGUERES - AULNIZEAUX.

   (b) STARTING POINT: Bend in the CRAMANT - AVIZE Road 600 metres due South of the R in CRAMANT.

   (c) Head of Column will pass Starting Point at 9.0.a.m.

   (d) ORDER OF MARCH: 2nd Bn Wiltshire Regiment, Brigade H.Q., 9th Bn Welch Regiment, 9th Bn R.W.Fusiliers, 59th Field Ambulance, 94th Field Coy. R.E.; No, 4 Coy., 19th Div. Train, 19th Bn M.G.Corps.

4. Guides will be sent to meet Units' Transport at the Eastern end of the villages in which they are to be billeted.

5. Brigade H.Q. will close at CRAMANT at 8.0.a.m. and re-open on arrival at BROUSSY LE GRAND.

6. Acknowledge.

H. Fraser
Captain

Brigade Major 58th Infantry Brigade.

Issued at 2.30.p.m.

Issued to all recipients of 58th Brigade Order No. 250.

SECRET.   F.   Copy No. 19.

58th Infantry Brigade Order No. 251.

29th June, 1918.

Ref. to 1/80,000
    CHALONS & ARCIS Sheets.

1. The 19th Division is to be transferred to the British Zone by rail.

2. The 58th Brigade Group composed as under will march on 30th June to the HAUSSIMONT, VASSIMONT Staging Area, preliminary to entraining at SOMMESOUS, in accordance with attached march table.

        58th Brigade H.Q.
        9/R.W.Fusiliers.   59th Field Ambulance.
        9/Welch Regt.   No. 4 Coy. 19th Div. Train.
        2/Wiltshire Regt.   94th Fld. Coy. R.E.
        58/T.M.Battery.   19th Bn M.G.Corps.

3. First line transport and baggage wagons will march with units.

4. Intervals of 200 yards will be maintained between Battalions and units and between units and their transport. Intervals of 50 yards will be maintained between each series of 10 vehicles.

5. Details as regards billeting in the staging area will be issued later, and also details as to the allotment of lorries to units.

6. On arrival in the new area units will at once report the exact location of their Headquarters and the number of men that fell out during the march.

7. Brigade H.Q. will close at BROUSSY LE GRAND at 9.15.a.m. on the 30th inst. and re-open on arrival in the new area at a place to be notified later.

8. Acknowledge.

                                                      Captain

                Brigade Major 58th Infantry Brigade.

Issued at 12.45.p.m.

    Copy to all concerned.

March Table to accompany O.O. No. 251.

Unit.	From.	To.	Starting Point.	Time of passing S.P.	Route.	Remarks.
58th Brigade H.Q.) 58th T.M.Battery)	BROUSSY LE GRAND.	HAUSSIMONT VASSIMONT Area.	Point where track crosses the BROUSSY - BANNES Rd. about half-way between BROUSSY & BANNES.	10.0.a.m.	BANNES to MORAINS les PETIT via track passing through the r of la Petit Ferme thence to ECURY - NORMEE - VASSIMONT.	
9/Welch Regt.	do.	do.	do.	10.6.a.m.	"	
9/R.W.Fusrs.	do.	do.	do.	10.18.a.m.	"	
2/Wilts Regt.	Le BESNIL.	do.	do.	10.30.a.m.	"	
No. 4 Coy. 19th Div. Train.	BROUSSY LE GRAND.	do.	do.	10.42.a.m.	"	
59th Fld. Ambce.	do.	do.	do.	10.47.a.m.	"	
19th Bn M.G.Corps.) 94th Fld.Coy.R.E.)	AULNAY					The 19th Bn M.G Corps & 94th Fld Coy. R.E. will march independent -ly under orders of the O.C. 19th Bn M.G.Corps so as to be clear of ECURY by 1.30.p.m

NOTES: (a) DRESS. Marching Order.
(b) There will be a halt for dinners about 1.p.m. (c). Cookers, water carts and mess carts should be at the head of Units' Transport to facilitate dinners being served quickly.

AMENDMENT No.1 to March Table accompanying
O. O. 251.

In column of "Remarks" delete "so as to be clear of ECURY by 1-30 p.m." and substitute "so as to be clear of MORAINS by 12 noon, and column should not make any long halt between MORAINS and ECURY."

29.6.1918.

J.W. Fraser — Captain,
Brigade Major, 58th Infantry Brigade.

Copy to all concerned.

HQ 58 Indep Bde
Vol 3 (1928...)
July 1918.

4

On His Majesty's Service.

Confidential.

D.A.G. G.H.Q. 3rd Echelon.

CONFIDENTIAL.

> HEADQUARTERS.
> 58TH BRIGADE.
> No. Bws 1141
> Date 2/8/18

Headquarters

    19th Division.

       Herewith War Diaries for July for units of 58th Infantry Brigade.

                              Brigadier General

                Commanding 58th Infantry Brigade.

2.8.18.

Army Form C. 2118.

WAR DIARY

INTELLIGENCE SUMMARY.

(Erase heading not required.)

Instructions regarding War Diaries and Intelligence Summaries are contained in F.S. Regs., Part II. and the Staff Manual respectively. Title pages will be prepared in manuscript.

Place	Date	Hour	Summary of Events and Information	Remarks and references to Appendices
VASSIMONT.	July 1st) 3rd)		Battalions entraining at SOMMESOUS and proceeding to British zone. Detraining at ANVIN and proceeding by march route to COUPELLE VIEILLE Area.	
COUPELLE VIEILLE.	4th		Brigade marched to billets in CAMPAGNE les BOULANNAIS Area. (Copy Bde. Order 252 attached and marked A).	A
CAMPAGNE.	5th to) 10th)		Battalions training under Battalion arrangements.	
	11th		Bde. moved by Bus route to LIGNY les AIRE Area (Copy Bde. Order 253 attached and marked B).	B
LIGNY les AIRE	12th to) 23rd.)		Battalions training under Battalion arrangements. Reconnaissance of MT. BERNENCHON - HINGES Ridge and BEUVRY - BETHUNE Ridge carried out by Bde. and Battns. and schemes for counter-attack prepared. Copies of these schemes are attached and marked C, D, E, F, G and H.	C, D, E, F, G, & H.
	24th to) 31st)		Battalions training under Battalion arrangements. Brigade Transport Competition held and won by 2nd Bn Wiltshire Regt. Brigade Inter-Platoon Competition held and won by 9th Bn Welch Regiment.	

2nd August, 1918.

for. Brigadier General

Commanding 58th Infantry Brigade.

A.

SECRET.   Copy No. 18

58th Infantry Brigade Order No. 252.

3rd July, 1918.

Ref. to ARMY Traffic Map, 1/100,000
and HAZEBROUCK 5A

1. The 58th Brigade Group will march to the CAMPAGNE Area to-morrow in accordance with the attached March Table.

2. First Line Transport and baggage wagons will accompany units on the march.

3. There will be no halt for dinners for main column up to CAMPAGNE. Units moving beyond this point may halt for dinners if they wish.

4. Units billeted on the FRUGES - VERCHOCQ Road will keep this road as clear as possible of troops and transport to allow troops of other Brigade Groups to pass.

5. Watches will be synchronized by means of a watch sent out to all units from Brigade H.Q. at 8.0.a.m.

6. The following distances will be maintained during the march :-

    Between Coys. 50 yards.
    Between Units and between units and their transport 200 yards.
    Between every 10 vehicles 50 yards.

7. Brigade H.Q. will close at WAILLY at 9.45.a.m. and will re-open at CAMPAGNE on arrival.

8. Acknowledge.

                                          _____ Captain

                            Brigade Major 58th Infantry Brigade.

Issued at 7.45.a.m.

Copies to all recipients of O.O. No. 251.

March Table to accompany O.O. No. 252.

Unit.	From.	To.	Starting Point.	Time of passing S.P.	Route.	Remarks.
9/Welch Regt.	COUPELLE VIEILLE	LEDINGHEM	Road junction ⅜ mile due N of P in COUPELLE VIEILLE.	10.38.a.m.	Via RUMILLY Cross roads ½ mile due N of the B in B de RENTY - CAMPAGNE 9/Welch thence via BEAUMONT.	
9/R.W.Fusrs.	WAILLY.	HAPPE & LEFAY.	do.	11.0.a.m.		
Brigade H.Q.	"	CAMPAGNE.	do.	11.12.a.m.		
58/T.M.Batty.	COUPELLE VIEILLE.	"	do.	11.16.a.m.		
2/Wilts Regt.	"	"	do.	11.19.a.m.		
No. 4 Coy,19th Divl. Train.	"	BEAUMONT.	do.	11.27.a.m.		
94th Fld.Co.R.E.	DRICKVILLE.		Road junction ½ mile due N of 3rd E in COUPELLE VIEILLE.	11.27.a.m.	Via ASSONVAL to main St. MARTIN-FRUGES Road to FAUQUEMBERGUES HERVARRE Chau. - La BUCAILLE.	
59th Fld.Amb.	½"	Le MESNIL.	Same as for Bde.H.Q.	-	Same as for Bde.H.Q to CAMPAGNE thence direct to Le MESNIL	March independently at a time to be decided by the O.C. Unit and communicated to Bde.HQ any route but the one shown is recommended
19th/M.G.Corps.	COUPELLE NEUVE.	VAUDRINGHEM.	-	-	via FRUGES - MONTE-VILLE - FAUQUEMBERGUES	

Notes:- 1. Dress - Fighting Order.
2. The usual ten minute halts will be observed ten minutes to every clock hour.

SECRET.

B

Addendum No. 1 to 58th Inf. Brigade Order No. 253.

10th July, 1918.

DRESS.- All ranks will wear Marching Order with Steel helmets.

BICYCLES.- No bicycles or cooking utensils will be carried in the buses with personnel.

[signature]
for Major

for Brigade Major 58th Infantry Brigade.

Issued to all recipients of 58th Brigade O.O. No. 253.

SECRET   Copy No. 18

58th Infantry Brigade Order No. 253.

July, 10th, 1918.

Ref. Map CALAIS 13 1/100,000.
HAZEBROUCK 5A 1/100,000.

1. 58th Brigade will move from CAMPAGNE Sub-area to FLECHIN Sub-area on 11th July.

2. Personnel will move by bus, transport by road.
   Lewis guns and 16 drums per gun will be taken with the personnel on the busses.

3. Transport will move in accordance with attached March Table and will march under the orders of the Brigade Transport Officer.

4. Arrangements for move of personnel will be notified by the Staff Captain.

5. 19th Division will come under orders of XIII Corps from 12 noon 11th July; but will continue to be in G.H.Q. Reserve.

6. 58th Bde.H.Q. will close at CAMPAGNE at 3.0.p.m. and will open at LIGNY les AIRE on arrival.

7. Acknowledge.

                                        H.W. Horn. Major for
                                                  Captain

                              Brigade Major 58th Infantry Brigade.

Issued at 11.a.m.

        Copy No. 1 G.O.C.
                 2 9.R.W.Fusrs.
                 3 9.Welch R.
                 4 2.Wilts Regt.
                 5 58.T.M.Bty.
                 6 94.Fld.Co.R.E.
                 7 59.Fld.Ambce.
                 8 No. 4 Co. 19th Div.Train.
                 9 Staff Captain.
                10 Bde.Transport Offr.
                11 Bde. Signal Offr.
                12 19th Div. "G"
                13 19th Div. "Q"
                14 56th Inf. Bde.
                15 57th Inf. Bde.
                16 A.P.M., 19th Div.
                17) War Diary.
                18)
                19 File.

March Table to accompany 58th Brigade O.O. No. 253

Unit.	From.	To.	Starting Point.	Route.	Hour to pass S.P.	Remarks.
Brigade H.Q.) 2/Wilts Regt.) 9/Welch Regt.)	CAMPAGNE CAMPAGNE LEDINGHEM	LIGNY les AIRE AUCHY au BOIS RELY	Cross roads ½ mile due N. of B in B de RENTY	FAUQUEMBERGUES – AUDINCTHUN – RECLINGHEM-LOIRES – FEBVIN BOULOGNATS – PALFART.	Head of column to pass S.P. at 8.0.a.m.	
9/R.W.Fusiliers.) 94th Fld.Coy.R.E.) 59th Fld. Ambce.)	HAPPE DRIONVILLE le MESNIL	LIGNY les AIRE le TIRMARD WESTREHEM	Road junction immediately E of the T in THIEMBRONNE.	WITLARETZ FAUQUEMBERGUES – [illegible] – AUDINCTHUN – RECLINGHEM-LOIRES – FEBVIN PALFART.	Head of column to pass S.P. at 8.45.a.m.	To join Bde.H.Q Column at FAUQUEMBERGUES
No. 4 Coy. 19th Divl. Train.	FAUQUEMBERGUES.	WESTREHEM	–	–	–	To march independently and to be clear of FAUQUEMBERGUES by 9.a.m.

NOTES:
1. Dress – Marching Order.
2. The whole Column will come under orders of the S.T.O. after passing FAUQUEMBERGUES.
3. There will be a long halt in the vicinity of DENNE BROEUCQ, at which animals will be watered and fed. They should again be watered at FEBVIN PALFART as watering facilities are bad in the new billeting area.
4. The following distances will be maintained during the march –
    (a). 100 yards between the transport of each unit.
    (b). 25 yards between every six vehicles.

SECRET   58th Brigade No. S.C. 8954.

ADMINISTRATIVE INSTRUCTIONS with reference to 58th Brigade Order No. 253 and 19th Division Q.559/C (attached).
------------::::--------

1. All units will detail an Officer to report to a representative of the Brigade Staff at 3.30 p.m. on the 11th instant at the Cross Roads just North of the I in LE MESNIL.

2. Units will be formed up by 3.45 p.m. as laid down in B.M.810 with the exception of the 2nd Bn Wiltshire Regt, who will be formed up on the MIEURIES - LEDINGHEM road facing North with the head of the column at the junction of that road and the SENLECQUES - LE MESNIL Road.

3. 1 Officer will travel on the front bus allotted to each unit and will report to a representative of Brigade H.Q. immediately on arrival at the debussing point.

4. Lorries for extra baggage are allotted as follows :-

   1 Lorry to each Battalion, to carry also that portion of the Brigade Canteen at present in each Battalion's village.

   1 Lorry for 58/T.M.Battery and Brigade H.Q.

   They will report to H.Q. of Units at 12.15 p.m. tomorrow and will be available for one journey only.

5. 1 Baggage wagon and 2 pairs of horses have been ordered to rejoin Battalions today.

6. Units will be responsible for carrying away tents which they have been lent by Brigade H.Q., unless they return them to Brigade H.Q. by 8 p.m. tonight.

                                           Major,
                         Staff Captain 58th Infantry Brigade.

Brigade H.Q.
   10th July 1918.

To all recipients of 58th Brigade Order No. 253.

SECRET.

ALL UNITS.
19th Div G.
58th Inf. Bde.
57th Inf. Bde.

> HEADQUARTERS.
> 58TH BRIGADE.
> No. Bm 982
> Date.

Reference my B.M. 910 dated 18.7.18, para. 4 (b).

Please paste the following over this para. as it stands at present:-

(b). Battalion Reserve of S.A.A. & Bombs.) to march Brigaded in rear
    Tool Limber.   ) of 9/Welch R. in the
    Maltese Cart.   ) following order :-
    1 Water Cart.   ) 2/Wiltshire Regt.,
    3 Cookers.   ) 9/R.W.Fusiliers,
    Officers' Mess Cart.   ) 9/Welch Regt.
                                                      Brigade H.Q.

And add the following at the bottom of the march table A(1) issued under my B.M. No. 959/1 of 19th inst.

Transport of Battalions will pass the Starting Point in the following order and at the following times :-

2nd Bn Wiltshire Regt........	Zero plus 30.	Route as above.
9th Bn R.W.Fusiliers.........	Zero plus 40.	"
9th Bn Welch Regiment........	Zero plus 45.	"
Brigade H.Q..................	Zero plus 50.	"

NOTE:-
    200 yds. between Units.
    25 yds. between every six vehicles.

                                                                           Major

20.7.18.   A/Brigade Major 58th Infantry Brigade.

50th Brigade No. B.M.919.

SECRET.

ALL UNITS.
19th Div. "G")
50th Inf. Bde.) For information.
57th Inf. Bde.)

Scheme for the assembly of "G" BRIGADE for counter-attack
on Mt. BERNENCHON — HINGES Ridge (to be known as Scheme "A".

Reference scheme for counter-attack on Mt. BERNENCHON — HINGES Ridge
issued under 19th Div. No. G.1996 (this office No. B.M.900 of 14.7.18)
and map attached thereto.

1. In the event of this move being ordered, the Brigade will assemble near ALLOUAGNE. The assembly area for each battalion is shown on Map A. Brigade H.Q. will be at.
T.M.B. will assemble immediately in rear of 9th Bn Welch Regt. about D.1.b.5.0.

2. On arrival at the assembly area the 9th Bn R.W.Fusiliers will post a picquet of 1 platoon in the vicinity of Railway Bridge in V.26.d.9.9. and the 2nd Bn Wiltshire Regt. a similar picquet on the road about D.2.d.2.8.

3. The march to positions of assembly will be in accordance with the attached Table "A".

4. Unless otherwise ordered, the following transport will accompany units and march as under :—

   (a) Coy. pack animals with ammunition.) in rear of Coys.
       Lewis Gun limbers.   )

   (b) Battalion reserve of S.A.A. & Bombs) to march brigaded in rear of 9th
       Tool limber.   ) Bn Welch Regt. in the following
       Maltese Cart.   ) order :—
       1 Water cart.   ) 2/Wiltshire Regt.
       2 Cookers.   ) 9/R.W.Fusiliers.
       Officers' Mess cart.   ) 9/Welch Regt.
) Brigade H.Q.

5. Half a G.S. Waggon will be provided by Brigade H.Q. for transport of T.M.B. cooking gear and mortars — which will be left under a guard of 2 men at T.M.B. H.Q. in present billets until the waggon with a guide arrives from Brigade H.Q.

6. Battalions will move as Fighting Battalions (numbers as laid down in O.B/1919) and in Fighting Order.
   The extra 50 rounds of S.A.A. will be issued from Battalion reserve on arrival at positions of assembly.
   (N.B.— Should the Brigade move by bus and not by march route this S.A.A. will be issued before starting).

7. Administrative H.Q. of Units with remainder of transport, will remain in present billets, pending orders as to their disposal from the Divn. The packs of Units will be collected (if this has not been done before the Battalion leaves) into one billet, with the exception of those of the surplus personnel, which will be retained by them. The Battalion Pack dump will be left under a guard of 1 N.C.O. and 3 men detailed from the surplus personnel.

8. SURPLUS PERSONNEL will be prepared to move to the Divisional Reception Camp but will await orders for this move.

9. 1 Lewis Gun per battalion will be left behind with surplus personnel.

10. In the event of Battalions moving by Bus all Lewis Guns (except 1 left with surplus personnel) and 32 L.G. Drums per L.G. Section will be carried with the troops in the buses. 8 drums per A.A. L.G. will be carried

11. The following messages will be issued by this office in connection with this scheme :-

 (a) "Stand by for Scheme A" -

   Units will at once make all arrangements to be ready to move off from billets at 15 minutes notice.

 (b) "Carry out Scheme A. Zero hour 12 noon."

   This message may or may not have been preceded by message (a). In either case Units will make all necessary arrangements and move off so as to pass the Starting Point in accordance with the March Table.

 (c) "Carry out Scheme A at once".

   This also may or may not have been preceded by (a) message. In either case units will on receipt of (c) move off as quickly as possible to positions of assembly by the routes already laid down but without reference to the order of march, or time of passing the Starting Point. Mounted officers from units will be sent forward to points where there is a possibility of clashing with other units, to prevent this happening. An Officer of the Brigade Staff will be at the Starting Point for this purpose.

   If message (c) is received, Lewis Gun limbers and Coy. pack animals will move in rear of Coys. Transport, however, referred to in para. 4(b) will stand by in billets ready to move off on receipt of further orders.

   Messages (a), (b) and (c) must be acknowledged at once.

   On receipt of either of these messages, each unit will detail an officer, mounted or on a bicycle, to report to Brigade H.Q. atn once. If, however, either (b) or (c) is received after (a), a second officer need not be sent.

12. Routes from billets to positions of assembly should be reconnoitred by Transport Officers.

13. A rear Echelon of Brigade H.Q. will remain open at LIGNY LES AIRE.

14. ACKNOWLEDGE.

(sd) H.W.HOUSE, Major

A/Brigade Major 50th Infantry Brigade.

15.7.18.

TABLE A(1)

Unit.	Starting Point.	Time of passing Starting Point.	Route.
58th Brigade H.Q.	Cross roads, T.21.a.7.2.	Zero hour.	FEREAY - AUCHEL - LOZINGHEM.
58th T.M.Battery.	do.	Zero plus 2.	do.
2/Wiltshire Regt.	do.	Zero plus 4.	do.
9/R.W.Fusiliers.	do.	Zero plus 14.	do.
9/Welch Regt.	do.	Zero plus 24.	do.

NOTES:

1. Zero hour will be included in the order for the move.

2. Should, however, units be ordered to move as quickly as possible, they will move off as soon as they are ready using the routes laid down but irrespective of the order of march, and the time of passing the Starting Point, where there will be a Staff Officer to prevent clashing.

3. Distances, unless otherwise ordered, will be as under:—

   (a) Between Companies 100 yards.
   (b) Between rear Coy. and Transport 100 yards.
   (c) Between Battalions 200 yards.

4. Transport of Brigade will pass the Starting Point in the following order, and at the following times :-

2nd Bn Wiltshire Regt.......	Zero plus 38.	
9th Bn R.W.Fusiliers.......	Zero plus 42.	Same route as above.
9th Bn Welch Regiment......	Zero plus 46.	"
Brigade Headquarters.......	Zero plus 50.	"

   Note: — 200 yards between Units.
   25 yards between every six vehicles.

D

Addendum to B.M.986 dated 20th July to be attached thereto.

When Brigades are ordered to move from Positions of Assembly to Positions of Deployment units will move to RESERVE POSITIONS as under :-

9/R.W.Fusrs. - to the vicinity of the cemetery in K.1.b. by Tracks Q. and Q.1.

9/Welch Regt.)
2/Wilts Regt.) to wood in K.1.a. - by tracks Q. and Q.2.
58/T.M.Bty.)

Brigade H.Q. remains unchanged.

Addendum to B.M.919 dated 15.7.18 to be attached thereto.

When Brigades are ordered to move from Positions of Assembly to Positions of Deployment Units will move to RESERVE POSITIONS as under:-

9/R.W.Fusrs. -   Vicinity of LENGLET.
9/Welch Regt. -   "   " LA VALEE
2/Wilts Regt. -   "   " LE HAMEL.
58/T.M.Bty.   -   "   " LENGLET.
Bde. H.Q.   -   "   " LENGLET.

The route in each case will be via B track.

<u>SECRET</u>.

HEADQUARTERS.
66TH BRIGADE.

SCHEME FOR THE ASSEMBLY OF 'C' BRIGADE FOR
COUNTER-ATTACK on BEUVRY - BETHUNE RIDGE
to be known as SCHEME "B".

20th July, 1918.

Reference Scheme for counter-attack on BEUVRY - BETHUNE Ridge issued under 19th Div. No. G.2008/2 (this office No. B.M.961) and map attached thereto.

1. In the event of this move being ordered the Brigade will assemble on the southern edge of the BOIS DES DAMES. The assembly area for each Battalion is shown on map referred to above.
Brigade H.Q. will be at LA BUISSIERE at J.5.d.1.0.

2. The march to the positions of assembly will be in accordance with Table B attached.
Route FERFAY - AUCHEL - MARLES LES MINES - Southern edge of BOIS DES DAMES.

3. Unless otherwise ordered the following transport will accompany units and march as under :-

    (a) Coy. pack animals with ammunition.)
        Lewis Gun limbers.   )in rear of Coys.

    (b) Battalion Reserve of S.A.A. & Bombs.)to march brigaded in rear of
        Tool limber.   )9/Welch Regt. in following
        Maltese Cart.   )order :-
        1 Water cart.   )2/Wiltshire Regt.
        3 Cookers.   )9/R.W.Fusiliers.
        Officers' Mess cart.   )9/Welch Regt.
                                           Brigade H.Q.

4. Half a G.S. Wagon will be provided by Brigade H.Q. for transport of T.M.B. cooking gear and mortars - which will be left under a guard of 2 men at T.M.B. H.Q. in present billets until the waggon with a guide arrives from Brigade H.Q.

5. Battalions will move as Fighting Battalion (numbers as laid down in O.B./1919) and in Fighting Order.
The extra 50 rounds of S.A.A. will be issued from Battalion reserve on arrival at positions of assembly.
(N.B: Should the Brigade move by Bus and not by march route this S.A.A. will be issued before starting).

6. Administrative H.Q. of Units with remainder of Transport, will remain in present billets, pending orders as to their disposal from the Divn. The packs of units will be collected (if this has not been done before the Battalion leaves) into one billet, with the exception of those of the surplus personnel, which will be retained by them. The Battalion Pack dump will be left under a guard of 1 N.C.O. and 3 men detailed from the surplus personnel.

7. SURPLUS PERSONNEL will be prepared to move to the Divisional Reception Camp but will await orders for this move.

8. 1 Lewis Gun per battalion will be left behind with surplus personnel.

9. In the event of Battalions moving by bus all Lewis Guns (except 1 left with surplus personnel) and 32 drums per L.G. Section will be carried with the troops in the buses. 8 drums per A.A. L.G. will be carried.

P.T.O.

10. The following messages will be issued by this office in connection with this scheme :-

   (a) "Stand by for Scheme B" -

   Units will at once make all arrangements to be ready to move off from billets at 15 minutes notice.

   (b) "Carry out Scheme "B". Zero hour 12 noon"

   This message may or may not have been preceded by message (a). In either case units will make all necessary arrangements and move off so as to pass the Starting Point in accordance with the March Table.

   (c) "Carry out Scheme "B" at once".-

   This also may or may not have been preceded by (a) message. In either case units will on receipt of (c) move off as quickly as possible to positions of assembly by the routes already laid down but without reference to the order of march, or time of passing the Starting Point. Mounted Officers from Units will be sent forward to points where there is a possibility of clashing with other units, to prevent this happening. An Officer of the Brigade Staff will be at the Starting Point for this purpose.

   If message (c) is received, Lewis Gun limbers and Coy. Pack animals will move in rear of Coys. Transport however referred to in para. 4(b) will stand by in billets ready to move off on receipt of further orders.

   Messages (a), (b) and (c) must be acknowledged at once.

   On receipt of either of these messages, each unit will detail an Officer, mounted or on a bicycle, to report to Brigade H.Q. at once. If, however, either (b) or (c) is received after (a), a second Officer need not be sent.

11. Routes from billets to positions of assembly should be reconnoitred by Transport Officers, and also suitable places for parking transport on arrival under cover from aircraft.

12. A rear Echelon of Brigade H.Q. will remain open at LIGNY-les-AIRE.

13. ACKNOWLEDGE.

                                                    H.W.Horne   Major

                                        A/Brigade Major 58th Infantry Brigade.

Issued to -
   9/R.W.Fusiliers.
   9/Welch Regiment.
   2/Wiltshire Regt.
   58/T.M.Battery.
   Staff Captain.
   Bde. Int. Offr.

   19th Div. "G")
   56th Inf. Bde.) For information.
   57th Inf. Bde.)

T A B L E "B"

Unit.	Starting Point.	Time of passing Starting Point.	Route.
58th Bde.H.Q.	Cross Roads, T.21.a.7.2.	Zero hour.	FERFAY - AUCHEL - LOZINGHEM *MARLES-LES-MINES*
58th T.M.Battery.	do.	Zero plus 2.	do.
2/Wiltshire Regt.	do.	Zero plus 4.	do.
6/R.W.Fusiliers.	do.	Zero plus 14.	do.
9/Welch Regt.	do.	Zero plus 24.	do.

NOTES:

1. Zero hour will be included in the order for the move.

2. Should, however, units be ordered to move as quickly as possible, they will move off as soon as they are ready using the routes laid down but irrespective of the order of march, and the time of passing the Starting Point, where there will be a Staff Officer to prevent clashing.

3. Distances, unless otherwise ordered, will be as under :-

    (a) Between Companies 100 yards.
    (b) Between rear Coy. and Transport 100 yards.
    (c) Between Battalions 200 yards.

4. Transport of Brigade will pass the Starting Point in the following order, and at the following times :-

    2nd Bn Wiltshire Regt........ Zero plus 38.   Same route as above.
    6th Bn R.W.Fusiliers........ Zero plus 42.
    9th Bn Welch Regiment....... Zero plus 46.
    Brigade Headquarters........ Zero plus 50.

    Note:- 200 yards between Units.
           25 yards between every six vehicles.

SECRET   E   58th Brigade No. B.M.971.

9th Bn. R.W.Fusrs.	94th Field Coy. R.E.
9/Welch Regt.	19th Div. "G".
2/Wilts Regt.	19th Div. "Q"
58/T.M.Bty.	56th Inf. Bde.
59/Fld. Amb.	57th Inf. Bde.
No.4 Coy. Train.	19th Div. Train.

Map ref.) HAZEBROUCK 5A. 1/1,000,000
) Sheet 36.A.   1/20,000

Herewith revised instruction for move of the 58th Infantry Brigade by March route   Bus, or tactical train.

Please destroy B.M.971 and B.M.971/1 previously issued.

ACKNOWLEDGE

H. W. House   Major

A/Brigade Major 58th Infantry Brigade.

21.7.18.

SECRET.   58th Brigade No. B.M. 971.

9th Bn R.W. Fusiliers.   94th Field Coy. R.E.
9th Bn Welch Regiment.   19th Div. "G".
2nd Bn Wiltshire Regiment.   19th Div. "Q"
58th Trench Mortar Battery   56th Inf. Bde.
59th Field Ambulance.   57th Inf. Bde.
No. 4 Coy. Div. Train.   19th Div. Train.
                        ----

1.   While the 19th Division is in G.H.Q. Reserve it will be held at 24 hours notice to move, the Brigade in the AUCHEL Area being held at 8 hours notice.

2.   In the event of the Division being ordered to move from the XIII Corps area, the move will be carried out wither by march route, bus, or tactical train, according to the portion of the front to which the Division is ordered and the tactical situation at the time.

3.   If ordered to move to Second Army, the move would be carried out by march route to the area BOESEGHEM - QUIESTEDE, BLESSY - LAMBRES.
      If required to move to an area further North the move would be carried out by bus or tactical train.

4.   If ordered to move to any other portion of the front the move would be carried out by bus or tactical train.

5.   Instructions for these moves are attached -

      (a) Scheme H for move by march route.
      (b) Scheme J for move by bus.

6.   On relief by another Division all orders and arrangements in connection with the above will be handed over.

7.   Units will move complete unless otherwise ordered. Surplus Personnel will, however, be earmarked so that, if necessary, it can be immediately detached from the Fighting Battalion on arrival at the destination in each case. Should the Surplus Personnel be ordered not to proceed with units, it will be ordered to join the Divisional Reception Camp, AUMERVAL.

8.   Baggage and Supply wagons will move with units.

9.   Acknowledge.

                                                              Major
                                    A/Brigade Major 58th Infantry Brigade.

Brigade H.Q.
   21st July, 1918.

         NOTE:
               No scheme for entraining will be issued at present.

SECRET.

Scheme for the move of the 58th Brigade
to the Second Army by
March Route, to be known as Scheme "H".

1. In the event of the Brigade being ordered to move by march all Units of the Brigade Group will march in Fighting order, packs and surplus baggage being stacked in one place in present billets and left under a guard of 1 N.C.O. and 3 men.

2. Starting Point and order of march are shown in the attached March Table "A".

3. Transport will march in rear of units.

4. The following distances will be observed :-

   Between Companies................... 100 yards.
   Between units and their transport... 100 yards.
   Between Battalions.................. 500 yards.
   Between each section of six vehicles 25 yards.

5. On receipt of message "Carry out Scheme "H", Zero hour - Acknowledge" Units will move off in accordance with attached Table "A".

6. Supply arrangements will be notified as early as possible after the orders for the move have been received.

7. One lorry will be ordered to report to the 58th T.M.Battery for transport of guns and stores.

                                          H.W. Stone   Major

                                    /Brigade Major 58th Infantry Brigade.

Brigade H.Q.
   21st July, 1918.

TABLE "A"

Unit.	Starting Point.	Time at which head of column will pass S.P.	Route.	Remarks.
58th Bde.H.Q.	Road junction, T.7.a.9.6.	Zero.	ESTREE BLANCHE - BLESSY - ROCQUETOIRE.	Destinations will be notified as soon as possible after the order to move has been received.
9/Welch Regt.	do.	Zero plus 4.	-do-	
9/R.W.Fusrs.	do.	Zero plus 19.	-do-	
2/Wilts Regt.	do.	Zero plus 34.	-do-	
58/T.M.Battery.	do.	Zero plus 45.	LIGNY-les-AIRE - Road junction T.7.a.9.6. - ESTREE BLANCHE - BLESSY - ROCQUETOIRE.	
59th Field Amb.	do.	Zero plus 50.	-do-	
No. 4 Coy.Train.	do.	Zero plus 60.	-do-	
ø94th Field Co.R.E	Cross Roads. S.6.d.9.8.	Zero plus 69.	ESTREE BLANCHE - BLESSY - ROCQUETOIRE.	

ø 94th Field Coy. will be formed up on the side road running East out of LA TIRMENDE, and not on the AUCHY - ESTREE BLANCHE Road.

SECRET.

Scheme for the embussing of the 58th Inf. Bde. Group to be known as Scheme "J".

1. In the event of the Division being ordered to move by bus to the Second Army or another area the embussing point for the 58th Inf. Bde. Group will be T.14.a.9.2. - S.6.d.9.7. (Sheet 36.A).

2. PACKS will be taken on the busses unless otherwise ordered. If packs cannot be taken on the busses owing to the tactical situation they will be dumped at the H.Q. of units and cleared under Divisional arrangements. A minimum of cooking utensils should be taken on the busses with the men. It might be necessary for the packs of the fighting personnel and the cooking utensils to be dumped on arrival at the destination, in which case they will be left under a guard of 1 N.C.O. and 3 men per unit.

3. On receiving the message "Carry out Scheme J - Zero hour - Acknowledge" Units will be formed up by zero hour in the following positions ready to embuss :-

    (a) 58/Bde.H.Q. - Facing N.E. on the LIGNY-les-AIRE - RELY road. Head of the Column to be 20 yds. S.West of the junction of that road and the AUCHY-au-BOIS - ESTREE BLANCHE Road.

    (b) 9/Welch Regt. - Facing S.W. Head of the column to be 20 yds. N.E. of the road junction at T.7.a.9.6.

    (c) 9/R.W.Fusrs. - In rear of Brigade H.Q.

    (d) 2/Wilts Regt. - Facing North, on the road between the WESTREHEM - ST.HILAIRE Road and the road junction at T.14.c.7.5. Head of the column to be at road junction T.14.a.6.2.

    (e) 58/T.M.Bty. - Facing East on the WESTREHEM - ST. HILAIRE Road. Head of column to be 20 yds. WEST of the road junction at T.14.a.6.2.

    (f) 59/Fld. Amb. - In rear of 58th T.M.Battery.

    (g) No.4 Coy.Train - In rear of 59th Field Ambulance.

    (h) 94/Fld Coy.R.E - On road running E. out of LA TIRMANDE. Column facing E, with its head 20 yds. W. of cross roads S.6.d.9.8.

4. Transport will move under orders to be issued when destination is known.

5. SUPPLY ARRANGEMENTS will depend on the destination of units and will be notified in due course.

6. Lorries for surplus baggage will be available as under; they will be despatched to units as soon as possible after order to move is sent out -

    Brigade H.Q.   ) 1 lorry.
    58th T.M.Battery.)

    9/R.W.Fusiliers.) 1 lorry.
    2nd Wiltshire R.)

    9/Welch Regiment.) 1 lorry.
    Brigade Canteen.)

7. Units will move complete (Fighting personnel, Administrative personnel and Surplus personnel) less personnel moving with transport, unless otherwise ordered.
    If surplus personnel does not move with units, they will proceed with full kit to Divl. Reception Camp, AUMERVAL.

P.T.O.

8. On receipt of orders to carry out Scheme J Units will issue 50 extra rounds of ammunition per man.

All Lewis Guns will be carried in the busses and 32 drums per L.G.Section.

If the surplus personnel remains behind, 1 Lewis gun will be left with it.

9. ACKNOWLEDGE.

H.W. Howe   Major

A/Brigade Major 58th Infantry Brigade.

21.7.18.

SECRET  58th Brigade No. B.M.971.

```
9th Bn R.W.Fusrs.      94th Field Coy. R.E.
9/Welch Regt.          19th Div. "G".
2/Wilts Regt.          19th Div. "Q"
58/T.M.Bty.            56th Inf. Bde.
59/Fld. Amb.           57th Inf. Bde.
No.4 Voy. Train.       19th Div. Train.
```

Map ref.) HAZEBROUCK 5A. 1/1000,000
) Sheet 36.A.   1/20,000

Herewith revised instruction for move of the 58th Infantry Brigade by March route   Bus, or tactical train.

Please destroy B.M.971 and B.M.971/1 previously issued.

ACKNOWLEDGE

H. W. House Major

A/Brigade Major 58th Infantry Brigade.

21.7.18.

SECRET.   58th Brigade No. B.M. 971.

9th Bn R.W. Fusiliers.   94th Field Coy. R.E.
9th Bn Welch Regiment.   19th Div. "G".
2nd Bn Wiltshire Regiment.   19th Div. "Q".
58th Trench Mortar Battery   56th Inf. Bde.
59th Field Ambulance.   57th Inf. Bde.
No. 4 Coy. Div. Train.   19th Div. Train.
----

1. While the 19th Division is in G.H.Q. Reserve it will be held at 24 hours notice to move, the Brigade in the AUCHEL Area being held at 8 hours notice.

2. In the event of the Division being ordered to move from the XIII Corps area, the move will be carried out wither by march route, bus, or tactical train, according to the portion of the front to which the Division is ordered and the tactical situation at the time.

3. If ordered to move to Second Army, the move would be carried out by march route to the area BOESEGHEM - QUIESTEDE, BLESSY - LAMBRES.
   If required to move to an area further North the move would be carried out by bus or tactical train.

4. If ordered to move to any other portion of the front the move would be carried out by bus or tactical train.

5. Instructions for these moves are attached -

   (a) Scheme H for move by march route.
   (b) Scheme J for move by bus.

6. On relief by another Division all orders and arrangements in connection with the above will be handed over.

7. Units will move complete unless otherwise ordered. Surplus Personnel will, however, be earmarked so that, if necessary, it can be immediately detached from the Fighting Battalion on arrival at the destination in each case. Should the Surplus Personnel be ordered not to proceed with units, it will be ordered to join the Divisional Reception Camp, AUMERVAL.

8. Baggage and Supply wagons will move with units.

9. Acknowledge.

                                                            Major
                                     A/Brigade Major 58th Infantry Brigade.

Brigade H.Q.
21st July, 1918.

   NOTE:
       No scheme for entraining will be issued at present.

DRAFT.

Scheme for the move of the 58th Brigade to the Second Army by March Route, to be known as Scheme "H".

1. In the event of the Brigade being ordered to move by march all Units of the Brigade Group will march in Fighting Order, packs and surplus baggage being stacked in one place in present billets and left under a guard of 1 N.C.O. and 3 men.

2. Starting Point and order of march are shown in the attached March Table "A".

3. Transport will march in rear of units.

4. The following distances will be observed :-

    Between Companies.................... 100 yards.
    Between units and their transport... 100 yards.
    Between Battalions................... 500 yards.
    Between each section of six vehicles 25 yards.

5. On receipt of message "Carry out Scheme "H", Zero hour - Acknowledge" Units will move off in accordance with attached Table "A".

6. Supply arrangements will be notified as early as possible after the orders for the move have been received.

7. One lorry will be ordered to report to the 58th T.M.Battery for transport of guns and stores.

                                       Major

                         ./Brigade Major 58th Infantry Brigade.

Brigade H.Q.
   21st July, 1918.

TABLE "A"

Unit.	Starting Point.	Time at which head of column will pass S.P.	Route.	Remarks.
58th Bde.H.Q.	Road junction, T.7.a.9.6.	Zero.	ESTREE BLANCHE - BLESSY - ROCQUETOIRE.	Destinations will be notified as soon as possible after the order to move has been received.
9/Welch Regt.	do.	Zero plus 4.	-do-	
9/R.W.Fusrs.	do.	Zero plus 19.	-do-	
2/Wilts Regt.	do.	Zero plus 34.	-do-	
58/T.M.Battery.	do.	Zero plus 45.	LIGNY-les-AIRE - Road junction T.7.a.9.6. - ESTREE BLANCHE - BLESSY - ROCQUETOIRE.	
59th Field Amb.	do.	Zero plus 50.	-do-	
No. 4 Coy.Train.	do.	Zero plus 60.	-do-	
∅94th Field Co.R.E	Crossroads. S6.d.9.8.	Zero plus 69.	ESTREE BLANCHE - BLESSY - ROCQUETOIRE.	

∅ 94th Field Coy. will be formed up on the side road running East out of LA TIRAMDE and not on the
AUCHY - ESTREE BLANCHE Road.

SECRET.

Scheme for the embussing of the 58th Inf. Bde. Group to be known as Scheme "J".

1. In the event of the Division being ordered to move by bus to the Second Army or another area the embussing point for the 58th Inf. Bde. Group will be T.14.a.9.2. - S.6.d.9.7. (Sheet 36.A).

2. PACKS will be taken on the busses unless otherwise ordered. If packs cannot be taken on the busses owing to the tactical situation they will be dumped at the H.Q. of units and cleared under Divisional arrangements. A minimum of cooking utensils should be taken on the busses with the men. It might be necessary for the packs of the fighting personnel and the cooking utensils to be dumped on arrival at the destination, in which case they will be left under a guard of 1 N.C.O. and 3 men per unit.

3. On receiving the message "Carry out Scheme J - Zero hour - Acknowledge" Units will be formed up by zero hour in the following positions ready to embuss :-

   (a) 5 58/Bde.H.Q. - Facing N.E. on the LIGNY-les-AIRE - RELY road. Head of the Column to be 20 yds. S.West of the junction of that road and the AUCHY-au-BOIS - ESTREE BLANCHE Road.

   (b) 9/Welch Regt. - Facing S.W. Head of the column to be 20 yds. N.E. of the road junction at T.7.a.9.6.

   (c) 9/R.W.Fusrs. - In rear of Brigade H.Q.

   (d) 2/Wilts Regt. - Facing North, on the road between the WESTREHEM - ST.HILAIRE Road and the road junction at T.14.c.7.5. Head of the column to be at road junction T.14.a.6.2.

   (e) 58/T.M.Bty. - Facing East on the WESTREHEM - ST. HILAIRE Road. Head of column to be 20 yds. WEST of the road junction at T.14.a.6.2.

   (f) 59/Fld. Amb. - In rear of 58th T.M.Battery.

   (g) No.4 Coy.Train - In rear of 59th Field Ambulance.

   (h) 94/Fld Coy.R.E - On road running E. out of LA TIRMANDE. Column facing E. with its head 20 yds. W. of cross roads S.6.d.9.8.

4. Transport will move under orders to be issued when destination is known.

5. SUPPLY ARRANGEMENTS will depend on the destination of units and will be notified in due course.

6. Lorries for surplus baggage will be available as under; they will be despatched to units as soon as possible after order to move is sent out -

          Brigade H.Q.   )
          58th T.M.Battery.) 1 lorry.

          9/R.W.Fusiliers.   )
          2nd Wiltshire R.   ) 1 lorry.

          9/Welch Regiment.)
          Brigade Canteen.   ) 1 lorry.

7. Units will move complete (Fighting personnel, Administrative personnel and Surplus personnel) less personnel moving with transport, unless otherwise ordered.
   If surplus personnel does not move with units, they will proceed with full kit to Divl. Reception Camp, AUMERVAL.

P.T.O.

8. On receipt of orders to carry out Scheme J Units will issue 50 extra rounds of ammunition per man.

All Lewis Guns will be carried in the busses and 32 drums per L.G. Section.

If the surplus personnel remains behind, 1 Lewis gun will be left with it.

9. ACKNOWLEDGE.

H.W. Howe   Major

A/Brigade Major 58th Infantry Brigade.

21.7.18.

SECRET.

All Battalions.
58/T.M.Battery.
Staff Captain.
Bde. Sig. Offr.

Map Refce: Sheet 44.B. N.E.
Sheet.36.A. S.E.

With reference to Scheme B, counter-attack on the BEUVRY → BETHUNE Ridge.

Herewith an outline of the attack of the Left (B) Brigade.

Please acknowledge receipt.

(Sd) H.W.HOUSE.
Major,
A/Brigade Major 58th Infantry Brigade.

22.7.18.

Copy to 19th Div. (for information).

APPENDIX I.

1. In the event of orders to move to Rear Positions of Assembly for Scheme B, Units will move to rear assembly positions as shown on attached map.

    Route :- AUCHEL - MARLES LES MINES - Southern edge BOIS DES DAMES.

APPENDIX II.

1. On receipt of orders to move to forward positions of assembly (Yellow line) Units will proceed in accordance with following Table.

Unit.	Rear position of Assembly.	Route.	Forward Assembly position.
Right Bn. 9/R.W.Fus.	Wood, E.26.d.2.2.	BLUE Route.	E.29.c.2.9. E.28.b.6.6.
Left Bn. 9/Welch R.	S.W. end of wood E.20.c.5.8.	RED Route.	E.28.b.6.6. E.22.d.2.3.
Reserve Bn. 2/Wilts R.	S. end of wood D.30.d.8.5.	RED & BLUE Route and thence BLUE Route.	E.27.central.

Brigade H.Q. - Les CHARMEUX CHAU.

SECRET
Ref. Map attached.

SCHEME "B" (Right (A) Brigade).

Counter-attack on BETHUNE - BEUVRY Ridge.

Outline of attack should 58th Bde. be ordered to take over the task allotted to A Brigade.

Preliminary Moves. 1. The moves of the Bde. to Positions of Assembly in the woods North of VAUDRICOURT, and from thence to the position of deployment (Yellow line) are dealt with in Appendix I and II.

Intention. 2. The attack will be delivered by A Infy. Bde. on the Right and B Infy Brigade on the left.

General Plan of Attack. 3. The attack will be delivered from the Position of deployment (Yellow line, K.18.a.7.6. to E.29.a.1.9.). Reserve Bn. at E.28.d. either in Eastern edge of VAUDRICOURT Wood or in the open low ground to the East of it.
Direction - boundaries - and objectives of attack are shown on attached map. (Note: Until the first objective is gained the Church at BEUVRY will be taken as the centre guiding point between the two assaulting battalions).
The attack will be carried out by 2 Assaulting Battalions in front and one Bn. in Reserve.

On the right - 9th Bn R.W.Fusiliers.
On the left - 9th Bn Welch Regiment.
in Reserve - 2nd Bn Wiltshire Regt.

Hd.Qrs. 4. Brigade H.Q. VAUDRICOURT CHATEAU, K.4.a.7.7.
Bde. Forward Station. Enclosure in F.19.b.7.2. and subsequently in BLUE Line.

Assaulting Battalions. With their Reserve Coys.

Reserve Battn.) With rear Coys. of Reserve Bn. as far as
T.M.Battery.) the ANNEQUIN - LAUNDRY Line.

Formations for Attack. 5. Each assaulting Bn. will be on a 3 Coy. front with one Coy. in reserve. Bde. Normal Formation for attack behind creeping barrage except that, leading line will be in section columns and not extended during initial advance vide. para. 8. Reserve Coy. 400 yards in rear of Assaulting Coys.

Objectives 6. The first objective (BLUE Line) will include the Northern edges of enclosures on the N. side of the BETHUNE - BEUVRY Road. On Right flank it will extend South of the BEUVRY Branch of the Canal.
The 2nd objective (RED line) will be approximately the BEUVRY - CAMBRIN Line.
After the capture of the RED Line (and as soon as Protective barrage permits) Posts will be pushed forward to localities marked by Red semi-circles on the map to secure the QUESNOY SPUR.

Barrage 7. In addition to heavy artillery fire on objectives the infantry attack will be covered by a creeping barrage. The line on which this barrage will come down will depend on whether the ANNEQUIN - LAUNDRY Line is still held by us or not.
A detailed barrage table will be issued later.
After the capture of the RED line a protective barrage will be put down in front of it. Arrangements will be made for this barrage to lift when the Posts are pushed forward.
The attack will also be covered by an overhead M.G. barrage.

SECRET.

SCHEME B. (Left(B)Brigade).

Counter-attack on BEUVRY - BETHUNE Ridge.

Outline of attack should 58th Brigade be ordered to take
over task allotted to B Brigade.

Intention. 1. The attack will be delivered by A Infy. Bde. on the Right and
B Bde. on the left.

General 2. The attack of B Bde. will be delivered from the Forward
plan of Assembly Line (E.29.c.2.9. to E.22.d.2.3.).
attack. Direction, Boundaries and objectives of attack are shown on
attached map. After having established the BEUVRY - CAMBRIN, line,
posts will be pushed forward to deny crossings of the Canal to
the enemy.

Moves to rear Positions of Assembly near GOSNY and HESDIGNEUL and
from there to forward Assembly Position (Yellow Line) are dealt
with in Appendix I and II.

The attack will be carried out by 2 Battalions in front and one
Battalion in Reserve.

9th Bn R.W.Fusiliers will attack on the Right.
9th Bn Welch Regt. will attack on the Left.
2nd Bn Wiltshire Regt. will be in Bde. Reserve.

Hd.Qrs. 3. Brigade H.Q. - VAUDRICOURT CHATEAU.(K.4.a 7.7.)
Adv. Bde.H.Q - QUARRY, E.22.d.4.0.
Assaulting Battalions' H.Q. - With Reserve Coys.
Reserve Battn.H.Q.)
T.M.Battery H.Q.) QUARRY, E.22.d.4.0.

Formations 4. Each assaulting Battalion will be on a 3 Coy. front.
for attack Each Coy. on a 2 platoon front with one platoon in support and
one in Reserve.
Each platoon in 2 lines -

20 yards between lines.
150 yards between waves.
400 yards between Assaulting and Reserve Coys.

Objectives. 5. The 1st Objective (BLUE line) will comprise the N.
edges of the enclosures on N. side of BEUVRY - BETHUNE Road.
The 2nd Objective (RED line) will comprise the Northern
slope of the BEUVRY Ridge on which the BEUVRY - CAMBRIN line is
situated.
After the capture of the RED line, posts will be pushed forward
to localities shown in red on the map to deny crossings of Canal
to the enemy.

Barrage. 6. In addition to heavy Artillery fire on objectives the Infantry
attack will be covered by a creeping barrage moving in lifts of
100 yards at rate of 100 yards in 5 minutes.
The barrage will probably come down on the line shown as a
dotted violet line on attached map.
A detailed barrage Table will be issued later.
After the capture of RED line a protective barrage will be put
down on the CANAL - arrangements will be made for this barrage to
lift when posts are pushed forward.

Details 7. (a). The attack from Forward Positions of Assembly will commence
of in Section Columns which will deploy into extended order when
attack. necessary. This will probably not be before reaching the Railway
running through E.17.d. and E.24.a.

(b). The leading 2 platoons of each assaulting Coy. will pass
through the first objective and capture the 2nd objective, Support
and Reserve Platoons of each Coy. will mop the first objective
where Reserve Platoon will remain, the Support Platoon moving
forward in support of the attack on the 2nd objective.

/After

- 2 -

After capture of RED line (and as soon as the barrage allows) support platoons of the Right Battalion will move forward and establish posts at F.2.c.5.2., F.1.d.7.0., F.8.a.6.1.; Support platoons of Left Battalion will establish posts at F.7.a.7.8., and E.12.b.5.7. and a post at about F.7.c.0.7. in Support.

Reserve Coys. will remain in neighbourhood of BETHUNE Locality South of BEUVRY - BETHUNE Road.

The Reserve Battalion will move forward 1,000 yards in rear of the assaulting Battalions to the neighbourhood of LAUNDRY POST.

Distribution of troops after the attack.
8. After capture of final objective the distribution will be as follows:-

Each Assaulting Battalion. - 3 Coys. each with 2 assaulting platoons in the RED line, 1 in outposts covering Canal crossings and 1 platoon in or in front of the BLUE line.

1 Reserve Coy. in BETHUNE Locality S. of the BEUVRY - BETHUNE Road.

Reserve Battalion.
In Brigade Reserve in LAUNDRY POST. Locality.

Main Line of Resistance.
9. The RED line will be the main line of resistance.
O's.C. Assaulting Battalions will use their Reserve Coys. to restore any partial loss of this line.

Machine Guns. 10. Machine Guns will be disposed as follows :-

(a) 1 Section with each Assaulting Battalion to go forward with the rear waves and establish positions in the RED line after capture.

(b) 2 sections to cover the advance of the Infantry from VERQUIN RIDGE by overhead fire on the BLUE LINE. After the capture of the BLUE line these 2 sections will become Brigade Reserve.

Stokes Mortars. 11. The 58th Trench Mortar Battery will remain in Brigade Reserve.

Liaison. 12. One Officer and 1 Runner from each assaulting battalion will be at Brigade H.Q. for liaison duties.

Ammunition. 13. 2 Limbers per battalion will form a Brigade Reserve near Brigade H.Q. Remaining limbers will push up as close as possible to Battn.H.Q. Empty limbers will be exchanged for full ones at Brigade H.Q.

Withdrawal. 14. There will be no withdrawal without written orders.

Major

A/Brigade Major 58th Infantry Brigade.

21.7.18.

Issued to - 9/R.W.Fusrs.   Staff Capt.
           9/Welch Regt.   Bde. Sigs. Offr.
           2/Wilts Regt.   19th Div. "G" (for inf).
           58/T.M.Bty.

Details of Attack.

8. (a). The attack from the Position of Deployment will commence in Section Columns which will deploy into extended order when necessary. This will probably not be before the dotted blue line is reached.

The rear wave will do any necessary mopping up to the BLUE line. There will be a pause on this line to re-organise and prepare for the further advance. During this pause the Reserve Coys. of Bns. will close up on the assaulting Coys. and will occupy and hold the BLUE line. When the barrage moves forward after the pause on BLUE line the 3 assaulting Coys. of each Bn. will continue the advance in their original formation to the 2nd objective (RED Line), which they will capture.

After the capture of the RED Line the Left Bn. will push forward strong posts as shown on map to secure the QUESNOY SPUR and to give observation to the Canal.

LE QUESNOY Keep should be held by at least two platoons.

(b). Reserve Coys. of Battalions will occupy and hold the BLUE line. The Reserve Coy. of the Right Bn. will be prepared to move forward to assist in clearing BEUVRY village if necessary, its place being taken by one Coy. of Reserve Battalion vide below.

(c). The Reserve Battalion will follow the assaulting battalions about 1,000 yards in Rear as far as the ANNEQUIN - LAUNDRY Line which it will occupy pushing one Coy. forward to the BLUE line to reinforce that line and, if necessary, release the Reserve Coy. of Right Bn. to assist in clearing BEUVRY village.

(d). During the advance from the BLUE to the RED line the flanks of the assaulting battalions will push steadily forward even though the portion moving through BEUVRY village itself may be held up so as to outflank the village and if necessary eventually isolate it. In such case troops on the flanks will assist those pushing through the village by getting in on the flanks and rear of the enemy.

(e). Assaulting Battalions will arrange to drop mutual Liaison posts at points of junction on the BLUE and RED lines and at suitable positions between those lines.

Distribution of troops after the attack.

9. After capture of the final objective and re-organisation the position will be held as follows :-

Each Assaulting Battalion. 2 Coys. in RED line with advanced posts holding LE QUESNOY SPUR.
One Coy. in support in position about 300 to 400 yards behind the RED line. One Coy. in Reserve in BLUE line.

Reserve Battalion. 3 Coys. in ANNEQUIN - LAUNDRY line with one platoon in S.P. in F.20.d.2.8. 1 Coy. in BLUE line (under orders of O.C. Right Bn).

Main line of Resistance.

10. The RED line will be the main line of resistance. O's.C. Assaulting Battalions will use their Reserve Coys. to maintain this line or to restore it in case of partial loss.

Machine Guns.

11. One section will follow each assaulting Battalion and will assist the advance on the BLUE line and subsequently the RED line by fire where possible. When RED line is captured they will occupy positions for the defence of that line.

The remaining 2 sections will move forward under the orders of O.C. Coy. with the RESERVE Bn. as far as the ANNEQUIN - LAUNDRY Line. When the BLUE line has been captured and the advance on RED line has commenced these 2 sections will move up and take up positions for the defence of the BLUE line paying special attention to the defence of the valley in F.14.d. and b. Two guns will occupy strong point in F.20.d.2.8. with the platoon of Reserve Bn.

- 3 -

Stokes Mortars.	12. Two mortars will follow the attack of Right Bn and take up a position in the vicinity of the bank in F.20.a. When the advance is continued from BLUE to RED line those mortars will take up positions whence the line of the Branch Canal bank can be enfiladed.
Whippet Tanks.	13. These will operate so as to protect the right flank of the Brigade. They will also assist if necessary in clearing BEUVRY village.
Liaison.	14. One Officer and one runner from each assaulting battalion will be with Bde. H.Q. for liaison duties.
Ammunition.	15. Two limbers per battalion will form a Bde. Reserve near Bde.H.Q. Remaining limbers will push up as close as possible to Bn.H.Q. Empty limbers will be exchanged for full ones at Bde.H.Q.
Withdrawal	16. There will be no withdrawal without written orders.

H W House.
Major

A/Brigade Major 58th Infantry Brigade.

Brigade H.Q.
22.7.18.

SCHEME "B". (A Bde.).

APPENDIX I.

If ordered to move to the positions of Assembly for A Brigade Units will move to Assembly positions in the woods North of VAUDRICOURT (K.4.a.) shown on attached map.
Bde.H.Q. to VAUDRICOURT CHATEAU (K.4.a.7.7.).

Order of March
    58th Brigade.H.Q.
    58th T.M.Battery.
    2/Wiltshire Regt.
    9/R.W.Fusiliers.
    9/Welch Regt.

Route: - AUCHEL - MARLES-les-MINES - SOUTHERN edge of BOIS DES DAMES - K.1.d.4.1. - K.1.b.3.2. - and thence by HESDIGNEUL - VAUDRICOURT Road.

APPENDIX II

1. On receipt of orders to move to the Positions of deployment (Yellow line) units will march independently as under. As far as possible VERQUIN will be avoided.

    (a) Right Bn. (9/R.W.Fus).

        Position of deployment - Right on cross roads K.6.a.7.9. Left on trench at E.29.d.7.6.
        Route.
        Debouch from E. edge of VAUDRICOURT wood in K.4.b. South of DROUVIN - VERQUIN Road, thence to slag heap in K.5.b.7.9., thence round both sides of slag heap.

    (b) Left Bn. (9/Welch R.).

        Position of deployment.- Right on trench at E.29.d.7.6. Left on track in E.29.a.
        Route:
        Debouch from E. edge of VAUDRICOURT wood in K.4.b. North of DROUVIN - VERQUIN Road, thence across country avoiding VERQUIN as much as possible.

    (c) Reserve Bn. (2/Wilts).

        Position of deployment - E.28.d. either in Eastern edge of wood or in the open low ground to the East of it.

        Route: Direct.

        M.G.Coy.- One section to follow each assaulting battalion and two sections the Reserve Bn. to their positions of deployment.

        T.M.B. - Two mortars with right assaulting battalion.
                Remainder stay at Bde.H.Q.

        Bde.H.Q. - Remain in VAUDRICOURT CHATEAU.

SECRET.   H.

SCHEME "A" (RIGHT (A) BRIGADE).

COUNTER-ATTACK ON MT. BERNENCHON - HINGES RIDGE.

Ref. attached map and map issued under
this office No. B.M.899 of 14.7.18.

Outline of attack should the 58th Brigade be ordered to
take over the task allotted to "A" Brigade.

Preliminary .. The moves of the Brigade to positions of assembly and from
Moves.   these to Line of Deployment (Yellow line) are dealt with in
                Appendices I and II attached.

Intention.   1. The attack will be delivered by "A" Infy. Bde. on the Right
                and "B" Bde. on the Left.

General   2. The attack of "A" Bde. will be delivered from the line of
Plan.   deployment (Yellow Line W.13.d.6.5. - W.7.central).
                Direction - boundaries and objectives of the attack are shown
                on the attached map. After having established the RED line -
                posts will be pushed forward to cover the Canal crossings.
                The attack will be carried out by 2 battalions in front and 1
                battalion in Reserve.

                9th Bn R.W.Fusiliers will attack on the right.
                9th Bn Welch Regiment will attack on the left.
                2nd Bn Wiltshire Regiment will be in Bde. Reserve.

H Q   3. Assaulting Bns. H.Q. - with Reserve Coy.
                Reserve Bn. H.Q.   - (1) With Bn. East of River CLARENCE.
                                      (2) With Coy. in SHROPSHIRE line in
                                          W.8.c.
                T.M.Battery - V.24.c.3.4.
                Brigade H.Q - ███████. V.23.a.2.6.

Formation of 4. Each assaulting Bn. will be on a 3 Coy. front. The Brigade
Attack.   Normal formation of attack behind a creeping barrage will be used.
                Distances.   One Coy. in Reserve.
                             20 yards between lines.
                             150 yards between waves.
                             400 yards between assaulting Coys. and Reserve Coys.

Objectives. 5. The first objective (BLUE line) comprises all the enclosures
                West of LANCASHIRE LINE.
                The second objective RED line comprises the SUFFOLK LINE, and
                the unconnected lengths of trenches running South to W.16.a.99.60.
                thence to DOVECOTE where it bends back along the PIONEER LINE.
                After the capture of the RED Line (and as soon as the
                protective barrage allows), posts will be pushed forward to
                localities shown on the map to deny crossings to the enemy.

Barrage.   6. A detailed BARRAGE TABLE will be issued later.

                (1). The attack will be covered by a creeping barrage which will
                move at the rate of a 100 yards in 5 minutes up to the BLUE Line -,
                and at 100 yards in 6 minutes from the BLUE Line to the
                final objective.
                     After capture of the final objective, a protective barrage
                will be put down. Arrangements will be made for this barrage to
                lift when posts are ready to be pushed forward.

                (2). Heavy Artillery will bombard the following points :-

                (a) before Zero LE VERTANNOY - Enclosure in W.8.d. - LE CAUROY -
                    HINGES. The Road from AVELETTE to the Road
                    d'HINGES.

                                                                        (b).

(b) after Zero CANAL CROSSINGS, lines of approach and selected points, keeping always at least 400 yards beyond the line of the creeping barrage.

Details of attack.

7. (a). The attack will be carried out as far as possible in section columns, deployment into extended order will not take place before reaching the line of the creeping barrage unless necessitated by rifle and M.G. fire.

(b). The leading waves of the assaulting Coys. will push right through to the final objective, pausing on the BLUE line 10 minutes to mop it as far as possible.

(c). The second wave will follow right through behind, mopping HINGES and SUFFOLK SWITCH and reinforcing the 1st wave on the final objective if necessary, after which it will also furnish Lewis Gun and rifle posts to be pushed out in front of the RED line.

(d). The Reserve Coy. of each Bn will halt on the BLUE line; it will complete the mopping of this area and consolidate the line.

(e). When the protective barrage lifts posts will be pushed out (1) by the Right Bn. to protect the right flank and command the road from the Canal to HINGETTE, (2) by the Left Bn. to the trenches in W.10.b. to deny the crossings of the CANAL to the enemy.

(f). The Reserve Bn. will move from its position near the River CLARENCE at Zero plus 130 and ~~will take the operation after the objective~~ will take up positions as follows (shown on map attached)

1 Coy. in SHROPSHIRE LINE, W.21.a. (protecting right flank).
1 Coy.   "   "   "   " W.8.d. and W.14.b.
1 Coy.   "   "   "   " W.8.c.
1 Coy. about W.8.central.

(g). The Assaulting Battalions will arrange to form liaison posts at points of junction in the BLUE and RED lines.

Distribution of troops after the attack.

8. After the capture of the final objective, and re-organisation, the positions will be held as follows :-

<u>Right Assaulting Battn.</u> - 3 Coys. in RED line with advanced posts. 1 Coy. in Reserve in or in front of BLUE Line.

<u>Left Assaulting Battn.</u> - 2 Coys. and 2 platoons of the 3rd Coy. in RED line with advanced posts. 2 platoons of the 3rd Coy. in Support in SUFFOLK SWITCH. 1 Coy. in Reserve in the BLUE line

<u>Reserve Battn.</u> - as shown in para. 7 (f).

9. The RED line will be the main line of resistance. O's.C. Assaulting Battalions will use their Reserve Coys. to maintain this line or to restore in case of partial loss.

M.G.Coy.

10. (a). One section of M.G's will follow each Assaulting Battalion. They will be used for the defence of the RED line particular attention being paid to the Southern flank.

(b). 2 sections will take up a position about W.14.c.3.2. from which they will cover the advance of the Infantry with overhead fire on (1) VERTANNOY, (2) HINGES. Later they will form Bde. Reserve, and move to positions in the BLUE Line.

Stokes mortars.

11. Stokes mortars will follow the right battalion to assist in the event of the infantry being held up in front of LE VERTANNOY or later in front of HINGES. Two out of the 4 remaining teams of the T.M.B. will carry for these two guns, the remaining 2 teams will be held in reserve about V.24.c.3.4.

Whippet Tanks.

12. Action of Whippet Tanks will be notified later.

(3).

Liaison. 13. An Officer and 1 runner from each assaulting battalion will be with Bde. H.Q. for liaison duties.

Ammunition 14. Two limbers per battalion will form Bde. Reserve, near Bde. H.Q., Remaining limbers will push up as close as possible to Bn. H.Q. Empty limbers will be exchanged for full ones at Brigade. H.Q.

Withdrawal. 15. There will be no withdrawal without orders.

16. Advanced Bde. Report Centre will be established at STINK INN (W.8.d.) as early as possible.

17. Acknowledge.

[signature]
Major

A/Brigade Major 58th Infantry Brigade.

23.7.18.

Issued to 9/R.W.Fusiliers.
9/Welch Regiment.
2/Wiltshire Regt.
58/T.M.Battery.
Staff Captain.
Bde. Sig. Offr.
19th Div. "G" (for information).

APPENDIX I.

The Brigade will move to rear positions of assembly in the BOIS du REVEILLON (as shown on map attached to Scheme A, issued with my B.M.899 dated 14.7.18.) as follows :-

    Brigade H.Q. - Town Major's office, LA BEUVRIERE.
    9/R.W.Fusiliers in D.2.b.
    9/Welch Regt. in D.9.c.
    2/Wilts Regt. in D.14.b.
    58/T.M.B. - West of 2/Wilts Regt. in D.14.a.

ROUTE: - FERFAY, AUCHEL - LOZINGHEM - ALLOUAGNE.

APPENDIX II.

The Brigade will move to a position of deployment between W.13.d.6.5. and W.7.central (Yellow line). Although it would probably be necessary for leading platoons to deploy on reaching the road through W.13.d. and a., and W.7.c. the Yellow line shows the approximate line on which the deployment of the Brigade would become complete. The pause on this line should, of course, be as brief as possible.

The Reserve Battalion and T.M.B. will assemble in the ground East of the River CLARENCE as shown on the map attached.

Bde.H.Q. will move to Orchard V.23.a.2.6.

ROUTE: - 9/R.W.Fusrs. - A. Track, A.2. Track then Tracks W.1 - 4.

    9/Welch Regt - B Track, B.1 Track, then tracks X.1 - 4.

    2/Wilts Regt) as for 9/R.W.Fusiliers in that order.
    58th T.M.Bty)

Movement will be by companies at 100 yards intervals, as far as CHOCQUES and LENGLET - thence by platoons at 50 yards intervals.

Vol. 38.

Headquarters
56th Inf. Bde.
(19th Div.)
August 1918

On His Majesty's Service.

16   9/1065

HEADQUARTERS 58TH BRIGADE.
No. Bmv 1656
Date 11-9-18

CONFIDENTIAL.

Headquarters
   19th Division.

   Herewith WAR DIARY for AUGUST for the undermentioned
Unit :-
   58th Infantry Brigade H.Qrs.

                                         Brigadier General

                                 Commanding 58th Infantry Brigade.

11.9.18.

Army Form C. 2118.

WAR DIARY
or
INTELLIGENCE SUMMARY.
(Erase heading not required.)

HQ 58 Infy Bde.

Place	Date	Hour	Summary of Events and Information	Remarks and references to Appendices
LIGHTLIES AIRE.	Aug. 1st		Brigade training. Battalions carrying out Company training.	
	2nd		-do-	
	3rd		-do-	
	4th		-do-	
	5th		-do-	
	6th		Brigade moved forward to relieve 3rd Divn. in HINGES SECTOR. 9th Bn R.W.Fusiliers moved by road to CHOCQUES being in reserve. 9th Bn Welch Regt. and 2nd Bn Wiltshire Regt. moved by bus to CHOCQUES and relieved 2nd SUFFOLKS 76th Brigade. Bde.H.Q. at ABBAYE (W.25.a.0.8) CHOCQUES. (Copy Brigade Order No. 254 attached).	A.
LINE, HINGES SECTION	7th		Enemy reported to be withdrawing - patrols sent out to keep in touch. Line advanced slightly but heavy fire encountered from VERTBOIS FM.	
		10.20pm.	Patrols report enemy seen at Q.35.a.3.8. and machine guns firing from Q.35.c.	
	8th	6.35am	Advance held up, enemy in considerable strength with M.G. and T.M. holding line running N. and S. roughly Q.29.c. Flank units unable to make headway.	
		11.45am	Orders from Divn. to occupy house and orchard at W.6.a.5.4. and push patrols along E. side of MURBRAUNT to outflank VERTBOIS FM.	
		4.45pm	Situation unchanged. Enemy holding FMS. at Q.35.b.2.8. and W.6.a.3.4.	
		7.15.pm	FM. at W.6.a.3.4. now in our possession.	
	9th	4.40pm	Heavy shelling S.W. VERTBOIS FM. Our artillery active from 2.30 - 3.50.p.m.	
		6.20pm	Our line now runs from Q.35.b.9.9. - Q.35.d.20.78 - Q.35.d.4.5. thence along TURBEAUTE to W.5.b.5.7. Q.35.d.2.9. not held by either side. Enemy M.G. active at Q.35.b.0.5.	
	10th	1.pm.	2 prisoners captured by 2nd Bn Wiltshire Regt. near VERTBOIS FM.	
			Line now runs in front VERTBOIS FM. along line of TURBEAUTE from N. Bde. boundary to W.5.b.5.7.	
		4.25pm	Situation normal. 9th Bn Welch Regt. relieved 2nd Wilts Regt. in front line. 9th R.W.Fusrs. moved up into position vacated by 9th Bn Welch Regiment. 2nd Wilts Regt. to Bde. reserve. (Copy Bde. Order No. 255 attached).	B.
	11th		Quiet day.	

A6945 Wt. W11422/M1160 350,000 12/16 D. D. & L. Forms/C/2118/14.

Army Form C. 2118.

WAR DIARY
or
INTELLIGENCE SUMMARY.
(Erase heading not required.)

Instructions regarding War Diaries and Intelligence Summaries are contained in F. S. Regs., Part II. and the Staff Manual respectively. Title pages will be prepared in manuscript.

Place	Date	Hour	Summary of Events and Information	Remarks and references to Appendices
LINE.	12th	4.30pm	Quiet day.	
	13th		Quiet day. Intermittent enemy shelling on right of Support Coy.	
	14th	4.30pm	Quiet day. 9th R.W.Fusrs. relieved 9th Welsh Regt. in front line, 2nd H.L.I. moved up to support, and 9th R.W.Fusrs. into Bde. Reserve. (Copy Bde. Order No. 255 attached).	C
	15th		Quiet day.	
	16th		-do-	
	17th		-do-	
	18th	4.30am	Quiet day. Slight hostile shelling of W.R.C. and C. Div. wire that Corps on left reports numerous explosions on all parts of Corps front. Five explosions on Div. front, at Q.24.d.3.7. and vicinity of PARADIS. Corps report 16th German Div. withdrawn and prisoners of 392 I.R. state they are withdrawing to a line W. of LESTREM with covering rearguard posts. Warning that some night affect our front. The 2nd Bn. 11th Regt. relieved the 9th R.W.Fusrs. in the front line, on the right. (Copy of Bde. Reserve (Copy of Bde. Order No. 267 attached).	D
			the SHROPSHIRE LINE. (Corps or Bde. Order No. ...) Orders are to send forward patrols as to Mormal of PARADIS road in Q.24.a. Outer Div. on left reports that strong patrols are to be sent forward to ascertain if any withdrawal has to battalions on this front.	
	19th			
		5.15pm	Enemy artillery active against CANAL LINE. Patrols have established Post at Q.36.c.9.5. and endeavouring to establish line along road in Q.35.a.b., and d.	
		11.50pm	Div. report line running from K.8.b.8.2. - N.1.d.9.9. - LA TOMBE WILLOT - VERTBOIS FM. No advance to be made by 57th Bde., beyond LESTREM LAWE until Bdes. on either flank come into line but will co-operate with them in endeavouring to outflank any hostile posts. Instructions to Res. to push R.G. well forward by daylight so as d.21 may be able to exercise personal control. (Copy Bde. Order No.258 attached).	
	20th		Patrols pushed forward by 2nd Wiltshire Regt. towards LESTREM LAWE. Enemy M.G. post in wood at Q.36.a.9.5. Patrols in contact with enemy at Q.36.b.6.7.	
		2.45pm	General line runs LONE FARM (R.62.a. and R.31.b.) to R.31.b.5.5. thence approximately due N. through Q.25.central. 2nd Wiltshire Regt. having been squeezed out, Bde. become Bde. in Reserve. (Copy Bde. Order No.258 attached).	E
RESERVE NEDGE	21st		Provisional orders for defence of sector to be taken over from 4th Div. issued (Copy B.M.1420 attached). Guides.	F

A6945 Wt. W14422/M1160 350,000 12/16 D.D. & L. Forms/C/2118/14.

Army Form C. 2118.

WAR DIARY
or
INTELLIGENCE SUMMARY.
(Erase heading not required.)

Instructions regarding War Diaries and Intelligence Summaries are contained in F.S. Regs., Part II. and the Staff Manual respectively. Title pages will be prepared in manuscript.

Place	Date	Hour	Summary of Events and Information	Remarks and references to Appendices
Reserve ASSAYE.	22nd		Quiet day.	
NOISY NOOK. V.12.b.2.6.	23rd		Orders for Brigade to take over new sector from 4th Division. (Copy Bde. Order No. 259 attached)	G.
Sht.36A. S.E.24th	24th		Quiet day. Orders for patrols to push forward and get into touch with enemy.	
	25th		Hostile artillery active on forward area in early morning, some gas shelling. Western line.	
	26th		A quiet day, hostile aircraft active. Our patrols active locating enemy posts.	
	27th		Some shelling of CANAL & GORDON Lines with H.E., otherwise a quiet day. The 9th R.W.Fusiliers relieved the 9th Bn Welch Regiment in the front line. (Copy Bde. Order No. 260 attached).	H.
	28th		The enemy commenced to withdraw from in front of the 9th Bn R.W.Fusrs., front line advanced to vicinity of ZELOBES. Hostile artillery quiet.(Copy Bde. Order No. 261 attached).	I.
	29th		Further withdrawal on the part of the enemy, line pushed to R.26.b.00.90. to R.26.b.7.2. Hostile artillery quiet., from the shelling that did take place it was evident that the bulk of the enemy's artillery had been moved back some distance.	
	30th		Enemy withdrawal continued, front line pushed forward to R.27.c.1.1. to West bank of River LAWE to R.27.c.5.9.	
	31st		Line advanced slightly and patrols crossed the LAWE. 2nd Wilts Regt. relieved the 9th R.W.F. in the front line. On relief 9th R.W.Fusrs. moved to HINGES. (Copy Bde. Order No. 262 attached).	J.
Brigade H.Q.				

11th Septr., 1918. Brigadier General

Commanding 58th Infantry Brigade.

SECRET　　　　　　　　　　　　　　　　　　　　　　　　Copy No. 18

58th Infantry Brigade Order No.254.

Ref. map 1/40,000.　　　　　　　　　　　　　　　　4th August, 1918.

1. The 58th Inf. Brigade will relieve the 76th Inf. Brigade in the HINGES Sector on the night of 6th/7th August.

2. Battalions will take over the line as follows :-

    Front Line .... 2nd Bn Wiltshire Regt.
    Support "   .... 9th Bn Welch Regiment.
    Reserve "   .... 9th Bn R.W. Fusiliers.

    The 2/Wiltshire Regt. and 9/Welch Regt. will move up by bus on the afternoon of the 6th inst. debussing S. of CHOCQUES on the CHOCQUES - ECQUES Road at 6.0.p.m.
    The 9/R.W.Fusiliers will move on the 6th inst. by march route via LILLERS.

3. The Battalions moving by bus should arrange to send forward their cookers to the debussing point so as to give their men a hot meal before moving into the line.

4. Troops debussing will conceal themselves as far as possible under trees etc. until dark.

5. All details of relief will be arranged between C.O's. concerned.

6. Orders as regards Advance parties and Surplus personnel will be issued later.

7. 76th Inf. Bde. H.Q. are at L'ABBAYE,W.25.a.0.8.

8. ACKNOWLEDGE.

　　　　　　　　　　　　　　　　　　　　　　　　　　Captain

　　　　　　　　　　　　　　　Brigade Major 58th Infantry Brigade.

Issued at 8.45.p.m.

    Copy No. 1 G.O.C.
             2 9.R.W.Fus.
             3 9.Welch R.
             4 2.Wilts R.
             5 58.T.M.B.
             6 58.Fld. Amb.
             7 No.4 Coy. Train.
             8 Staff Capt.
             9 Bde. Transport Offr.
            10 Bde. Int. Offr.
            11 Bde. Sig. Offr.
            12 56th Inf. Bde.
            13 57th Inf. Bde.
            14 76th Inf. Bde.
            15 19th Div. "G"
            16 File.
            17) War Diary.
            18)

Addendum No. 1 to 58th Bde. Order No. 254.

5th August, 1918.

1. The 2/Wiltshire Regt. will relieve the 1/Gordon Highlanders in front line. Bn. H.Q. N.10.a.1.1.
   The 9/Welch Regt. will relieve the 2/Suffolk Regt. in Support. Bn. H.Q. V.15.b.65.95.
   The 9/R.W. Fusiliers will move into Reserve. Bn.H.Q. D.5.c.7.9.
   O.C. 58/Bde. will assume command of the line on completion of relief.

2. Debussing orders for units moving by bus will be issued separately.

3. The Debussing Point will be - Head of Column at LE BOUDOU V.29.c.8.2. and not as previously stated. 76th Bde. H.Q. are being notified of this change by this office.
   Guides as arranged by Bn Commanders will meet Bn Commanders at the debussing point.

4. Units will not leave the debussing point until 8.p.m. Bns. will move up by platoons at 100 yards intervals 2/Wiltshire Regt. leading.

5. The 9/R.W.Fusiliers with Cookers and water-carts will move by march route to the Reserve Bn. Area. 2 Companies V.30.c., 2 Companies D.5.b.
   Route:- BOURECQ and LILLERS.
   Bn. will march so as to arrive at LE BOUDOU V.29.c.8.2. at 5.30.p.m. where guides will meet them.
   A representative of 76th Brigade H.Q. will hand over to O.C. 9/R.W.F all defence schemes and programmes of work.

6. The transport of battalions not required at debussing point or in Reserve Bn. Area with Administrative H.Q. and surplus personnel will march under Battalion arrangements.
   Route:- FERFAY - AUCHEL.
   2/Wiltshire Regt. will leave AUCHY by 10.a.m.
   9/Welch Regiment   "   "   RELY by 10.a.m.
   9/R.W.Fusiliers   "   "   LIGNY by 10.30.a.m.

7. Troops and Transport will maintain the following distances on the march :-
   Between Coys........... 100 yards.
   Between unit & Transport........ 100 yards.
   Between every 6 vehicles......... 25 yards.

8. Lewis Guns of Battalions moving by bus will be taken in the busses. Twenty drums per gun will be taken into the line. Lewis Gun limbers will meet Battalions at the debussing point to take guns into the line.

9. The Front Line and Support Battalions will take over the Defence Schemes, Work and wiring schemes, Aeroplane Photos of the Battalions they relieve.

10. Battalions will render to Bde. H.Q. a map showing detailed dispositions by posts, Coy. and Platoon H.Q. by 2.0.p.m. 7th inst.

11. Battalions will render reports in accordance with the schedule laid down for the Bns. they relieve.
    The "Stand to" strength return will reach Bde.H.Q. by 9.am. daily.

12. Relief complete will be reported to Bde.H.Q. by the code words "ORDER No.121 NOTED".

13. Bde.H.Q. will close at LIGNY-les-AIRE at 4.p.m. and re-open at on arrival at L'AURIE W.25.a.0.8.

14. Acknowledge.

_____ Captain
Brigade Major 58th Inf. Brigade.

Issued at 9.p.m.
Issued to all recipients of B.O.254.

SECRET. B. Copy No. 20

58th Brigade Order No. 255.

Reference to
Sheet 36.A. 1/20,000. 9th August, 1918.

1. Unless the tactical situation should not permit of it the following inter-Battalion reliefs will take place on the night of 10th/11th August.

    9th Bn Welch Regt. will relieve the 2nd Bn Wiltshire Regt. in the Front Line.

    2nd Bn Wiltshire Regt. after relief will move into Brigade Reserve.
    Two Companies - SHROPSHIRE Line W.15.d.
    Two Companies and Hd.Qrs. - CHOCQUES.

    9th Bn R.W.Fusiliers will relieve the 9th Bn Welch Regt. in Support.
    At least 1 Company of the 9th Bn Welch Regt. will remain in the CANAL Line until relieved by 9th Bn R.W.Fusiliers.

2. All details of relief, and arrangements for guides, will be made between Battalion Commanders concerned.

3. Units will hand over all trench stores, defence schemes, aeroplane photos, maps and documents relating to the area.

4. O.C., 2nd Bn Wiltshire Regt. will arrange to have all the reconnaissances for the counter-attack schemes for Reserve Battn. carried out as soon as possible.

5. Completion of relief will be wired to Brigade H.Q. using code words:-
    "VACANCY NOT REQUIRED"

6. Front and Support Battalions will render a disposition report to Brigade H.Q. by 2.0.p.m. August, 11th.

7. ACKNOWLEDGE.

    Captain
    Brigade Major 58th Infantry Brigade.

Issued through Signals at
    1.0p.m.

    Copy No. 1 9.R.W.Fusrs.
            2 9.Welch R.
            3 2.Wilts R.
            4 58.T.M.Bty.   14 12th Inf. Bde.
            5 G.O.C.   15 Left Group R.A.
            6 Staff Capt.   16 "   "   M.G.
            7 Bde. Sig. Offr.   17 94th Fld. Coy. R.E.
            8 Bde. Int. Offr.   18 58th Fld. Amb.
            9 B.B.O.   19 No.4 Coy. Train.
           10 B.T.O.   20) War Diary.
           11 19th Div. "G"   21)
           12 56th Inf. Bde.   22 File.
           13 57th Inf. Bde.

SECRET.   Copy No. 2...

58th Infantry Brigade Order No.256.

13th August, 1918.

Ref. to Sheet 36.A
1/20,000.

1.   The following reliefs will take place on the night of the 14th/15th August.
   The 9th Bn R.W.Fusiliers will relieve the 9th Bn Welch Regt. in the front line.
   9th Bn Welch Regt. after relief will move into Brigade Reserve.
   1 Coy - SHROPSHIRE LINE, W.15.d.
   3 Coys. and Hd.Qrs. - CHOCQUES.
   2nd Bn Wiltshire Regt. will relieve the 9th Bn R.W.Fusiliers in Support.
   At least 1 Company of the 9th Bn R.W.Fusiliers will remain in the CANAL Line until relieved by the 2nd Bn Wiltshire Regt.

2.   All details of relief, including guides, will be made between Battalion Commanders concerned.

3.   Units will hand over all Defence Schemes, Aeroplane photos, maps, and documents relating to the area.

4.   All trench and area stores will be handed over on relief, and receipts obtained forwarded to Bde.H.Q. by 8.0.p.m. 15th inst.

5.   O.C., 9th Bn Welch Regiment will arrange to have all the reconnaissances for the counter-attack schemes for Reserve Battalion carried out as soon as possible.

6.   Completion of relief will be wired to Brigade H.Q. using code word "CERTAINLY".

7.   Front and Support Battalions will render a disposition map Scale 1/20,000 to Bde.H.Q. by 2.0.p.m. August 15th. Front Battalion will also show positions of Vickers Guns and L.T.Ms allotted to it.

8.   ACKNOWLEDGE.

                                                                    Captain

                                         Brigade Major 58th Infantry Brigade.

Issued through Signals at 1.30.p.m.

   Copy No. 1 9.R.W.Fusrs.
           2 9.Welch R.
           3 2.Wilts R.
           4 58.T.M.Bty.   13 57th Inf. Bde.
           5 G.O.C.   14 12th Inf. Bde.
           6 Staff Capt.   15 Left Group R.A.
           7 Bde. Sig. Offr.   16   "   "   M.G.
           8 Bde. Int. Offr.   17 94th Fld. Coy.R.E.
           9 B.B.O.   18 58th Fld Amb.
          10 B.T.O.   19 No.4 Coy. Train.
          11 19th Div. "G".   20) War Diary.
          12 56th Inf. Bde.   21)
                                             22 File.

SECRET.   Copy No. 20

58th Infantry Brigade Order No. 257.

17th August, 1918.

Ref. to Sheet 36.A
1/20,000

1. The following reliefs will take place on the night of the 18th/19th August :-

    The 2nd Bn Wiltshire Regt. will relieve the 9th Bn R.W.Fusiliers in the front line.

    9th Bn R.W.Fusiliers after relief will move into Brigade Reserve.
    1 Coy. - SHROPSHIRE LINE, W.15.d.
    3 Coys. and Hd.Qrs. - CHOCQUES.

    9th Bn Welch Regt. will relieve the 2nd Bn Wiltshire Regiment in Support.
    At least 1 Company of the 2nd Bn Wiltshire Regt. will remain in the CANAL LINE until relieved by the 9th Bn Welch Regiment.

2. All details of relief, including guides, will be made between Battalion Commanders concerned.

3. Units will hand over all Defence Schemes, Aeroplane photos, maps, and documents relating to the area.

4. All trench and area stores will be handed over on relief, and receipts obtained forwarded to Brigade H.Q. by 8.0.p.m. 19th instant.

5. Completion of relief will be wired to Brigade H.Q. using code words "LEAVE GRANTED".

6. Front and Support Battalions will render a disposition map to Bde.H.Q. by 2.0.p.m. August 19th. Front Battalion will also show positions of Vickers Guns and L.T.M's allotted to it.

7. ACKNOWLEDGE.

, Captain

Brigade Major 58th Infantry Brigade.

Issued through Signals at 10.30.a.m.

Copy No. 1 9.R.W.Fusrs.   12 56th Inf Bde.
        2 9.Welch Regt.   13 57th Inf Bde.
        3 2.Wilts Regt.   14 10th Inf Bde.
        4 58.T.M.Bty.   15 Left Group R.A.
        5 G.O.C.   16   "   "   M.G.
        6 Staff Capt.   17 94th Fld.Coy.R.E.
        7 Bde. Sig. Offr.   18 58th Fld Amb.
        8 Bde. Int. Offr.   19 No. 4 Coy. Train.
        9 B.B.O.   20) War Diary.
       10 B.T.O.   21)
       11 19th Div. "Q"   22 File.

SECRET.

Addendum No. 1 to 58th Infantry Brigade
Order No. 258.

20th August, 1918.

The 2nd Bn Wiltshire Regiment will keep in constant touch with the situation by means of a patrols going forward and visiting the Coys. of the Battalions in front of them.

[signature]
Captain

Brigade Major 58th Infantry Brigade.

Issued to all recipients of 58th Brigade O.O.258.

SECRET

E

Copy No. 12

58th Brigade Order No.258.

20th August, 1918.

Refce to Sheet 36.A. S.E.

1. The general line now runs LONE LANE (R.32.a. and R.31.b.), to R.31.b.5.8. thence approximately due N. through R.25.central.
    The 8th Bn Gloucestershire Regt. (19th Division) are in touch with 2nd Seaforth Highlanders (4th Div) about R.31.b.5.8.

2. The 2nd Bn Wiltshire Regiment having been squeezed out of its front the Brigade will become the Reserve Bde. of the 19th Division.

3. The 2nd Bn Wiltshire Regiment will move to positions as under, Care being taken that no undue movement takes place during the move -

    One Coy. on the line LE VERTBOIS FM. Q.35.b.2.8. to Farm at W.6.a.3.4.

    Three Coys. in the EDINBURGH and ABERDEEN LINES.

    Battalion H.Q. to old position at W.10.a.1.1. with forward Report Centre at W.4.d.2.9.

4. The 9th Bn R.W.Fusiliers and 9th Bn Welch Regiment will remain in their present positions.

5. The four L.T.M's and one section Machine guns will remain under orders of O.C., 2nd Bn Wiltshire Regt. and will move under his orders to locations within his new lines which will be reported to Brigade H.Q.

6. Completion of move of the 2nd Bn Wiltshire Regiment will be reported to Brigade H.Q. using Code word "AMAZON".

7. ACKNOWLEDGE.

                                                          Captain

Brigade Major 58th Infantry Brigade.

Issued through Signals at 2.45.pm.

    Copy No. 1 9.R.W.Fusrs.
             2 9.Welch Regt.
             3 2.Wilts Regt.
             4 58.T.M.Bty.
             5 19th Div. G.
             6 56th Inf. Bde.
             7 57th Inf. Bde.
             8 10th Inf. Bde.
             9 Staff Capt.
          10 Left Group R.A.
          11 Left Group M.G's.
          12)War Diary.
          13)
          14 File.

SECRET. 58th Bde. B.M.1420. Copy No. 14.

58th INFANTRY BRIGADE.

PROVISIONAL DEFENCE ORDERS FOR NEW SECTOR.

Boundaries. 1. The Boundaries of the Brigade Sector are as shown on attached Map "A".

Organisation of Front. 2. The front is organised for defence in two Zones :-

    (a). The Outpost Zone, comprising the area East and exclusive of the front line of the Battle Zone.

    (b). The Battle Zone. The front system of the Battle Zone with which the Brigade is immediately concerned consists of the area between the Front Line of the Battle Zone and the RESERVE and CANAL LINE both lines ~~exclusive~~ inclusive.

Dispositions. 3. The Line will be held as follows :-

    (a). One Battalion (with 1 section Vickers guns and 2 Light Trench Mortars attached) holding the Outpost Zone.

    (b). Two battalions side by side holding the 1st System of the Battle Zone. The dividing line between Bns. is shown on Map "A".

Outpost Battalion. 4. The Outpost Battalion will hold the Outpost Line as under :-

    (i). Two Companies side by side forming the picquet line and immediate supports. Two, or if necessary, 3 platoons of each Coy. will form the picquet line, the remainder being in immediate support about 200 yards behind.

    Two Companies holding the Outpost Line of Resistance. The approximate points at which the Outpost Line of Resistance will join that of the Units on Right and Left will be notified as soon as possible.

    The 4 Vickers Guns and 2 L.T. Mortars will be disposed primarily for the defence of the Outpost Line of Resistance but can be moved by O.C. Battalion for any special purpose.

    H.Q. Outpost Battalion at present Q.29.d.2.9.

Battle Zone Battalions. 5. (a). The two Battalions holding the First System of the Battle Zone will be disposed side by side. It is the intention to eventually hold the Battle Zone as under :-

    (i). A line of strong points each garrisoned by a platoon (in some cases 1 Vickers gun in addition) approximately along the Line of the Front Line of the Battle Zone. There will be two or three of these strong posts 500 to 600 yds. apart on each Battalion front. They will be prepared and wired for all round defence, and will be so sited or built that they will not mask fire from the Line of retention. These posts will be held at all costs and there will be no retirement from them.

    (ii). Two full Coys. from each battalion plus any platoons not required for strong points as in (i) will hold the Line of retention, which is the RESERVE and CANAL Line. This line will be held along its whole length by section posts or L.G. Teams so that the interval between any two posts will never be more than 30 to 40 yards.

- 2 -

(iii). One Company from each battalion will be behind the Line of retention as a Counter-attacking Company. In the case of the Right Battalion this Coy. will be in GORDON Trench. In the case of the Left Battalion a suitable position will have to be found probably somewhere about Q.31.b. These Coys. will not be responsible for the defence of any line but will be disposed with a view to counter-attack. They will be prepared to counter-attack on any portion of their Battalion front. Right Battalion Counter-attacking Company will also be prepared to counter-attack on right portion of Line of Retention of Left Battalion, i.e. the portion on the near side of the Canal. Probable counter-attacks to be most carefully reconnoitred, routes marked, and counter-attacks practised both by day and night.

(b). Until, however, the Strong Points are ready the Battle Zone will be held as under on each Bn front :-

1 Coy. holding front line disposed in posts of ½ platoons or sections along the front.

2 Coys. holding Line of Retention.

1 Coy. Counter-attack.

In other respects the arrangements laid down in (a) above will apply.

H.Q. Right Battn....... HINGES, W.10.a.1.1.
H.Q. Left Battn....... HALF-WAY HOUSE, W.2.b.4.5.
Brigade H.Q............ NOISY NOOK, V.12.b.2.6.
moving shortly to STINK INN, W.3.d.2.6.

M. Guns & T. Mortars. 6. Trench Mortars of 58th L.T.M.Battery (less the 2 attached to Outpost Battn), will be disposed for the defence of the Line of Retention. Machine Gun Defence is being arranged by 19th M.G.Battalion.

General Policy. 7. (a). A policy of vigorous patrolling will be adopted by the Outpost Battalion, in order to locate the enemy, secure identifications, and to ensure that any pronounced thinning of the enemy's Outpost Line will be at once apparent.
Should the enemy commence a further withdrawal O.P. Battalion will automatically become the advanced guard and will follow up keeping in touch with the enemy, harassing his rearguards and forcing them to withdraw before they are ready. The 4 Vickers Guns and 2 Trench Mortars will remain attached to the Battalion. The present policy is to be one of vigorous activity on the part of forward troops, but in which, as far as possible, undue losses are to be avoided.

(b). The 2 Battalions in the Battle Zone will have the Forward Area and routes to Outpost Line thoroughly reconnoitred so as to be able to advance rapidly if required owing to a withdrawal of the enemy or for any offensive action on our part.

Action in case of enemy attack. 8. In case of an enemy attack

(a) Outpost Battalion.
The picquet line will hold up the enemy if possible. In the case of small attacks or raids local counter-attacks from immediate support will recapture any posts temporarily lost. In the event of a heavy attack forcing the picquet to fall back they will do so on to the line of resistance of the Outposts. There will be no withdrawal from this line except on the order of the Battalion Commander.
The Battalion Commander will not order a withdrawal unless it is certain that the enemy is attacking in force and on a large front, and it is evident that the outpost line of

resistance/

Resistance cannot be maintained. In this event he will withdraw fighting, harassing and delaying the enemy, and inflicting as many casualties on him as possible in order to disorganise and break up his attack before it reaches the Battle Zone. The Outpost Battalion will after passing through the Front System of the Battle Zone re-organise in rear of the Line of Retention and become Brigade Reserve.

(b). Battalions holding Battle Zone.

(a). The Strong Points in front of the Line of Retention will fight to the last. There is to be no withdrawal from them.

(b). Troops holding the Line of Retention will maintain their position at all costs. There is to be no withdrawal from this line. Should the enemy penetrate into any portion of the Line of Retention the Counter-attacking Companies will be launched in counter-attack without hesitation to restore the line.
Unless, however, troops from in rear have arrived to take their place, or the situation is well in hand, troops in or in rear of the Line of Retention will not be used to counter-attack in front of that line.

(c). Each Battle Zone Battalion will send an Officer and Runners to the H.Q. of O.P. Battalion to keep it in touch with any changes in the situation and the progress of the attack.

(d). It is very important that the troops holding the strong points and the Line of Retention understand that if the Outpost troops are forced to withdraw, they will pass through the Line of Retention and reform behind it. Under no circumstances must troops holding strong points or the Line of Retention become involved in this withdrawal.

9. ACKNOWLEDGE.

, Captain

Brigade Major 58th Infantry Bde.

Brigade H.Q.

21st August, 1918.

Copy No. 1 9.R.W.Fusrs.
2 9.Welch R.
3 2.Wilts R.
4 58.T.M.Bty.
5 19th Div. "G".
6 Left Group Arty.
7 19th M.G.Battn.
8 56th Inf. Bde.
9 10th Inf. Bde.
10 57th Inf. Bde.
11 C.R.E., 19th Div.
12 O.C. Bde. Signals.
13 Bde. Transport Offr.
14) War Diary.
15)
16 File.

SECRET. 58th Brigade No. B.M.1420/1.

All Units.   19th Division "G".
56th Inf. Bde.   C.R.E., 19th Divn.
57th Inf. Bde.   O.C., Bde. Signals.   19th M.G. Battn.
Left Group R.A.   231st Inf. Bde.
                    Bde. Transport Offr.

Addendum to 58th Brigade PROVISIONAL DEFENCE ORDERS, B.M.1420 para. 4.

1. 4 18 pdrs. and 2 4.5 Howitzers forming a composite battery known as the "Outpost Battery" are located as under.

    H.Q. .... Q.34.b.6.9.
    2 18 pdrs .... Q.34.b.3.3.
    2 18 pdrs .... Q.29.c.1.5.
    2 Hows .... Q.28.d.7.8.

    A Forward O.P. is established at R.25.a.3.7.

2. The Outpost Battery will cover the Outpost Zone, and carry out harassing fire on enemy communications, etc. It will act in close liaison with the Outpost Battalion and will engage any favourable targets which may present themselves.

3. In the event of an enemy withdrawal the O.P. Battalion automatically becomes the Advanced Guard Battalion and the Outpost Battery will act as part of the Advanced Guard under the orders of O.C. that Battn.

                                               Captain
                        Brigade Major 58th Infantry Brigade.

24.8.1918.

SECRET   G   Copy No. 22

58th Infantry Brigade Order No.259.

21st August, 1918.

Reference to Sheet 36.A. S.E.

1. On the 23rd instant the 19th Division will take over that portion of the 4th Divisional front South of the line shown in RED on Map "A" already forwarded with Provisional Defence Orders issued under B.M.1420 dated 21.8.18.

2. On August 23rd and the night August 23rd/24th the 58th Inf. Bde. will take over the sector shown as the Left Bde. on Map "A". That portion North of the present Divisional boundary will be taken over from 10th Inf. Bde. Any troops S. of the new Brigade Boundary may be withdrawn.

3. 9th Bn Welch Regiment will be Outpost Battalion and will take over from 2nd Bn Seaforth Highlanders.
2nd Bn Wiltshire Regt. will be Right and 9th Bn R.W.Fusiliers Left Battle Zone Battalions. Battalions will hold their sectors as laid down in Provisional Defence Orders already forwarded under B.M. No. 1420.
In cases where the relief is not carried out platoon by platoon relieving Companies will ensure that they have satisfactorily taken over the line within the limits for which they are responsible before the troops holding that portion of the line withdraw.

4. The relief will be carried out in accordance with the attached Table. All other details of relief except those mentioned in the attached table to be arranged between C.O's concerned.

5. The 4 Machine Guns of 19th M.G.Battalion attached to the Outpost Battalion will relieve the 4 machine guns attached to the Outpost Battalion of the 10th Inf. Bde. These guns may subsequently be moved by the O.C. Outpost Battalion to any positions he may select.

6. All details for relief of the Light Trench Mortars will be arranged between Battery Commanders. The guns in the Outpost Line will be relieved at one hour's intervals.
Relief of guns in HARRISON Trench to be complete by 3.p.m.

7. All Maps, Aeroplane Photos, Documents relating to the sector, Programmes of work and Trench stores will be taken over and receipts given for what is taken over.

8. The 9th Bn Welch Regiment will send forward an Advance Party consisting of 1 Officer per Coy, 1 N.C.O. per Platoon and 1 Offr. and 1 N.C.O. from Battalion H.Q. to remain in the line for 24 hours before the arrival of their Battalion. Guides will meet this party at Q.34.b.65.90. at 8.0.p.m. August 22nd.
Battalion Commanders of the Battalions in the Battle Zone positions will make their own arrangements for sending advance parties.
All advance parties to be rationed up to and including the 24th instant.

9. Units will render a disposition map to Brigade H.Q. by 12 noon August 24th. Outpost Battalion will show positions of Machine Guns and L.T.Mortars allotted to it. Positions of Anti-aircraft L.G's will also be shown by all battalions.

10. Completion of relief and in the case of 2nd Bn Wiltshire Regt. completion of dispositions will be wired to Brigade H.Q. using code word "PARIS".

11. Brigade H.Q. will close at L'ABBAYE at 6.0.p.m. August 23rd and will re-open at NOISY NOOK V.12.b.2.6. at the same hour.

12. Administrative Instructions are being issued separately by the Staff Captain.

P.T.O

12. ACKNOWLEDGE.

[signature]

Captain

Brigade Major 58th Infantry Brigade.

Issued through Signals at 11.p.m.

Copy No. 1 9.R.W.Fusrs.
       2 9.Welch R.
       3 2.Wilts R.
       4 58.T.M.Bty.
       5 G.O.C.
       6 Staff Capt.
       7 Bde.Sig.Offr.
       8 Bde.Int.Offr.
       9 B.B.O.
      10 B.T.O.
      19th Div. 'G'
      12 56th Inf. Bde.
      13 57th Inf. Bde.
      14 10th Inf. Bde.
      15 Left Group R.A.
      16 "   "   M.G.
      17 94th Fld. Coy.
      18 58th Fld. Amb.
      19 No. 4 Coy. Train.
      20 19th M.G.Bn.
      21) War Diary.
      22)
      23 File.

Relief Table to accompany 58th Brigade Order No.259.

Unit.	Relieve.	Position.	Route.	Meet guides at	Time of meeting guides.	Remarks.
9th Bn Welch Regiment.	2nd Seaforth Hrs.	Outpost Battn.	HINGES Road	Junction of HINGES Road & FORD LANE, Q.34.d.4.6.	9.p.m.	) Number of) guides to) be settled) between
9th Bn R.W.Fusiliers.	1st R. Warwickshire Regiment.	Left Battn. in Battle Zone.	GONNEHEM MOORLAND Road.	Cross roads LES HARISOIRS, N.2.b.0.6.	2.p.m.	) C.O's) concerned.)
2nd Bn Wiltshire Regt.	2nd D. of Wellington Regiment.	Right Battalion in Battle Zone.	-	-		Relief to commence at 3.p.m.

NOTE: A distance of 100 yards will be maintained between platoons during relief.

SECRET.

Addendum No. 1 to 58th Infantry Brigade
Order No.259.

22nd August, 1918.

1. In the event of an attack or preliminary bombardment developing during the relief, troops of the 58th Inf. Bde. Sth. of the CANAL will man the nearest trenches and report their whereabouts to 10th Inf. Brigade H.Q.
   Troops of the 58th Inf. Bde. N. of the CANAL will man the nearest trenches and put themselves under the orders of the Battalion Commander whom they are relieving.

2. Platoons moving by daylight will move at intervals of 200 yards instead of 100 yards as previously stated.

Captain
Brigade Major 58th Infantry Brigade.

Issued to all recipients of 58th Inf. Bde. O.O.259.

SECRET Copy No. 19

58th Infantry Brigade Order No. 260.

August 25th, 1918.

Ref. to Sheet 36.A. S.E.

1. The 9th Bn R.W.Fusiliers will relieve the 9th Bn Welch Regt. in the Outpost Line on the 27th/28th August.
   On relief 9th Bn Welch Regiment will move to positions in the Battle Zone vacated by 9th Bn R.W.Fusiliers.

2. All details of relief will be arranged between C.O's concerned.

3. (a). All maps, aeroplane photos, and documents relating to the area, programmes of work, trench and area stores will be handed over and receipts given.

   (b). All daily working parties being found by the 9th Bn R.W.Fusrs. will be taken over by the 9th Bn Welch Regt.

4. Battalions will forward a map showing their dispositions by platoons to reach this office by 12 noon 28th inst. Outpost Battn. dispositions will include positions of the section of M.G's and L.T.M's attached to it. Maps will be returned to Battalions if desired.

5. In order that the line of retention may not be completely unoccupied during the relief the O.C. 2/Wiltshire Regiment will arrange for their counter-attacking Company to occupy this line when vacated by the 9th Bn R.W.Fusiliers. Details to be arranged between C.O's.
   It will return to its counter-attacking position as soon as the first Company of 9th Bn Welch Regt. arrives in the Line of Retention.

6. Completion of relief to be wired to Brigade H.Q using following code words:-
   9th Bn R.W.Fusiliers......... ARRAS.
   9th Bn Welch Regt............ SOISSONS.

7. ACKNOWLEDGE.

Captain
Brigade Major 58th Infantry Brigade.

Issued through Signals at 8.0.p.m.

Copy No. 1 9.R.W.Fusrs.
2 9.Welch Regt.
3 2.Wilts Regt.
4 58.T.M.Bty.
5 G.O.C.
6 Staff Capt.
7 Bde. I.O.
8 Bde. T.O.
9 Bde. Sig. Offr.
10 19th Div 'G'
11 56th Inf. Bde.
12 57th Inf. Bde.
13 229th Inf. Bde.
14 230th Inf. Bde.
15 58th Fld. Amb.
16 82nd Fld. Coy. R.E.
17 No. 4 Coy. Train.
18) War Diary.
19)
20 File.

SECRET

Copy No. 14.

58th Infantry Brigade Order No. 261.

28th August 1918.

Ref: Map Sheet 36A S.E. 1/20.000.

1. The Divisional front is being advanced to the approximate line R.33.d.7.5 - R.27.d.0.2 - R.20.c.9.2.

2. The Brigade front will be advanced tonight and will be established by tomorrow morning on the line R.27.d.0.2 - R.27.c.7.7 - R.27.c.1.8 - along the North and East side of the road leading to CROIX MARM USE.
   Brigades on both flanks are also advancing their line.
   Junction will be established with 56th Brigade at Road Junction R.27.d.0.2 and with 177th Brigade at R.20.c.9.2.

3. Outpost line of resistance will remain as at present till new line is established unless O.C. 9th R.W.Fusiliers finds it necessary to move Reserve Coys. forward to support leading Coys.

4. Care must be taken to throw back defensive flanks to join units on flanks until they are up in line.

5. Time is left to O.C. 9R.W.Fusiliers provided the line is established by 5 a.m.

6. Patrols will be pushed forward from new line to establish touch with enemy.

7. Acknowledge.
   9/R.W.Fusiliers to acknowledge by wire immediately.

, Captain,

Brigade Major 58th Infantry Brigade.

Issued through Signals at 6.30 p.m.

Copy No			
1	9/R.W.Fus.	9.	56th Bde.
2	9/Welch.	10.	57th Bde.
3	2/Wilts.	11.	177th Bde.
4	58/T.M.Bty.	12.	Left Group, R.F.A.
5	G.O.C.	13.	Left Group, M.G.
6	Staff Captain.	14)	
7	B. I. O.	15)	War Diary.
8	19th Div "G".	16.	File.

SECRET J. Copy No. 19.

58th Inf. Brigade Order No.362.

29th August, 1918.

Reference Sheet
36A S.E. 1/20,000.

1. The 2nd Bn Wiltshire Regiment will relieve the 9th Bn R.W.Fusrs. in the Outpost Line on the night 31st August/1st September. On relief the 9th Bn R.W.Fusiliers will move to positions in the Battle Zone vacated by 2nd Bn Wiltshire Regiment.

2. All details of relief will be arranged between O.C's concerned.

3. (a) All maps, aeroplane photos, and documents relating to the area, programmes of work, trench and area stores will be handed over and receipts given.

   (b) All daily working parties being found by 2nd Bn Wiltshire Regt. will be taken over by 9th Bn R.W.Fusiliers.

4. Battalions will forward a map showing their dispositions by platoons to reach this office by 12 noon 1st Septr. Outpost Battn. dispositions will include position of the section of M.G's and L.T.M's attached to it. Maps will be returned to Battalions if desired.

5. In order that the Line of Retention may not be completely unoccupied during the relief the O.C., 9th Bn Welch Regiment will arrange for the three platoons of the Counter-attacking Company on the West side of the Canal to occupy this line when vacated by the 2nd Bn Wiltshire Regt. Details to be arranged between C.O's. The three platoons will return to their Counter-attacking positions as soon as the first Coy. of the 9th Bn R.W.Fusiliers arrive in the Line of Retention.

6. Completion of relief to be wired to Brigade H.Q. using following code words :-

   9th Bn R.W.Fusiliers........ WELL.
   2nd Bn Wiltshire Regiment.... DOME.

7. ACKNOWLEDGE.

                                          Captain

                              Brigade Major 58th Infantry Brigade.

Issued through Signals at 8.p.m.

Copy No. 1 9.R.W.Fus.
        2 9.Welch R.   11 56th Inf. Bde.
        3 2.Wilts R.   12 57th Inf. Bde.
        4 58.T.M.Bty.   13 177th Inf. Bde.
        5 G.O.C.   14 178th Inf. Bde.
        6 Staff Capt.   15 58th Fld. Amb.
        7 Bde. I.O.   16 82nd Fld. Coy. R.E.
        8 Bde. T.O.   17 No.4 Coy. Train.
        9 Bde. Sig. Offr.   18) War Diary.
       10 19th Div. 'G'   19)
                               20 File.

19

WO 58 Supply Btly
(19ᵃ Bde)
Vol 39
September 1918

14

On His Majesty's Service.

D.A.G.
G.H.Q.
3RD Echelon.

WAR DIARY or INTELLIGENCE SUMMARY.

Army Form C. 2118.

(Erase heading not required.)

HEADQUARTERS,
58TH BRIGADE.
No. B.M. 968
Date 10/10/18

Place	Date	Hour	Summary of Events and Information	Remarks and references to Appendices
	Septr. 1st.		Brigade Headquarters move to X.2.a.5.8. (LOCON) from STINK INN. 2nd Wilts Regt. as Outpost Coy. move forward about 1000 yards and occupy a line in R.30.a. and c. and R.36.a. In touch with enemy along the whole line. No captures - casualties 3 wounded. Ordered to push forward at daylight to conform with advance of 57th Brigade on Right. 177th Inf Bde. on left in line with 58th Bde.	
X.2.a.5.8.	2nd		Situation at early morning unchanged. Still in close touch with enemy. Warning order issued for an attack on 3rd instant in conjunction with Divisions on Right and Left. Operation Order issued at 3.30.p.m. 9th Bn Welch Regt. are moved up on right of 2nd Wilts Regt. 9th R.W.Fusiliers in Brigade Reserve (See Bde. Order No. 264 marked A and attached).	A.
	3rd		Zero hour 5.30.a.m. Attack commenced under creeping barrage of shrapnel. Completely successful captures 53 prisoners including 2 Officers some Light Machine Guns and 1 T.M. Casualties 10 killed 44 wounded one Officer wounded. Detailed account of the attack is attached and marked B Final line established LANSDOWNE POST - PONT LOGY - CURZON POST - EUSTON POST - ROUGE CROIX EAST POST with patrols pushed forward to keep touch with the enemy. Later in the day efforts made to establish posts in TILLELOY SOUTH POST for the purpose of preventing enemy removing guns. TILLELOY SOUTH POST is found occupied by enemy. Heavy M.G. fire continuaed. Captured guns are removed by the enemy. Operation Order issued for further advance, on 9th inst. to Old British front line with B Line as intermediate objective. 58th Bde. Transport moved from CHOCQUES to HINGES.	B.
	4th		"B" Line reached by 9th Welch Regt. and 2nd Wilts at 7.30.a.m. Posts established in MOATED GRANGE FARM. 9th R.W.F. moved up two Companies to occupy Outpost Line of Resistance. Casualties 10 killed and 12 wounded. Brigade Headquarters moved to WELLINGTON POST R.29.b.2.1. 2.p.m. Orders issued 2.40.p.m. for the relief of 58th Bde. by 57th Bde. on night 4th/5th.G.161 marked C and attached).	C.
R.29.b.2.1.	5th		Relief complete 1.22.a.m. 9th Welch Regt. moved to bivouacs S. of LOCON. 9th R.W.F. move to bivouacs in ESSARS Area. 2nd Bn Wilts Regt. move to CANAL BANK between AVELETTE and HINGES Bridges, with Headquarters at GORDON HOUSE. 9th Welch report gas booby traps in O.B.L. caused 31 gas casualties in 1 Coy.	
STINK INN.	6th) 10th)		Training under Battalion arrangements. 2nd Wilts proceeded by bus to BOMY for a tactical scheme under Corps arrangements. Orders issued for relief of 57th Bde. in the line by 58th Bde. Provisional Defence Orders issued 9th inst. (Corps attacked and marked C.I.)	

Army Form C. 2118.

WAR DIARY
or
INTELLIGENCE SUMMARY.
(Erase heading not required.)

Instructions regarding War Diaries and Intelligence Summaries are contained in F.S. Regs., Part II. and the Staff Manual respectively. Title pages will be prepared in manuscript.

Place	Date	Hour	Summary of Events and Information	Remarks and references to Appendices
STINK INN	11th		On the evening Septr 11th the 58th Bde. relieved the 57th Bde. in the left sector of the Divnl. front. Relief complete by 4.45.a.m. Final dispositions 9th R.W.F. Right front Bn, 9th Welch left front Bn, 2nd Wilts support.	D
R.34.b.9.7.	12th		Quiet day and night.	
	13th		From 9.45. to 10.30.a.m. gas bombardment in vicinity of PONT LOGY.	
	14th		From 9 - 10.a.m. gas bombardment of PONT LOGY. 2nd Wilts relieved 9th Welch in left sub-sector relief complete 12.15.a.m.	E
	15th		Post of 9th R.W.F. at M.35.d.85.15. rushed and garrison captured, otherwise quiet day.	
	16th		Quiet day.	
	17th		Quiet day in forward area some shelling of battery positions and LES HUIT MAISONS.	
	18th		A Quiet day.	
	19th		A quiet day, the 9th Welch relieved the 9th R.W.F. in the right sub-sector.	F
	20th		A quiet day. The 57th Bde. attacked the DISTILLERY S.17.central and SHEPHERD'S REDOUBT, both were captured, prisoners 1 Officer and 129 O.R. Little retaliation on our front.	
	21st		A quiet day intermittent shelling of Bde. area by hostile artillery. 3/30.a.m. hostile attack captured NORA TRENCH held by 57th Bde. Orders for the relief of the 58th Bde. in the Left Sector of the Divisional front by the 56th Bde. 9th R.W.F. on relief move to ESSARS, 2nd Wilts to CANAL BANK (Bn.H.Q. GORDON HOUSE, HINGES). 9th Welch to LOCON, 58th T.M.B. to LONG CORNET W.23.b.75.15.	G
	22nd		Quiet day on Bde. sector. Our aircraft very active. Hostile artillery shelled Bde. area intermittently.	

Army Form C. 2118.

WAR DIARY
or
INTELLIGENCE SUMMARY.

(Erase heading not required.)

Instructions regarding War Diaries and Intelligence Summaries are contained in F. S. Regs., Part II. and the Staff Manual respectively. Title pages will be prepared in manuscript.

Place	Date	Hour	Summary of Events and Information	Remarks and references to Appendices
W.23.b.75.15.	23rd		Relief of 58th Bde. by 56th Bde. complete 1.20.a.m. Brigade Headquarters moved to LONG CORNET Sheet 36 W.23.b.80.15.	
	24th		Units resting and bathing; weather fine.	
	25th		Units training. During the night some intermittent shelling of back areas by hostile artillery with H.E. shrapnel.	
	26th		Intermittent shelling of LOCON Area with H.E. shrapnel during the early morning. Warning Order received.	
		9.20.a.m.	The 58th Bde. to relieve the 57th Bde. in the line the night 27th / 28th.	
		9.45am	Warning Order issued to Units by wire.	
		7.30pm	Orders for relief of 57th Bde. by the 58th Bde. issued. Order for Bde. relief cancelled with exception of 9th Welch Regt. who were ordered to relieve the 10th R.War Regt on the night 27th/28th this unit coming under the command of G.O.C. 57th Bde. *Provisional Defence scheme (attd.)*	H
	27th		58th Bde. ordered to relieve 57th Bde. in the Right Sub-sector of the Div. front on night 28th/29th.	I
X.28.a.30.60	28th		Bde. H.Q. closed LONG CORNET 5.p.m. and re-opened LOISNE CHATEAU X.28.a.30.60. Bde. relief reported complete 11.40.pm.	
	29th		Quiet day on the Brigade front.	
		6pm	Operation Order 272 issued. The two forward battalions 9th R.W.F. and 9th Welch Regt to push forward and establish general line S.5.c.5.5. S.11.a.7.9. S.11.a.7.1. S.17.d.8.7. S.11.d.8.3. in conjunction with the 56th Bde. attack on the general line of the DES LAIES DITCH. During afternoon intermittent shelling of Whole Bde. area.	J
	30th		Zero hour. The Right Group Artillery put down an effective barrage M.G's and 58th L.T.M.B. Stokes co-operated. All objectives obtained. Three light M.G's were captured by the 9th Welch Regt. The 9th R.W.F. captured 1 Heavy M.G. Casualties 3 Officers wounded 8 O.R. killed 39 wounded. After the operation the whole of the Bde. area was quiet for the day and night. The Operation Order issued for the relief of 58th Bde. by 230th Bde. 74th Div. on night Octr. 1/2nd.p.m. Bde. and C.O's 230th inf. Bde. reconnoitre the Bde. area.	K
3.10.18.				

Brigadier General
Commanding 58th Infantry Brigade.

SECRET.   A   Copy No. 22

58th Infantry Brigade Order No.264.

2nd September, 1918.

Ref. Map Sheet 36A. S.E. & S.W.
1/20,000 - AUBERS Sheet 1/10,000
and attached map.

GENERAL IDEA.   1.   The 19th Division in conjunction with Divisions on both flanks will attack to-morrow morning 3rd inst.
Zero hour will be notified later.
The 58th Infantry Brigade will be on the Left, the 57th Infantry Brigade on the Right, 59th Division on Left of 58th Inf. Brigade.

JUMPING OFF LINE.   2.   As shown on attached map, issued to Units of 58th Inf. Brigade only. 2nd Bn Wiltshire Regiment will make every
OBJECTIVES & BOUNDARIES.   effort to establish this line to-day where not already on it. There will be a pause of 5 mins. on 1st objective.
A Liaison Post with 59th Division will be established at M.20.d.5.0.

PLAN OF ATTACK   3.   Attack will be carried out by 2 Battalions with 1 Battn. in Brigade Reserve. -

      On right.............. 9th Bn Welch Regiment.
      On Left............... 2nd Bn Wiltshire Regt.
      In Brigade Reserve.... 9th Bn R.W.Fusiliers.

DISPOSITIONS.   4.   Each Assaulting Battalion will attack with 3 Coys. in front line, 1 Coy. in Battalion Reserve.
Each Assaulting Coy. in two waves, 2 platoons in each wave, approximately 300 yds. distance between waves.
Each wave in two lines, 1 L.G.Team or Rifle Section forming 2nd Line.
Leading line of 1st wave in extended order. All remainder in blobs till necessary to deploy.

HEADQUARTERS.   5.
      9th Bn Welch Regiment...... R.28.d.9.0.
      2nd Bn Wiltshire Regt...... R.23.b.3.8.
      9th Bn R.W.Fusiliers....... About R.23.b.75.90.
      Brigade Hd.Qrs............. X.2.a.5.8.

Forward Battalions will establish Advanced Hd.Qrs. in WELLINGTON POST, R.29.b.3.1., as early as possible after Zero and subsequently in vicinity of R.30.c.5.9.
Brigade Forward Station will move with and be established at 2nd Bn Wiltshire Regt. H.Q.

ASSEMBLY.   6.   9th Bn Welch Regiment will to-night take over from 2nd Bn Wiltshire Regt. the right portion of the front from M.25.d.0.7. to Right Brigade Boundary, and will be formed up ready for attack by 3.30.am.
2nd Bn Wiltshire Regiment will re-adjust on the Left Front from from Left Brigade Boundary to M.25.d.0.7. and will be formed up ready for attack by same hour.
Completion of assembly will be reported to Brigade H.Q. by code words :-
      9th Bn Welch Regiment.... CARDIFF.
      2nd Bn Wiltshire Regt.... DEVIZES.

Reserve Companies of Battalions will assemble on line of Queen Mary's Road and will move forward to the jumping-off line at Zero after which they will be used at discretion of O's.C. Battalions. If necessary, portions of them must be used to form defensive flanks.

Reserve Battalion will be assembled WEST of LOCON - LESTREM ROAD in Sq. R.26.d. and R.32.b. by 5.30.a.m.
O.C. Battalion or Adjutant will be at Brigade H.Q. at 6.0.a.m.

BARRAGE. 7. Attack will be carried out under a creeping barrage details of which will be forwarded later. Pace 100 yds. in 2 minutes. There will also be a M.G. Barrage.

MACHINE GUNS. 8. Two Vickers Guns will follow rear wave on each flank of the Brigade. If necessary during the advance they will be prepared to form defensive flanks should troops on either flank be held up. After capture of final objective they will take up positions for its front line defence by direct fire.

TRENCH MORTARS. 9. 2 Mortars will move forward by bounds in rear of centre of each Battalion and be prepared to deal with any points holding up the attack. Carrying party of 30 will be provided by 9th Bn R.W. Fusiliers.

CONSOLIDATION. 10. After capture of final objective the position will be consolidated in depth and the front line will, if necessary, be thinned. Final disposition - 2 Coys. in depth in front. One Coy. in support about or in front of 1st objective (GREEN Line). One Coy. in Reserve in rear of GREEN Line.

PATROLS. 11. As soon as protective barrage beyond final objective admits strong patrols will be pushed forward by 9th Bn Welch Regiment to LORETTO Post and by 2nd Bn Wiltshire Regt. to ROUGE CROIX Posts.

AMMUNITION. 12. Orders re ammunition and bombs are being issued separately.

WATCHES. 13. Watches will be synchronised at 6.0.p.m. and midnight.

14. ACKNOWLEDGE.

F.H. Fraser.
Captain

Brigade Major 58th Infantry Brigade.

Issued through Signals at 3.30.p.m.

Copy No.			
1	9.R.W.F.	12	56th Inf. Bde.
2	9.Welch R.	13	57th Inf. Bde.
3	2.Wilts Regt.	14	178th Inf Bde.
4	58.T.M.Bty.	15	A.D.M.S., 19th Div.
5	G.O.C.	16	No.4 Coy. Train.
6	Staff Capt.	17	Left Group R.A.
7	Bde. I.O.	18	" " M.G. (2)
8	Bde. Sig. Offr.	19	19th M.G. Battn.
9	Bde. T.O.	20	82nd Fld. Coy. R.E.
10	19th Div. G.	21)	War Diary.
11	19th Div. Q.	22)	
		23	File.

"B"

REPORTS ETC.

Time.	From.	Information.
5.30.a.m.	F.O.O.	Barrage good - shrapnel bursting low.
5.40.a.m.	F.O.O.	So far no enemy barrage.
5.50.a.m.	F.O.O.	Infantry seen at M.25.d.9.5.
6.13.a.m.	F.O.O.	Reports from R.36.a.4.0. infantry well up on 1st objective - prisoners coming in freely.
6.15.a.m.	F.O.O.	9/R.W.F. ordered to move up to position R.28.a.9.9. - R.28.c.4.3. Two companies in front on line (W) of LAWE, 2 Coys. in rear. Bn.H.Q. to R.27.b.45.20.
6.20.a.m.	F.O.O.	Infantry at M.26.d.3.4.
6.25.am.	9/Welch R.	First objective gained - enemy opposition weak. Prisoners coming in - Prisoners from 102 R.I.R.
6.32.a.m.	F.O.O.	Infantry well on way to 2nd objective - very little opposition.
6.40.a.m.	F.O.O.	Infantry about 200 yards off 2nd objective - prisoners coming in well.
6.45.a.m.	2/Wilts R.	Prisoners reported 1 L/Cpl. 8 O.R. 102 R.I.R. 23rd R.D. (1 prisoner wears 392 R.I.R on shoulders but has 102 R.I.R. in paybook.)
6.50.a.m.	F.O.O.	Report from M.27.a.6.9. - prisoners coming in well.
7.2.a.m.	F.O.O.	Report from M.27.b.6.3. Infantry going strong 300 yards in front of him.
7.14.a.m.	2/Wilts R.	Report from O.C. Left Coy. states he is at M.26.b.2.7. and infantry in front of him.
7.45.a.m.		Battalions ordered to try and establish line M.21.d.8.0. - LORETTO POST, in line with left and right.
8.10.a.m.		Further orders issued to Battalions (received from Div) to take up a general line on ROUGE CROIX East POST - EUSTON POST - CURZON POST - PONT LOGY.

C.

LOPA	LIBE	
LOHO.	FUWA.	JEQI.
LOTO.	BUJA.	

G.161.   4.9.18.

BUZA will be relieved by BUJA to-night AAA QOFO will take over from LOHO and LOTO AAA Guides at the rate of 1 per platoon and 1 per Coy. H.Q. to be at the following places at 8.p.m. LOHO at Bn.H.Q. M.33.b. 2.6. LORETTO POST AAA LOTO at X Roads at M.26.d.7.6. AAA Bn.H.Q. QOFO will be at LORETTO HO. AAA On relief LOHO will move to S. end of LOCON LOTO to CANAL BANK detailed instructions will be issued later AAA LOPA will come into BUJA Bde. Reserve and will move to R.29. and 35. move not to commence before 12 midnight and to be complete by 4.a.m. dispositions at discretion of Battalion Commander AAA LIBE may withdraw forward guns after 9.p.m. to W.8.d.9.4. Forward guns of FUWA will come under orders of BUJA and will report their dispositions to them AAA Booby trap parties will be handed over on relief. AAA Relief complete to be wired to Bde.H.Q. using names of respective Battalion Commanders as code words arrival in reserve area will also be reported AAA ACKNOWLEDGE.

From - BUZA

Time - 2.40.p.m.

SECRET.   Copy No...7...

58th Infantry Brigade.

Provisional Defence Orders for Right Sub-sector of Divisional Front.

Boundaries. 1.(a) Boundaries are as shown on attached Map 'B'.

(b) The dotted Yellow Line shows approximately the General Line on which the front line posts are. There is an Advanced Post near SEVEN SISTERS.

(c) The dotted Green Line shows the approximate Outpost Line of Resistance.

(d) The dotted Black Line shows the Line of Retention.
 The numbers show the positions where platoon breastwork posts are to be made, three for each Coy. on this line.
 The positions of counter-attacking platoons of each Coy. are not shown.

Organisation 2. (a) The Outpost Zone consists of the Outpost Line of
of the front Resistance and the area to the East of it.

(b) The Battle Zone consists of the area between the Outpost Zone and the Line of Retention (inclusive).

Dispositions.3.   The Line will be held as follows :-

Two front Battalions side by side holding the Outpost Zone.
 Dividing line between battalions as shown on map.
 One Battalion holding Line of Retention.

Front Bns. 4. The Front Battalions will eventually hold the Outpost Zone as under :-

(i) Two Coys. from each Bn. forming the Picquet Line and immediate Supports, three or two platoons of each Coy. forming Picquet Line and one or two platoons the immediate Support. The Picquet Line will be held by Platoon Posts or groups of Posts, i.e., the Platoon may be divided into two or more posts but they will be close together so as to form a definite locality for the defence of which the Platoon will be responsible.

(ii) Remaining two Coys. of each Battalion holding the Outpost Line of Resistance, three platoons of each Coy. in Line of Resistance and one platoon in immediate support for counter-attack.

In addition a proportion of Vickers Guns and 4 Light Trench Mortars will be disposed for the Defence of the Outpost Zone, normally for the defence of the Outpost Line of Resistance.   Each Front Battalion has, however, authority to move 2 Vickers Guns and 2 Mortars in its area to any position required for a special purpose.

NOTE: At present it may be advisable to modify the above to some extent until the situation becomes more settled. Thus it may be found necessary to put more than 2 Coys. into the Picquet Line and immediate supports. In this case the number of Coys. holding the Line of Retention must be correspondingly reduced. Battalion Commanders will therefore use their discretion as to the way they hold the Line on taking over according to the actual conditions, reporting their dispositions as soon as possible.

/Positions

- 2 -

Positions where trenches (especially BICZER TRENCH) come in from the enemy direction must be specially guarded as the enemy may very likely attempt bombing attacks down them. The Distillery gives the enemy very good observation over our lines and it is therefore likely he will try to retake it. The Line in this vicinity must be held sufficiently strongly to prevent this.

Bn. in Line of Retention. 5. The Battalion in the Line of Retention will have all four Companies holding the Line. Each Coy. will have 3 platoons in the Line and one in close support for counter-attack. Platoons in the Line will be in Platoon or ½ Platoon posts.

Counter-Attacking Platoons. 6. All Counter-attacking Platoons will have ground over which they might have to attack most carefully reconnoitred and routes marked and prepared if necessary. They will practise counter-attacks where possible both by day and night.

Hd. Qrs. 7. Headquarters are at present as under :-

    Brigade Hd. Qrs. ... ... LOISNE CHATEAU, X.28.a.
    Bde. Forward Station. ... EPINETTE POST N., S.13.d.7.7.
    Right Front Battalion ... S.15.c.7.5.
    Left Front Battalion. ... S.10.a.5.4.
    Reserve Battalion ... ... X.17.a.9.4.
    Trench Mortar Battery ... X.17.a.7.5.

Trench Mortars & Machine Guns. 8. Two Mortars in area of each front Battalion. Normally for defence of Outpost Line of Resistance but may be moved by O.C. Battalion concerned if required for any special purpose.
    Remainder in rear sited for defence of Line of Retention.
    Machine Gun Defence is being arranged by O.C. 19th M.G.Bn.

General Policy. 9.(a). A policy of vigorous patrolling will be adopted by the 2 front battalions in order to locate the enemy, secure identifications, and ensure that any pronounced thinning of the enemy's Outpost Line will be at once apparent.
    Every opportunity is to be taken of gaining ground, and advancing the line.
    Should the enemy commence a further withdrawal he will be immediately followed up by leading two Coys. of both front battalions who will keep touch with him, harassing his rear guards and forcing them to withdraw before they are ready.

(b). The Reserve Battalion will have forward area and routes to the Outpost Line thoroughly reconnoitred so as to be able to advance rapidly if required owing to a withdrawal of the enemy or for any offensive action on our part.

Action in case of Enemy Attack. 10. In case of an enemy attack :-

(a). <u>Front Battalions</u>.
    The Picquet Line will hold up the enemy if possible. In the case of small attacks or raids local counter-attacks from supporting platoons will recapture any posts temporarily lost. In the event of a heavy attack forcing the Picquets to fall back they will do so on to the Line of Resistance of the Outposts. The Outpost Line of Resistance will be held to the last and all the resources of the two front battalions will be employed for the maintenance of this line.

(b). <u>Battalion holding Line of Retention</u>.
    There is to be no withdrawal from this line which must be maintained at all costs. Should the enemy penetrate any portion of the Line of Retention the Counter-attacking platoons will be launched in counter-attack without hesitation to restore the line.

- 3 -

Unless, however, troops from the rear have arrived to take their place, or the situation is well in hand, Troops in or in rear of the Line of Retention will not be used to counter-attack in front of that Line.

(c). The Reserve Battalion will send an Officer or N.C.O. with 2 Runners, to the H.Q. of each front battalion to keep it in touch with any changes in the situation and the progress of the attack.

10. ACKNOWLEDGE.

[signature]
Captain

Brigade Major 58th Infantry Brigade.

Brigade H.Q.
   26th September, 1918.

Copies to 1 9.R.W.Fusrs.
          2 9.Welch R.
          3 2.Wilts R.
          4 58.T.M.Battery.
          5 19th Div. 'G'.
          6)War Diary.
          7)
          8 File.

C.1.

58th Brigade No. B.M.1643.

SECRET

Copy No...6...

58th INFANTRY BRIGADE.

Provisional Defence Orders for Left Subsector of Divl. Front.

Boundaries. 1. Boundaries are as shown on attached map. A.

Organisation of Front. 2. (a) The Outpost Zone consists of the Outpost Line of Resistance (B Line) and the area to the East of it.

(b) The Battle Zone consists of the area between the Outpost Zone and the Line of Retention (inclusive).

Dispositions. 3. The Line will be held as follows :-

2 Front Battalions side by side holding the Outpost Zone. Dividing line between Battns. is shown on Map A.

1 Battn. holding the Line of Retention.

Front Battalions. 4. The Front Battalions will hold the Outpost Zone as under :-

(i) Two Coys. from each Battalion forming the Picquet Line and immediate supports (with advanced observation posts where necessary). Three platoons of each Coy. in Picquet Line and one in immediate support for counter-attack.

(ii) Remaining two Coys. of each Battalion holding Outpost Line of Resistance. Three platoons of each Coy. in Line of Resistance and one in immediate support for counter-attack.

In addition, a proportion of Vickers Guns and four Light Trench Mortars are disposed for the defence of the Outpost Zone. Each Front Battalion has authority to move 2 Vickers Guns and 2 Mortars in its area to any position required for a special purpose.

Battn. in Line of Retention. 5. The Battalion in the Line of Retention will have all 4 Coys. holding this line. Each Coy. will have 3 platoons in the Line and one in close support for counter-attack. Coys. will be disposed by platoons along the Line, each platoon being in two half platoon posts not more than about 50 yards apart.

Counter-Attacking Platoons. 6. All Counter-attacking platoons will have ground over which they might have to attack most carefully reconnoitred and routes marked and prepared if necessary. They will practise counter-attacks where possible both by day and night.

Head-Quarters. 7. Headquarters are at present as under, but these are liable to alteration :-

Brigade H.Q............... R.34.b.8.7.
Right Front Battn........ M.32.d.3.3.
Left Front Battn......... M.28.d.9.2.
T.M.Battery.............. M.31.d.7.8.
Reserve Battalion........ M.36.c.3.0.

Trench Mortars & M. Guns. 8. Two Mortars in area of each Front Battalion. Normally for defence of Outpost Line of Resistance but may be moved by O.C. Battalion concerned if required for any special purpose. Remainder in rear sited for defence of Line of Retention. Machine Gun Defence is being arranged by O.C., 19th M.G.Battn.

- 2 -

General Policy.

9.(a). A policy of vigorous patrolling will be adopted by the 2 front battalions in order to locate the enemy, secure identifications, and ensure that any pronounced thinning of the enemy's Outpost Line will be at once apparent.

Every opportunity is to be taken of gaining ground, and advancing the Line.

Should the enemy commence a further withdrawal he will be immediately followed up by leading two Coys. of both front battalions who will keep touch with him, harassing his rear guards and forcing them to withdraw before they are ready.

(b). The Reserve Battalion will have forward area and routes to the Outpost Line thoroughly reconnoitred so as to be able to advance rapidly if required owing to a withdrawal of the enemy or for any offensive action on our part.

Action in case of Enemy Attack.

10. In case of an enemy attack.

(a). Front Battalions.

The Picquet Line will hold up the enemy if possible. In the case of small attacks or raids local counter-attacks from supporting platoons will recapture any posts temporarily lost. In the event of a heavy attack forcing the Picquets to fall back they will do so on to the Line of Resistance of the Outposts. The Outpost Line of Resistance will be held to the last and all the resources of the two front Battalions will be employed for the maintenance of this line.

(b). Battalion holding Line of Retention.

There is to be no withdrawal from this line which must be maintained at all costs. Should the enemy penetrate any portion of the Line of Retention the counter-attacking platoons will be launched in counter-attack without hesitation to restore the line.

Unless, however, troops from the rear have arrived to take their place, or the situation is well in hand, Troops in or in rear of the Line of Retention will not be used to counter-attack in front of that Line.

(c). The Reserve Battalion will send an Officer or N.C.O. with 2 runners, to the H.Q. of each front battalion to keep it in touch with any changes in the situation and the progress of the attack.

11. ACKNOWLEDGE.

, Captain

Brigade Major 58th Infantry Brigade.

Brigade H.Q.

9th September, 1918.

Copy No. 1 9.R.W.Fusrs.
2 9.Welch R.
3 2.Wilts R.
4 58.T.M.B.
5 19th Div. G.
6) War Diary.
7)
8 File.

SECRET.   Copy No. 24

            58th Infantry Brigade Order No.266.

                                              9th September, 1918.

Ref. map Sheet 36A. S.E. & S.W.
     1/20,000.

1.   The 58th Inf. Brigade will relieve the 57th Inf. Brigade on the night of the 10th/11th September in the Left Subsector of the 19th Divisional Sector.
      On relief Battalions will be disposed as under :-

      9/R.W.Fusrs. will be right front Battn. relieving 10/R.War. Regt.
      9/Welch Regt. will be left front Battn. relieving 8/Gloucester Regt.
      2/Wilts Regt. will be in support relieving 3/Worcester Regt.

2.   All details of relief will be arranged between C.O's concerned.

3.   Battalions will move up by platoons at 100 yards intervals. No relieving troops will cross the LA BASSEE - ESTAIRES Road before 8.15.p.m.

4.   All Defence orders, Aeroplane photos, trench maps, work programmes and trench stores will be taken over and receipts given. Copies of lists of trench stores taken over will be sent to Bde.H.Q. by 6.p.m. 11th inst.

5.   All units will forward disposition reports showing dispositions by platoons to reach Bde.H.Q. by 12 noon 11th inst.
      O.C., 58th T.M.Battery will report locations of guns.

6.   Battalions will hand over all arrangements as regards training facilities to relieving units.

7.   Administrative Instructions are being issued by the Staff Capt.

8.   Relief complete will be wired to Brigade H.Q. using code word "YORK".

9.   Brigade H.Q. will close at STINK INN at 5.p.m. and re-open at R.34.b.8.7. on arrival.
      Command of the sector will pass to G.O.C. 58th Inf. Bde. on completion of relief.

10.   ACKNOWLEDGE.

                                              F.H. Fraser.
                                              _____, Captain

                                      Brigade Major 58th Infantry Brigade.

Issued through Signals at 8.0.a.m.

          Copy No. 1 G.O.C.
                   2 9.R.W.Fus.   14 82/Fld. Co.R.E.
                   3 9.Welch R.   15 No. 4 Coy. Train.
                   4 2.Wilts R.   16 8S/Bde.R.F.A.
                   5 53.T.M.B.   17 19th M.G.Bn.
                   6 Depot, 9/R.W.F.   18 O.C., Left Group M.G
                   7   "   9/Welch R.   19 Staff Capt.
                   8   "   2/Wilts R.   20 Bde. Sig. Offr.
                   9 19th Div. 'G'   21 Bde. T.O.
                  10 19th Div. 'Q'   22 Bde. Gas Offr.
                  11 56th Inf. Bde.   23) War Diary.
                  12 57th Inf. Bde.   24)
                  13 A.D.M.S, 19th Div.   25 File.

SECRET.   E   Copy No. 26

53th Infantry Brigade Order No. 267.

13th September, 1918.

Ref. to AUBERS & LESTREM
Sheets, 1/10,000.

1. The 2nd Bn Wiltshire Regt. will relieve the 9th Bn Welch Regt. in the Left Sub-sector on the night 14th/15th September.
   On relief the 9th Bn Welch Regiment will take over the positions in the Line of Retention vacated by the 2nd Bn Wiltshire Regt. and will be in Brigade Reserve.

2. All details for relief will be arranged between Commanding Officers concerned. No relieving troops will cross the LA BASSEE Road before 8.0.p.m.

3. All Aeroplane photos, Maps, and Trench Stores will be handed over on relief.

4. Programmes of work will be handed over by the Battalions concerned. O.C., 9th Bn Welch Regiment will send back an Officer to take over, in daylight, the work in progress on the Line of Retention. Details as regards working parties for Line of Retention will be arranged direct with O.C., 82nd Field Coy. R.E. Half a day's work will be carried out on the Line of Retention on the afternoon of the 15th instant.

5. O.C., 9th Bn Welch Regt. will send back representatives from each Coy. (either Officers or N.C.O's) to take over, in daylight, the bivouacs at present occupied by 2nd Bn Wiltshire Regt. and reconnoitre the routes from there to the stand to positions in the Line of Retention as in some cases these positions are some distance apart.

6. Battalions will render disposition reports to reach this office by 12 noon 15th instant.

7. Relief complete will be wired to Brigade H.Q. using code word "COMMISSION".

8. ACKNOWLEDGE.

                                                F.H. Fraser
                                                        Captain

                                        Brigade Major 53th Infantry Brigade.
Issued through Signals at 8.0.am.

```
Copy No. 1  9.R.W.Fusrs.
         2  9.Welch Regt.
         3  2.Wilts R.
         4  Depot,9.R.W.F.
         5    "    9.Welch R.
         6    "    2.Wilts R.
         7  58.T.M.B.
         8  G.O.C.
         9  Staff Capt.
        10  Bde. T.O.
        11  Bde. Gas Offr.
        12  19th Div. G.
        13  19th Div. Q.
        14  56th Inf. Bde.
        15  57th Inf. Bde.
        16  C.R.A., 19th Div.         22 O.C. 19th Div Train.
        17  C.R.E., 19th Div.         23 O.C. No.4 Coy. Train.
        18  A.D.M.S.,   do.           24 176th Inf Bde.
        19  88th Bde. R.F.A.          25) War Diary.
        20  82nd Fld. Co. R.E.        26)
        21  19th M.G.Bn.              27 File.
        22  O.C. Left Group M.G's.
```

SECRET.   F.   Copy No. 27.

58th Infantry Brigade Order No. 268.

17th September, 1918.

Ref. AUBERS & LESTREM
Sheets 1/10,000.

1. The 9th Bn Welch Regiment will relieve the 9th Bn R.W.Fusrs. in the Left Sub-sector on the night 18th/19th September.
   On relief the 9th Bn R.W.Fusiliers will take over the positions in the Line of Retention vacated by the 9th Bn Welch Regt. and will be in Brigade Reserve.

2. All details for relief will be arranged between Commanding Officers concerned. No relieving troops will cross the LA BASSEE Road before 8.0.p.m.

3. All Aeroplane photos, maps, and Trench Stores will be handed over on relief.

4. Programmes of work will be handed over by the Battalions concerned. O.C., 9th Bn R.W.Fusiliers will send back an Officer to take over, in daylight, the work in progress on the Line of Retention. Details as regards working parties for Line of Retention will be arranged direct with O.C., 82nd Field Coy.R.E. Half a day's work will be carried out on the Line of Retention on the afternoon of the 19th inst.

5. O.C., 9th Bn R.W.Fusiliers will send back representatives from each Coy. (either Officers or N.C.O's) to take over, in daylight, the bivouacs at present occupied by 9th Bn Welch Regt. and reconnoitre the routes from there to the stand to positions in the Line of Retention as in some cases these positions are some distance apart.

6. Battalions will render disposition reports to reach this office by 12 noon 19th inst.

7. Relief complete will be wired to Brigade H.Q. using code word "CONTENT".

8. ACKNOWLEDGE.

                                        Captain
                        Brigade Major 58th Infantry Brigade.

Issued through Signals at 12.30.p.m.

Copy No. 1 9.R.W.Fusrs.
        2 9.Welch R.
        3 2.Wilts R.
        4 Depot, 9.R.W.F.
        5   "   9.Welch R.
        6   "   2.Wilts R.
        7 58.T.M.B.
        8 G.O.C.
        9 Staff. Capt.   19 88th Bde. R.F.A.
       10 Bde. T.O.   20 82nd Fld. Co.R.E.
       11 Bde. Gas Offr.   21 19th M.G.Bn.
       12 19th Div. G.   22 O.C. Left Group M.G's.
       13 19th Div. Q.   23 O.C. 19th Div. Train.
       14 56th Inf. Bde.   24 O.C. No. 4 Coy.   "
       15 57th Inf. Bde.   25 177th Inf. Bde.
       16 C.R.A., 19th Div.   26 O.C. Bde. Signals.
       17 C.R.E., 19th Div.   27) War Diary.
       18 A.D.M.S., 19th Div.   28)
                                      29 File.

SECRET. G. Copy No. 28

58th Infantry Brigade Order No.269.

21st September, 1918.

Ref. to Sheets
36.A. S.E. & 36.S.W.
1/20,000.

1. The 58th Infantry Brigade will be relieved in the Left Sector of the Divisional front by the 56th Infantry Brigade on the night Septr. 22nd/23rd.
   On relief the Brigade will be disposed as follows :-

9th Bn R.W.Fusrs..... ESSARS.	2nd Bn Wilts Regt.... CANAL BANK.
9th Bn Welch Regt.....LOCON.	58th T.M.Battery..... W.8.d.9.5.

2. All details for relief will be arranged between C.O's concerned.

3. All Defence Orders, L.G. A.A. Positions, Aeroplane photographs, Trench and Area stores will be handed over on relief and receipts obtained. The two front line battalions will hand over all information they have obtained concerning MAUDLIN TRENCH, any enemy posts and wire in front of it.

4. The 9th Bn Welch Regt. will move back to LOCON by march route.
   Lorries have been asked for to move the 9th Bn R.W.Fusiliers to ESSARS.
   Lorries or trains have been asked for to move the 2nd Bn Wilts Regt. to HINGES.

5. Relief complete will be wired to Brigade H.Q. using the code words "ORDER No. 962 RECEIVED".

6. Command of the sector will pass to G.O.C., 56th Inf. Bde. on completion of relief.

7. 58th Inf. Brigade H.Q. will close at R.34.b.9.7. on completion of relief and re-open on arrival at LONG CORNET.

8. ACKNOWLEDGE.

J.W. Fraser
Captain,

Brigade Major 58th Infantry Brigade.

Issued through Signals at 12.30.pm.

Copy No.1 9.R.W.Fusrs.	16 56th Inf. Bde.
2 9.Welch R.	17 57th Inf. Bde.
3 2.Wilts R.	18 177th Inf. Bde.
4 Depot, 9/R.W.F.	19 C.R.A, 19th Div.
5 " 9/Welch R.	20 C.R.E, -do-
6 " 2/Wilts R.	21 A.D.M.S, -do-
7 58.T.M.B.	22 88th Bde. R.F.A.
8 G.O.C.	23 82nd Fld. Co.R.E.
9 Staff Capt.	24 19th M.G.Battn.
10 Bde. Transport Offr.	25 Left Group M.G's.
11 Bde. Int. Offr.	26 O.C., 19th Div. Train.
12 Bde. Gas Offr.	27 No. 4 Coy. Train.
13 Bde. Signal Offr.	28) War Diary.
14 19th Div. G.	29)
15 19th Div. Q.	30 File.

SECRET   Copy No 28

58th Infantry Brigade Order No. 271.

Ref to RICHEBOURG and
LOCON Sheets - 1/10,000.

27th September 1918.

1. The 58th Inf. Brigade (less 9/Welch R) will relieve the 57th Inf. Brigade (Less 10/R.Warwick.R) in the Right Sub-Sector of the Divisional front on the night 28/29th Sept.

2. The 9/R.W.Fus will relieve the 8/Glosters on the Right.
The 2/Wilts R will relieve the 3/Worcesters in support, relief to be complete by 8.30 p.m.
The 58/T.M.Battery will relieve the 57/T.M.Battery.
The 9/Welch R. will return to the command of G.O.C. 58th Brigade on completion of relief.

3. All details for relief will be arranged between C.Os. concerned.

4. Trains are being arranged to convey the 2/Wilts and 58/T.M.Bty to LE TOURET.

5. All Defence Orders, Aeroplane Photographs, Trench Maps, Trench and Area stores will be taken over. The Battalion in Support will also take over all arrangements for working parties required for work on Line of Resistance.

6. All Battalions will forward a Disposition Map showing dispositions by platoons, Lewis Guns and Anti-Aircraft Lewis Guns. O.C. 58/T.M.Battery will forward a map showing positions of his Mortars. The above maps will be forwarded so as to reach this office by 12 noon September 29th. Any subsequent alterations in dispositions will be reported by 9 a.m. each day.

7. Relief complete will be wired to Brigade H.Q. using the code words "YES LATER".

8. Brigade H.Q. will close at LONG CORNET at 4.30 p.m. 28th inst and re-open at LOISNE CHATEAU at the same hour.
G.O.C. 58th Inf. Brigade will take over command of the sector on completion of relief.

9. ACKNOWLEDGE.

                                                    F.W. Fraser, Captain,
                                        Brigade Major 58th Infantry Brigade.

Issued through Signals at 8.30 p.m.

Copy No			
1. 9/R.W.Fus.		16. 56th Inf. Bde.
2. 9/Welch.		17. 57th Inf. Bde.
3. 2/Wilts.		18. 165th Inf. Bde.
4. Depot, 9/R.W.Fus.		19. C.R.A. 19th Div.
5. Depot, 9/Welch.		20. C.R.E. do
6. Depot, 2/Wilts.		21. A.D.M.S. do
7. 58/T.M.Bty.		22. Right Group, Arty.
8. G.O.C.		23. 81st Fd. Coy, R.E.
9. Staff Captain.		24. 19th M.G. Battn.
10. Bde Transport Offr.		25. Right Group, M.Gs.
11. Bde Int. Officer.		26. O.C. 19th Div Train.
12. Bde. Gas Officer.		27. No. 4 Coy, Train.
13. Bde. Signal Offr.		28)
14. 19th Div "G".		29) War Diary.
15. 19th Div "Q".		30. File.

I.

SECRET.   Copy No. 28.

58th Infantry Brigade Order No.270.

Ref. to RICHEBOURG &
LOCON Sheets - 1/10,000.

26th September, 1918.

1. The 58th Inf. Brigade will relieve the 57th Inf. Brigade in the Right Sub-sector of the Divisional front on the night 27th/28th September.
   Relief to be carried out in accordance with attached Table.

2. All details for the relief will be arranged between C.O's concerned.

3. All Defence Orders, Aeroplane Photographs, Trench maps, Trench and Area stores will be taken over. The Battalion in Support will also take over all arrangements for working parties required for work on Line of Retention.

4. All Battalions will forward a Disposition Map showing dispositions by platoons, Lewis Guns and Anti-aircraft Lewis Guns. O.C. 58th T.M.Battery will forward a map showing positions of his Mortars. The above maps will be forwarded so as to reach this office by 12 noon September 28th. Any subsequent alterations in dispositions will be reported by 9.0.a.m. each day.

5. Relief complete will be wired to Brigade H.Q. using the code words "FAIR AND WARMER".

6. Brigade H.Q. will close at LONG CORNET at 4.30.p.m. 27th inst. and re-open at LOISNE CHATEAU at the same hour.
   G.O.C. 58th Inf. Brigade will take over command of the sector on completion of relief.

7. ACKNOWLEDGE.

                                                        Captain
                                        Brigade Major 58th Infantry Brigade.

Issued through Signals at 2.p.m.

       Copy No. 1 9.R.W.Fusrs.   16 56th Inf. Bde.
              2 9.Welch R.   17 57th Inf. Bde.
              3 2.Wilts R.   18 165th Inf. Bde.
              4 Depot, 9/R.W.F.   19 C.R.A., 19th Div.
              5 Depot, 9/Welch R.   20 C.R.E.,   do.
              6 Depot, 2/Wilts R.   21 A.D.M.S., do.
              7 58/T.M.Bty.   22 Right Group Arty.
              8 G.O.C.   23 81stFld. Co. R.E.
              9 Staff Capt.   24 19th M.G. Battn.
             10 Bde. Transport Offr.   25 Right Group M.G's.
             11 Bde. Int. Offr.   26 O.C. 19th Div. Train.
             12 Bde. Gas Offr.   27 No. 4 Coy. Train.
             13 Bde. Signal Offr.   28) War Diary.
             14 19th Div. 'G'   29)
             15 19th Div. "Q".   30 File.

Relief Table to accompany 58th Inf. Brigade Order No. 270.

Unit.	From.	To.	Relieve.	Route.	Batta. H.Q.	Remarks.
9/R.W.Fusiliers.	LA MOTTE	Right Front.	9/Gloucester R.	Route "B" or RUE du BOIS.	S.15.c.7.5.	By march route.
9/Welch Regt.	LOCON.	Left Front.	10/R. Warwicks.	-	S.10.a.5.4.	By train from LOCON.
2/Wiltshire Regt.	HINGES.	Support.	3/Worcester Regt.	-	X.17.c.9.4.	By train from near HINGES. Relief to be complete by 8.0.p.m.
58/T.M.Battery.	V.23.c.95.85.	-	57/T.M.Battery.	-	X.17.c.7.5.	By train from HINGES.

SECRET. Copy No. 10

58th Infantry Brigade Order No. 272.

29th September, 1918.

Ref. to map
36.S.W.3 1/10,000

1. At Zero hour to-morrow morning 56th Inf. Brigade will capture the General Line of the DES LAIES DITCH.

2. At the same Zero hour Right Group Artillery will put down an 18-pdr. barrage along line from S.11.c.8.4. to S.17.b.8.1.
Zero plus 3 lift to Line from S.11.d.0.5. to S.18.a.0.1.
Zero plus 5 lift to Line from S.11.b.25.20. along SUSAN TRENCH to S.11.d.85.30. to S.18.a.5.1.
Zero plus 20 lift to Line of SOPHIA TRENCH - BIEZ Farm - S.18. central.
Zero plus 30 Cease fire.

Rates of fire.

Zero to Zero plus 3.... 4 rounds per gun per minute.
Zero plus 3 to Zero plus 10... ... ... 3 " " " " "
Zero plus 10 to Zero plus 25... ... ... 2 " " " " "
Zero plus 25 to Cease Fire. ... ... 1 round " " " "

4.5 Howitzers.

2 Hows: Zero to Zero plus 20 on German front and Support Lines in S.11.b.
2 Hows: dealing with BICZER TRENCH.
1 How: Pumping Station S.12.c.5.1.
1 How: Orchard S.18.d.0.6.

Heavies are also co-operating.

3. O.C. Right Group Machine Guns will arrange to put an M.G. Barrage down from Zero to Zero plus 20 on Eastern half of Square S.18.c.
At Zero plus 20 this barrage will lift to area Eastern half of Square S.18.d. till Zero plus 30 when fire will cease.
M.G's will also fire on area BICZER TRENCH DU BIEZ Farm from Zero to Zero plus 20.

4. 58th T.M.B. will assist in dealing with BICZER TRENCH.

5. Under cover of above barrages both front line Battalions will push forward strong fighting patrols and will establish the General Line S.5.c.5.5. - S.11.a.7.9. - S.11.a.7.1. - S.17.d.8.7. - S.17.d.8.3.
Attached map shows this General Line and the approximate points (Red Circles) at which Platoon Posts will be established.
This line will be eventually held by 2 Coys. of each Battn. one Coy. in Support, and one Coy. in Outpost Line of Resistance.

6. When the barrage lifts off SUSAN TRENCH and the road in S.18.a. and c. strong patrols will push forward and establish themselves on this line if possible. These patrols should not be taken from the platoons detailed to form the platoon posts.

/7.

- 2 -.

7. 2 Green Very Lights fired from Front Line will be the signal for counter-preparation should the enemy be seen to be preparing to counter-attack.

8. Watches will be synchronised by Brigade Signal Officer at 11.0.p.m.

9. Zero hour 7.30.a.m.

10. ACKNOWLEDGE.

F.W. Fraser, Captain

Brigade Major 58th Infantry Brigade.

Issued through Signals at 8.0.p.m.

Copy No. 1 9.R.W.Fusiliers.
2 9.Welch Regt.
3 2.Wiltshire R.
4 58.T.M.Battery.
5 Right Arty. Group.
6 Right M.G. Group.
7 56th Inf. Bde.
8 165th Inf. Bde.
9 19th Div. 'G'.
10) War Diary
11)
12 File.

SECRET.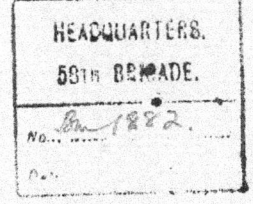

STOKES MORTAR CO-OPERATION REFERENCE
PARA. 4 of O.O. 272.

Two Mortars in Shepherd's Redoubt trained on to BICZER TRENCH.

<u>Zero.</u> One minute gunfire (15 - 20 per minute) from both Mortars:-

<u>No.1</u> firing on to junction of Ditch and BICZER TRENCH at S.17.b.35.97.

<u>No.2</u> firing on to trench junction at S.11.d.47.10.

<u>Zero plus 1 to Zero plus 15.</u>

Both Mortars slow rate of searching fire along trench from S.11.d.47.10. to S.11.d.70.25.

<u>Zero plus 15 to Zero plus 17.</u>

Both Mortars gunfire at full range traversing from BICZER at S.11.d.70.25. to LIST TRENCH at S.11.d.6.3.

(signed), Captain

Brigade Major 58th Infantry Brigade.

29.9.18.

Issued to all recipients of O.O. 272.

K. WD.

SECRET.   Copy No. 33

58th Infantry Brigade Order No. 273.

Ref. to RICHEBOURG   30th September, 1918.
1/10,000.
HAZEBROUCK 5A) 1/100,000.
LENS 11   )

1. The 58th Inf. Brigade Group will be relieved by the 230th Inf. Bde. Group, 74th Division, in the right sub-sector of the Divisional front on the night October 1st/2nd in accordance with the attached Tables.

2. The 58th Inf. Brigade Group will be composed of the following Units :-

    58th Brigade H.Q.   59th Field Ambulance.
    9/R.W.Fusrs.   5th Bn S.W.Bord. (P).
    9/Welch Regt.   31st Mobile Vet. Section.
    2/Wilts Regt.   No. 3 Section D.A.C.
    58/T.M.Battery.   No. 4 Coy. Divisional Train.
    81st Field Coy.R.E.

3. All details of relief will be arranged between C.O's concerned. Relief of 2nd Bn Wiltshire Regt. will be completed by day in accordance with train arrangements.

4. Units in the Line will hand over:- Provisional Defence Orders, B.M.1878, Instruction with regard to Operation to be carried out by "C" Special Coy. R.E., all Trench maps, Aeroplane photos, Trench and Area stores. O.C. 2nd Bn Wiltshire Regt. will hand over all arrangements for work on Line of Retention.

5. Relief complete will be wired to Brigade H.Q. using the code words "WEATHER CHANGEABLE".
    Arrival in PERNES AREA and numbers falling out on line of march will also be reported.

6. Brigade H.Q. will close at LOISNE CHATEAU on completion of relief and re-open on arrival at PERNES.
    G.O.C. 230th Inf. Bde. will assume command of the sector on completion of relief.

7. The surplus personnel of the Bde. (less 2nd Wilts R) will march to BURBURE under orders of Major P.H.BRADBURY, M.C. 9/Welch R. leaving transport lines at 10.00 a.m. and rejoin their respective units. Route HINGES - CHOCQUES - ALLOUAGNE. Orders for surplus personnel of 2/Wilts R. will be issued later.

8. ACKNOWLEDGE.

                                                        Captain
                                    Brigade Major 58th Infantry Brigade.

Issued at 8.0.pm. through Signals.

Copy No. 1 9.R.W.F.   11 G.O.C.   20 230 Inf.Bde.
          2 9.Welch R.   12 Staff Capt.   21 166.Inf.Bde.
          3 2.Wilts R.   13 Mc. Int. Offr.   22 19th Div. G.
          4 58.T.M.B.   14 D. B. O.   23 19th Div. Q.
          5 81.Fld.Co.R.E.   15 B. G. O.   24 C.R.A.
          6 59.Fld. Amb.   16 D. T. O.   25 C.R.E.
          7 5.S.W.B. (P)   17 Major BRADBURY,   26 A.D.M.S.
          8 31.Mob.Vet.Sectn.   9/Welch R.   27 A.P.M.
          9 No.3 Sec.D.A.C.   18 56.Inf. Bde.   28 O.C. Train.
         10 No.4 Co. Div.Train.   19 57.Inf. Bde.   29 Depot,9.R.W.F.
                        30 Depot, 9.Welch R.   33) War Diary.
                         31   "   2.Wilts R.   34)
                         32 Bde. Q.M.S.   35 File.

Ref. to HAZEBROUCK 5A & LENS 11 1/100,000.

March Table for move of 1st Line Transport, on 1st October.

Unit.	From.	To.	Starting Point.	Head of Column to pass S.P. at.	Route.	Remarks.
9/R.W.Fusrs. Transport.	LINNET LANE.	SACHIN.	Junction of LINNET LANE & LOCON ROAD.	09.00.	LOCON - BETHUNE - CHOCQUES - MARLES-les-MINES - PERNES.	
2/Wilts Regt. Transport.	do.	SAINS les PERNES.	-do-	09.50.	-do-	
Brigade H.Q. Transport.	do.	PERNES.	-do-	09.10.	-do-	
9/Welch Regt Transport.	do.	PRESSY.	-do-	09.13.	-do-	
5/S.W.Bord. Transport.	X.1.b.6.1.	FIEFS.	Junction of WILLOT LANE & LOCON ROAD.	09.23.	-do-	To be formed up on WILLOT LANE.
81/Fd.Coy. Transport.	X.8.b.9.3.	BOYAVAL.	LOCON CHURCH	09.35.	-do-	To be formed up on LOCON CHURCH - SWING BRIDGE ROAD.
No.3 Sectn. D.A.C.	W.27.c.4.3.	PERNES.	X Roads due S. of L in VEEDIN LES BETHUNES.	10.35.	-do-	To be formed up off main road and join Col. in rear of 81st Fld. Coy. R.E.
31st M.V.S.	BELSAGE FM.	do.	-do-	10.45.	-do-	March in rear of No.3 Sectn. D.A.C.
No.4 Coy. Train.	CHOCQUES.	MAREST.			BURBURE - FERFAY - AUMERVAL - PERNES.	March under orders of O.C. Coy. to be clear of CHOCQUES 10.00

P.T.O.

Relief Table to accompany O.O. 273.

Unit.	From.	To.	Relieved by.	Remarks.
9/R.W.Fusrs.	Right Front Line Battn.	BURBURE.	10th Buffs.	By train from LE TOURET to BURBURE.
9/Welch Regt.	Left Front Line Battn.	do.	16th Sussex.	-do-
2/Wilts Regt.	Support Battalion.	do.	15th Suffolks.	By train from LE TOURET & EMPEROR'S ROAD to BURBURE.
58/T.M.Battery.	Line.	do.	230th T.M.Bty.	By train from LE TOURET to BURBURE.
58/Bde.H.Q.	LOISNE CHATEAU.	PERNES.	230th Bde.H.Q.	By train and lorry.

NOTES: (1) Billets will be found in BURBURE.

(2) Cookers will meet Units in BURBURE.

(3) 9/R.W.Fusrs., 9/Welch Regt., and 58th T.M.Bty. will be allowed to rest approximately for 6 hours in BURBURE before moving off to the PERNES Area.

March Table to accompany O.O. 273.

Unit.	From.	To.	Hour of March.	Route.	Remarks.
5/S.W.B.(P)	SURBURE.	FIEFS.	On arrival at BURBURE Stn.	AMETTES – NEDONCHELLE.	
2/Wilts R.	do.	SAINS Les PERNES.	On arrival at BURBURE Stn.	FERFAY – AUMERVAL – SACHIN.	Tea to be served in vicinity of BURBURE Stn.
9/R.W.Fus.	do.	SACHIN.	To be clear of SURBURE by 13.30 2nd October.	FERFAY – AUMERVAL.	
9/Welch R.	do.	PRESSY.	Not to leave BURBURE before 14.00 2nd October.	FERFAY – AUMERVAL – PERNES.	To march in rear of 9/R.W.Fusrs.
58/T.M.Bty.	do.	MAREST.	Not to leave BURBURE before 14.15 2nd October.	do.	To march in rear of 9/Welch Regt.
81/Fd.Coy. R.E.	X.10.d.1.9	BOYAVAL.	On arrival at BURBURE Stn.	AMETTES – NEDONCHELLE – FIEFS.	
59/Fd.Amb. & Transport.	PONT DU REVEILLON.	do.		MARLES-les-MINES – PERNES.	Under orders of O.C. 59th Field Ambce.

NOTES: (1). The usual intervals of 100 yards between Coys., and 500 yards between Battalions and similar formations will be observed when on the march.

(2). The strictest march discipline will be maintained throughout the march.

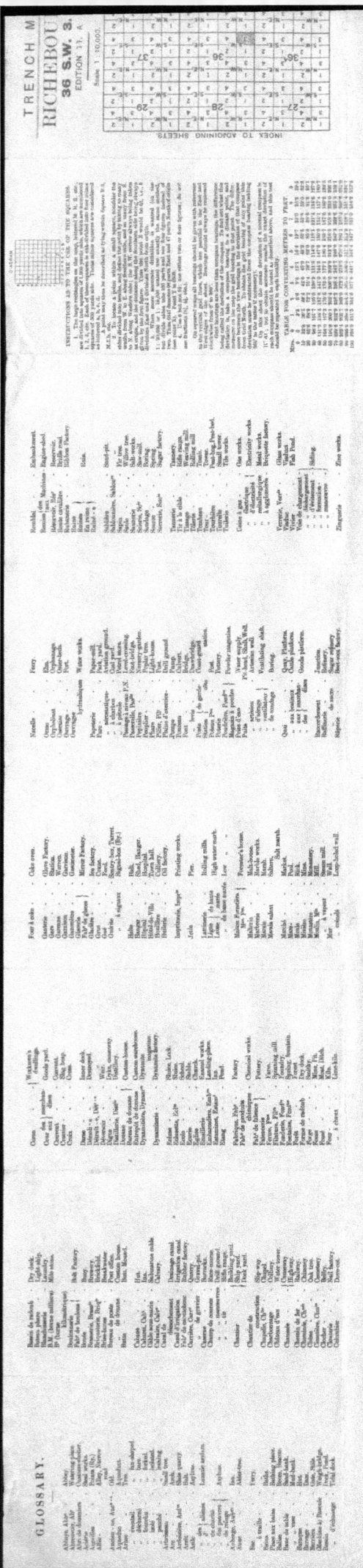

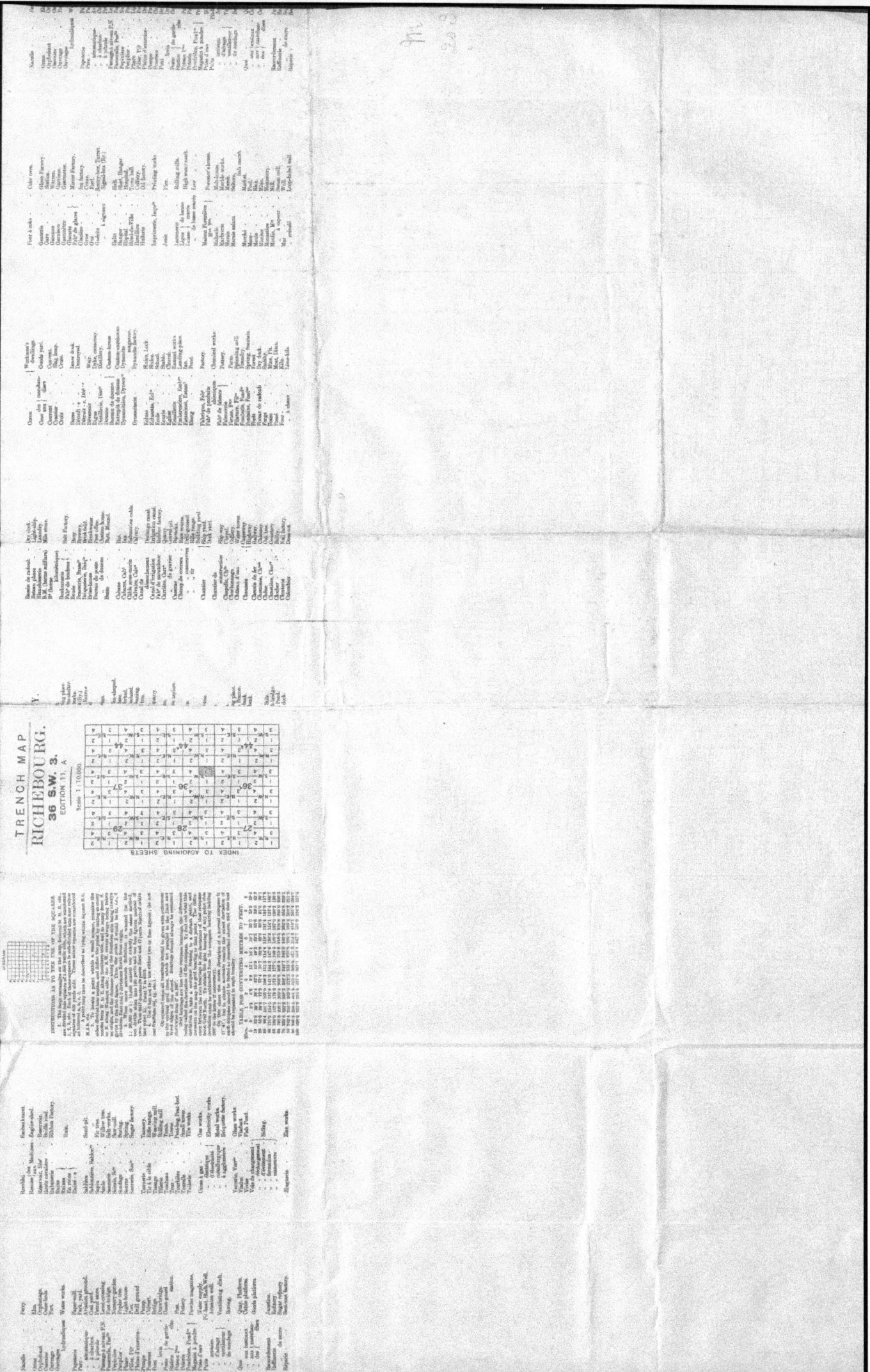

19

58th Inf Bde. (1948th)
October 1961
O.T.T
Vol I

28

On His Majesty's Service.

Army Form C. 2118.

WAR DIARY

INTELLIGENCE SUMMARY.

(Erase heading not required.)

Instructions regarding War Diaries and Intelligence Summaries are contained in F. S. Regs., Part II. and the Staff Manual respectively. Title pages will be prepared in manuscript.

Place	Date	Hour	Summary of Events and Information	Remarks and references to Appendices
X.28.a.30.60.	Octr. 1st	0700	Quiet day on Bde. front, light shelling of forward area and considerable shelling of back areas. Hostile party attempted bombing raid on our posts in BICZER TRENCH, they were driven off by bombs and rifle fire.	
PERNES.	2nd	0700	Relief of 58th Infy Bde. by 230th Bde. complete. 58th Bde.H.Q. established at PERNES. Battns. travelled by march route from BURBURE to PERNES Area via FLORINGHEM and AUMERVAL after resting for 4 hours in billets at BURBURE.	A See 58th Bde Order 273.
	3rd		All Units resting and bathing. Weather fine. 19th Division (less Artillery) ordered to move to Third Army, XVII Corps. Bde. Order No. 274 issued 17.30 hrs.	B.
	4th		58th Bde. Group entrained with a portion of the transport. Entrained PERNES Station. Remainder of transport by road under the orders of the Bde. Transport Officer. Units detrained SAULTY Station and marched to billets in BARLY Area. 58th Bde.H.Q. established in BARLY CHATEAU.	Map Sht. LENS 11
BARLY.	5th		Orders received for the move of 58th Bde. Group to the GRAINCOURT Area. Transport by march route on 6th inst. and personnel by bus on 7th inst. (O.O.275 attached & March Order No.3 marked C).	C.
	6th		Transport of Bde. Group marched to BOISLEUX AU MONT and BOYELLES. Winter time came into force from night of 5th/6th Octr.	
	7th		Personnel of Bde. Group embussed BARLY 13.30 and proceeded to debussing point where CANAL DU NORD cuts main BAPAUME - CAMBRAI Road. From this point units marched to camping area allotted (Squares K. 4 and 5. E. of GRAINCOURT). 58th Bde.H.Q. established in dug-out in MAMMOUTH TRENCH.	Map sheet 57.C.N.E.
K.4.d.50.45.	8th	1800	Bde. Group marched to CANTAING via GRAINCOURT and LA JUSTICE. XIX Divn. now becomes Divn. in support to XXIV Div. of XVII Corps. 58th Bde.H.Q. established L.3.b.05.50. All units billeted in area L.2.b. and d. and L.3.a. and c.	D. O.O.276
	9th		The enemy reported retiring. The Bde. were ordered to be prepared to move forward at short notice.	
	10th	1030	In the event of the 19th Division being ordered to advance through the 24th Divn and become the leading Divn. the 58th Inf. Bde., 2nd N.Z. Bde.R.F.A., 2 M.G. Coys., 94th Fld. Coy. R.E. and the Divl. Mounted Detachment are ordered to form the advanced guard of the Division.	E. O.O.277 Map shts. (57c. NE, 57b. NW.

A6945 Wt. W11422/M1160 350,000 12/16 D. D. & L. Forms/C/2118/14.

Army Form C. 2118.

WAR DIARY
INTELLIGENCE SUMMARY.
(Erase heading not required.)

Instructions regarding War Diaries and Intelligence Summaries are contained in F. S. Regs., Part II. and the Staff Manual respectively. Title pages will be prepared in manuscript.

Place	Date	Hour	Summary of Events and Information	Remarks and references to Appendices
	10th	1730	The 58th Bde. moved from CANTAING Area to Squares A.18 and 24 by march route via NIERGNIES Bde.H.Q. established RUE GAUCHET A.24.a.40.40.	F O.O.278.
	11th		Weather wet. Units engaged in clearing up billets and clearing roads of dead horses etc. in immediate vicinity of billets.	
CAGNONCLES T.28.d.45.25.	12th		The 58th Bde. moved via CAMBRAI ANNEXE Station - FACTORY B.8.b.9.8. - LA BABOTTE to CAGNONCLES All Units billeted in the village which was found very dirty but only slightly damaged,T.28.d. 55.45. Occasional H.V. shells of small calibre fell on the northern outskirts of the village throughout the night.	G O.O.279.
	13th		Weather fine - units employed on light work cleaning up village while standing by at short notice to move if necessary.	
	14th		Units training near billets in case orders should be received to move forward.	
	15th	1000	Representatives from 17th Infy Bde. 24th Divn. came to reconnoitre billets occupied by the 58th Infy Bde.	
		2000	Orders received that the 19th Division will relieve the 24th Divn. in the line on 17th inst.	
	16th		Bde.H.Q closed CAGNONCLES 13.30 re-opened RIEUX 17.30. The move was carried out in the form of an attack over open-country 2/Wilts Regt on the right, 9/Welch Regt. on the left, 9/R.W.F. in support. Personnel of Bde.H.Q. moved in rear of the support battalion. Transport moved by road under/of the Bde. T.O.	H O.O.280
RIEUX	17th		Units training near/ billets and ready to move at short notice. Orders received that the 58th Infy Bde. will take over from the left battn. of the 57th Bde. 10/R.War. Regt. on the night of Octr. 18/19th.	
		1800	Conference was held at 58th Bde.H.Q. G.O.C. XIX Div. C.R.A. XVII Corps, G.O's.C. 57 and 58 Bdes.	
	18th		58th Bde. moved by march route via AVESNES-lez-AUBERT to ST. AUBERT 9/R.W.F. and 2/Wilts R. behind the 10th R. War. Regt. in the line, the 9/Welch moved into support at AVESNES-lez-AUBERT	J O.O.281

Army Form C. 2118.

WAR DIARY
or
INTELLIGENCE SUMMARY.
(Erase heading not required.)

Instructions regarding War Diaries and Intelligence Summaries are contained in F. S. Regs., Part II. and the Staff Manual respectively. Title pages will be prepared in manuscript.

Place	Date	Hour	Summary of Events and Information	Remarks and references to Appendices
ST. AUBERT.	19th		The 19th Divn. ordered to attack and capture the high ground E. of the R. SELLE. The 57th Bde. to attack on our right and the 4th Divn. on our left.	O.O.282
	20th		The 58th Bde. attacked at 02.00 hrs. the R. SELLE was successfully crossed and all objectives taken. Objectives being reached the line was consolidated and strong patrols pushed forward.	See Narrative App. I.
V.9.a.8.8.		0430	Adv. Bde.H.Q. established at V.9.a.8.8.	
HAUSSY		1600	Bde.H.Q. moved forward and were established in HAUSSY, V.11.b.3.6. HAUSSY was intermittently shelled with H.E. and Gas throughout the day and during the night.	
	21st		HAUSSY persistently shelled throughout the day and night with Gas and H.E. Intermittent shelling of whole Bde. Area Both front line battalions 9/R.W.F. and 2/Wilts R. pushed patrols well forward (See narrative Appendix I). 9/Welch R. relieved 2/Wilts R. in the front line.	
	22nd		Considerable shelling of Bde. area, persistent shelling of HAUSSY with Gas and H.E. Weather bad heavy rain from early morning until late in the afternoon. Patrols from front line units came in contact with considerable machine gun fire.	
SANDPITS V.5.a.4.3.		15.30	Bde.H.Q. closed at HAUSSY 15.30 hrs. and moved to SAND-PITS V.5.a.4.3. Orders received for relief of 19th Divn. in the line by 61st Divn. In accordance with above orders Bde. Order No. 283 was issued for the relief of 58th Bde. by the 182nd Bde. on the night of 23/24th Octr.	O.O.283
	23rd		Considerable hostile aircraft and artillery activity.	
		10.30	Warning order received that in order to make our line conform with that of the 57th Bde. on our right it might be necessary to advance our line to the railway running through P.18 and Q.13.	
		16.00	Orders were received at noon to carry out this minor operation under a barrage at 16.00 hrs This was successfully carried out by the 9/Welch Regt. and the 9/R.W.Fusrs. Prisoners captured 20 O.R. 2 of whom were wounded.	
	24th	0515	Relief of 58th Bde. by the 182nd Bde. complete 03.15 hrs. Bde.H.Q. moved to RIEUX. Bde.H.Q. established at U.19.d.0.6. Units of Bde. on relief moved by march route over-land where possible to billets in RIEUX.	
RIEUX.		1430	Bde.H.Q. moved across village to new headquarters U.20.d.2.8.	
	25th		Units resting and training under battalion arrangements.	

Army Form C. 2118.

WAR DIARY
or
INTELLIGENCE SUMMARY.
(Erase heading not required.)

Place	Date	Hour	Summary of Events and Information	Remarks and references to Appendices
RIEUX	26th		Units bathing. Training under Battalion arrangements.	
	27th		-do-	
	28th	1430	During morning training under battalion arrangements. Demonstration by aeroplane flying at different altitudes, a few selected Lewis Gunners from each Bn. were practising with Camera Guns.	
	29th		Units training under battalion arrangements.	
	30th		-do-	
24.11.1918.				

Lieutenant Colonel
Commanding 58th Infantry Brigade.

Map "A"
Haspres
Sommaing sur Ecaillon
Vendegies sur-Ecaillon
Berme
St. Martin
Saulzoir
Ravin Brûlé
Chaussée Brunehaut
PRACTICE TRENCHES
Montrécourt
Montrécourt Wood
Escarmain
Haussy
Vertain
St. Aubert
St. Vaast
St. Python
Romeries
Maison Bleue
Maison Druon
Maison Blanche
P
Q
V
W
Field Survey Bn. [10869]. 14-10-18
Scale 1 : 20,000

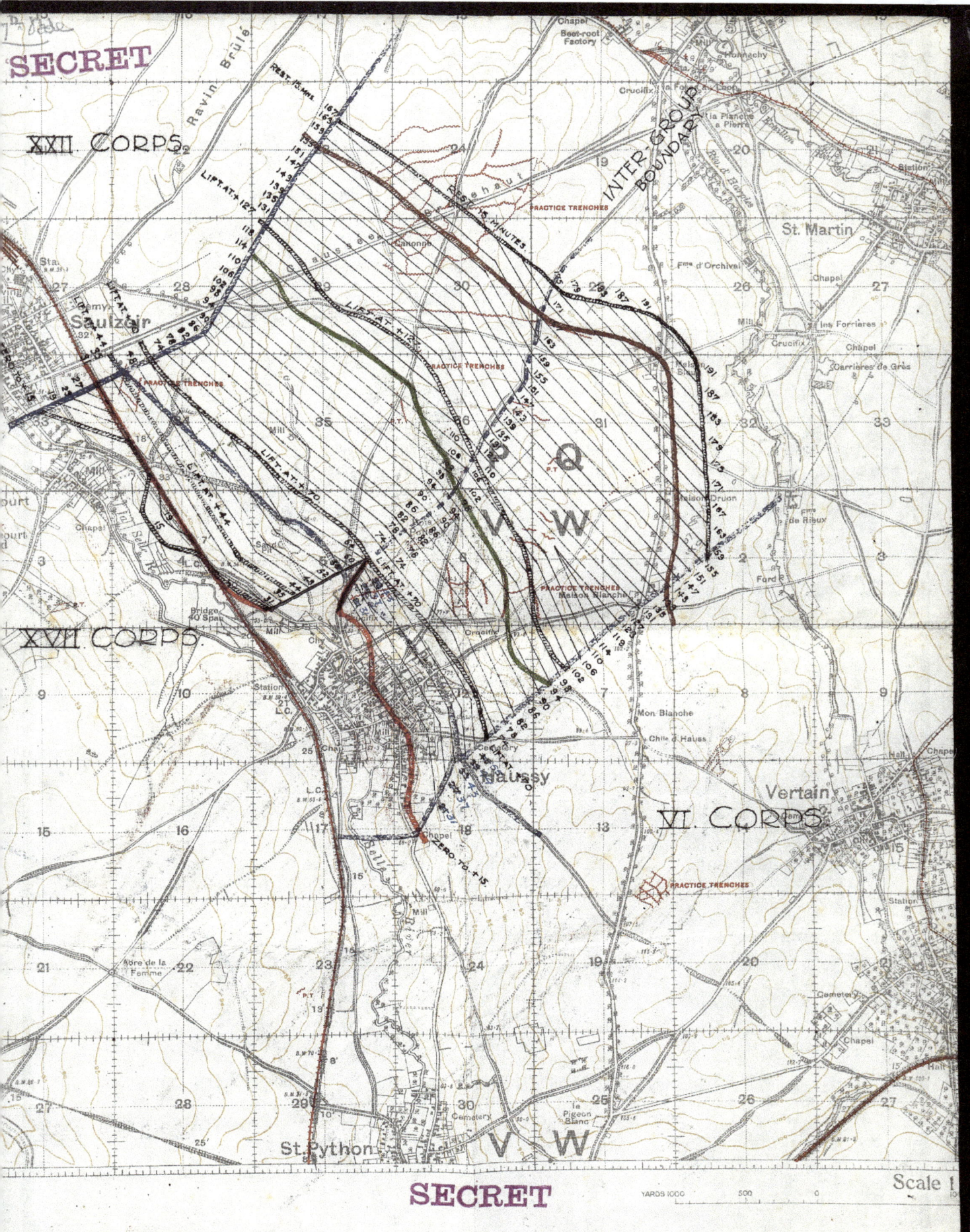

SECRET.   B   War Diary   Copy No. 28.

58th Infantry Brigade Order No.274.

3rd October, 1918.

Ref. to LENS 11
1/100,000.

1. The 19th Division (less Artillery) will be transferred to Third Army XVII Corps.

2. The 58th Brigade Group composed as under will move on October 4th. Personnel and proportion of transport by train. Remainder of transport by road in accordance with attached March Table.

58th Bde.H.Q.	81st Field Coy R.E.
9/R.W.Fusrs.	59th Field Ambulance.
9/Welch R.	No.4 Coy. Train.
2/Wilts Regt.	No.3 Section D.A.C.
58th T.M.B.	31st Mob Vet. Sec.
19th D.H.Q.	

3. The entraining station for the 58th Brigade Group will be PERNES. Entrainment will be carried out in accordance with attached Entraining Table "A".

4. Lewis Guns will be carried on the limbers proceeding by train. Three A.A. Lewis Guns will accompany Battalions moving by train. If necessary three ordinary Lewis Guns will travel on the half limber usually allotted to the A.A. Lewis Guns.

5. Dress for personnel moving by train will be "Marching Order".

6. Each Unit will detail an Officer to report to an Officer of the Bde. Staff at PERNES Station 1½ hours before the time of departure of his unit's train with the exact entraining strength of his unit.

7. The 9th Bn R.W.Fusiliers will detail one Coy. for loading and off loading duties. This Coy. will report to the R.T.O. 3 hours before the departure of the Transport Train.

8. Supply arrangements will be in accordance with the attached Table "B".

9. Advance parties will travel on kit lorries details of which will be issued later. Unless otherwise ordered they will report to the Staff Captain at BARLY Church on arrival in the new area.

10. The transport proceeding by train will arrive at the entraining station 3 hours before the scheduled time of departure and the personnel 1 hour.

11. Entrainment of all Units must be completed half an hour before the time of departure of trains.

    Breast ropes for horse trucks must be provided by units. D.A.D.O.S. has been ordered to procure a supply from which units will draw.

12. Once a unit has been entrained no man will be allowed to leave his truck, unless permission is obtained from O.C. Train.
    Picquets to be detailed by O.C. Train will be provided at all stops for each end of the train, to prevent troops leaving.
    On arrival at the detraining station the "Fall In" will be sounded on which troops will detrain quickly and in silence.

13. All doors of covered trucks and carriages, on the right hand side of the train, when on the main line, will be kept closed.

14. All Units will reconnoitre their entraining stations.

15. ACKNOWLEDGE.

F.W. Fraser Captain
Brigade Major 58th Infantry Bde.

Issued through Signals at 8.30.p.m.

Copy No. 1 9.R.W.Fusrs.
2 9.Welch R.
3 2.Wilts R.
4 58.T.M.B.
5 81.Fld.Co.R./.
6 59.Fld.Amb.
7 No.4.Coy. Train.
8 No.3 Sec. D.A.C.
9 31.M.V.S.
10 G.O.C.
11 Staff Capt.
12 Bde. Sig. Offr.
13 Bde. Int. Offr.
14 Bde. Transport Offr.
15 Bde. Gas Offr.
16 Bde. Bombing Offr.
17 56th Inf. Bde.
18 57th Inf. Bde.
19 19th Div. G.
20 19th Div. "Q"
21 C.R.E.
22 A.D.M.S.
23 O.C. 19th Div. Train.
24 A.P.M.
25 Sergt. i/c M.M.P. (2).
26 Bde. Q.M.S.
27 R.T.O. PERNES.
28) War Diary.
29)
30 File.

March Table to accompany 58th Inf. Brigade Order No. 274.

Unit.	From.	To.	Starting Point.	Head of Column passes S.P. at	Route.	Remarks.
19th D.H.Q. Transport.	AUCHEL.	PENIN.	Cross roads VALHUON.	08.00	VALHUON - BRYAS - MARQUAY - AVERDOINGT.	
58th Bde.H.Q. Transport. 31/Mob.Vet.Sec.	PERNES.	"	"	08.07	"	⎫ Will march as ⎬ one unit. ⎭
No.3. Section D.A.C.	"	"	"	08.17	"	
9/Welch Regt. Transport.	PRESSY.	"	"	08.20.	"	
2/Wilts. R. Transport.	SAINS LES PERNES.	"	"	08.23.	"	
9/R.W.Fusrs. Transport.	SACHIN.	"	"	08.26.	"	
81/Fld.Co.R.E. Transport.	BOYAVAL.	"	"	08.29	"	
59/Fld. Ambce. Transport.	"	"	"	08.34.	"	
No.4 Coy. Train.	MAREST.	"	"	08.38.	"	

NOTES:
1. The B.T.O. 58th Inf. Brigade will be i/c the Column.
2. The 2nd Wilts Regt. will detail a suitable Officer to ride on and report to Captain TAPP, M.C. at Sub-Area Commandant's office PENIN at 10.00. Each Unit will send forward an N.C.O. during the march to get touch with this Officer.
3. The following intervals will be maintained throughout the march - 100 yards between Units. 50 yards between every 10 vehicles.
4. The strictest march discipline will be maintained throughout the march.
5. DRESS: Marching Order, soft caps, steel helmets will be carried on the left shoulder, overcoats at discretion of T.O's but if one man of a unit wears one all must.

ENTRAINING TABLE "A"

Train	Type	Unit	Strength		Time departure of train
No. 1.	Personnel.	19th Div. H.Q.	30 Off.	600 O.R.	14.46.
		58th Bde. H.Q.	6 "	90 "	
		2nd Wilts Regt.	28 "	720 "	
		58 T.M.Battery.	6 "	50 "	

Train	Type	Unit	Horses	Vehicles	Time departure of train
No. 2.	Transport.	19th Div H.Q.	3 horses.	3 axles.	17.46.
		58th Bde H.Q.	4 L.D.)	2 limbers.	
			10 Riders.)		
	Personnel.	Each Battn.	10 Riders.)	3 Cookers,)	
			11 L.D.)	4 L.G.Limbers.)	
			6 H.D.)	1 Water Cart,)	
				1 Mess Cart.)	
		81st Fd Coy.	4 L.D.)	1 Water Cart.)	
			4 Riders.)	1 Limber.)	
		59th Fd. Ambce.	4 L.D.)	1 Water Cart.)	
			4 Riders.)	1 Limber.)	
		9/R.W.Fus.	1 Company (Loading party).		
		59th Fd. Ambce.	8 Offrs. 200 O.R.		

Train	Type	Unit	Strength		Time departure of train
No. 3.	Personnel.	9/R.W.Fus (less 1 Coy)	20 Off.	500 O.R.	20.46.
		9/Welch.	26 "	730.	

Notes. (1) O.s. C. Trains will be as follows :-

    No. 1.   G.O.C.
    No. 2.   Lt.Col D. Mackenzie, D.S.O.
    No. 3.   Lt.Col H.Ll.Jones, D.S.O.

(2) Accommodation on the trains is as follows :-

<u>Personnel</u>   1900.

<u>Transport</u>   17 flats. 30 covered trucks.

SECRET.   C   Copy No. 28

            58th Inf. Brigade Order No. 275.
            ────────────────────────────────
                                          5th October, 1918.

Ref. map LENS 11
1/100,000.

1.   19th Division, less Artillery, is moving on the 6th and 7th insts.

2.   The 58th Brigade Group will be constituted as under:-

            58th Infy. Bde.   No. 5 Section D.A.C.
            81st Field Coy. R.E.   No. 4 Coy. Train.
            59th Field Ambulance.   31st Mob. Vet. Section.

        Transport of all units will move under the orders of the B.T.O., which will be issued separately, to BOISLEUX AU MONT and BOYELLES Area on the 6th inst.
        Personnel of the Group will move by bus on the 7th inst. with the head of the Column at the N. entrance to BARLY on the AVESNES - BARLY Road.
        Detailed orders for embussing will be issued later.

3.   The O.C. 2nd Bn Wiltshire Regt. will detail an Officer to report to Captain TAPP, M.C. at the Area Commandant's Office BOISLEUX AU MONT at 12.00 on the 6th inst. to be allotted billets. If possible this will be the same Officer as was detailed for the same duty on the 4th inst.

4.   The following will be the allotment of lorries for blankets, Officers' valises and Officers' and Mens' cooking gear :- *for the move on the 7th inst*

            Brigade H.Q.   1 lorry.
            Each Battn.   2½ lorries.
            T.M.B.   ½ lorry.
            81/Fld Coy.   ½ lorry.
            59/Fld Amb.   ½ lorry.

        Hours of reporting will be notified later.

5.   Surplus personnel will move by bus and not with the transport.

6.   Orders concerning advance parties will be issued later.

7.   All Lewis Guns (except 1 Anti-aircraft gun per Bn) and 12 drums per gun, and Stokes Mortars will be carried with the men in the busses.

8.   Dress for embussing will be Full Marching Order.

9.   Acknowledge.

                                          H.W. Hume.
                                          ─────────
                                              Major for
                                              Captain

                              Brigade Major 58th Infantry Brigade.

Issued through Signals at 21.30

    Copy No. 1 9/R.W.F.   16 Bde. Bombing Offr.
            2 9.Welch R.   17 56.Inf. Bde.
            3 2.Wilts R.   18 57.Inf. Bde.
            4 58.T.M.B.   19 19th Div. G.
            5 81.Fld. Co.   20 19th Div. Q.
            6 59.Fld. Amb.   21 C.R.E.
            7 No.4 Co.Train.   22 A.D.M.S.
            8 No. 3 Sec. D.A.C.   23 O.C. Div. Train.
            9 31.M.V.S.   24 A.P.M.
           10 G.O.C.   25 Sergt. i/c M.M.P.
           11 Staff Capt.   26 Town Major, BARLY.
           12 Bde. Sig. Offr.   27 Bde. Q.M.S.
           13 Bde. Int. Offr.   28) War Diary.
           14 Bde. Transport Offr.   29)
           15 Bde. Gas Offr.   30 File.

SECRET.

MARCH ORDERS No. 3.

Ref. map LENS 11
1/100,000.

1. The 58th Brigade Group of Transport composed as under will move to-morrow 6th instant in accordance with the attached March Table.

H.Q. 58th Bde.	59.Field Ambulance.
9.R.W.Fusrs.	No. 3 Sec. D.A.C.
9.Welch R.	31st Mob. Vet. Sec.
2.Wilts R.	No.4 Coy. 19th Div. Train.
81.Fld. Co. R.E.	

2. DRESS: Marching Order. Soft caps, steel helmets on left shoulder, overcoats at discretion of T.O's but if one man of a unit wears one all must do so.

3. DISCIPLINE. The strictest march discipline will be observed. Several cases were noticed to-day of men hanging on to wagons and marching away from their wagons on the left of the road. The N.C.O. at the rear of each unit must be made to bear in mind that he is put there for the purpose of maintaining discipline.

4. HALTS: The usual halts will be observed. The halt at 12.50 will last until 13.00. Animals will be watered and fed at this halt.

5. INTERVALS: 100 yards between Units.
   50 yards between every ton wagons.

6. BILLETING: Each unit will send forward a N.C.O. to report to Captain TAPP, M.C., A.S.C. at Area Commandant's office at BOISLEUX-AU-MONT at 12.00 for billeting there.
   These N.C.O's will return and meet their units at FICHEUX and guide them to their billets.

                                         Captain
                          Transport Officer, 58th Inf Brigade.

5.10.18.

Issued to all recipients of O.O.275.

March Table in conjunction with March Order No. 3.

Unit.	From.	To.	Starting Point.	Time.	Route.	Remarks.
No.3 Sec. D.A.C.	GOUY.	LOISLEUX AU MONT and BOYELLES.	Road Junction Eastern end of HOMCHIET.	11.00.	HAUTEZ-les-LOGES MRTRENCOURT - BLAIRVILLE - FICHEUX.	
2/Wilts Regt.	"	"	"	11.10.	"	
No.4 Coy.A.S.C.	"	"	"	11.13.	"	
58/Bde.H.Q.	BARLY.	"	"	11.17.	"	
9/Welch Regt.	"	"	"	11.19.	"	
59/Fld. Ambce.	"	"	"	11.22.	"	
9/R.W.Fusrs.	SOMBRIN.	"	"	11.26.	"	
81/Fld.Co.R.E.	"	"	"	11.29.	"	
31/Mob. Vet. Section.	"	"	"	11.34.	"	

NOTE: Attention is drawn to the fact that winter time is in force on 6.10.18.

SECRET.   Copy No. 11

58th Infantry Brigade Order No. 278.

Reference to Sheet 57c. N.E.
1/20,000.

1. The 19th Division becomes Division in Support.

2. The 58th Brigade will move to-night to area L.3. and 4.

    Route – GRAINCOURT – CANTAING Road.

    Starting Point – Road junction K.5.c.25.95.

    Cookers and L.G. Limbers march with Companies; remainder of Transport in rear of Battalions.

    Bde.H.Q. and 58th T.M.Battery will pass S.P. at 18.00.
    2nd Bn Wiltshire Regiment   "   "   "   " 18.04.
    9th Bn Royal Welch Fusrs.   "   "   "   " 18.12.
    9th Bn Welch Rgt.   "   "   "   " 18.20.

    Distances between Coys. – 50 yards.
    "   "   Bns. – 200 "

    Connecting files must keep in touch with units in front.
    Packs will be carried.

3. Advance parties will be at the Western entrance of CANTAING (L.3.a.9.4.) at 17.00 and await the arrival of the Staff Captain.

4. ACKNOWLEDGE.

                                        [signature]
                                                    Captain

                                        Brigade Major 58th Infantry Bde.

Issued through Signals at 4.30.p.m.

    Copy No. 1 9.R.W.F.
             2 9.Welch R.
             3 2.Wilts R.
             4 58.T.M.B.
             5 19th Div. G.
             6 56th Bde.
             7 57th Bde.
             8 B.T.O.
             9 B.I.O.
            10 Staff Capt.
            11) War Diary
            12)
            13 File.

"E"

SECRET.

Amendment No. 1 to 58th Inf. Brigade Order No.277.

Para. 6:   For "Divisional Mounted Detachment" read "No.3 Troop,
           A Squadron, 6th Dragoon Guards".

Para. 7:   For "Divisional Mounted Detachment (less 1 section)"
           read "No.3 Troop, A Squadron, 6th Dragoon Guards".

                                                    _____, Captain

12.10.18.   Brigade Major 58th Infantry Brigade.

        Issued to all recipients of O.O.277.

SECRET.

Addendum No. 1 to 56th Inf. Brigade Order No. 277.

Para. 6, after "Divl. Mounted Detachment" add

"H.Q. and Bearer Division (less 1 sub-division) of 57th Field Amb."

Para. 7, after "Divl. Mounted Detachment" add

"1 Bearer Sub-division of 57th Field Ambulance."

                                                            Captain

10.10.18.   Brigade Major 56th Infantry Brigade.

SECRET.   Copy No. 20.

58th Infantry Brigade Order No.277.

10th October, 1918.

1. From all information to hand the enemy is carrying out a retirement on a large scale. A vigorous pursuit has been ordered along the whole Army front.

2. The pursuit by the XVII Corps is to be carried out with the utmost determination. The hostile rearguards are to be attacked as soon as located. The one aim and object of all ranks should be to get at the enemy's main forces and bring them to battle.

3. Corps boundaries are as shown on map issued on 9.10.18.

4. At present the 19th Division is in support to the 24th Div. Group.

5. The strictest march discipline of all arms is to be enforced. Troops are to move off the roads to halt whenever possible.

6. In the event of the 19th Division being ordered to advance through the 24th Division and so become leading group the Advanced Guard to the Division will consist of :-

    58th Infantry Brigade.
    2nd N.Z. Bde. R.F.A.
    2 Machine Gun Coys.
    94th Field Coy. R.E.
    Divl. Mounted Detachment.

7. In this event the Vanguard will probably consist of the following troops, the whole under the command of the O.C. Battalion:-

    1 Battalion.
    1 Sec. T.M.B.
    2 Sec. R.F.A.
    1 M.G. Coy.
    1 Sec. 94th Field Coy. R.E.
    Divl. Mounted Detachment (less 1 section).

   Every Battalion Commander will consider the handling of this force. Attention is directed to the diagram "An Infantry Brigade acting as an Advanced Guard" which shows a suggested formation for the Vanguard advancing when not in close touch with the enemy.

8. The Vanguard must act with the greatest vigour and boldness. Its duty is to drive in weak forces of the enemy and so avoid delaying the Main Guard. When the enemy is met with in strength the Vanguard will force the enemy to disclose his dispositions and hold him to his ground while dispositions for attack are made by troops in rear.

9. If ordered to move in fighting order Troops of 58th Bde. will dump haversacks with surplus kit and greatcoats rolled in bundles. The Pack will be carried but containing only fighting kit and leather jerkin when issued.

10. ACKNOWLEDGE.

                                                    Captain
                                   Brigade Major 58th Infantry Bde.

Issued through Signals at 1030 hours.

Copy No.			
1 9.R.W.F.	8 B.T.O.	15 C.R.E.
2 9.Welch R.	9 B.I.O.	16 O.C. Div.Train.
3 2.Wilts R.	10 B.B.O.	17 O.C. No.4 Coy.Train.
4 58.T.M.B.	11 56.Inf.Bde.	18 19th M.G.Bn.
5 G.O.C.	12 57 -do-	19 Bde.Q.M.S.
6 Staff Capt.	13 19th Div.G	20) War Diary.
7 Bde. Sig. Offr.	14 19th Div.Q.	21)
		22 File.

SECRET.   F   Copy No. 8

58th Infantry Brigade Order No. 278.

Refce. Sheet 57c.N.E.
       Sheet 57b.N.W.
       1/20,000.

1. The 58th Brigade will move to Squares A.18. and 24. to-day 10th inst:
   Route via CANTANEUX MILL (F.30.a.).
   Starting Point - Road junction at L.3.a.95.45.

   Bde.H.Q.)
   T.M.B.   ) will pass Starting Point at 13.30. hours.
   2/Wilts R.   "   "   "   "   "   13.35. "
   9/R.W.F.   "   "   "   "   "   13.45   "
   9/Welch R.   "   "   "   "   "   13.55   "
   Bde. Transport "   "   "   "   "   14.10   "

2. L.G. Limbers, Cookers, Water carts, A.A. Limbers, Mess Carts, Maltese Cart and Pack animals will march with Battalions, remainder of transport under orders of Bde. T.O. in rear of column.

3. Dress: Marching Order.

4. Units will report their arrival in new area and location of Headquarters.

5. Brigade Headquarters will close at CANTAING at 14.00 hours and re-open on arrival at RUE GAUCHET on arrival.

6. Acknowledge.

                                          [signature]
                                          Captain

                              Brigade Major 58th Infantry Brigade.

   Copy No. 1 9/R.W.Fusrs.
           2 9/Welch R.
           3 2/Wilts R.
           4 58/T.M.Battery.
           5 G.O.C.
           6 Staff Capt.
           7 19th Div. G.
           8) War Diary.
           9)
          10 File.

SECRET.   Copy No... 23

58th Inf. Brigade Order No. 279.

Ref. to 57.B. N.W.
1/20,000.   12th October, 1918.

1. The 58th Brigade and 94th Field Coy. R.E. will move to CAGNONCLES to-day. The 19th M.G. Battalion will move to CAURIOR.

   Route: Via. CAMBRAI STATION - FACTORY, B.8.b.9.8. - LA BAHOTTE.
   Starting Point: Road junction A.18.b.2.5.

   Bde. H.Q.)
   58/T.M.B) will pass Starting Point at 14.15 hours.
   2/Wilts R.   "   "   "   " " 14.20   "
   9/R.W.F.   "   "   "   " " 14.30   "
   9/Welch R.   "   "   "   " " 14.40   "
   Bde. Tpt.   "   "   "   " " 14.55   "
   94/Fld.Co.R.E. "   "   "   " " 15.05   "
   19th M.G. Battn. march independently to be clear of Eastern outskirts of CAMBRAI by 16.00 hours.

2. "A" Echelon Transport will march with Units. "B" Echelon Transport will be Brigaded in rear under B.T.O.

3. Units of 58th Bde. will send a guide to Bde.H.Q. to guide lorries to Blanket dumps.

4. Units will report arrival and location of H.Q. on reaching CAGNONCLES.

5. F.G.C.M. for trial of Pte. SHENTON, 9th Bn Welch Regt. and Pte. MITCHELL, 2nd Bn Wiltshire Regt. will be indefinitely postponed if no orders to the contrary have been received by units by 13.30 to-day.

6. Brigade H.Q. will close at A.24.a.4.4. at 13.30. hours and re-open on arrival at CAGNONCLES. An Officer of Brigade H.Q. at A.24.a.4.4. will remain until communication is established at CAGNONCLES.

7. ACKNOWLEDGE.

                                                    Captain
                                        Brigade Major 58th Infantry Brigade.

Issued through Signals at 13.15 hours.

    Copy No. 1 9/R.W.F.
             2 9/Welch R.
             3 2.Wilts R.
             4 58.T.M.B.
             5 G.O.C.
             6 Staff Capt.
             7 Bde. Sig. Offr.
             8 B.T.O.
             9 B.I.O.
            10 B.B.O.
            11 19th Div. G.
            12 19th Div. Q
            13 56th Inf. Bde.
            14 57th Inf. Bde.
            15 A.D.M.S.
            16 C.R.E.
            17 O.C. Div. Train.
            18 O.C. No.4 Coy. Train.
            19 A.P.M.
            20 O.C. Div. Mtd. Detachment.
            21 19/M.G.Bn.   24 War Diary.
            22 Liaison Offr. R.A.M.C.   25 File.
            23 War Diary

SECRET.
H
Copy No. 23

58th Infantry Brigade Order No. 280.

15th October, 1918.

Ref. to 51.C. S.W.
57.B. N.W.
1/20,000.

1. The tactical situation permitting the 19th Division will relieve the 24th Division in the line on the 17th October.

2. The 58th Inf. Brigade will move to RIEUX to-morrow 16th instant. Personnel will move in the afternoon in accordance with scheme being issued. Transport of Units will move under the orders of the Brigade Transport Officer via B.5.d. and C.1.a. Starting Point Road junction B.5.c.9.2. Head of Column to pass Starting Point at 14.00 hours.

3. Units will take over accommodation at present occupied by Units of 17th Brigade as under with certain modifications.

    9th Bn R.W.Fusiliers from 1st Bn Royal Fusiliers.
    9th Bn Welch Regt.   "   8th Bn Queen's.
    2nd Bn Wiltshire Regt. "   3rd Bn Rifle Brigade.
    58th T.M.Battery.   "   17th T.M.Battery.

4. Advance parties will report for instructions as to modifications mentioned in para. 2 to Staff Captain at the Church RIEUX at 11.00. hours.

5. Lorries will report as follows for blankets -

    At H.Q. 9th Bn R.W.F. 09.15.   1 lorry.
    " H.Q. 9th Bn Welch Regt.   1 lorry.
    2nd Bn Wiltshire Regt. and 58th T.M.Battery 1 lorry each on completion of journey by 9th Bn R.W.Fusrs. and 9th Bn Welch Regt.

6. Brigade H.Q. will close at CAGNONCLES at 13.30. hours and re-open at RIEUX on arrival.

7. ACKNOWLEDGE.

                                        Captain

                    Brigade Major 58th Infantry Brigade.

Issued through Signals at 08.00 hours 16.10.18.

    Copy No. 1 9.R.W.F.
            2 9.Welch R.   14 A.D.M.S.
            3 2.Wilts R.   15 A.P.M.
            4 58.T.M.Bty.   16 56th Inf. Bde.
            5 G.O.C.   17 57th Inf. Bde.
            6 Staff Capt.   18 17th Inf. Bde.
            7 Bde. Sig. Offr.   19 O.C. 19th Div. Train.
            8 B.T.O.   20 O.C. No.4 Coy. Train.
            9 B.I.O.   21 Bde. Q.M.S.
           10 B.B.O.   22 Sergt. i/c M.M.P.
           11 19th Div. G.   23) War Diary.
           12 19th Div. Q.   24)
           13 C.R.E.   25 File.

SECRET.   J   Copy No. 21

58th Brigade O.O. 281.

18th Octr., 1918.

Ref. to 51.A. S.E.
51.A. S.W.

1. The 58th Inf. Bde. will take over the front of the left Bn 57th Inf. Bde., 10/R.War. Regt. on the night Octr. 18/19th as under :-

   On right, 2nd Bn Wilts Regt. disposed as follows -
   One platoon WEST of River approximately V.4.a. and c.
   Three platoons about V.8.d. and V.9.c.
   One Coy. approximately V.7.b. and c. Two Coys. East end of ST. AUBERT. Bn.H.Q.

   On left. 9th Bn R.W.Fusrs. disposed as follows :-
   Two platoons in MONTECOURT about V.3.b. Two platoons in Sunken Road P.32.c. One Coy. approx. V.1.c. and d. Two Coys. E. end of ST. AUBERT. Bn.H.Q. V.13.b.0.7.

   Reserve, 9th Bn Welch Regt. in AVESNES and 58th T.M.B. in ST. AUBERT.

   Inter-Bn. Boundary V.7.central - cross tracks V.3.c.central (incl. to right Bn). - Rly. V.4.a.8.9.

2. All details for the relief of the forward Battalions will be arranged between C.O's concerned. 9th Bn Welch Regt. will be clear of RIEUX by 15 hours.

3. Touch will be gained and maintained by means of Liaison Posts by 2nd Wilts R. with troops of 57th Bde. and by 9/R.W.F. with troops of 4th Div.
   Patrols will also work along the W. bank of R. SELLE within Bde. Boundaries.

4. The two forward Bns. will render disposition reports to reach this office by 12.00 hours 19th inst.

5. Six Sappers of 178 Tunn. Coy. R.E. will be attached to Bde.H.Q. for the purpose of searching for mines and booby traps. Should Units require their services they will indent on Bde.H.Q.

6. Completion of relief will be wired to this office using code word COMMAND.

7. Bde.H.Q. will close at RIEUX at 15.00 hours and re-open at U.18.d.1.1. on arrival.

8. ACKNOWLEDGE.

                                            Captain
                        Brigade Major 58th Infantry Brigade.

Issued through Sigs. at 09.30 hours. 18.10.18.

Copy No. 1 9.R.W.F.   14 57th Inf. Bde.
         2 9.Welch R.   15 C.R.A.
         3 2.Wilts R.   16 C.R.E.
         4 58 T.M.B.   17 A.D.M.S.
         5 G.O.C.   18 D.A.P.M.
         6 Staff Capt.   19 O.C. Div. Train.
         7 Bde. Sig. Offr.   20 O.C. No.4 Coy. Train.
         8 B. T. O.   21) War Diary.
         9 B. I. O.   22
        10 B. B. O.   23 File.
        11 19th Div. G.
        12 19th Div. Q.
        13 56th Inf. Bde.

SECRET.   Copy No. 24

                    53th Bde. Order No. 282.

Ref. to 51.A. S.E.
       51.A. S.W.   18th October, 1918.

INTENTION.   1.   On 20th Octr. the Division in conjunction with Divisions
                  on both flanks will capture the high ground E. of the River
                  SELLE. 57th Bde. will attack on our Right 4th Division on
                  our left.
                       The attack consists of two phases -

                  (a) The bridging of the River SELLE and capture of line of
                  Railway and high ground in P.34.a. and d. and V.5.a.

                  (b) The capture of the high ground marked on map as final
                  objective.

BOUNDARIES   2.   Boundaries and objectives are shown on attached map which
AND   also shows the times at which the Infantry advance from each
OBJECTIVES.   Intermediate Objective and finally arrive at Final Objective.
                       The "Jumping Off" Line will be the Left Bank of the
                  River SELLE.
                       Liaison Posts will be established with flank units at
                  points marked L.P.

DISPOSITIONS.3.   The attack will be carried out by 2 Bns. in front and
                  one in reserve.
                            On Right........ 2nd Bn Wiltshire Regt.
                            On Left......... 9th Bn R.W.Fusrs.
                            In Reserve...... 9th Bn Welch Regt.

                       Each front Bn. will attack with two assaulting Coys.
                  One Coy. in Support and one in Reserve.

BRIDGING.   4.   The 94th Field Coy.R.E. will throw 10 bridges across the
                  River. These will probably have to be placed in position
                  at ZERO under cover of the opening barrage but it may be
                  possible to place some of them in position beforehand. The
                  approximate position of these bridges is shown on map
                  previously issued to Bns. The Southern 5 bridges (1 to 5)
                  are allotted to Right Bn., the Northern 5 (6 to 10) to
                  Left Bn.
                       Leading platoons of each leading Coy. will be assembled
                  with their respective bridging parties at Zero close to the
                  site where bridges are to be thrown. Remainder will be
                  assembled at convenient positions behind. As soon as
                  possible after Zero the leading platoons will cross and as
                  soon as the barrage permits will occupy the line of the
                  Railway. Remaining troops of Assaulting Bns. will follow
                  closely, the object being to get the whole of the Assaulting
                  Bns. East of the River as quickly as can be. The importance
                  of the Infantry crossing the River and forming up rapidly
                  behind the barrage cannot be over-estimated. There must be
                  No hesitation.
                       From the Railway the attack will be continued in
                  Attack Formation.

RESERVE BN. 5.   The Reserve Bn. will on 19th October move to a position
                  of readiness about Squares V.8.d. and 14.b. To be in
                  position by 22.00 hours. Position to be reconnoitred on
                  morning of 19th. The Bn. will be prepared to move across
                  the River when ordered to the Line of the Road in P.34.d.
                  and   V.5.a.

- 2 -

ARTILLERY ARRANGEMENTS. 6. The attack will be carried out under a creeping Artillery and M.G. Barrage.

18-Pr. Creeping Barrage will open at Zero on the Black line shown on attached map and will remain there till Zero plus 15 when it will start to creep forward at the rate of 100 yards in 4 minutes straightening out over the Railway and halting for 9 minutes on Protector 200 yards beyond it. It will then continue to move forward at 100 yards in 4 minutes till it reaches Protector 200 yards beyond 2nd objective where it will rest till Zero plus 70 minutes. It will then move forward at same rate of advance to Protector beyond 3rd Objective where it will rest till Zero plus 127 minutes. It will then continue at same rate till it reaches Protector to Final Objective where it will remain for 15 minutes when barrage fire will cease.

Strong patrols will then be pushed forward by both Bns. to the Railway South of SOMMAING to capture any guns that may be West of the Railway. One Battery will be pushed across the River SELLE as soon as bridges are ready and will closely support the infantry, especially for anti-Tank defence.

MACHINE GUNS. 7. In addition to the M.G's detailed for the creeping barrage 1 Coy. will go forward with the Bde. as forward guns.

One section will follow the attack closely in each Bn. sector. These guns will get on to the high ground of 3rd Objective as quickly as possible to cover the advance on final objective. Right section from about P.36.c., Left section working forwards to about P.29.d. As soon as final objective is taken these two sections will take up position for the defence of the Objective by direct fire. Guns should be sited to bring cross fire to bear across the valley in P.25.a. and the slopes in P.24.d.

One section will follow further in rear in each Bn. sector on the outer flanks and will be prepared to form defensive flanks should the attack of Bdes. on the flanks be held up. The Right guns should find suitable positions on the slopes V.5.b. and 6.a. and P.36.c. The Left Section will send two guns as quickly as possible to a position on the spur near LE TORDOIR, the remaining guns pushing on to the slopes in P.29.c. and a. to cover the valley in P.28.d. and 29.a.

When the Flanks are secure these 2 sections will be disposed for defence in depth back to the high ground about the Line of 3rd Objective.

TRENCH MORTARS. 8. Light Trench Mortars will deal with certain selected targets at Zero. One Mortar will move forward with each Bn. to deal with enemy machine guns impeding the advance. When the final objective is taken these Mortars will take up positions to cover the Sunken Roads in Q.25.c. and P.30.a.

DIRECTION. 9. General compass direction of attack must be known by all Officers.

To assist in maintenance of direction one round of Thermite shell (which gives a big flame) will be fired at each lift of the barrage to mark the flank of each attacking Bn.

As the barrage lifts on to Protective Barrage over each objective to allow Infantry to come on to it a salvo of Thermite shells will be fired by Artillery along the front.

CONSOLIDATION.	10. The Final Objective is the line to be held. The 2 leading Coys. of each Bn. will consolidate in depth on Final Objective and in rear of it with outposts in front to command all hollows and roads leading up to our line from the HARPIES Valley and Railway South of SOMMAING. Practice trenches in front of final objective must be mopped up. The two rear Coys. will consolidate in depth on the 3rd Objective and in front of it. The greatest efforts must be made to get dug in before daylight. Commanding Officers will organise the consolidation on the ground. Rifle Grenade Signals showing 3 Green Lights will be fired on reaching the final objective. These will be issued to Bns. on 19th inst.
CONTACT AEROPLANES.	11. Contact Aeroplanes will call for flares at - Zero plus 5 hours. Zero plus 6 hours. Zero plus 7 hours. Flares are to be lit by the most advanced infantry on or near the final objective. A counter-attack plane will be in the air from daylight onwards.
HEADQUARTERS.	12. Bn. Battle Hd.Qrs. will be established about Square V.9. by 21 hours on 19th. Forward Hd.Qrs. of both Bns. will be established on high ground near the MILL (P.35.c.) when 3rd Objective is taken. Brigade Forward Command Post will be established about V.9.c.9.8. by daylight on 20th. This will subsequently move to a position near the SAND PIT in V.5.a. Bde. Forward Station - MILL in P.35.c.
COUNTER-ATTACK.	13. The possibility of an enemy counter-attack with Tanks must be borne in mind. The infantry must concentrate their attention on stopping the enemy infantry following the Tanks. The tanks themselves will be put out of action by Artillery, Trench Mortars and selected Machine Guns.
COMMUNIC-ATIONS.	14. Visual signalling will probably be the best and most reliable means of communication and must be made full use of.
WATCHES.	15. Watches will be synchronised by Bde. Signalling Officer at 17.00 hours 19th Octr.
	16. Zero hour will be 02.00 hours on morning of 20th Octr.
	17. Secrecy regarding the above operation is essential. Information regarding them is to be kept back from troops in the Line as much as possible, and information given them should be the minimum compatible with the carrying out of their Task.
	18. ACKNOWLEDGE.

F.H. Fraser,
Captain

Brigade Major 53th Infantry Brigade.

Issued through Sigs. at 23.45 hours.

Copy No. 1 9/R.W.Fusrs.
2 9.Welch R.
3 2.Wilts R.
4 58.T.M.Bty.
5 G.O.C.
6 Staff Capt.
7 Bde. Sig. Offr.
8 B.I.O.
9 B.T.O.
10 B.B.O.
11 19th Div. G.
12 19th Div. Q.
13 56th Inf. Bde.
14 57th Inf. Bde.
15 10th Inf. Bde.
16 O.C. Left Group R.A.
17 O.C. 19th M.G.Bn.
18   -do-
19 C.R.E.
20 C.R.A. 19th Div.
21 A.D.M.S.
22 O.C. Train.
23 O.C. No.4 Coy. Train.
24) War Diary.
25)
26 File.

Maps issued to units of 58th Inf Bde only.

SECRET.   Copy No...11.

58th Infantry Brigade Order No. 283.

Ref. 51.A. S.E.)
     51.A. S.W.) 1/20,000.   22nd October, 1918.

1. 19th Div. (less Artillery) will be relieved by 61st Div. on 23rd/24th October.

2. 58th Bde. will be relieved by 182nd Bde. On relief units of the 94th Field Coy. R.E. and 19th Bn M.G. Corps less 2 Coys. will move to RIEUX via MONTRECOURT and St.AUBERT. Infantry as far as practicable will move across country. When moving along a road distances of 100 yds. between Coys. and 200 yds. between Bns. will be maintained.

3. Relief will be carried out as follows :-
   Reserve Bn will be relieved on evening 23rd Octr. Front Line Bns. will be relieved early morning of 24th by attacking Bns. of 61st Div. passing through them and forming up on their 'jumping off' line. As soon as 61st Div. troops are formed on this line all infantry in rear of 'jumping off' line will be withdrawn.
   61st Div. will endeavour to complete the forming up by 02.15 hours on 24th inst. At 03.15 hours advanced posts in front of 'jumping off' line will be withdrawn through troops of 61st Div. and at that hour command of front will pass to relieving Bns.
   Further details will be issued later.

4. 2nd Wilts Regt. will report relief complete by code words "BOOKS RECEIVED". Method of reporting front line Bns. relief will be issued later.

5. Orders for T.M.Battery will be issued later.

6. 94th Field Coy. R.E. on relief will move to RIEUX in accordance with orders already issued by C.R.E.

7. Administrative Instructions have been issued by Staff Captain.

8. ACKNOWLEDGE.

                                                Captain

                        Brigade Major 58th Infantry Brigade.

Copy No. 1 9.R.W.F.
         2 9.Welch R.   8 94th Field.Coy.R.E.
         3 2.Wilts R.   9 19th M.G. Bn.
         4 T.M.B.   10 Staff Captain.
         5 57th Inf. Bde.   11) War Diary.
         6 10th   -do-   12)
         7 182nd   -do-   13 File.

WO 95 36 Inf Bde
Mar 1918. (19th Div.)
1704/4/1

On His Majesty's Service.

Army Form C. 2118.

WAR DIARY
or
INTELLIGENCE SUMMARY.
(Erase heading not required.)

Instructions regarding War Diaries and Intelligence Summaries are contained in F. S. Regs., Part II. and the Staff Manual respectively. Title pages will be prepared in manuscript.

Place	Date	Hour	Summary of Events and Information	Remarks and references to Appendices
RIEUX	Novr. 1st		Brigade Tactical Scheme (See Appendix). A Conference of Commanding Officers was held at 58th Bde. H.Q.	A.
SOMMAING	2nd	0730 1430	58th Bde.H.Q. moved to HAUSSY. 58th Bde.H.Q. moved to SOMMAING via VENDEGIES.	B.
	3rd) 8th)		Brigade concentrated in SOMMAING and VENDEGIES final preparations being made for operations next day. For account of operations see narrative.	C.
HOUDAIN	9th		The Brigade (less 9th Welch) billeted in HOUDAIN and BREAUGIES. Troops resting and cleaning. Weather fine.	D.
	10th		Brigade (less 9th Welch) march to ETH. Bde.H.Q. was established in the Chateau. 9th Welch marched from MALPLAQUET to HOUDAIN. Weather fine.	E.
ETH	11th		At 09.45 hrs, an order was received from division stating hostilities would cease from 11.00 hrs on Monday 11th. See Appendix. 9th Welch moved from HOUDAIN to WARGNIES le GRAND and rejoined the Bde.	
	12th		Bde. resting and cleaning up. Weather cold but fine.	
	13th		Bde. resting; late in the evening orders were received for the Bde. to move back to BERMERAING.	F.
	14th		Bde. marched to BERMERAING. 9/R.W.F., 9/Welch, Bde.H.Q. and T.M.B. billeted in BERMERAING 2/Wilts Regt. in ST. MARTIN.	G.
	15th		March of Bde. continued to AVESNES lez AUBERT.	
AVESNES	16th		Bde. cleaning up. Weather very cold.	
	17th		Church parades for all denominations. Combined Voluntary Thanksgiving Service in the afternoon. Weather very cold.	

Army Form C. 2118.

WAR DIARY
or
INTELLIGENCE SUMMARY.
(Erase heading not required.)

Instructions regarding War Diaries and Intelligence Summaries are contained in F. S. Regs., Part II. and the Staff Manual respectively. Title pages will be prepared in manuscript.

Place	Date	Hour	Summary of Events and Information	Remarks and references to Appendices
AVESNES.	18th) 21st)		Battalions carrying out training under Bn arrangements. Weather cold.	
	22nd		G.O.C. inspected the 2/Wilts R. and 9/Welch R. Two Coys. in drill order, two Coys. in marching order. Weather fine.	4
	23rd		G.O.C. inspected the 9/R.W.F. and 58/T.M.B.	
	24th		Orders received for the Bde. to move to the CANDAS Area. Personnel and proportion of transport by rail, main transport by road.	7
	25th		Bde. moved to CAMBRAI prior to entrainment. Transport of Bde. Group moved to HAPLINCOURT en route for new area under B.T.O.	
CAMBRAI	26th		Bde. in CAMBRAI. Transport of Bde. Group marched from HAPLINCOURT to ALBERT.	
	27th		-do- -do- Orders received that Bde. would proceed to new area by bus and not by rail. Transport of Bde. Group arrived in new area.	7
	28th		Bde. in CAMBRAI. 9/R.W.F. and 9/Welch each ordered to send away 100 miners for immediate demobilization.	
	29th		Personnel of Bde. Group moved by bus to CANAPLES Area. Remaining transport moved by road. See Bde. Order No. 292. Bde. billeted as follows - Bde.H.Q. and 9/Welch at HALLOY les PERNOIS, 9th R.W.F. and 58th T.M.B. CANAPLES, 2/Wilts FIEFFES and MONTRELET.	
HALLOY les PERNOIS.	30th		Bde. in billets. Cleaning up and organizing the area.	

2.12.18.

[signature]
Lieutenant Colonel
Commanding 58th Infantry Brigade.

Reference 19th Div. No. 1,000

58th Bde. No. 1001.

Ref. attached 1/20,000 Map.

INTENTION. 1. On 1st Novr. the 58th Bde. in conjunction with 56th Bde. on the Right (imaginary) and B Division on the Left (imaginary) will capture the Ridges lying between the RIOT DU PONT AVAQUES and COURIOR and will outflank COURIOR by seizing the high ground to the South of it in B.15, 20 and 21.

The enemy's Main Line of Resistance is believed to run along the Ridge running North and South through B.11.b., B.12.c., and B.18.a. with Outposts holding the ridges in front.

OBJECTIVES. 2. The Objectives and Boundaries of the Bde. and dividing Line between Bns. are shown on attached map. Also the halts of the barrage and the times at which it lifts off the protector to each objective. The barrage will move between objectives at the rate of 100 yards in 2 minutes. Liaison Posts with Flank Bdes. will be established at Points marked on the Map. Those in rear of 3rd objective will be withdrawn by order of the Bn. Commander concerned when satisfied that touch is satisfactorily established on final objective.

DISPOSITIONS. 3. The attack will be carried out by 2 Bns. in front and 1 in Reserve.

    On Right.   2nd Bn Wiltshire Regt.
    On Left   9th Bn Welch Regt.
    In Reserve.   9th Bn R.W. Fusiliers.

Each Bn. will attack up to the 3rd Objective with 2 Coys. in front, 1 in Support, and 1 in Reserve.

From the 3rd Objective the 2nd Bn Wiltshire Regt. will push forward a 3rd Coy. to occupy the final objective from the CEMETERY in B.16.b. inclusive to Left Boundary of Bn. at B.15.d.8.5. The valley between these two points will be lightly held by Infy. Posts the main defence being cross fire from slopes near the CEMETERY and the Spur in B.16.a. and c. Machine Guns will also assist in this vide para. 6.

Final dispositions will be 3 Coys. holding final objective - one Coy. in Reserve about B.11.c.

From the 4th Objective the 9th Bn Welch Regt. will attack the final objective from Left Boundary to House in B.15.c.9.9. exclusive with 2 Coys. 1 Coy. will attack this House and form the flank back to B.15.d.8.5. Final dispositions 3 Coys. holding final objective, 1 Coy. in Reserve behind Spur in B.22.a.

RESERVE BN. 4. Will be assembled by Zero in Valley in C.3.d. and be prepared to move forward when ordered to a position of readiness in Valley in B.12.a. and c. Bn. Commander will be with Brigadier by Zero plus 15 minutes.

ARTILLERY. 5. The attack will be covered by a Creeping Artillery and M.G. Barrage. Timings of Artillery Barrage are shown on map.

MACHINE GUNS. 6. One Coy. of Machine Guns is allotted to the Bde. as forward guns. Two sections will operate on each Bn. front. One section will closely follow the advance to the top of each Ridge and cover the advance of the Infantry to the next Ridge as long as possible with direct overhead fire, the sections leapfrogging through each other if necessary for this purpose. The section in rear will also specially watch the outer flank of the Bde. and be prepared to cover the flank should troops on that flank be held up.

/On.

- 2 -

On arrival on Final Objective one section of guns in Right Bn. Sector will take up position to cover the valley of the GRAND RIOT (B.16.) with cross fire, one section will take position on Spur in B.11.b. In Left Bn. Sector 1 section will take up positions to cover the final objective with direct fire the special localities to be watched being the road on Left Flank and the corner of the Salient in B.15.a. One section will take up position in rear about Spur in B.21.b.

LIGHT TRENCH MORTARS. 7. One Mortar will move forward with each Bn to deal with any points of resistance impeding the advance. When final objective is captured one Mortar will take up position to cover LE CATEAU - CAMBRAI Road, 1 Mortar to cover Eastern exits from COURIOR.

CONSOLID- ATION & PATROLL- ING. 8. The Final Objective is the Line to be held. It will be consolidated by the 3 Coys. of each Bn. holding it in depth. Commanding Officers will personally see that consolidation is properly organised. If situation admits outposts will be pushed forward to command any ground not covered from the Final Objective.

As soon as barrage fire ceases fighting patrols will push forward to ascertain the situation. Should COURIOR be found to be evacuated the Spur in B.9.c. and 15.a. will be occupied.

R.E. 9. Two sections R.E. are allotted to the Bde.
One section will follow the attack and will ramp or bridge the Streams in the valleys to make them passable for Field Guns and Limbers. Crossing places to be clearly marked. They will also cut any necessary gaps through wire for vehicles.
One section will construct a strong defensive post in the vicinity of the CHATEAU in B.20.b.
The O.C., R.E. will arrange to have the 'jumping off' line, as shown on map, taped out by 9.0.a.m. on 1st Novr.

CONTACT AEROPLANE. 10. A Contact Aeroplane will call for flares at Zero plus 2 hours and Zero plus 3 hours. Flares will be lit, and in addition flappers and helmets waved by the leading Infantry.

HEAD- QUARTERS. 11. Advanced Bde. H.Q. as shown on map.
Bde. Forward Station in Road in C.2.d.9.2. moving forward to each successive ridge when captured approximately along the Dividing Line between Bns. Final position on Spur in B.17.a.
Both Bn.H.Q. will be in Road in C.2.d. and 3.c. at Zero. Battalion Commanders with Forward Command Posts will move forward with or near their Reserve Coys. They will carry flags to indicate their position.

WATCHES. 12. Will be synchronised by Bde. Sig. Officer at 07.30 hours on 1st Novr.

13. ACKNOWLEDGE.

Captain

Brigade Major 58th Infantry Brigade.

31.10.18.

SECRET.   Copy No. 24

                    58th Brigade Order No. 284.

                                                    1st November, 1918.
Ref. to 51.A. 1/40,000.

1.   The 58th Bde. Group composed as under will move to HAUSSY
and MONTRECOURT in accordance with attached March Table on
November 2nd:-

         58th Inf. Bde.   19th Bn M.G.C. (less 2 Coys).
         94th Fld. Coy. R.E.   58th Fld. Amb.

2.   Personnel will move across country as much as possible, East
of the ST. AUBERT - Villers - en - CAUCHIES Road units moving
across country will march independently to their Billets. Units
will be clear of above mentioned Road by 09.00 hours.

3.   The 58th Bde. Group will move to VENDEGIES on Novr. 3rd.
Move to be complete by 06.00 hours. Further details later.

4.   Brigade H.Q. will close at RIEUX at 06.30 hours on Novr. 2nd
and re-open on arrival at HAUSSY.

5.   ACKNOWLEDGE.

                                            F.W. Fraser
                                                    Captain

                                    Brigade Major 58th Inf. Brigade.

Issued through Sigs. at 14.45 hours.

Copy No. 1 9.R.W.Fusrs.   15 D.A.P.M.
         2 9.Welch R.   16 No.4 Coy. Train.
         3 2.Wilts R.   17 94th Fld. Coy.R.E.
         4 58.T.M.B.   18 58th Fld. Amb.
         5 G.O.C.
         6 Staff Capt.   19 C.R.E.
         7 B.T.O.   20 C.R.A.
         8 B.Sig. Offr.   21 A.D.M.S.
         9 B.I.O.   22 19th Bn M.G.C.
        10 B.B.O.   23 19th Div. Train.
        11 19th Div. G.   24) War Diary.
        12 19th Div. Q.   25)
        13 56th Inf. Bde.   26 File.
        14 57th Inf. Bde.

March Table to accompany 58th Brigade Order No. 284.

Unit.	From.	To.	Starting Point.	Time of passing Starting Point.	Route.	Remarks.
Bde.H.Q. personnel.	RIEUX.	HAUSSY.	N. & S. Grid Line of U.14. and 20.Central.	07.40 hours.		To march across country.
9/R.W.F. personnel.	do.	"	-do-	07.45 hours.		To march across country 200X S. of CHAUSSEE BRUNEHAUT.
58/T.M.B.	do.	"	-do-	do.		Follow 9/R.W.F.
9/Welch R.	do.	"	-do-	do.		To march across country 200X S. of the 9/R.W.F.
2/Wilts R.	do.	"	-do-	do.		To march across country 200X S. of 9/Welch R.
58/Bde Transport Brigaded.	do.	"	Bend in RIEUX – AVESNES Road at U.20.d.0.3.	06.45 hours.	Via AVESNES & ST. AUBERT.	To march under orders of B.T.O. to be clear of ST. AUBERT by 08.15hours.
58/Fld. Amb.	do.	MONTRECOURT.	do.	07.00 hours.	do.	To march under orders of O.C. 58/Fld. Amb. and to clear ST. AUBERT by 08.30 hours.
94/Fld. Co. R.E.	do.	MONTRECOURT.	do.	07.08 hours.	do.	To march under orders of O.C. 94/Fld. Coy and clear ST. AUBERT by 08.38 hours.
19th Bn M.G.C. (less 2 Coys).	do.	HAUSSY.	do.	07.14 hours.	do.	To march under orders of O.C. 19th Bn M.G.C. and clear ST. AUBERT by 08.44 hours.

P.T.O.

NOTES:

(a) Dress: Marching Order.

(b) Following intervals to be maintained - 100 yards between Coys., 100 yards between Units' Transport and 25 yards between every six vehicles.

(c) Personnel of Battalions of 58th Bde. will enter HAUSSY in the following order - 9/R.W.F. and 58/T.M.B., 9/Welch Regt., 2/Wilts Regt.

(d) Personnel of 19th Bn M.G.C., 94th Field Coy. R.E. and 58th Field Ambulance will march off the roads as much as possible.

SECRET.   Copy No. 27

58th Infy. Bde. Order No. 285.

Ref. Special map attached.

1. On 4th Novr. 19th Division will attack and capture objectives shown on attached map.
   The attack on BLUE objective will be carried out by 56th Bde. That on the GREEN and RED objectives by 56th Bde. on the Right and 58th Bde. on the Left. The 32nd Bde. of 11th Division will attack on the Left of 58th Bde.

2. The Divisional and Bde. Boundaries are shown on the attached map. Also the Dividing Line between Bns.
   The Sunken Road in L.12.b. and G.7.d. is inclusive to the Bde.
   The lines showing objectives are purely diagrammatic, the Tactical features in the neighbourhood form the real objectives.
   Similarly Boundary lines are only intended as a guide to frontages. They may always be crossed for tactical purposes when necessary.

ASSEMBLY & FORMING UP FOR ATTACK.

3. (a) The Brigade will assemble on night of 3rd/4th Novr. as follows :-

   Two leading Bns. in Squares L.19.c. and K.24.d. approximately as shown on map, under cover of the Spur in L.19.c. and a.
   Reserve Bn. in Square K.30.a. The Reserve Bn. of 56th Bde. is assembling in L.25.a. and the Southern portion of L.19.c.
   Assembly positions are to be carefully reconnoitred on morning of 3rd Novr. and positions marked if necessary.
   Positions selected for Bn.H.Q. to be reported as soon as possible.
   The 2 Forward Sections of Machine Guns and the L.T.M.B. will select suitable assembly positions on morning of 3rd Novr. and report locations to Bde.H.Q.

   (b) At Zero hour the two leading Bns. will advance in rear of the Reserve Coy. of the Left Bn. of 56th Bde. They will, by means of Officers, keep in the closest touch with the situation on front of Left Bn. of 56th Bde. They will form for attack just behind the crest of the Hill marked 106.7 in Square L.16.a. and b. and advance from this Line so as to be formed up close under the barrage forming the protector to the BLUE Line in ample time to advance behind the barrage when it commences to move forward at Zero plus 135 minutes. It is of vital importance that Bns. are in position to follow the barrage up to time and if necessary they will push through the Reserve and Supporting Coys. of the Left Bn. of 56th Bde. during the advance in order to close up. All ranks must understand that 56th Bde. are not advancing beyond the BLUE Line in our Sector and they must push straight through them and form up under the barrage ready for it to lift.

   (c) Reserve Bn will follow the two leading Bns. at approximately 1000 yards distance as far as the hill in L.16.a. and b. and will be prepared to move forward from there as ordered. This Bn. will also be prepared, if ordered, to pass through the two leading Bns. on the GREEN Line and establish itself on the high ground East of the villages ETH and BRY.

4. The attack from the BLUE Line will be carried out by 2 Bns. in front and one in Reserve.

On Right.	9th Bn Welch Regt.
On Left.	2nd Bn Wiltshire Regiment.
In Reserve.	9th Bn R.W.Fusiliers.

   The Right Bn. will attack on a two Coy. front with one Coy. in Support and one in Reserve.
   The Left Bn. will advance from the BLUE Line on a one Coy. front pushing up a second Coy. on its Left as soon as there is room, and, if necessary, a 3rd Coy. to extend the Left to join

up with the right of 32nd Brigade at G.2.a.0.5 where a liaison post will be established. During the advance the Coys. echeloned on the Left flank will be specially on the look out for a possible counter-attack in a Southerly direction down the PETIT AUNELLE River Valley. The Reserve Company will eventually establish itself in a selected position about L.12.a. and G.7.b. with the special object of guarding this Valley.

The Reserve Bn. will move as indicated in para. 3 (c).

Liaison Posts shown on the map will be established by Bns. concerned from the BLUE Line onwards. 2nd Bn WILTSHIRE Regt. will have a party told off to take over the L.P. at L.11.c.2.7. from 56th Bde. as soon as possible after BLUE Line is reached. This party should be sent forward from Reserve Coy.

ARTILLERY ARRANGEMENTS. 5. The attack will be covered by a Creeping Barrage of Field Artillery and Machine Guns. Up to the BLUE objective the Barrage will advance at the rate of 100 yards in 4 minutes. A pause of about 15 minutes will be made on the protector to the BLUE Line. The Barrage will lift off this protector at Zero plus 135 minutes. From the BLUE to the GREEN Objective the rate of advance will be 100 yards in 5 minutes.

On arrival at the GREEN Objective a pause of half an hour will be made during which troops will re-organise and consolidate. Barrage fire will then cease and the Right Bn. will push forward its line to the RED Line. Strong patrols will at the same time be pushed forward to seize the River crossings at BRY (Right Bn) and ETH (Left Bn). If the situation admits patrols will be pushed on the high ground East of these two villages and an Outpost Line established on this high ground.

In order to assist in keeping distance a round of Thermite shell will be fired at each alternative lift of the barrage (and 200 yds. beyond the latter) along the boundary of each attacking Bn. up to the BLUE Objective. From the BLUE to the GREEN Objective Smoke will be substituted for Thermite. As the barrage comes down on the Protector to each objective a few rounds of Thermite will be fired along the whole Divl. front.

MACHINE GUNS. 6. 2 Sections are allotted to the Bde. as forward guns. One Section will work in each Bn. sector. Their object will be to cover the advance of the attacking infantry by direct fire wherever this is possible. In the Right Sector two guns will be pushed forward as early as possible to the Spur in G.8.d. and 9.c. to cover the further advance on to the RED Line. In the Left Sector the guns will be disposed with special regard to the protection of the left flank and for defence against a counter-attack up the valley of the PETIT AUNELLE River. When this flank is secure guns may be moved forward to cover the advance of patrols towards the River crossings at ETH and BRY.

LIGHT TRENCH MORTARS. 7. 2 Mortars on Pack as long as possible will follow advance of leading Bns. They will be prepared to deal with opposition from Sunken Roads about L.11.d. and will eventually take up positions 1 to cover Sunken Road in G.9.a. and c. and one to cover Sunken Road in G.2.a. and the valley of the PETIT AUNELLE.

2 Mortars with extra ammunition will be in Reserve on Limber.

CONSOLIDATION. 8. The GREEN and RED Line will be consolidated. Leading Coys. will consolidate in depth. Reserve Coy. or Coys. of Right Bn will be about the Line of the Road in G.8.a. and c.

Reserve Coy. of Left Bn. will be disposed for defence of the valley of the PETIT AUNELLE.

Battalion Commanders will arrange the consolidation on the ground.

Rifle Grenade Signals showing three Greens will be fired by leading Coys. on reaching the GREEN Objective.

R.E. 9. One section of R.E. is allotted to the Bde. and will be employed for construction of Adv. Bde. H.Q. for the Bde. and Artillery Group.

P.T.O /10.

- 3 -

SPECIAL INFORMATION.	10.	Leading Bns. will obtain and forward to Bde.H.Q. as early as possible information as to the nature of the obstacle formed by the PETIT AUNELLE River and later by the SART Stream if patrols succeed in reaching it.
HEAD- QUARTERS.	11.	Position of Bde.H.Q. at Zero will be notified later. Bde. Forward Station will be at K.30.b.8.2. moving forward to vicinity of ST. HUBERT and later to about L.16.central.
		When GREEN Objective is captured Bde. Forward Station will be established in Sunken Road in G.8.a.
		On capture of BLUE Objective Bde. H.Q. will move to vicinity of ST. HUBERT.
CONTACT AEROPLANE.	12.	A Contact Aeroplane will call for flares at -

Zero plus 2 hours.
Zero plus 3 hours.
Zero plus 4 hours.

Front line troops will light flares, wave white flappers, etc.

A Counter-attack aeroplane will be in the air from daylight onwards.

WATCHES. 13. Will be synchronised at an hour to be notified later.

14. Zero hour will be notified later.

ACKNOWLEDGE.

F.W. Lane (?)

Captain

Brigade Major 58th Infantry Brigade.

Issued through Sigs. at 16.00 hours on 2nd Novr. 1918.

Copy No. 1 9.R.Q.Fusrs.   15 32nd Inf. Bde.
         2 9.Welch R.   16 Left Group R.F.A.
         3 2.Wilts Regt.   17 D.A.P.M.
         4 58.T.M.B.   18 No.4 Coy. Train.
         5 G.O.C.   19 94th Field Coy.R.E.
         6 Staff Capt.   20 58th Fld. Amb.
         7 B.T.O.   21 C.R.E.
         8 B.I.O.   22 C.R.A.
         9 B.B.O.   23 A.D.M.S.
        10 Bde. Sig. Offr.   24 19th Bn M.G.C.
        11 19th Div. 'G'   25 19th Div Train.
        12 19th Div. 'Q'   26) War Diary.
        13 56th Inf. Bde.   27)
        14 57th Inf. Bde.   28 File.

Addendum No. 1 to 58th Bde. Order No. 285.
----

1. Ref. para. 11. -
    Bde.H.Q. will be established at the CHATEAU K.35.a.1.9. by 1700 Hours on Novr. 3rd.   It will move to vicinity of ST. HUBERT when BLUE Objective is taken.

2. Ref. para. 13.
    Watches will be synchronised by Bde. Signal Offr. at 1700 hours and 23.00 Hours on Novr. 3rd.

3. Ref. para. 14.
    Zero hour will be 05.30 hours on Novr. 4th.

    ACKNOWLEDGE.

                                        [signature]
                                                        Captain

3.11.18.   Brigade Major 58th Infantry Brigade.

    Issued to all recipients of O.O. 285.

SECRET.

Addendum No.2 to 58th Bde. Order No. 285.

MACHINE GUNS.
1. "B" Coy. 19th Bn M.G.C. will co-operate with the Bde, 2 sections will act as forward guns.
Remaining 2 sections under O.C. 'B' Coy will move forward at Zero behind the Reserve Battalion to the high ground about L.16.b.3.2. with a view to covering the advance of the Bde. from the BLUE Line.
When the GREEN Line has been captured these guns will move forward to the high ground in L.12.c.

2. After capture of the RED Line O.C. 'B' Coy. will co-ordinate the consolidation in depth of all 16 guns.
O.C. 'B' Coy. will make his H.Q. with the Right attacking Bn (9th Bn Welch Regt) and will detail a Liaison Officer to work with the Left attacking Bn (2nd Bn Wiltshire Regt).
Thus either Bn. Commander may have the use of a proportion or of all the rear guns on application to the Coy. Commander or Liaison Officer as the case may be.

R.E.
3. 1 Section of the 94th Field Coy. R.E. will be allotted to the Bde. to extemporise bridges across the AUNELLE River. If possible bridges to take Pack animals will be extemporised at G.7.b.35.10. and G.7.b.5.6. approx.
The Officer i/c Section will keep in close touch with the O's.C. the Attacking Bns.

Captain,
3.11.18.
Brigade Major 58th Infantry Brigade.

Issued to 9/R.W.Fusrs.
9/Welch Regt.
2/Wilts Regt.
58/T.M.Bty.
19th Bn M.G.C.
94/Field Co.R.E.

SECRET.

Addendum No. 3 to 58th Brigade Order No. 285.

1. The enemy having retired attacking Bn.s will now assemble on the line of the JENLAIN - CURGIES Road from L.11.c.75.00. to L.11.c.2.6. Bns. will move to assembly positions forthwith relieving troops of 56th Bde. on this line. Arrival in assembly positions to be reported with the least possible delay.

2. Reserve Bn will move to position near Fme de WULT forthwith and at Zero to L.16.a.

3. Forward sections of Machine Guns and 58th T.M.B. will conform.

4. The barrage will open at Zero (05.30 hours) on the ♣ 165 line (which is about 600 yards beyond the road) and remain on this line for 10 minutes then move forward 100 yards in 5 mins. as laid down.

5. Bde. Forward Station is at Fme. de WULT. A Forward Station will be established at approximately L.16.central by Zero.

                                                    Captain

                       Brigade Major 58th Infantry Brigade.

3.11.18.

         Issued to 9.R.W.Fusrs.
                  9.Welch R.
                  2.Wilts R.
                  58.T.M.B.
                  56.Inf. Bde.
                  32.Inf. Bde.
                  93. Bde. R.F.A.
                  19th Bn M.G.C.
                  B Coy. 19th Div. M.G.C.
                  94.Field Coy.R.E.
                  19th Div. G.

SECRET.

NARRATIVE of OPERATIONS
from November 3rd to 9th 1918.

1. On the morning of 2nd November 19th Division Order No. 252 was issued ordering an attack on the morning of 4th November with the following objectives :-
   (a) The high ground just West of and overlooking JENLAIN.
   (b) The Spur West of and overlooking the villages of ETH and BRY.

   This attack to be carried out under a creeping barrage. Subsequently patrols were to be pushed forward to seize the River crossing at ETH and BRY and, if the situation allowed, to establish an outpost line on the high ground N.E. of those villages.

   The attack on the first objective was to be carried out by the 56th Brigade. From this objective onwards the attack was to be carried out by 56th Brigade on the Right and 58th Brigade on the Left.

   On the night 2/3rd November 56th Brigade took over the line on the Divisional front and 58th Brigade was concentrated in VENDEGIES and SOMMAING.

2. During the 3rd November the 56th Brigade were able to push forward and by the afternoon it became evident that they had advanced well forward towards JENLAIN. This necessitated a considerable modification of original plans. Battalions were therefore ordered up at once into the Assembly positions originally decided on North and North West of MARESHES, and moved off between 4 and 4.30 p.m. Brigade H.Qrs. moved to the Chateau South of ARTRES. By about 4.30 p.m. information was received that the 56th Brigade had reached JENLAIN and, in consultation with G.O.C. 56th Brigade, it was decided to jump off for the attack next morning from the Line of the main LE QUESNOY - VALENCIENNES road. Battalions were therefore ordered to move forward and take over the Line of this road within their respective boundaries from the troops of 56th Brigade holding it, and to form up for attack on this Line.

   This movement presented very considerable difficulties. The night was intensely dark, it was raining heavily, and the advance was necessarily carried out without any guides and over ground which had not been reconnoitred. It was, however, extremely well carried out by battalions and by 01.15 hours on 4th November the Brigade was formed up ready to attack, 9/Welch R. on the Right and 2/Wilts R. on the Left along the line of the LE QUESNOY - VALENCIENNES Road, 9/Royal Welch Fus. in Reserve near the FME. DE WULT. Brigade H.Qrs. was established at FME. DE WULT by 05.30 hours.

3. At ZERO hour, 06.00 hours on 4th November, the barrage opened and the attack commenced. A heavy mist was lying in the valleys which did not clear for several hours. Owing to the fact that the Brigade front at the commencement of the attack was only about 500 yards wide, but expanded rapidly to nearly 2000 yards on the objective, the Left Battalion, 2nd Wilts Regt. started on a one Company front which was increased to a two Company front after crossing the PETIT AUNELLE River. The 9/Welch R. advanced on a two Company-front throughout. The reserve Battalion, 9/Royal Welch Fus. moved at Zero to a position on the high ground overlooking JENLAIN. The enemy Artillery retaliation to our barrage was not heavy except in certain places. FME. DE WULT was fairly heavily shelled for about half an hour and there was a good deal of gas about JENLAIN and both East and West of it. Little opposition was met with up to the PETIT AUNELLE River which proved to be a more serious obstacle than was expected being a deep stream running between high banks some 10 yards across.

After crossing the river considerable Machine Gun fire was encountered but was overcome without great difficulty, the German gunners in most cases running away and abandoning their guns before the Infantry could get to close quarters. A number of machine guns were captured but very few prisoners.

On the extreme right touch was not established with 56th Brigade on the RED and GREEN Line till about an hour after the GREEN Line had been taken, when a Liason Post was established at O.9.d.0.0.

About ten minutes after the barrage fire ceased, heavy machine gun fire was opened on the Ridge in G.2. and G.8. from the villages and the slopes to the East of them. The Ridge was also subjected to severe shelling. Shelling and machine gun fire on this Ridge continued severe throughout the day.

Meantime as soon as Barrage fire had ceased patrols had been pushed forward to secure the river crossings and to get onto the high ground East of the villages of ETH and BRY. The 2nd Wilts R. patrols captured nine prisoners in the outskirts of ETH, but were unable to penetrate further owing to Machine Gun fire. A later attempt by this Battalion to clear the village with two strong platoons was also unsuccessful, the platoons suffering heavy losses from shell and machine gun fire. Patrols from the 9th Welch R. reached the outskirts of BRY but were heavily fired on and forced to withdraw.

At 12 noon the Reserve Battalion, 9th R.Welsh Fus. was ordered to the area West of the PETIT AUNELLE River about Square L.12.a. and c. and Brigade Headquarters moved to CHATEAU d'en HAUT FM.

4. It being evident that the occupation of the High ground East of the villages was impossible without artillery support. An attack under a barrage was ordered on the whole Division Front to take place at 16.30 hours. The objective given for this attack was the WARGNIES-la-MARLIERE Road as far North as LA MAISON BLANCHE, thence swinging back to gain touch with 11th Division who were to attack simultaneously to capture the 100·6 Hill in Square A.27.b. It had been hoped to get smoke put down on the slopes East of the villages but this could not be arranged in time. This attack was carried out by the same two leading Battalions, the two rear Companies in each case being passed through the leading Companies which followed in support. The Reserve Battalion moved at Zero plus 5 minutes to the position vacated by the leading Battalions. The enemy reply to our barrage was heavy and very prompt, coming down on the Ridge in G.8. within two minutes of Zero. The attack was also met by heavy machine gun fire the moment it started. Both Battalions however pushed on though suffering heavy casualties. The Support and Reserve Companies of the 9th Welch Regt suffered most severely. The 2nd Wilts Regt. also met with considerable opposition in the village of ETH itself, and also from machine gun fire from their left flank as the attack by 11th Division did not materialise. Eventually the Right Company of the 9th Welch Regt. established itself on the objective (the WARGNIES-la-MARLIERE Road) where touch was gained with 56th Brigade. The Left Company swung back to join 2nd Wilts Regt. who had captured ETH and established a line on the slopes East of it, but were unable to gain the crest of the spur. The left of 2nd Wilts Regt. was unable to get touch with anyone as (owing apparently to their orders not reaching them in time) the 32nd Brigade of the 11th Division had not attacked at all. The Support Company therefore formed a defensive flank to protect the Left and Rear of the Battalion. About 50 prisoners were captured during this attack.

5. At 06.26 hours, 5th November, the advance was continued under a light barrage. The Line of the WARGNIES-la-MARLIERE Road was reached without opposition. Thereafter there was some slight machine gun fire mostly from the Left flank. Brigade Headquarters moved to WARGNIES-le-GRAND about mid-day. Meantime the 9th R.W.Fus. had been ordered forward to pass through the two leading Battalions and continue the advance on the whole Brigade Front.

The Battalion passed through the leading Battalions approximately on the line of the Road in G.6.c. and 12.a. There was a little spasmodic machine gun fire from small parties of the enemy but no serious opposition until the high ground in H.3.a. was reached. Attempts to push on over this crest to the spur in H.9.a. and the village of BETTRECHIES were stopped by heavy machine gun fire from a number of machine guns firing from the spur in H.9.a. It was by this time getting dark, it had been raining almost uninterruptedly all day and the going was very heavy. The troops were therefore re-organised on this line and touch was established with 56th Brigade on the Right and 11th Division on the Left. As soon as it was quite dark two strong patrols were sent forward to try and effect a footing on the Ridge in H.9.a. They were fired at from machine guns all along this Ridge and were unable to get on to it. It was therefore decided to put down a barrage and continue the advance at Dawn. The 2nd Wilts Regt. took up a position in Support S.E. of ROISIN about G.6.c. and G.12.a. The 9th Welch Regt. moved into Reserve in Eastern outskirts of BRY.

6. At 05.00 hours on 6th November Brigade Headquarters moved to a Farm East of BRY in G.11.d.

At 06.00 hours the 9th R.W.Fus. in conjunction with 56th Brigade on their Right attacked under a light barrage and captured the village of BETTRECHIES with little opposition. Before dawn the 2nd Wilts Regt. had been moved forward to a position East of MEAURAIN whence two Companies at ZERO took the positions in H.2.b. and H.3.a. to protect the Left flank and Rear of 9th R.W.Fus. as it was understood that the 32nd Brigade of the 11th Division on the Left were not attacking. As a matter of fact the 32nd Brigade did attack and touch was established with them by 9th R.W.Fus. about Northern edge of BETTRECHIES. A line was established by 9th R.W.Fus. round the Eastern side of the village but all attempts to push across the River HOGNEAU and on to the high ground to the East of it failed, although patrols succeeded in getting down to the river bank and one platoon established itself close to the river in H.10.a. opposite the Station. Eight machine guns allotted to the Battalion for this attack were used partly to protect the Left flank and partly to cover the Eastern slopes of the valley of the HOGNEAU after the capture of the village. Twelve more machine guns were sent up later to keep the BOIS DANCADE and BOIS D'UGIS under fire. Enemy machine gun fire from the BOIS DANCADE, the station, and the Eastern slopes of the valley was heavy throughout the day and BETTRECHIES itself was very heavily shelled during the day and the following night. MEAURAIN was also heavily shelled and a considerable number of casualties caused among the civilians there.

7. About mid-day on 6th November 56th Brigade were ordered to carry out an attack during the afternoon on the spur in H.10.c. and, swinging up their Right, to advance to the Line of the BETTRECHIES-HOUDAIN Road thus outflanking the BOIS DANCADE. This was subsequently cancelled, 57th Brigade relieved 56th Brigade during the night 6th/7th November and 57th Brigade carried out the attack at 06.00 hours on 7th November. 9th R.W.Fus. kept the BOIS DANCADE and slopes East of it under heavy rifle and machine gun fire during the operation, and, as soon as the barrage covering 57th Brigade advance permitted, pushed across the river and occupied the village of BELLIGNIES and the line of the BELLIGNIES - BAVAY Road without opposition, the enemy having retired during the night. Owing to the narrowing of the Front the 57th Brigade now took over the whole Divisional Front, the 9th R.W.Fus. being ordered to protect their left flank as the troops North of the river were far behind. The Battalion therefore occupied a defensive flank extending from the village of BELLIGNIES to the spur immediately North of the village of HOUDAIN, where they were in touch with the Left flank of 57th Brigade. During the morning of 7th November the 9th Welch Regt. were moved forward into BETTRECHIES and the 2nd Wilts Regt. were concentrated about the S.Eastern end of MEAURAIN. Brigade Headquarters moved to LA FLAMENGERIE about 09.00 hours.

Page 4.

8. Under instructions received from Division the 9th Welch R. were placed at the disposal of 57th Brigade from 06.00 hours on 8th November and in accordance with orders from 57th Brigade moved at 05.00 hours to BREAUGIES and subsequently became Left Supporting Battalion to that Brigade. The 57th Brigade continued the advance Eastwards on morning of 8th and in order to secure their Left flank the 9th R.W.Fus. extended their flank to HONS-HERGIES and by mid-day were disposed:- one Company about Southern end of BELLIGNIES, one Company North of HOUDAIN, one Company by MARBLE WORKS in I.7.c. and one Company round HONS-HERGIES. From those positions patrols pushed Northwards across the river and reconnoitred HERGIES and MICLOT-POLLET which were found clear of the enemy. The 2nd Wilts Regt. had in the meantime been directed from NEAURAIN on HOUDAIN but were subsequently stopped at BREAUGIES Brigade Headquarters moved to BREAUGIES at 09.00 hours and subsequently at 16.00 hours to HOUDAIN.

The 11th Division were now coming up North of the river and 56th Brigade were moving up to connect between 57th Brigade and 11th Division. As the flank became secure Companies of the 9th R.W.Fus. were withdrawn in succession and moved to HOUDAIN. The last Company from HONS-HERGIES arrived about midnight at which hour the dispositions of the Brigade were:-

    Brigade H.Q. & 9th R.W.F.   in   HOUDAIN.
    2nd Wilts R. & 58th T.M.B.   in   BREAUGIES.
    9th Welch R. still attached to 57th Brigade.

9. These dispositions remained unchanged during the 9th and on 10th the Brigade (less 9th Welch Regt) moved back to ETH. 9th Welch Regt. moved to HOUDAIN and the following day to WARGNIES-le-GRAND where they rejoined the Brigade.

10. The villages occupied by the Brigade during the advance viz:- ETH, BRY, BETTRECHIES and BELLIGNIES all contained many civilian /s

11. Casualties to the Brigade during these operations were:-

    Officers.   1 killed 15 wounded.
    Other ranks.   58 "   295 "   7 missing 10 gassed.
    TOTAL - 384.

12. A number of machine guns and trench mortars were captured but there was no time to collect them during the battle, subsequently 5 Heavy machine guns, 10 Light machine guns and 2 Trench mortars were collected in the vicinity of ETH and BRY. There was no opportunity for searching other parts of the battlefield.

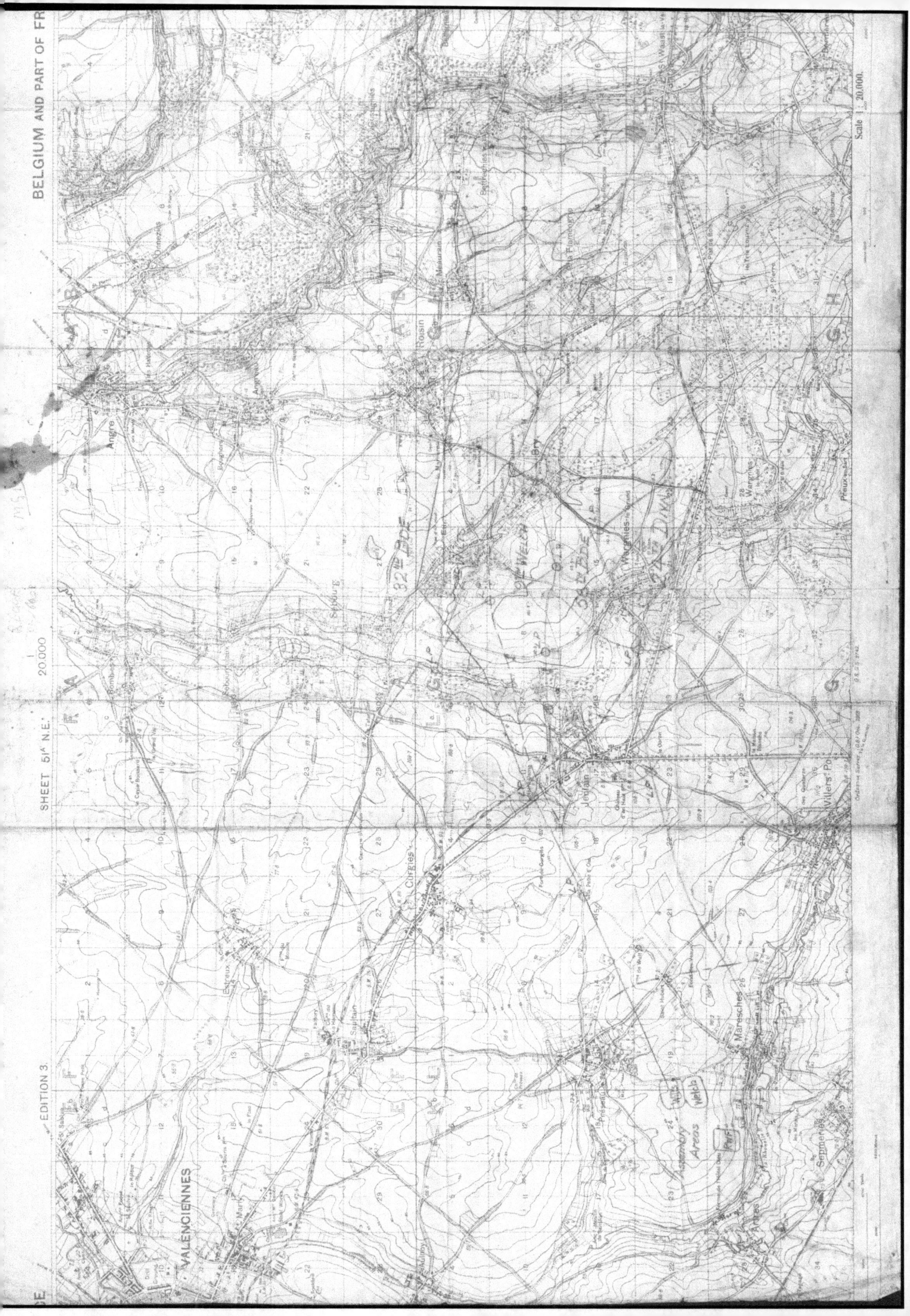

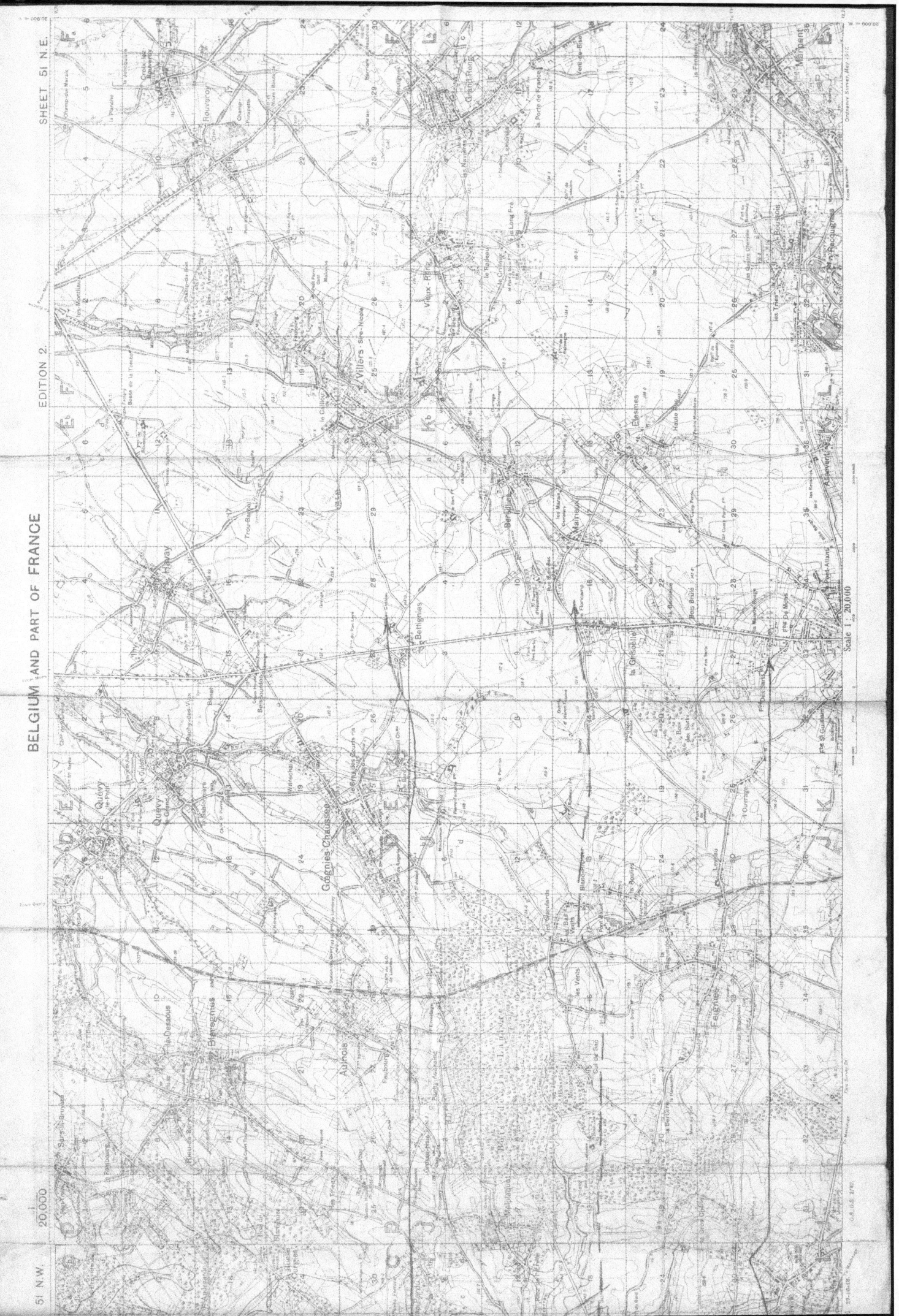

B.M

OBJECTIVE MAP

SECRET   Copy No. 22

58th Brigade Order No. 286.

Ref: to Sheet 51 N.W. 1/20,000.

1. The 58th Brigade (less 9/Welch) 58th Field Ambulance, and No 3. Section, D.A.C. will move to ETH on Nov. 10th in accordance with attached March Table.

2. All transport of units will march in rear of units. Surplus Personnel and Transport of 9/Welch will remain in HOUDAIN and await the arrival of their Battalion. On Nov. 11th the 9/Welch will move to ETH passing the Starting Point at H.18.b.6.1. at 09.15 hours, and march via same route as used by 58th Brigade on 10th instant.

3. Dress - Marching Order.

4. The following intervals will be maintained :- 500 yards between units, 100 yards between Companies or corresponding units, 25 yards between every 6 vehicles. There will be no halting in Villages or on main lorry routes.

5. Lorries. No lorries will be available for transport of blankets or overcoats etc. As soon as baggage waggons have dumped present loads in new billets they should be sent to pick up Greatcoats and Haversacks,. Blankets being collected as soon after as possible.

6. Billeting certificates. Certificates will be completed in the usual way for all billets in the present area.

7. Advance parties. Will meet Staff Captain at ETH Church at 09.00 hours 10th instant.

8. ACKNOWLEDGE.

                                                            Captain,
9.11.18.   Brigade Major 58th Infantry Brigade.

Issued through Signals at 22.45.hours.

        Copy No. 1 9/R.W.Fus.   14. 56th Inf. Bde.
             2 9/Welch.   15. 57th Inf. Bde.
             3 2/Wilts.   16. C.R.E. 19th Div.
             4 58/T.M.Bty.   17. A.D.M.S. do
             5 Depot, 9/Welch.   18. 58th Fd. Ambce.
             6 G.O.C.   19. No 3 Sect. D.A.C.
             7 Staff Captain.   20. No. 4 Coy, Train.
             8 Bde Signalling Offr. 21. O.C. 19th Div Train.
             9 Bde Transport Offr.   22) War Diary.
            10 Bde. Int. Offr.   23)
            11 Bde. Bombing Offr.   24. File.
            12 19th Div "G".
            13 19th Div "Q".

March Table to accompany 58th Brigade Order No. 286.

Unit.	From.	To.	Starting Point.	Time pass Starting Point.	Route.	Remarks.
58/T.M.Battery.	BREAUGIES.	ETH.	H.11.b.2.1.	09.15 hours.	BETTRECHIES - LA PERCHE ROMPUE LA HOULETTE.	
2/Wilts Regt.	do	do	do	09.18 hours.	do	
58th Brigade H.Q.	HOUDAIN.	do	H.18.b.6.1.	09.15 hours.	do	
9/R.W.Fusiliers.	do	do	do	09.19 hours.	do	
No.3 Sect, D.A.C.	do	do	do	09.35 hours.	do	Leaves Column at BETTRECHIES
58th Fd. Ambce.	do	do	do	09.55 hours.	do	

COPY.

PRIORITY.

To 58th Inf.Brigade.   11th November 1918.

The following message received from Corps:-

"Hostilities will cease from 11.00 hours today. Troops will stand fast in their present positions. Defensive precautions will be taken. No intercourse of any sort with the enemy."

From 19th Divn.   (Sgd) W.S.SCAMMELL,Captain,
07.45 hours.   General Staff.

SECRET 58th Brigade Order No. 287.　　　　　　Copy No 22

Ref: Map Sheet 51A & 51.
1/40,000.

1. 58th Brigade Group composed as under will move to BERMERAIN and ST.MARTIN tomorrow Nov. 14th in accordance with attached March Table :-

        58th Infantry Brigade.
        No. 3 Section, D.A.C.
        No. 4 Coy, Train.

2. Transport will move with units. A and B Echelons will march together in rear of Battalions.

3. Administrative Instructions are being issued separately by the Staff Captain.

4. Brigade H.Q. will close at ETH Chateau at 10.00 hours and re-open on arrival at BERMERAIN.

5. ACKNOWLEDGE.

                                                                          Captain,

Nov. 13th 1918.　　　　Brigade Major 58th Infantry Brigade.

Issued through Signals at 23.30 hours.

Copy No. 1   9/R.W.Fus.
         2   9/Welch R.
         3   2/Wilts R.
         4   58/T.M.Bty.
         5   G.O.C.
         6   Staff Capt.
         7   Bde.Signalling Offr.
         8   Bde. Transport Offr.
         9   Bde. Int. Offr.
       10   Bde. Bombing Offr.
       11   19th Div. "G".
       12   19th Div. "Q".
       13   56th Inf. Bde.
       14   57th Inf. Bde.
       15   C.R.E.
       16   A.D.M.S.
       17   D.A.P.M.
       18   No 3 Sec. D.A.C.
       19   No. 4 Coy, Train.
       20   O.C. 19th Div. Train.
       21)
       22) War Diary.
       23   File.

March Table to accompany O.O. No. 287.

Unit.	From.	To.	Starting Point.	Time head of column passed starting point.	Route.	Remarks.
9/N.Cch.	WARGNIES le GRAND.	BERMERAIN.	Cross Roads G.22.d.00.15.	11.00 hours.	WARGNIES LE PETIT les QUATRE VENTS R.5.c.	
58th Bde H.Q. and 58th T.M.B.	ETH.	do	do	10.20 hours.	do	
9/R.W.Fus.	ETH.	do	do	10.24 hours.	do	
2/Wilts.	ETH.	do	do	10.34 hours.	do	
No.3 Sec. D.A.C.	ETH.	do	do	10.44 hours.	do	
No 4 Coy. Train.	LA FLAMENGERIE.	do	Cross Roads. G.22.d.00.15.	11.45 hours.	do	

Note (a) Dress – Marching Order. Leather Jerkins may be carried on the lorries.

(b) Following intervals will be maintained :– 200 yards between units, 100 yards between Coys. and Battalions, and their transport, 25 yards between every 6 vehicles.

SECRET.

58th Brigade Order No. 288.

Copy No. 23

Ref. Map Sheet. 51A.
1/40,000.

1. The 58th Brigade Group composed as under will move to AVESNES-les-AUBERT tomorrow, November 15th (see March Table attached).

        58th Inf.Brigade.
        59th Field Ambulance.
        No.3 Section D.A.C.
        No.4 Coy.Div.Train.

2. The Transport of the 58th Infantry Brigade will march Brigaded under orders of the Brigade Transport Officer.
    Order of march same as for the dismounted personnel.

3. When possible dismounted personnel will march clear of roads.

4. **Billeting Parties.** Will meet Staff Captain at Town Major's Office, AVESNES at 10.00 hours 15th instant.

5. **Lorry Arrangements.** Will be notified later.

6. Brigade Headquarters will close at BERMERAIN at 08.00 hours and re-open at AVESNES on arrival.

7. ACKNOWLEDGE.

                                              Captain,

Nov. 14th 1918.   Brigade Major, 58th Infantry Brigade.

Issued through Signals at 21.30 hours.

        Copy No. 1.   9th R.W.Fus.
                2.   9th Welch R.
                3.   2nd Wilts R.
                4.   58th T.M.Bty.
                5.   G.O.C.
                6.   Staff Captain.
                7.   Bde.Sig.Offr.
                8.   Bde.Transport Offr.
                9.   Bde.Int.Offr.
              10.   Bde.Bombing Offr.
              11.   19th Div. "G"
              12.   19th Div. "Q".
              13.   56th Inf.Bde.
              14.   57th Inf.Bde.
              15.   C.R.E., 19th Div.
              16.   A.D.M.S., 19th Div.
              17.   D.A.P.M., 19th Div.
              18.   No.3 Sect.D.A.C.
              19.   No. 4 Coy.Train.
              20.   59th Field Amb.
              21.   O.C., 19th Div.Train.
              22)
              23)   War Diary.
              24.   File.

March Table to accompany O.O. No.288.

Unit.	To.	Starting Point.	Time head of column passes starting point.	Route.	Remarks.
2nd Wilts R. personnel	AVESNES-les-AUBERT	Q.20.c.99.80.	09.53 hours.	CHAUSSEE BRUNHAUT.	Route to Starting Point via Road Q.21.c. Q.20.d.
58th Bde.H.Q.	-do-	Q.14.d.7.1.	09.51 hours.	VILLERS-EN-CAUCHIE	
53th T.M.Bty.					
9th Welsh R. Personnel	-do-	-do-	09.53 hours.		Route to Starting Pt. via Rd. Q.21.c.Q.20.d.
9th R.W.Fus. Personnel	-do-	-do-	09.59 hours.		-do-
58/Bde.Transport. Brigaded.	-do-	Q.20.a.99.80.	10.05 hours.		-do-
Hq.3 Sqn.D.A.C.	-do-	-do-	10.20 hours.		
No.4 Coy.Train	-do-	-do-			Will join tail of Column behind No.4 Coy.Train as it passes 59th Fld.Amb. Camp on CHAUSSEE BRUNHAUT
59th Fld.Amb.	-do-	-do-	10.40 hours.		

Note (A) Dress - Marching Order.
(B) Following intervals will be maintained:- 200 yards between Units, 100 yards between Companies, 50 yards between every 6 vehicles.
(C) The strictest march discipline is to be maintained during the march.
(D) The 1st Halt after passing the Starting Point will be at 10.50 hours.

SECRET.

58th Brigade Order No. 289.

Copy No. 26

Ref. to maps
LENS 11 &
VALENCIENNES 12
1/100,000.

1. The 19th Div. will move to BEAUQUESNES - CANDAS Area on Novr. 24th, 25th and 26th.

2. The 58th Bde. Group will be composed as under for the purpose of the move only :-

58th Inf. Bde.
59th Field Ambulance.
No.4 Coy. 19th Div. Train.
19th Div. Reception Camp.
81st Field Coy. R.E.
82nd Field Coy. R.E.
94th Field Coy. R.E.

3. The transport of all units of Bde. Group (less portion moving by rail) will move by road, dismounted personnel of Bde. Group by train.

4. Orders for the move of transport will be issued separately.

5. Orders for entrainment of the Dismounted Personnel and proportion of transport will be issued separately. Entraining Station will be CAMBRAI VILLE.

6. March to the entraining station will be carried out as follows. Route Main St. VAAST - CAMBRAI Road.

Train No.7. The transport to proceed by train will parade in the following order on the main CAMBRAI - St. VAAST Road at 16.30 hours Nov. 26th Head of Column to be at cross roads due S. of the H in HALTE S. of AVESNES-lez-AUBERT.

Bde.H.Q., 9/R.W.Fusrs., 9/Welch Regt., 2/Wilts Regt., 59/Fld. Ambce., 19th Div. Reception Camp, 94th Fld. Coy.R.E.

The transport from 81st Field Coy.R.E. proceeding by train will join the end of the column at the cross roads ½ mile E. of the S in CAGNONCLES at 16.45 hours Novr. 26th.

The similar transport of the 82nd Field Coy.R.E. will join the end of the column at the Sugar Factory N.W. of CAURIOR at 18.00 hours Novr. 26th.

The whole of the above transport will be under the command of Lieut. C.F. CURTIS, 58th Bde.H.Q., who will be responsible for entraining and detraining the transport.

Personnel of Bde.H.Q. will pass the cross roads S. of the H in HALTE S. of AVESNES at 18.00 hrs. on Novr. 26th. Route same as for transport.

Train No.8. Personnel 9/R.W.Fusrs (less 1 Coy), 9/Welch Regt., 58th T.M.B. Route main CAMBRAI - St.VAAST Road.
The 9/R.W.Fus. will pass the cross roads due S. of the E in HALTE S. of AVESNES at 22.00 hrs. Novr. 26th.
The 9/Welch Regt. will pass same point at 22.08 hrs. Nov.26th.
The 58/T.M.B.   "   "   "   "   "   22.18 hrs.   "   "

Train No.9. Personnel 2/Wilts Regt., 81st, 82nd, and 94th Field Coys.R.E., 59th Field Ambulance, 19th Div. Reception Camp.
Route and Starting Point same as for Train No.8.
2/Wilts Regt. will pass the Starting Point at 02.00 hrs.Nov.27th.
94/Coy.R.E.   "   "   "   "   "   "   02.08   "   "   "
59/Fld. Amb.   "   "   "   "   "   "   02.12   "   "   "
19/Div. Rec. Camp "   "   "   "   "   02.16   "   "   "

Personnel of 81st Coy.R.E. will march independently via NAVES so as to arrive at entraining station at 05.00 hrs. Novr. 27th.
Personnel of 82nd Coy.R.E. will march independently passing the Sugar Factory at 03.45 hrs. Novr. 27th.

- 2 -

7. Lieut. Col. L.F. SMEATHMAN, D.S.O., M.C. will be O.C. No. 7 Train.
   Major L. HAMMILL, D.S.O., M.C. will be O.C. No. 8 Train.
   Lieut. Col. MACKENZIE, D.S.O. will be O.C. No. 9 Train.

8. Dress:- Marching Order, caps will be worn.

9. Bde. H.Q. will close at AVESNES at 16.00 hrs. on Novr. 26th and re-open on arrival in the new area at a place to be notified later.

10. ACKNOWLEDGE.

F.H. Fraser

Captain

Brigade Major 58th Infantry Brigade.

Issued through Signals at 7.0.p.m., Novr. 23rd.

Copy No. 1   9.R.W.F.
         2   9.Welch R.
         3   2.Wilts R.
         4   58.T.M.B.
         5   G.O.C.
         6   S.C.
         7   B.T.O.
         8   B.Sig.O.
         9   19th Div. G.
        10   19th Div. Q.
        11   56th Inf. Bde.
        12   57th Inf. Bde.
        13   A.P.M.
        14   81.Fld.Coy.R.E.
        15   82. -do-
        16   94. -do-
        17   O.C. 19th Div. Train.
        18   No.4 Coy. Train.
        19   59.Fld. Amb.
        20   19th Div. Reception Camp.
        21   No.2 Group Lovatt's Scouts.
        22   Major P.H. BRADBURY, M.C., 9/Welch R.
        23   Major W.S. SHEPHERD, M.C., 2/Wilts R.
        24   R.T.O., CAMBRAI.
        25) War Diary
        26)
        27   File.
        28   No 3 S.A.C.

SECRET.

Addendum No. 1 to 58th Bde. Order No. 289.

1. The transport of the 58th Bde. Group (less portion moving by rail) will move to CAMBAS Area under orders of Captain J.H. EAVES, A.S.C.

2. The 58th Bde. Transport Group will be composed as under and will move to Divnl. Starting Point at SUGAR FACTORY 1,000 yds. N.W. CAURIOR which will be passed at 09.20 hrs. in accordance with attached March Table.

   Transport, 58th Inf. Bde.   Transport, 81/Fld. Coy.R.E.
   "   59/Fld. Ambce.   "   82/   -do-
                               "   94/   -do-
   No. 4 Coy. 19th Div. Train. No. 3 Sec. D.A.C.

3. Captain H.G. PERCIVAL, M.C. will be in command of the 58th Bde. Transport Group.

4. Orders for the moves on Novr. 26th and 27th will be issued by Captain J.H. EAVES.

5. O.C., 2/Wilts Regt. will detail one Officer (mounted) to report to G.S.O.3 19th Div. as Billeting Representative of the 58th Bde. Transport Group at SUGAR FACTORY, 1,000 yds. N.W. CAURIOR at 07.30 hrs. on Novr. 25th.

6. ACKNOWLEDGE.

                                            [signature]
                                                    Captain

                        Brigade Major 58th Infantry Brigade.

Issued to all recipients of 58th Bde. Order No.289, & No. 3 Sec., D.A.C.

Ref. to Map. VALENCIENNES Sheet 12.

March Table to accompany Addendum No.1 to 58th Brigade Order No. 289.

Date.	Unit.	To.	Starting Point.	Hour Head of Column passes Starting Pt.	Route.	Remarks.
Novr.25th	58th Bde.H.Q.	HAPLINCOURT & BERTINCOURT Area.	Cross roads due S. of H in HALTE South of AVESNES-lez-AUBERT.	08.00 hrs.	Road through T of STA (CAMBRAI) - Southern outskirts CAMBRAI - Fbg. de PARIS - N end of MAIS-NIERES - MARCOING - RIBECOURT - FLESQUIERES - HAVRILCOURT - HERMIES.	
"	9/R.W.Fusrs.	"	-do-	08.02 hrs.		
"	9/Welch R.	"	-do-	08.05 hrs.		
"	2/Wilts R.	"	-do-	08.08 hrs.		
"	59/Fld. Amb.	"	-do-	08.11 hrs.		
"	94/Fld.Coy.R.E.	"	-do-	08.14 hrs.		
"	No.3 Sec.D.A.C.	"	-do-	08.18 hrs.		
"	No.4 Coy. Train.	"	-do-	08.33 hrs.		
"	81/Fld Coy.R.E.	"	-	-		Will join tail of Column as it passes Cross roads ½ mile E. of S in CAGNON-CLES at 08.45 hrs.
"	82/Fld Coy.R.E.	"	-	-		Will join tail of Col. as it passes Sugar Factory 1,000 yds. N.W. of CAURIOR at 10.10 hrs.

P.T.O.

NOTES:

a. Following distances to be maintained throughout march.
   Between sections of 12 vehicles   50 yards.
   "   transport of units   100 yards.
   "   Secs. of D.A.C.   100 yards.

b. Dress - Marching Order, caps will be worn.

SECRET.

Amendment No.1 to 58th Bde. Order No. 289.
---

1. Times of departure of trains allotted to Bde. Group have been altered, see 19th Div. Q/759/G already issued.
   A further alteration has been made in that No.7 train is now a personnel train and No. 9 Train is now a Type Omnibus Train.

2. Para. 6 is cancelled and the following substituted :-

   March to entraining station will be carried out as follows:-

Date.	Unit.	To.	Starting Point.	Hour head of Col. passes S.P.	Route.
Train No.7 Nov. 27th	2/Wilts R.	CAMBRAI VILLE	X Roads due S of E in HALTE S of AVESNES.	08.30 hrs	Main CAMBRAI - ST.VAAST Road.
" "	94/Fld.Co. R.E.	"	"	08.38	"
" "	59/Fld.Amb.	"	"	08.42	"
" "	19/Div.Rec. Camp.	"	"	08.46	"
" "	58/T.M.B.	"	"	08.48	"

Personnel of 81/Fld. Coy.R.E. will march independently via NAVES so as to arrive at entraining station at 11.30 hrs Nov. 27th.
Personnel of 82/Fld. Coy.R.E. will march independently passing the Sugar Factory N.W. of CAURIOR at 10.15 hrs. Novr. 27th.
Personnel of No. 2 Group Lovatt's Scouts will march independently via VILLERS en CAUCHIES and NAVES arriving at the entraining station at 11.30 hrs 27th Novr.

Date.	Unit.	To.	Starting Point.	Hour head of Col. passes S.P.	Route.
Train No.8 Nov. 27th	9/R.W.F.	CAMBRAI VILLE	X Roads due S of E in HALTE S of AVESNES.	12.30 hrs.	Main CAMBRAI - ST.VAAST Road.
" "	9/Welch R.	"	"	12.38	"

Train No.9. Transport to proceed by train will parade in the following order on the CAMBRAI - ST. VAAST Road at 15.00 hrs. Novr. 27th. Head of Column to be at cross roads due S. of the H in HALTE S. of AVESNES-les-AUBERT:-

Bde.H.Q., 9/R.W.F., 9/Welch R, 2/Wilts R, 59/Fld. Ambce., 19th Div. Reception Camp, 94/Field Coy.R.E.

Transport of 81/Field Coy.R.E. moving by rail will join the end of the Column at the cross roads ½ mile E. of the S in CAGNONCLES at 15.15 hrs Novr. 27th.

The similar transport of the 82/Fld. Coy.R.E. will join end of column at the Sugar Factory N.W. of CAURIOR at 16.30 hrs Novr. 27th.

The whole of the above transport will be under the command of Lieut. C.F. CURTIS, 58th Bde.H.Q., who will be responsible for the entrainment and detrainment of the above transport.

Personnel of Bde.H.Q. will pass the cross roads S. of the H in HALTE S. of AVESNES at 16.30 hrs. Novr. 27th. Route same as for transport.

P.T.O.

3. Para. 8 "DRESS" add Leather Jerkins will be worn.

4. Para. 9 is cancelled and the following substituted:-
    "Bde.H.Q. will close at AVESNES at 16.00 hrs. Nov. 27th and re-open on arrival in the new area at a place to be notified later."

                                                    Captain
                            Brigade Major, 58th Infantry Brigade.

24.11.18.

Issued to all recipients of 58th Bde. Order No.289.

SECRET.   Copy No. 15

58th Brigade Order No. 290.

Ref. to VALENCIENNES   24th November, 1918.
Sheet 12, 1/100,000.

1. The 58th Brigade Group composed as under will move to CAMBRAI in accordance with attached March Table on the 25th inst, taking over billets vacated by 183rd Bde.

    58th Inf. Bde.   59th Field Ambce.
    94th Fld. Coy. R.E.

2. The 58th Bde. Group Transport will move as already ordered. Transport moving by rail will march with units.

3. Billeting Parties composed as follows will report to Lieut. C.F. CURTIS, 58th Bde.H.Q., at Area Commandant's Office CAMBRAI at 10.00 hrs. 25th inst.

    Battalions...... 1 Officer and 5 Other Ranks.
    Other Units..... 1 Officer and 1 Other Ranks.

4. Four lorries are allotted to the Brigade which will report at Bde.H.Q. at 08.30 hrs. to-morrow 25th inst. They will be available for two journeys and will be allotted as follows :-

    9/R.W.Fusrs........ 1 lorry.
    9/Welch Regt...... 1 "
    2/Wilts Regt...... 1 "

    Guides from these units will report at Bde.H.Q. at 08.30 hrs. 25th inst.

    One Lorry for T.M.B. and 94th Fld. Coy.R.E. Guides from these units will report at 08.30 hrs. 25th inst. This lorry will return to Bde.H.Q. after unloading at CAMBRAI and be used by Bde.H.Q. for second journey.

5. Bde.H.Q. will close at AVESNES at 10.00 hrs. 25th inst. and re-open on arrival at CAMBRAI.

6. ACKNOWLEDGE.

                                                  F.W. Fraser
                                                  Captain

                                   Brigade Major 58th Infantry Brigade.

Issued through Sigs. at 23.00 hrs.

    Copy No.1 9.R.W.Fusrs.
           2 9.Welch R.   10 19th Div. Q.
           3 2.Wilts R.   11 56. Inf. Bde.
           4 58.T.M.B.   12 57. Inf. Bde.
           5 G.O.C.   13 D.A.P.M. 19th Div.
           6 B.S.O.   14 Area Comdt. CAMBRAI.
           7 94.Fld.Co.R.E.   15) War Diary.
           8 59.Fld. Ambce.   16)
           9 19th Div. G.   17 File.

                                                     P.T.O.

March Table to accompany 58th Brigade Order No.290.

Unit.	To.	Starting Point.	Hour head of column passes S.P.	Route.	Remarks.
58th Bde.H.Q.) 58th T.M.B.)	CAMBRAI.	X Roads just S of E in HALTE S. of AVESNES-lez-AUBERT.	10.15 hrs.	Main CAMBRAI - ST. VAAST Road.	To march under O.C. 58th T.M.B.
94/Fld. Coy.R.E.	"	"	10.18 "	"	
9/Welch Regt.	"	"	10.25 "	"	
2/Wilts Regt.	"	"	10.33 "	"	
9/R.W.Fus:rs.	"	"	10.43 "	"	
59/Fld. Ambce.	"	"	11.00 "	"	

NOTES:

(a). The following intervals to be maintained -

    100 yds. between Coys.
    100 yds. between Units and their transport.

(b).- DRESS: Marching Order, Caps and Leather Jerkins to be worn.

(c).- The usual halts will be observed ten minutes to every clock hour.

SECRET.   Copy No. 23

58th Brigade Order No.291.

Ref. to maps
LENS 11 & VALENCIENNES 12
1/100000.
Sheet 57B 1/40,000.   26th Novr., 1918.

1. 58th Bde. Order No.289 and Amendment is cancelled.

2. The dismounted personnel and the proportion of transport moving by rail of the 58th Bde. Group will entrain at CAMBRAI VILLE Station on Novr. 28th.

3. Composition of trains and march to entraining station will be as under:-

Train No.7	Unit.	Date.	S.P.	Time Head of Col. passes S.P.	Remarks.
	2/Wilts R.	28.11.18	CAMBRAI VILLE Station A.11.c.5.9.	11.10 hrs.	
	58/T.M.B.	"	"	11.15 "	
	59/Fld. Amb.	"	"	11.16 "	
	19th Div. Rec. Camp	"	"	11.18 "	
	81/Fld.Co. R.E.	"	"	11.19 "	
	94/Fld.Co. R.E.	"	"	11.21 "	
	82/Fld.Co. R.E.	"	"	11.23 "	
	No.2 Group Lovatt's Scouts.	"	"	11.25 "	

Train No.8					
	9/R.W.F.	"	"	15.10 "	
	9/Welch R.	"	"	15.20 "	

Train No.9 - Transport of Bde. Group proceeding by train will arrive at the Station Yard xx A.11.c.5.9. at the following times:-

Bde. H.Q.   )
19/Div.Rec. Camp)   17.17 hrs.
9/R.W.F............. 17.19 "   81/Fld.Coy.R.E.)
9/Welch R........... 17.21 "   82/Fld. Coy.R.E.) 17.28 hrs
2/Wilts R........... 17.23 "   94/Fld. Coy.R.E.)
59/Fld. Amb......... 17.25 "

On arrival at the station the whole of the above transport will come under the command of Lieut. C.F.CURTIS, 58th Bde.H.Q. who will be responsible for its entrainment and detrainment.

Units will be held responsible for their transports' knowing the route to the entraining station.

4. Personnel of Bde.H.Q. will arrive at CAMBRAI Station at 19.25 hrs Novr. 28th.

5. The following Officers will be in command of trains :-

No.7 Train.... Lieut. Col. Mackenzie, D.S.O.
No.8 Train.... Major L. HAMILL, D.S.O., M.C.
No.9 Train.... Lieut-Col. L.F. SHEATHMAN, D.S.O., M.C.

P.T.O.

6. DRESS: Marching Order, Caps and Leather Jerkins will be worn.

7. Bde.H.Q. will close at CAMBRAI at 17.00 hrs on Novr. 28th and re-open on arrival in the new area.

8. ACKNOWLEDGE.

                                            Captain

                         Brigade Major 58th Infantry Brigade.

Issued through Sigs. at 13.00 hrs.

```
Copy No. 1  9.R.W.F.
        2  9.Welch R.
        3  2.Wilts R.
        4  58.T.M.B.
        5  G.O.C.
        6  S.C.
        7  B.Sig.O.
        8  19th Div. G.
        9     -do-  Q
       10  56.Inf.Bde.
       11  57.  -do-
       12  D.A.P.M., 19th Div.
       13  81 Fld.Coy.R.E.
       14  82  -do-
       15  94. -do-
       16  59.Fld.Amb.co.
       17  19th Div. Reception Camp.
       18  No.2 Group Lovat's Scouts.
       19  Major P.H.BRADBURY, M.C. 9/Welch R.
       20  Major W.S.SHEPHERD, M.C., 2/Wilts Regt.
       21  R.T.O., CAMBRAI.
       22) War Diary.
       23)
       24  File.
```

SECRET Copy No 23

58th Brigade Order No. 292.

Ref: to VALENCIENNES 12
and LENS 11.

1. 58th Brigade Order No. 291 is cancelled.

2. The 58th Brigade Group (dismounted personnel) will move to the CAMDAS area by bus on the 29th inst. Transport at present with units will move by road on the same date.

3. Units will parade in column of route already told off in batches of 25 ready to embuss as under on the main CAMBRAI - LE CATEAU Road at 08.45 hours.

```
58th Brigade H.Q.)  Head of column to be at junction of CAMBRAI
58th T.M.Battery.)  LE CATEAU and CAMBRAI ST VAAST Roads.
9/R.W.Fusiliers.    60 yards S.E. of above road junction.
9/Welch Regt.       550    "   "    "    "    "    "    "
2/Wilts Regt.      1050    "   "    "    "    "    "    "
59th Fd Ambce.     1550    "   "    "    "    "    "    "
No.2 Group,
  Lovats Scouts.   1600    "   "    "    "    "    "    "
94th Fd.Coy,R.E.   1620    "   "    "    "    "    "    "
81st  "   "   "    1640    "   "    "    "    "    "    "
82nd  "   "   "    1700    "   "    "    "    "    "    "
19th Div.Rec.Camp. 1760    "   "    "    "    "    "    "
```

Troops will parade off the road as much as possible.
One officer or Senior N.C.O. is to travel on each bus or lorry.
25 O.R. will travel on each bus or lorry.

4. Dress :- Marching Order. Caps and Greatcoats to be worn. Blankets will be carried in the pack and leather jerkins rolled on top of the pack secured by the pack straps.

5. Embussing officer. Major P.H.Bradbury, M.C. 9/Welch Regt. will act as embussing officer for the Brigade. He will meet the D.A.Q.M.G. at the embussing point (the above mentioned cross roads) at 08.30 hours on 29th inst. One officer will be detailed by each unit to act as unit embussing officer. These officers will report to Major P.H.BRADBURY, M.C. at 08.30 hours at the embussing point.

6. Debussing Points. Will be notified to units before moving off. Units billeting parties will meet them at the debussing point.

7. Lorries for kit. 6 lorries are allotted to the Brigade Group as under :-

```
           9/R.W.Fus.      1 lorry.
           9/Welch R.      1 lorry.
           2/Wilts R.      1 lorry.
```
Each of these units will send a guide to Brigade H.Q. at 08.00 hours on Nov. 29th.
```
           94th and 82nd Fd Coys, R.E.    1 lorry.
           81st Fd Coy, R.E. and)
           Lovat's Scouts.      )         1 lorry.
           Bde H.Q. and T.M.Bty.          1 lorry.
```
Each of these units will have a guide at Brigade H.Q. at 08.00 hours on Nov. 29th.

Units will be responsible that the lorry drivers conveying their baggage are given instructions (in writing) as to where they are to report in the new area. It is hoped to be able to notify units on the 28th inst. the exact villages in which they will be billeted. If this has not been done units will arrange a meeting point with their lorries and will send guides to this point immediately on arrival in new area.

8.   The transport of the Brigade Group proceeding by road will march under orders of Lieut. C.C.Marston, M.C. 9/R.W.Fus. and will parade in the following order on the main CAMBRAI - ST VAAST Road head of column to be at the junction of this road and the CAMBRAI - LE CATEAU Road ready to move off at 08.15 hours Novr. 29th.

    Units will ensure that their transport knows the route to this point.

    (Brigade H.Q.
    (T.M.Battery.
    (19th Div. Reception Camp.
    9/R.W.Fusiliers.
    9/Welch Regt.
    2/Wilts Regt.
    (59th Fd. Ambce.
    (81st Fd. Coy, R.E.
    (82nd Fd. Coy, R.E.
    (94th Fd. Coy, R.E.

Distances of 50 yards between units will be maintained throughout the march.

    Units bracketed together will march as one group.

9.   ACKNOWLEDGE.

    Captain,
    Brigade Major 58th Infantry Brigade.

27th Nov. 1918.

Issued through Signals at 20.00 hours.

Copy No.			
1	9/R.W.Fus.	13	81st Fd. Coy, R.E.
2	9/Welch.	14	82nd Fd. Coy, R.E.
3	2/Wilts.	15	94th Fd. Coy, R.E.
4	58/T.M.Bty.	16	59th Fd. Ambce.
5	G.O.C.	17	19th Div. Rec. Camp.
6	Staff Capt.	18	No 2 Group, Lovat's Scouts.
7	Bde.Sig.Offr.	19	Major P.H.Bradbury, M.C.
8	19th Div "G".	20	Lt. C.C.Marston, M.C.
9	19th Div "Q".	21	R.T.O. CAMBRAI.
10	56th Bde.	22)	
11	57th Bde.	23)	War Diary.
12	D.A.P.M. 19th Div.	24	File.

Vol. 42.

Headquarters,
58 2 Inf Bde
(19th Div.)
November 1918

On His Majesty's Service.

WAR DIARY
or
INTELLIGENCE SUMMARY.
(Erase heading not required.)

Army Form C. 2118.

Instructions regarding War Diaries and Intelligence Summaries are contained in F.S. Regs., Part II. and the Staff Manual respectively. Title pages will be prepared in manuscript.

Place	Date	Hour	Summary of Events and Information	Remarks and references to Appendices
HALLOY-les-PERNOIS.	Jany 1st) 2nd) 3rd)		Battalions of the Bde. carried out training.	
	4th		2/Wilts Regt. carried out a "Trooping of the Colours" parade. Dispersal draft of 50 O.R. left the Bde.	
	5th		Church Parades.	
	6th		Training in the morning, games in the afternoon.	
	7th		-do-	
	8th		-do-	
	9th		-do-	
	10th		-do-	
	11th		Dispersal draft of 19 O.R. left the Bde.	
	12th		Church Parades. Dispersal draft of 1 Offr. 28 O.R. left the Bde.	
	13th		Training in the morning, games in the afternoon. Dispersal draft of 3 Offrs 37 O.R. left the Bde.	
	14th		Training in the morning, games in the afternoon. Dispersal draft of 2 Officers 35 O.R. left the Bde.	
	15th		Practice Ceremonial Parade for Presentation of Colours, 9/R.W.F. & 9/Welch Regt. Dispersal draft of 1 Offr. 34 O.R. left the Bde.	
	16th		Training.	
	17th		Practice Ceremonial parade for presentation of Colours. Bde. cross country run won by 9/Welch R.	
	18th		Training. Dispersal draft of 1 Offr. 31 O.R. left the Bde.	
	19th		Church parades. Dispersal draft of 1 Offr. 34 O.R. left the Bde.	
	20th		Practice ceremonial parade for presentation of Colours. Dispersal draft of 1 Offr. 23 O.R. left the Bde.	
	21st		Training. Dispersal draft of 1 Offr. 28 O.R. left the Bde.	
	22nd		Presentation of Colours by Divl. Commander to 9/R.W.F. and 9/Welch Regt. (Div. Commdr: Major—General G.D. JEFFREYS, C.B., C.M.G.). Dispersal draft of 1 Offr. 33 O.R. left the Bde.	
	23rd		Training and games. 2/Wilts played the 3rd Worcesters in the semi final for the Divl. Commdr's Cup, Worcesters won 2 goals to nil.	
	24th		Training and games.	
	25th		Training and games. Dispersal draft of 1 Offr. 49 O.R. left the Bde.	
	26th		Church parades. Dispersal draft of 2 Offrs. 41 O.R. left the Bde.	
	27th		Training and games. Dispersal draft of 2 Offrs. 41 O.R. left the Bde.	
	28th		Training and games. Dispersal draft of 1 Offr. 37 O.R. left the Bde.	

Army Form C. 2118.

WAR DIARY
or
INTELLIGENCE SUMMARY.
(Erase heading not required.)

Place	Date	Hour	Summary of Events and Information	Remarks and references to Appendices
HALLOY-les-PERNOIS.	29th		Training and games. Dispersal draft of 1 Offr. 39 O.R. left the Bde.	
	30th		Training and games.	
	31st		Training and games.	
Brigade H.Q.				
4th February, 1919.				

for Brigadier General

Commanding 58th Infantry Bde.

Army Form C. 2118.

WAR DIARY
or
INTELLIGENCE SUMMARY.
(Erase heading not required.)

Headquarters,
58th Infantry Brigade

4th February 1919.

Army Form C. 2118.

WAR DIARY
or
INTELLIGENCE SUMMARY.

(*Erase heading not required.*)

Instructions regarding War Diaries and Intelligence Summaries are contained in F. S. Regs., Part II. and the Staff Manual respectively. Title pages will be prepared in manuscript.

Place	Date	Hour	Summary of Events and Information	Remarks and references to Appendices
HALLOY-les-PERNOIS.	Feb. 1st to 9th.		The Battalions of the Brigade carried out Military and Educational training during the mornings. Games of all descriptions being played during the afternoons.	
-do-	10th		H.R.H. The Prince of Wales visited the Brigade Area. The Brigade Staff and Battalion Commanders assembled at Brigade Headquarters to meet H.R.H.	
-do-	11th to 22nd		Military and Educational Training continued.	
-do-	23rd		Brigade Headquarters, 9th R.W.F. and 9th Welsh moved by lorry to Camps at VILLERS-l'HOPITAL. The transport of the above Units moved by road, Route:- St.LEGER - DOMART - St.HILAIRE - EPECAMPS - BERNAVILLE - PROUVILLE - MAIZICOURT - BEAUVOIR RIVIERE.	
-do-	24th		2nd Wilts moved by lorry to VILLERS-l'HOPITAL. Transport moved by road using the same route as the transport of Units moving on the 23rd. inst.	

VILLERS-l'HOPITAL.	25th to 28th		Brigade in VILLERS-l'HOPITAL.
			
			During the month the following dispersal Drafts were sent to the Corps Concentration Camp :-
			
			        Offr. O.R. Offr. O.R. Offr. O.R.
			Feb.1st. - 51 Feb.7th. 1 54 Feb.14th. - 18
			" 2nd. 1 62 " 8th. 1 77 " 15th. - 10
			" 3rd. 1 51 " 9th. 1 82 " 16th. - 24
			" 6th. 1 41 " 10th. 1 50 " 21st. 1 36
			                          " 13th. - 29 " 28th. - 28	

WAR DIARY
or
INTELLIGENCE SUMMARY.
(Erase heading not required.)

Army Form C. 2118.

The following drafts of retainable personnel left Battalions:-

Feb.18th. 9th Welsh 4 Officers and 100 O.R. to the 6th S.W.B. 30th Division, DUNKIRK.
" 27th. 2nd Wilts 2 Officers and 124 O.R. to the 2/5th Glouc'r Regt. 61st Division, ROUEN.
" 28th. 9th R.W.F. 2 Officers and 93 O.R. to the 26th Bn.R.W.F. 59th Division, DUNKIRK.

Lieut-Colonel.

Commanding 58th Infantry Brigade.

Army Form C. 2118.

WAR DIARY
or
INTELLIGENCE SUMMARY.
(Erase heading not required.)

Place	Date	Hour	Summary of Events and Information	Remarks and references to Appendices
VILLERS-l'HOPITAL.	March -		Demobilization of releasable Officers and O.Rs. continued throughout the month. Retainable men were sent to the Army of Occupation as they became available. The following dispersal drafts were sent to Corps Concentration Camp:- March 7th -- Off. 18 O.Rs. March 21st 11 Off. 11 O.Rs. " 14th 1 " 22 O.Rs. " 28th 1 " 9 O.Rs.	
	Mch. 12th		2 Officers and 46 O.Rs. proceed to join 1/6th Welsh, 1st Division, Army of Occupation.	
	19th		Headquarters, 19th Division ceased to exist from midnight 18/19th March, in accordance with instructions the remnants of the 19th Division were administered by the 58th Brigade H.Q. which was maintained at full strength for this purpose. Headquarters, 58th Brigade moved to FROHEN-LE-GRAND.	
FROHEN-LE-GRAND.	30th		The Cadre "A" of the 2nd Bn.Wiltshire Regt. entrained at CANDAS for the Base en route for ENGLAND. Strength 5 Officers and 88 other ranks.	

Captain.
for Brigadier-General,
Commanding 58th Infantry Brigade Cadre Group.

JUNE 1919.

Headquarters 58th Infantry Brigade

WAR DIARY
—or—
INTELLIGENCE SUMMARY.
(Erase heading not required.)

Army Form C. 2118

Place	Date	Hour	Summary of Events and Information	Remarks and references to Appendices
FROHEN-LE-GRAND	4.6.19	—	H.Qrs. 58th Inf. Bde. moves to CANDAS.	
CANDAS	16.6.19	—	Personnel and stores of Cadre of 58th Inf. Bde. move to MONDICOURT.	
MONDICOURT	17.6.19	—	Cadre entrained at 12.05 hrs and arrives at LE HAVRE at 00.30 hrs. 18.6.19	
LE HAVRE	18.6.19	—	Cadre in Camp at HARFLEUR from 18.6.19 to 20.6.19	
"	20.6.19	—	Cadre embarkes for U.K.	

J H Fraser
Captain
Brigade Major, 58th Infantry Brigade Cadre.

20.6.19

Army Form C. 2118.

WAR DIARY
or
INTELLIGENCE SUMMARY.

(Erase heading not required.)

Instructions regarding War Diaries and Intelligence Summaries are contained in F. S. Regs., Part II. and the Staff Manual respectively. Title pages will be prepared in manuscript.

Place	Date	Hour	Summary of Events and Information	Remarks and references to Appendices
HALLOY les PERNOIS.	Decr. 1st.) 8th.)		Battalions carrying on training and education.	
	9th		Inspection of Bde. Transport by Lt.-Colonel Commanding Bde.	
	10th 11th			
	12th		9/R.W.F. and 9/Welch R. moved to BERTEAUCOURT, 2/Wilts R. to St. LEGER les DOMART. Bns. moved under their own arrangements. These moves were carried out on account of the billets being better in new area.	
	13th		58th T.M.B. moved to HALLOY les PERNOIS.	
	14th		Training under Battalion arrangements.	
	15th		Church Parades. Bde. Commander attended Divine Service with 9/Welch Regt.	
	16th 21st)		Training under Battalion arrangements.	
	22nd		Church Parades. Bde. Commander attended Divine Service with 2/Wilts Regt.	
	23rd) 24th)		Training under Battalion arrangements.	
	25th		Xmas Day. Div. Commdr. and Bde. Commdr. attended Divine Service with 9/R.W.F. and afterwards both visited all Battalions. One hour's Parades under Battalion arrangements, remainder of day given up to Recreation.	
	26th 27th) 28th)		Training under Battalion arrangements.	
	29th		Church Parades. Bde. Commdr. attended Divine Service with 9/Welch Regt.	
	30th		115 Miners demobilised from the Brigade. Lecture by Lieut-Colonel H.F.MONTGOMERY, D.S.O. - G.S.O. 1, 19th Division.- on "Organisation of a Division".	

Army Form C. 2118.

WAR DIARY
or
INTELLIGENCE SUMMARY.
(Erase heading not required.)

Instructions regarding War Diaries and Intelligence Summaries are contained in F. S. Regs., Part II. and the Staff Manual respectively. Title pages will be prepared in manuscript.

Place	Date	Hour	Summary of Events and Information	Remarks and references to Appendices
HALLOY les PERNOIS.	31st.		Training under Battalion arrangements.	
			Brigade H.Q.	
			9th January, 1919.	
			[signature] for Lieutenant Colonel	
			Commanding 58th Infantry Brigade.	

www.ingramcontent.com/pod-product-compliance
Lightning Source LLC
Chambersburg PA
CBHW081428300426

44108CB00016BA/2325